44

P9-BZK-839

LC

THE RELIGION OF ANCIENT ISRAEL

THE
RELIGION
OF
ANCIENT ISRAEL

by

TH. C. VRIEZEN

THE WESTMINSTER PRESS
PHILADELPHIA

COPYRIGHT © 1963 W. DE HAAN N.V., ZEIST AND VAN LOGHUM SLATERUS N.V., ARNHEM, NETHERLANDS

ENGLISH TRANSLATION © 1967 LUTTERWORTH PRESS, 4 BOUVERIE STREET, LONDON EC4

This book originally appeared as *De godsdienst van Israël*

The English translation is by the Rev. Hubert Hoskins, and the Publishers are indebted to Dr. H. H. Rowley and Dr. R. E. Clements for editorial help

Library of Congress Catalog Card No. 67-22703

Published by The Westminster Press
®
Philadelphia, Pennsylvania

Printed in Great Britain

Contents

		Page
I	INTRODUCTION	7
II	ISRAEL'S RELIGION AGAINST THE BACKGROUND OF THE RELIGIONS OF THE ANCIENT EAST	22
	Israel and the surrounding world	22
	Some parallel phenomena that illustrate the relationship	25
	Cohesive and distinguishing aspects of the ancient Semitic religions in general	31
	The religion of Egypt	45
	The religion of Babylon	47
	The Phoenician-Canaanite religion	50
	The Aramaean religion	56
	The religion of some Transjordanian peoples	59
	The Edomites	64
	The religion of the North Arabian tribes	65
	The character of Israel's religion	71
III	RELIGIOUS LIFE AT ABOUT THE YEAR 1000	79
	Yahweh, the God of Israel	80
	Holy places	83
	Some social factors	99
IV	THE PREHISTORY	103
V	YAHWEH	124
VI	THE VICTORY OF YAHWISM	154

5

VII NEW FORMS OF LIFE, STATE AND RELIGION 179

VIII THE GREAT PROPHETS 194

IX REFORMATION AND DOWNFALL 228

X REGENERATION AND RECOVERY 240

XI CENTRALIZATION AND DISINTEGRATION .. 263

NOTES 277

ABBREVIATIONS 309

INDEXES 311

CHAPTER 1

Introduction

M Y PURPOSE IN what follows is to offer a picture of the
religion of Israel with respect not only to its historical
development but to its essence and inmost character as well.
Neither aim is an easy undertaking. Whether the investigator con-
centrates on the historical course taken by this religion or sets out to
shed some light on what it is essentially, in itself, the difficulties that
ensue are equally great.

With regard to the second task a modern phenomenologist has
said, 'the true nature of religion is a holy mystery, an enigma that one
can only guess at. Our speculations may be correct, more or less; but
the heart and centre of belief is a secret known only to the believer
himself.'[1]

Now when we come to deal with the religion of ancient Israel, even
though we are not Israelites we are not talking about something that
is essentially foreign to us. Although in a fashion different from that of
Jews whose way of life is based much more directly on the Old
Testament, there has always been in this western Christendom of ours
a vital connexion with the world of ancient Israel. Through many and
various channels, church, synagogue and even art, the Old Testament
as the record of ancient Israel's religion has imprinted itself deeply
upon the way we believe and think, the way we live, and even the way
in which we manage our political affairs. The religious confrontations
and events to which it testifies very largely determine even now the
character of our spiritual and mental outlook. It was not for nothing
that a historian of culture like Allard Pierson began his book on
Spiritual Forefathers with a brief account of Israel. The very title
adumbrates the notion that it is possible to share, in terms of our own
experience, the essential elements of this religion, in modern western
Europe, even twenty centuries after the most crucial, initial stages of
its development were concluded.

On the other hand, this does not mean, as so many people think, that getting to grips with the religion is therefore easy. To read a book like the Old Testament is more difficult than is often supposed. Small wonder that many who are quick to open the Bible soon shut it up again, because they have the feeling of being set down in a strange world, which they do not understand, even when they have before them a new translation of the Bible in the most up-to-date language.

People who have this experience with the Old Testament are often closer to the mark than those who, relying on a certain measure of general familiarity with the biblical narratives, skim through the book in a casual way and think that in so doing they are taking the whole thing in their stride. The truth is that there is an enormous distance, in time, place, culture and modes of thinking and belief, between our world and the world of ancient Israel.

The book was written over a period between two and three thousand years ago in the world of the ancient Near East—in a world very strange to us, and where life and thought were dominated by Semitic civilization. What men believed then—and the manner of their belief—was conditioned by experiences, attitudes and circumstances known to us only in part, and was couched in a language with which, as a channel of expression, we never become fully conversant, even if we have been dealing with it over a considerable period. These factors are calculated to ensure that, so far as ancient Israel's religion is concerned, it is and always will be true that we know in part.

In a broad sense, the problem of grasping the essential character of the faith of Israel is nothing new. We find it in ancient Israel itself, although on quite a different level, of course, from the primarily intellectual concern with literary and historic problems that engage us. For instance, we have prophets contending over what was the will and purpose of God, in the conflict of Jeremiah with Hananiah in 593 B.C., or of Elijah with Ahab in about 860.*

The Old Testament is full of argument about God and his activity, so that one can trace within Israel itself a progressive development in religious thinking, although this is not to say that there could not be regress as well as progress. Religion in Israel was always on the move, and in process of change.[2] As we explore the area constituted by Israel's religion, we shall see that it does not confront us with a cut-and-dried system of religious ideas and assured beliefs, but much

---

* Cf. Jer. 28 and 1 Kings 17f., respectively. From this point on, for dates which are before Christ the customary indication by the letters 'B.C.' will be dispensed with.

more with a process of spiritual growth, a strenuous endeavour to comprehend the God of Israel better and better. So strong indeed is this impression that we may be permitted to wonder whether we ought to speak of the religion of Israel in the singular at all. It has been conceived in so many different ways during the long period of Israel's existence as a people that one may well ask whether it is possible to point to one religious idea in it that is paramount.

With this in mind, we would do well to take to heart what was said not so very long ago by Professor S. H. Hooke:[3] he condemns the free-and-easy use of the general expression, 'the religion of Israel', as though such a thing did indeed exist and as though everyone means the same thing by it. Formulas such as the one just mentioned, or for that matter like 'true Yahwism' or 'the religion that finds expression in the Old Testament', are too vague. We must distinguish clearly between the phases of religion in ancient Israel which are so disparate in many respects, certainly in the later period, but still more so, earlier. It is evident that there are three forms of religion which stand in line of succession, and indeed side by side, regarding which it is hardly possible to say what common factor there is between them: (a) the religion of the patriarchs, (b) that of the ancient Hebrew tribes who remained in Canaan and whose religion was an amalgam of that of the patriarchs and that of the Canaanites, and (c) the religion of the Israelites who took part in the exodus and were 'in the wilderness'. We may assume that these forms of religion displayed important differences, even though we cannot hope to delineate them accurately. Hooke goes on to say, 'How far there was some common and central element in these three historically separate strands which caused them to blend and ultimately develop into what might be called the "official" religion of Israel is a difficult question.' In other words, he is really denying in principle that there is a specific, standard form of the Israelite religion to which one can point. It was always in process of development and subject to continuous change.

There is a lot of truth in that. Any student of Israel is going to reach the conclusion that her religion presents a motley array and appears in a great variety of forms and that between various phases of it the disparity is very considerable indeed. Still, it is questionable whether one has to take the business of separation so far that a basic link between them, at least in certain instances, becomes impossible to maintain. The question is worth pondering carefully, at any rate as regards the first period that Hooke refers to—the patriarchal age (*a*)—and to a great extent also for the period of the ancient Hebrew tribes between the time of the patriarchs and of the judges (*b*). Because the data on the religion of the patriarchs are so hard to evaluate with any degree of certainty, we are in a position to state only a few tentative conclusions about (*a*)—and then with the utmost caution; and of (*b*) also, although there are of course a number of fixed points in the Genesis and Judges narratives to which one can refer, we can offer only a very incomplete picture. It is not unlikely that for both periods we shall have to reckon with fairly sharply divergent types of religious life.

But then one would have to add to this that in some sense both periods reflect prehistorical, preliminary stages of Israel's religion. They represent, that is, the religion of the Hebrew tribes in the era prior to the emergence of the people of Israel. One cannot speak of a religion of Israel, in the full sense of the term, until there is an entity, a people of Israel; and as this was formed only during the period of the judges, it is only from then on that a religion of Israel can really be said to exist.

Where Hooke's category (*c*) is concerned—the religion of those tribes which lived through, and experienced, the Mosaic period—the case is different again. Here too it is to a considerable extent true to say that we cannot reconstruct it; but (as Hooke himself would allow) this much is certain: that the main features of this form of religion persisted in the official religion of Israel of a later time. That is plain from the fact that the principal critics and implementers of Israelite religion—the later prophets—based themselves on it and were for ever appealing to it. The most distinctive feature of this form of religion is that Yahweh, who is later on to dominate the spiritual life of the people of Israel and their existence as a nation, now makes his appearance. I would want to say, therefore, that if we set aside the earliest phases of Israel's religion which it is difficult for us to reconstruct in view of the lack of adequate literary data to which an assured date can be assigned, and which we can regard as preliminary, we can envisage it, in broad outline, as a single entity. That is still true, even when we fully recognize that the religion assumed many divergent forms of expression in the course of the centuries and that some of those forms incorporated elements so very alien in character that we are bound to describe them rather as syncretistic than as typical of Israel.

In this respect Israel's religion is not at all different from all other

religions of the ancient world and of our modern era, whether it be
the Babylonian-Assyrian and Egyptian religions or Christianity and
Islam. The Babylonian-Assyrian religion, like that of Egypt, presents
in the various stages of its existence a great multiplicity of aspects;
yet both religions have a character of their own. The way in which
these various aspects are commingled, even where the two religions
show an intrinisic affinity and agreement, is such that one has to
recognize the peculiar and unique character of both. That is just as
true of Christianity. In what a variety of forms *that* appears! We have
only to think of the religion of the Coptic monks, of the medieval
scholastics, of the mystics, Reformers, Quakers and Methodists, who
all have certain common traits that point to one essential element as
their ultimate source. As soon as we look at this conglomeration of
Christian groups together and compare it with Islam or Buddhism,
Parseeism or the religion of the Druses, to name just a few religions,
major and minor, it once again becomes, in spite of its diversity, very
plainly and recognizably a distinct community *vis-à-vis* those other
religions. There may perhaps be little outward difference between a
Coptic chapel and an Islamic mosque; and the ceremonies conducted
in them may have many things in common. Even so, there is as much
need to distinguish between them as between a Jewish synagogue and
a Calvinist church, although in both the walls are bare; and there is a
large affinity, outwardly at least, between the respective liturgies used
when a religious service is under way.

Outward forms are a determinative factor for a religion only up to
a certain point. There was a lengthy period during which the religion
of Israel countenanced the ancient holy places scattered up and down
the land; but there came a time when, because they had become a
hotbed of thriving syncretism, they were abolished, and then it was
only at one place in Jerusalem that sacrifices were allowed to be made.
This gave quite a different look, outwardly, to the religion of Israel;
and also modified its internal structure. Yet this does not mean that
what is known as the Deuteronomic Reform totally altered the
character of Yahwism. The religion *after* the Reform remained in
essentials what it had been before.

The best way to get an idea of the distinctive character of Israel's
religion, as bearing the stamp of Yahwism, is to compare it with those
attaching to the religions of the other peoples of the ancient East.[4]
This we shall do, therefore, in the succeeding chapter, where our aim
will be to etch in the general contours of Israelite religion, as dis-

tinguished from the oriental religions of the ancient world, which were so different in their essential nature, however much they may at times resemble and remind us of it.

To anticipate somewhat at this point, I would maintain that Israel's religion can best be typified by one word, by a name: Yahweh. It is this that dominates completely all the source-material that we possess for this religion: the Bible. This name occurs more frequently than any other noun or verb in the book. It has been calculated that it is used more than 6800 times, as against the 2500 occurrences of the general term for 'god', *Elohim*. Even in the old pre-exilic documents the name is that most often employed. It is possible that if we had more records from the sanctuaries of Northern Israel the proportion would be different, although it is not at all likely; for even there, during the period of the kings, the majority of theophorous personal names were formed with the Yahweh-name. One may take it as being predominant, therefore, even in North Israelite circles. This fact, based on a statistical examination of linguistic usage in the texts, accords entirely with the unconditional status of Yahweh in Israel's religion.[5] Although we cannot speak in terms of an explicit mono-theism (not *ab initio*, at any rate), Yahweh as Israel's God is without partner or competitor. He is not merely the head of a pantheon; he is 'God alone'. That is why the Old Testament can from time to time speak of God under various appellations (*El, Elohim, Eloah*); and in every case it is clear that Yahweh is meant. The word *El* does not function as a kind of determinative of Yahweh. There is not a god, Yahweh, beside other gods: in so far as these are taken for granted, they are not comparable with Yahweh; the notion of incomparability is applicable in the Old Testament to Yahweh alone. Yahweh tolerates no other at his side. He has no partner. He is a jealous God, as a recurrent formula has it, that expresses just how intolerable is any failure to recognize Yahweh's absolute uniqueness. In the religion of Israel, therefore, we find an element of intolerance that is essentially foreign to the polytheism of the ancient East. Elijah can order the killing of the priests of Baal under the very eyes of Ahab; and this has nothing to do with the clash of politics, as it would have done in, say, Egypt or Babylon. There too the priestly faction of one city might well be involved in conflict with that of another; but such cases are different in kind from that of Elijah in Israel, where the issues were purely religious in character. For Elijah certainly cannot be regarded as a political figure. Polytheism is by its very nature tolerant, relativist, syncretistic. In Israel's religion, as in its derivative, Christianity, and in Islam, which originated under the influence of both, there is a streak of intolerance, because the religious relation, in both a national and a personal context, is dominated by the God who makes himself known as the unconditioned, the absolute One, to those who believe in him. From the moment that Yahwism makes its appearance on the scene of history until now, that is fundamentally how it has been. Because of this, it has a strong resistance to every kind of syncretism and tends to assume an imperialist attitude towards all other religions. In principle they are rejected, even though this or that component of the religions competing with Yahwism may be absorbed by it. As soon as Yahwism encounters other religions there is a protracted struggle; and in the event some elements get accommodated, others expelled. Obviously, this issue was not one to be settled in the short term; it took centuries, in fact, for the process to be finally completed. Perhaps one ought even to say that it never was concluded, but only broken off abruptly at the time of the exile.

It would appear, therefore, that we can confidently ascribe to Yahwism a character all its own. As I said, this is a thesis which I intend to elaborate in the chapters that follow, first by making a comparison with the other religions of the ancient East, and then by means of a more detailed typology of Israel's religion in the earliest period at which it presents itself clearly to us.

That is, in effect, the period of the earliest monarchy, the time of Saul and David, the age in which Yahwism, along with the people of Israel themselves, had really 'dug in'. In their day Israel left behind her the period of sharp division among the tribes and embarked on one in which she came to be united as a people and achieved her own independent existence as a nation. More and more the old pastoral mode of life gave way to agriculture; and life in cities began to develop too. The need to enter upon a distinctive existence as an independent state gradually made itself felt.

A written record has come down to us from this period, or from very soon after it, which tells the story of the earliest monarchy and of the rise of David's dynasty. It is the first detailed source offering enough material, in the religious sphere, among others, to form the basis for an outline of the structure of Israel's religion. At all events it yields more substance for a descriptive account than does the Song of Deborah, which might form, as it does in Buber's celebrated sketch of *The Prophetic Faith*,[6] a possible starting-point. For the Song stands too much on its own as an extraordinary, spontaneous outburst of thanksgiving for victory won after a crucial battle to serve as a point of departure for a considered view of a religion in its historical framework. Naturally, it is of the first order of importance as a record, aesthetically as well as historically and in a religious context; and so it will prove extremely useful when we come to probe more deeply into the early course of events.

The fact that we have to delve so far back into history in order to get sufficient data for an outline of Israel's religion, going as far back as the earliest years of the life of Solomon,[7] illustrates very clearly the nexus of problems presented by the Israelite source-material.

There are definite reasons why it is exceptionally difficult to handle the Old Testament as history in a fair and responsible way. The chief reason is that in the course of history many of the ancient sources were re-issued after having first been worked over—that is, meddled with—by an editorial hand. The fact that they were read and re-read and passed on, and were evidently, therefore, a vital factor, culturally speaking, has had its big advantages, but also a number of drawbacks. One advantage has been that these sources have remained extant and not been lost or fallen into oblivion (as in the rather damp climate of Palestine might otherwise have been the case; for inscribed records, even of clay, did not readily stay in good condition in the soil there). But it is a drawback, from our standpoint, at any rate, that because of the additions and alterations introduced from time to time by revisers it is very difficult to sort out which parts of the transmitted historical documents are primitive and which are not. This can be done up to a point with the aid of stylistic research and criticism; but the criteria employed for this are not infallible and not easy to apply. The result is that although a fair amount of material from early Israel has survived, it is a tiresome and often highly uncertain business to prise this out of the textual context into which it was placed at some later period and thus to make it available for purposes of historiography. In that respect we are much better off where the Egyptian and Babylonian-Assyrian literature is concerned. Indeed it is possible in the latter case, on the basis of the archaeological evidence or of the study of letter-formation and the rules of grammar, to date a large number of the surviving texts fairly accurately. Again, the texts written in those languages are found singly, and only very seldom found bundled together as a collection, so that each literary unit can be quite clearly distinguished from its fellows.

By a combination of literary and historico-critical study and research over the past two centuries a certain amount of progress has been made with our understanding of the textual matter presented by the Old Testament; but a lot of questions remain concerning the time at which these sources originated. Despite all the work that has been done on the texts, informed opinion among scholars differs as regards the dating of this or that document, sometimes by as much as a hundred years.

It is when it comes to the earliest period that things are most difficult. One may question whether we have any authentic information at all that derives from the time of the patriarchs (c. 1700–1300). No one can answer with certainty. It is not impossible that in the stories of the patriarchs some very ancient bits of tradition have been preserved that do indeed go back to the patriarchal age. Some take the view that in many instances these stories are based on a written or oral tradition, accommodated perhaps to the form of epic songs, like the epics of the kings, Keret and Dan'el, in a Ugaritic context (see ch. 4, n. 12). This hypothesis may well be correct; but we can have no certainty about it, especially if we go on to press the question as to precisely which parts date from that early period and which do not. It is true that in recent decades various new possibilities have opened up of comparing these most ancient biblical texts with others found in the course of excavations in Nuzi, Mari and Ugarit. This has confirmed that the conditions of life depicted in the stories of the patriarchs, as well as the nomenclature of persons and places, tally with those which, as we now know, were prevalent in the middle of the second millennium; and it of course strengthens in certain respects the authority of the texts containing the patriarchal narratives, from a historical standpoint. Even so, it is still not enough to enable us to decide here and now what the value of the biblical texts as a source of history really is. Although the impression grows that the patriarchal period is being brought within the reach of the historiographer, it just is not documented well enough at the moment for us to have no misgivings on the score of accurate scholarship in presenting a picture of it. All that in fairness one can do is make some vague and tentative suggestions, based on a number of viable hypotheses.

Although perhaps not to the same large degree of uncertainty, the position is parallel with respect to the Mosaic period. Here again, a great many questions remain unsettled. As a matter of fact, recent years have seen the growth of, if anything, a sharper vein of criticism

directed at the received view of the tradition bearing on this period—
the 'received view' being that previously accepted among critico-
literary scholars, the reliability of which is now being called in
question.[8] Whereas until quite recently the figure of Moses has fairly
generally been linked with the story of the deliverance from Egypt and
the revelation on Sinai, for some time now the historical character of
this traditional association has been sharply contested. There are
those who will have nothing, or hardly anything, of a religion founded
in the wilderness, of a Mosaic background to certain Israelite institutions. A good many would argue that textual evidences of Moses'
period simply do not exist.

Now it appears to me that the critical method employed here is one
that is bound, because of its analytical character, to yield negative
results;[9] but these are owing rather to the method and the way in
which it is applied to the investigation of the sources than to the
sources themselves. I am myself firmly convinced that one can vindicate rather more of the tradition than is often supposed and that we
can place a fair measure of confidence at any rate in the oldest parts
of it. As to the figure of Moses, it is more reasonable to assume that a
personality so central to the course of history has attracted a whole
number of traditions to himself (a lot of major personages in history
have done that, after all) than that such a major figure has been
created almost entirely by the tradition itself, as some of the latest
critics would have us believe.[10]

Without sanctioning the tradition *en bloc* or wanting in any way to
shelter it under a protective wing, I must say how noticeable it has
been during the span of my academic labours over the past forty years
that as our knowledge of the ancient East has advanced, so the
tradition has been vindicated in various respects and to an unexpected
degree. Admittedly, this has not been true all along the line (one may
recall the story of the fall of Jericho in the Book of Joshua, which so
far from being confirmed by the excavations there, has had very grave
doubt thrown upon it);[11] but still in many instances it has been so.
One can cite various finds of the patriarchal period, Ugaritic texts
which provide data explaining certain passages in the prophets, such
as Ezekiel 14 and Isaiah 27. One thinks of the name Dan'el in
Ezekiel 14, which we meet with in the Ugaritic literature and which
was known, therefore, in Phoenicia eight hundred years before
Ezekiel. Priest-prophets such as Ezekiel (and Jeremiah), and others
too, do in fact appear to have had ancient traditions at their disposal

that had been preserved either from written sources or through oral transmission. One can confidently postulate this of the earliest historiographers as well. The distance in time between the Mosaic period (*c.* 1225) and the earliest compiler of tradition, J (*c.* 900), is relatively short. When we consider that the main contents of the traditions which he committed to writing must have acquired a fixed form, orally, long before he recorded them, we can only conclude that the traditions which he collected and edited go back to pretty near the time of the events which they relate. This is a case where only a few centuries separate the facts themselves from the recorded account. If, then, the earliest traditions have a very good backing of history, that is proportionately less true of the later recensions of those traditions: for example, that of the deuteronomic school (of the 7th or 6th century) and that contained in the priestly code (of the 6th century and later). There the tradition is increasingly coloured by new theological insights. On the other hand, these recensions are of great value in their turn, when we want to know what those subsequent theological ideas were.

Here it is possible to offer only a few general considerations, without going into detail. Even when we get to the chapter on the Mosaic period, we shall not be able to do more than delve a little further into a number of points at issue. In passing, we may venture just one observation on the question whether any authentic texts dating from this period exist or not. It is impossible to determine with complete certainty that any such texts have come down to us; but we may reckon with the possibility that in its most primitive form the decalogue should be attributed to that period. The situation is best reflected in a characteristic remark of L. Köhler's, uttered some few decades ago in a critical survey of the most recent literature on the decalogue:[12] namely, that whilst a Mosaic provenance cannot be proved, there is nothing that rules it out as a possibility. The question is therefore whether the burden of proof rests with those who accept the tradition or with those who reject it. If all historical traditions had to be corroborated by a number of independent witnesses before they could be accepted as historical data, the outlook for ancient history in general would be pretty poor! Of course, what is possibly or probably historical within a tradition must always be tested and checked against the status of the sources in which it occurs; but it is not necessary to discard every tradition that cannot be confirmed on the evidence of other contemporary sources. It would be hypercritical to insist on that. Still, anyone who adopts a more open attitude to the tradition is of course taking a certain risk and is bound to recognize that in so far as his historical account is based partly on traditions not fully tested as evidence it does contain hypothetical elements. He takes this risk as part of the bargain and consoles himself with the thought that somebody else who does his history-writing on the basis of fully corroborated traditions alone runs the risk of letting all sorts of crucial aspects slip and of mutilating his version of events through his neglect of elements that could enrich it. Historiography is always a matter of reconstruction; which in turn is grounded on a number of presuppositions which have to do not only with the business of *evaluating* the texts from a historical and critical standpoint, by the use, naturally, of a strict and systematic method of investigation, but also with a personal vision, which is the product, in part, of the historian's own turn of mind. Whether one likes it or not, there can be no writing history without a personal element of this sort. In the preliminary stages of his work every historian must start by examining his sources as rigorously as he can. That is the first thing he has to do, because it enables him to gauge the historical reliability of the data with which he has to work and to handle them with that always in view. When it comes to the reconstructive process of building everything into a whole, and to evaluating the sources, ineradicable personal factors will obviously have a part to play. To admit, in so many words, the presence of this personal element does not mean giving *carte blanche* to arbitrary personal 'insights' on an *a priori* basis or putting intuition above enquiry and research. It does, however, involve the sober recognition that writing history without making any personal decisions just is not a workable proposition.[13] That applies also to my attempt in the subsequent pages to write an account of the history of Israel's religion. It is as well that the reader know this in advance and know too that the author is himself keenly aware of it and also of the provisional nature of the results of his investigation.

In the preceding paragraphs we have made a number of observations on the subject of tradition, with a view to exposing the difficulties involved in using it for historical purposes, which the data for the earliest periods served very well to illustrate. When it comes to the later periods, the situation is rather different; for the nearer one gets to the time of the kings, the greater the flow of contemporary sources begins to be. The period of the judges is still full of problems; but after that, things improve.

This is not to say, of course, that from the time of the monarchy on, all the data that a historian might wish for are simply lying there ready for him to use. However much the sources may gain in historical trustworthiness, still they have been shaped to fit certain schemata of a later period, sometimes cut about or recast, often supplied with glosses of various sorts. All the same, a great deal of authentic material has survived, even in quite late recensions.

The worst of it is, however, that the textual evidences are so very incomplete, in the sense that they are really all out of the same drawer and therefore give a decidedly one-sided picture. To be specific, all the documents to reach us have been through the hands of the priesthood of the second temple at Jerusalem; and the truth is that this priestly caste handed down only such material as was acceptable to the later official—one might also say the orthodox—Jewish faith. Of texts associated with the earlier religious centres at such temples as those of Shechem, Bethel, Beersheba, Dan, Peniel, nothing has survived, unless it be perhaps the legends in the oldest Genesis-narratives regarding their foundation, but nothing more, either about the priesthood or the temple furnishings, the forms of sacrificial worship or the history of these things. There is one temple, that at Shiloh, which constitutes a part-exception to this, apparently because the Jerusalem priesthood saw itself as having inherited the Shilonic traditions. The later material is therefore important, certainly, but one-sided.

On the basis of the evidence provided in the Old Testament one can come up with an historical account of Israel's religion—but then only from the standpoint of the Jerusalemite tradition. Only here and there (and then mainly within the prophetic writings) do elements appear which give a fleeting impression of the kind of religious issues and insights that existed elsewhere, away from Jerusalem; and these are set in a highly polemical atmosphere. Outside of the prophetic writings we find precious little, aside from a few scattered general references to the Bethel-cult during the earlier period of the monarchy, whose 'calf worship' comes under heavy attack in the historical sources, i.e. on the part of their deuteronomic editors. But these pointers are so indeterminate that they are open to varying interpretations.

Still, if we want to construct a picture of religion in ancient Israel as a whole which is to be as reliable as we can make it, we must certainly do our best to bring these 'forgotten' or slighted forms of the religion into the record.[14] To that end it is essential to make all we can, not only of the scanty textual evidences but especially of the archaeological data, and at the same time to examine and sift the material offered for comparison by the Canaanite-Phoenician religion —always asking ourselves to what extent the material may help to explain this or that phenomenon in the non-Jerusalemite temple rites.

Where this last method is concerned we have to tread with very great caution; for we cannot simply use whatever non-Israelite sources may tell us in order to fill in the gaps in our knowledge of extra-Jerusalemite religious practices.

We have to remember that it is only in respect of certain periods (and certain places too) that the sources make any positive mention of Baal-worship. It applies in the case of Samaria at the time of Ahab and Jezebel, for instance, but not to other sanctuaries in Northern Israel at that period. We find all kinds of syncretistic forms of Yahwism flourishing there in various guises; and it may be, of course, that in certain instances (periods) these came pretty close to old-Canaanite Baalism. One may suspect that this was true, for example, of the Bethel-cult during the final days of the kingship in Northern Israel— and that, not simply because of a few revealing utterances on the part of Amos and Hosea but more especially in view of what we know about certain features of the religion of the 5th century Jewish colony at Yeb-Syene in Southern Egypt, which ought probably to be seen as a 'residue' of the late-Israelite cult at Bethel (see p. 261ff.). What happened with other holy places that we mentioned earlier is not at all certain. In general we may assume that the priesthood drifted with whatever chanced to be the prevailing tide; and that would have been determined mainly by the course of political events, by what the nations dominant at the time decided to do. To what extent the religion of 'the man in the street' was affected by the official temple cults is a question that must be asked and can only be answered in quite vague and general terms. Considering what the experience was in the time of Elijah and Isaiah, we might say that a hard core, a 'remnant', clung loyally to the ancestral faith in Yahweh, while the great mass of the people must undoubtedly have trimmed their sails to the wind.

This brings us back to where we started with this introduction. All kinds of difficulties confront the investigator. Any account of Israel's religion must be riddled with uncertainties and evidential lacunas, so that we are bound to fall far short of our ultimate goal. Although this may be disappointing, it is more than compensated for by the fact that through our study we can begin to see in a quite new way what it is that gives its distinctive character to the religion of ancient Israel. We do not find in the records a neatly tailored religious system; but those records do bring us face to face with 'a faith in the making', fortified in a struggle waged on many fronts and spiritually enriched and enhanced through being obliged by the impact of crucial events in history to be perpetually letting go outward forms and looking for new channels of self-expression.

So far, then, from being a 'closed' religion that one can bring under a single formula, it is a faith which through many shifts and changes of form and aspect reveals itself as a vital force that has given occasion, time and time again, for new growth.

CHAPTER 2

Israel's Religion Against the Background of the Religions of the Ancient East

Israel and the surrounding world

ONE CANNOT HOPE to give a true-to-life picture of Israel's religion without indicating its proper place within the world in which and out of which it arose. That world did not merely constitute the 'backcloth' to Israel's history; nor were the religions to be found in it merely so many items of scenery—'stage props' against which the drama of Israel was played out. On the contrary, that world was part and parcel of the Israelite outlook and understanding of life. The surrounding countries and their religions were fellow-players on this stage.

Just as there can be little understanding of Israel's secular history apart from that of the lands of the Euphrates, Tigris and Nile, Arabia, Syria and Asia Minor, so one can hope to understand little of her religion without having some idea of the religions of the peoples round about. Israel was certainly not autochthonous in what has come to be recognized as her fatherland—the land of Canaan; and she always remained conscious of that fact, in contrast to the other peoples of the Near East who, although they were just as much interlopers, apparently identified themselves with the earlier inhabitants who did regard themselves as native and indigenous. As we can see from the Genesis narratives, the original territory of the ancient Hebrew tribes, out of whom Israel grew, lies mainly to the east of the Syrian-Arabian desert, in the area comprising Northern Mesopotamia. The tribes which gave birth to this nation lived everywhere—and yet nowhere—in the regions environing the Fertile Crescent. Contact with Edom and the surrounding Arabian world was for Israel as normal as with the countries of Northern Syria and Northern Mesopotamia. Where religion is concerned, there are affinities in both directions.

22

If this, then, is the case with her beginnings, with her earliest history, the story is much the same as regards later periods, and in particular the last phase of ancient Israel's history; for once again she is scattered far and wide—to Egypt, to Assyria, Babylon, Asia Minor, Persia, Arabia and yet further afield—overspilling in every direction the borders of that Semitic circle from which she took her origin and which formed her background. Israel's destiny interlocks with that of all the Semitic peoples and in part even with non-Semites: Philistines, Hittites, Persians and Hamites (in so far as one must consider Egypt non-Semitic and in so far as various sorts of African communities played a part in Egypt's history), and later with Greeks and Romans.

It is the same with her religion and its history: it cannot be understood, at any rate during the period of ancient Israel's existence, without some familiarity with her developing environment. This thesis has been successfully propounded over many years now and needs to be insisted upon over and over again.[1] More than fifty years ago J. Hehn wrote in the preface to his book *Die biblische und die babylonische Gottesidee*:[2] 'It is only within the setting of its environment in the ancient East that the special character of the Israelite religion emerges clearly, and only then that one can begin to understand her own distinctive place in the story.'

It is the same with colours: although in a good light one can see them quite well, one can define them with real precision only when they are put side by side and inspected within the graduated scale of related shades as a whole.

What fully justifies our using the comparative method is that it gives us a keen eye for the distinctive character of this or that religion. To apply the method correctly, however, is by no means a simple matter; and it has given occasion for so many *faux pas* that a lot of people will have nothing to do with it any more. The chief reason has been that in making the comparison it was usual to take as one's point of departure those features that are conspicuously akin and on that basis to declare the one religion straightaway identical with, or deriving from, the other.[3] Over and over again this turned out to be wrong. Religions may employ the same ideas and yet differ profoundly from one another in their essential nature.

It is better to take note of the points of difference, on both sides, which such comparisons reveal. In that way the peculiar character of each religion is best brought out. Yet even this should not be carried too far; for we have to be on the look-out for the common traits as well as the divergences. However much the distinguishing characteristics that we discover may help us to classify religions according to type, there is more to every religion than just those elements that stand out because they are 'different'. G. E. Wright[4] quite justly observes that 'comparative religion is indeed one of the most difficult of disciplines because of the necessity of balancing details within a total perspective'. To get a fair comparison between religions one has not only to weigh the details one against the other but also have an eye to the major strands of thought governing the thing as a whole and to the place that the individuating ideas occupy within the whole. Only by taking into account the motifs which regulate the whole, together with the parallels and differential elements that find expression in it, are we going to exploit the method to any good effect.

Where Israel is concerned, we can be sure of one thing: as in her judicature and social structure, her psyche and world view, so too in her religion she had many things in common with the peoples all around her and with the Canaanites whose territory she invaded. The story in Genesis 14 of Abraham's seeking a blessing from the El Elyon of Melchizedek, the priest-king of pre-Israelite Jerusalem, admirably illustrates this point and shows that Israel remained for a long time sensible of the fact. The story is even an implicit admission that Israel (in the person of Abraham) was on the receiving end. The tithes paid by Abraham were given in honour of the El Elyon of Melchizedek.

We have to remember that Israel was a young nation, that at least a thousand years of civilization in Egypt and Babylon had come and gone before she appeared on the scene, that she was almost a thousand years junior to the Phoenician and Canaanite peoples, that she was one of the latest combinations of tribes disgorged by the Syrian-Arabian desert, and that these were still semi-nomadic when Egypt had attained her 18th dynasty and the high point of civilization in Babylon was already in the remote past. She owed her culture and (in the main, at any rate) her language to one of the junior nations of the Near East, the Canaanites. She herself emerged as a nation between 1230 and 1000; and her period of greatest prosperity was between 970 and 930.

This does not imply that Israel had no mind of her own or that her religion had no distinctive character. The contrary was the case and this really does mean something! Her political cast as well as her culture and religion exhibit certain crucial aspects that mark her off quite clearly from all the surrounding peoples. The hard centre of this was her relationship to her God. This it was that gave rise to elements in the pattern of her religious life and mental outlook which were altogether new and produced a religion and a way of envisaging the world that are to be counted among the noblest achievements of the mind and spirit of man.

Yet for all this, the pattern is itself inconceivable as something totally independent of the religious culture which constitutes Israel's environment. A whole variety of forms typical of the Semitic religions are to be found as much beyond the confines of Israel as within, especially as regards cultic matters: the rites and terminology of sacrifice, for example, temple furnishings, psalms and so forth. But in the personal sphere too many forms of expression are the same, because these peoples showed themselves possessed of the same temperament, the same psychic roots. That much is clear from the tenor of their psalms, their wisdom literature and other group reactions at the mental level to, for instance, events in history. There is even a resemblance between certain basic structural elements in their religions, even when these, for all that they were cast, initially, in a similar mould, developed, as indeed they often did, in a different direction with each of the various religions. As regards this point, it is worth taking a bit of trouble to show, by means of a few examples selected more or less at random, how elements of one sort or another which occur in other religions are present in Israel too, but have come to signify something quite different there.

Some parallel phenomena that illustrate the relationship

It should be enough for the present to consider this under three heads (although we shall need to come back to the ideas themselves later on in a different connexion): (a) the personal character of Israel's religion; (b) prophetism, and (c) the attitude of the divine being to the destruction of the holy city.

(a) The point has been made not a few times in various studies of the psalms in the Bible that the personal relationship to God here makes a very good showing as compared with that in the Babylonian psalms. Whereas in the Bible God is addressed in a forthright manner as 'my God', the hymns and prayers invoking the gods of Babylon proceed by way of a barrage of honorific titles. This has been dubbed a 'boot-licking' attitude: it only goes to show that the Babylonian deities had to be 'buttered up' in this fashion before their devotees dare come to them with their petitions.[5] Assyriologists,[6] basically, at any rate, with justice on their side, have demurred at this. They argue that the use of honorifics is accounted for by the strictly formal character of the cultic worship practised in the great temples of Babylon and Assyria. The psalmists there are to be looked for among the official ministers of the cult, who knew what the appropriate titles of the gods were; whereas in Israel the psalms came much more from the hands of private individuals. Moreover, it can be shown that in some Babylonian psalms and prayers there is sounded a distinct note of personal affection, which suggests that even in them a spiritual rapport with the gods is not to be discounted altogether. This is definitely reflected in the attitude taken to particular deities, as is evident from the celebrated hymn to Ishtar,[7] for instance; and again in the prayer of King Ashurbanipal to Nabu one can detect a warm, personal tone.[8] But the question is, of course, whether this kind of thing extends beyond the relationship of the king to the deity or beyond a relationship to certain quite special gods. The examples cited by Ravn undoubtedly give that impression.

It would seem that in the Babylonian sphere of culture there were three possible avenues to a relationship of a more personal kind:

1. Even as far back as the Sumerian epoch—as S. N. Kramer has pointed out[9]—one comes across evidence, in connexion with a number of Sumerian rulers, for a relationship with a personal deity. Apparently, such personal gods were intermediary figures between the 'great man' and the world of great gods.

2. Such intermediaries were held in the later Babylonian world to be in attendance upon every individual: the personal god is 'democratized' and becomes the friend of every Tom, Dick and Harry. His chief job is to convey his clients' supplications to the great gods themselves. One may conclude, therefore, that the personal gods, with whom people were in direct contact, have to be seen as belonging to the lower reaches of the divine world. What their precise position was is not clear. Whether we are to regard it, as W. G. Lambert[10] would seem to do, as being about on a par with that of the 'patron saint' in Christendom who is not invariably treated by his protégés with all that amount of respect, either, we cannot be sure; but it may be so.

3. There is a further group of personal gods: namely, those whom we may call *theoi patroioi* (gods of the fathers). As well as in the

old-Assyrian and Babylonian texts, we encounter them too in the milieu of the Syrian-Arabian desert, on the borders of the Arabian and the East Semitic civilization. Here we have gods who disclosed themselves to this or that individual, stayed in touch with him and were venerated by that person and his family—were even named after him. They could live on as family gods. In some instances the family gods of high-ranking individuals are identified with one or other of the great gods.[11]

If we reckon up the account, it would appear, then, that in the East Semitic world there are three categories that enable us to speak of direct, personal relations to and with divine beings: where these latter are the tutelary gods of nobles or princes, where at a later period they are the personal patrons of actual individuals, and where (in certain areas) they are family gods bearing the name of the head of a family. Again, it is sometimes the case that there is a more infelt relationship, especially where persons of high rank or birth are concerned, between certain of the great gods and their worshippers.

In the religion of Israel the situation is different again. There it is a clear case of *a personal relationship with the most high God*, with Israel's one and only God in person. He is directly accessible. Not only kings (like David, in 1 Sam. 30:6) may call upon him, but all who are in distress (Ps. 25:2; 35:23f.; 69:4; 71:12; 84:4, 11; 86:2, 12; 143:10, *passim*); and this even a non-Israelite can attest (Ruth 2:16) or can experience simply as one of the 'facts of life' (Gen. 16:13f.). In other words, there is in Israel an absolute immediacy about the relationship between God himself, in the highest sense of that term, and the individual human being; whereas with the Babylonians the personal relationship (except in the case of kings) is only possible on a lower level; so that the divinity with whom the individual man is concerned functions as a mere intermediary between that man and the great gods (or one of them) and thus serves to accentuate the contrast between the two.

The fact that the personal element in Israel's religious life differs functionally from any counterpart in the rest of the ancient Semitic world is important for the very reason that we ought probably to conclude, with A. Alt,[12] that in the oldest Hebrew tribal society this element is still playing a role akin to what we were speaking of (under 3) in regard to the North Eastern Semitic milieu. In its historic roots, therefore, the special personal relationship must have affinities with the type of relations to be encountered in that milieu;

and yet in the case of Israel something grew out of this element, something altogether different from what we find elsewhere, in that there it came to be subsumed within a wholly new form of theistic belief, namely Yahwism.

(b) The second example that we cited was prophetism. Here again there are elements of the familiar Israelite phenomenon that clearly have their cognates in the world of the ancient East: on the one hand in an ecstatic form among the Phoenicians,[13] and on the other in a far more rational form in the Mari-texts—that is, in the milieu of Northern Syria and Mesopotamia. But notwithstanding all the similarities, as soon as one considers the substance of the messages conveyed in Mari and of those for which the prophets of Israel stand, the divergence is so great that compared with it all the parallel elements are as nothing. Furthermore, Israelite prophetism, at least in its classical period, exhibits such an evident continuity that every possibility for comparison over and above that goes by the board, even though there are remarkable affinities to be adduced at the formal level.[14] One is bound, therefore, to refer to parallel phenomena, but also to recognize that the differences of religious function between them are so very large as to yield but one final verdict: that only in Israel did the prophetic element develop of its own accord into a wholly distinctive religious phenomenon—so much so that it is not only unique over against the religions of the ancient East but has even remained without parallel in the whole of world history.[15]

(c) Our third point too, regarding the reaction of the divine being to the destruction of his or her holy city, is well worth looking into. Here again, whilst a description of the formulas may suggest a kinship, the differences in religious outlook regarding the gods and their behaviour are as wide as the sky.

Someone who knows the Old Testament and looks upon it as an utterly unique piece of literature may be inclined to stare a bit on reading in the Mesha-inscription (c. 845, Moabite) that 'Omri, king of Israel, chastised Moab many years, because Chemosh[16] was wroth with his land'; 'but'—it says later on—'Chemosh restored it in my days'.[17] From this it would appear that the eclipse of Moab was attributed to the anger of Chemosh, who is evidently assumed to have turned his back on his country; later on, in Mesha's time, he 'turned again'—and so Mesha is able to triumph over Israel. Afterwards, the first thing he did was to build a sanctuary for Chemosh in gratitude for the deliverance. This appears in the preamble to the text (showing that we are to understand it as a temple inscription): 'I made this high place for Chemosh-in-Krhh, in token[18] of his help, because he saved me from every setback[19] in the sight of all that hate me.' The very phraseology reminds one in a number of ways of certain Old Testament utterances, sharing with them, as it does, recognition of the fact that the god's anger was the reason for the city's downfall. Perhaps that anger was attributed (by implication—the text does not say this in so many words) to a neglect of the cult of the god—and that was why Mesha put an end to it by building him a temple on the high ground near Dibon.

One can read similar texts with a provenance in the Assyrian-Babylonian world:[20] that is to say, where the victors inform us that the gods had forsaken the defeated city in a fit of anger at the transgressions of the ruling prince—his neglect of the cult, especially, as well as his failure to uphold justice and the law. This is what we are told in the case of the Assyrian kings Tukulti-Ninurta I and Esarhaddon after their conquest of Babylon,[21] and again in connexion with the king of Persia after his capture of the same city.[22] As a matter of fact, we find the same view expressed sometimes by the defeated kings themselves. Thus, for example, according to Tukulti-Ninurta, the Babylonian king, when he sees his downfall approaching, makes confession of his sins.[23] Nabonidus himself recognizes that the wrath of the gods has been 'openly shown' toward Babylon by their having deserted their sanctuaries.[21]

The same consciousness that the sins of king and people may be the reason for decline and downfall is present among the Hittites. Hence it is the duty of kings, by maintaining the cult and the moral decrees (the honouring of pledges made on oath), to ward off the anger of the country's gods.[24] The thought of divine retribution in the form of a plague is very plainly expressed in a prayer of King Murshilish (c. 1325), who puts the blame on his father's treachery toward Egypt, with which country that monarch had concluded an alliance.[25]

It is true that among the Hittites the idea also occurs that disasters may come about quite apart from any question of guilt on men's part—thus not as a judgment of the gods but as a result of their carelessness or indifference.[26] Even so, the paramount cause is human guiltiness, arising from sheer neglect of the cult.[27]

With the Sumerians things seem to have been different. At all events, W. G. Lambert points out[28] that in Sumeria the gods always side with their own cities: if a city or a sanctuary is razed, the gods are plunged into grief.[29] The deity is evidently regarded in this case as entirely 'national': he or she is a part of the nation as a unit, and the disaster is not imputed to any judgment enacted by the nation's own god. The god of the victorious city is roundly cursed, therefore, by that of the losers.

The Sumerians apart, it would seem that up to a point there was an agreed notion among the peoples of the ancient East as to how the deity who made his judgment known in the course of events sized things up in the religious and ethical sphere. The god might be angry with his people, might withdraw and abandon the holy city. This tallies with the Israelite way of thinking; but still there is a broad cleavage between Israel and the rest of the ancient East when the idea comes to be worked out in practice. Those countries in general looked to identify the guilt mostly[30] at the level of cultic observance, Israel in the religio-ethical sphere. What is yet more important: in other parts of the ancient East the judgment was assessed *post hoc*, in the light of the course events had taken; whereas in Israel it was stated most emphatically in advance by the prophets, as something that no one could avert or evade. What we have there are not later reflections following upon the execution of the sentence, but rather insights of a spiritual kind going before the judgment itself. Even *before* Amos could have known that Tiglath-Pileser III would appear on the scene, he was proclaiming that the Northern Kingdom would be 'taken away' to the North, beyond Damascus (5:27). The later prophets too were always doing this kind of thing. It was upon their religious and moral sense that they based their prognostications of doom; and this sets their preaching in a very different light from the historical and political reflections of the Semites to the East. It assumes too a quite different function, as admonition and as a solemn call to reform. The divine being is not inexorably fixed upon 'executing his wrath', but rather their message becomes the ground of an appeal for contrition. God will do everything he can to rescue men from their predicament. More even than the motives for the divine wrath cited by the prophets, this serves to demonstrate the ethical character of the Israelite religion. Let us add as a rider to this that the bond between Yahweh in Israel and the city in which he is worshipped is never as profound as elsewhere. Yahweh is never described as God of Jerusalem, for instance: such a direct involvement between him and a city made by human hands (as might occur elsewhere in the ancient East) is in principle not feasible in Israel (see p. 22f.).

From these three examples one thing is perfectly clear: it is that like (homologous)[31] elements may occur in the various religions, which yet differ entirely in the place they occupy and in the significance properly attaching to them and which may in fact function in totally divergent ways.

The fact that although their origin is one and the same their operative effect in Israel is quite other than in the world around her must help us especially to see that Israel's religion is structured on a wholly different pattern. Indeed, it is owing to the character of each religion considered individually that a given element produces one result in one case, whilst a similar or cognate element has in the case of another religion a quite different outcome.

It would be easy enough to set beside the items already mentioned many further evidences of a similar kind; and this would show, time and again, the extent to which elements in the religions, whilst having a close, mutual affinity, nevertheless hold a quite different place in them. To name only a few: creation, sin, the hereafter, ritual observances, and so on.

Cohesive and distinguishing aspects of the ancient Semitic religions in general

We must now move on and consider in brief outline the main aspects of the religions of the world in which Israel grew up. It has become increasingly clear that, discounting the religion of the nomads from among whom the progenitors of Israel had come, all the religions with which Israel had to do while she was developing into a national community were religions of husbandry, of the soil. It is no longer permissible to regard them as nature religions, although they did of course enshrine not a few elements of primitive nature worship.[32] Except in particular aspects, the people did not identify their gods *simpliciter* with natural forces. The process by which the powers of nature were personified and anthropomorphized was in full swing.[33] It is good not to lose sight of this fact; for previous generations have failed sufficiently to understand and acknowledge this background to the growth of a religious consciousness in Israel. According to them Israelite civilization and religion began *a limine*, as it were. This was a mistake. When we consider that civilization in this part of the world had begun thousands of years before Christ and, four or five millennia before the start of our era, had led in a number of places to the establishment of villages and sometimes of urban communities,[34] we can no longer envisage this corner of the world between 2000 and 1000 as being either barbarous or backward. The high standard of art that had been attained in many centres by the beginning of the third millennium, in Mesopotamia as well as in Palestine and Egypt, fills us with astonishment, every time a fresh discovery is made.

Each of the religions in question is a complex entity in which, however obvious the elements of diversity may be, we notice the same thing that we saw when speaking of Israel in connexion with these religions: namely, that each has numerous traits that are to be found among the others and yet in greater or less degree can have a differing function within the context of this or that religion. It is impossible to say that one thing is the typifying mark of each: that Egyptian religion is essentially 'provision for the dead'; that the Babylonian religion is 'astral', the Phoenician a fertility cult, the Arabian simply 'moon worship'. In all these statements there is a core of truth; and yet such a one-sided characterization must yield a false picture of each religion in itself as well as of the religions conjointly and in relation to one another. The features aforementioned are typical, of course, and even salient, but listed side by side in this way they give a one-sided and therefore misleading idea of the ancient East, of the very complex world which in fact it was. They obscure also those common elements that typify the ancient East as a whole.

First, then, something about a few of the common traits. Before we come to consider these, however, we must hoist another warning signal. In recognizing that the ancient Eastern religions do present some basic features in common, we have to be cautious about the idea of which a great deal has been heard in recent decades (although not, without dissent), that at any rate in so far as its origin is Semitic or has been influenced by Semitic civilization, the whole of the ancient East represents a single pattern of religion. Some scholars have gone so far as to suppose, for example, that certain rites from Babylon can be used without more ado to fill in what are alleged to be gaps in our knowledge of Hebrew ritual. This is insupportable, both with regard to the facts and as a method. All the common, basic features that one may detect in various quarters, and this applies to the whole Near Eastern world, often turn out to be much more homologous than analogous, although they may sometimes be analogous too. Even when certain elements are taken over by this side or that, they do not always assume the same function then that they had in the context from which they have been borrowed.

The considerable confusion that results when these things are not borne in mind is very much in evidence over the question of the character of kingship in the ancient East.[35] Various scholars have argued that not only in Egypt but in Babylon, in Phoenicia and even in Israel kings were held to be divine beings. They would everywhere observe near enough the same ceremonies that we have come to know so well from the Babylonian festival of the New Year.[36] Their divine status must have been conferred on them at their enthronement. The argument, where the Old Testament is concerned, is based on certain (coronation) psalms, such as Psalm 2 and Psalm 110; and much is made of Psalm 45:7f., where the king is himself addressed as God might be. This latter case is matter for dispute;[37] whilst in the coronation psalms, so called, the word-play on the king's being 'a son of God' is to be regarded as an adoption formula. This no more presupposes an apotheosis of the king than Israel is thought of as being divinized when, as a people, she is referred to in some divine utterance as 'my son' (Hos. 11:1). There is nothing in Israel to suggest that the Egyptian idea of a divine kingship has been adopted, even though all sorts of elements in the coronation ritual may remind one of Egyptian ceremonial and are in fact borrowed from it.[38] Neither in the case of Phoenicia nor of Babylon is there demonstrable proof of such a notion. Quite the contrary. In both those countries the kingship had a peculiar place and a distinctive function which at one period of history meant one thing and at another something else again.[39] For the evidence regarding the other peoples the reader can only be referred to the experts mentioned in note 35 (cf. p. 279). In any case, an account of the several religions will make it clear that the conditions underlying the divine kingship that one finds in Egypt are present nowhere else. In Egypt it is wholly intrinsic to the structure of the state and the religion, whereas in the other countries it would in both connexions be simply anomalous.

The following are some of the important religious elements found everywhere throughout the ancient East, even though their significance is not everywhere the same: (a) the pantheon, with a single divinity at its head, (b) the god who dies and rises again, and (c) the notion of a 'three-storeyed universe'.

(a) Although the figures of the gods themselves repeatedly change places or contend for each other's divine authority, in Babylon and

C

Phoenicia as well as in Egypt one does find a head of the pantheon. In Egypt this is Re or Amon, although there was a period during which the Aton-religion of Amenophis IV (Ikhnaton) attempted to oust Amon-Re worship[40] and though Isis, according to the myth, succeeded in wheedling out of Re his secret name and thus in having his absolute power at her disposal, which gave her opportunity and ability to practise her magic without let or hindrance.[41] It would appear that in this poem Re is seen as a 'superannuated' god, a *deus otiosus*. Yet even up to and during the latest period the sun-god, under the name of Amon, remained the principal god of Egypt; and in the Graeco-Roman age he came to be identified with Zeus and Jupiter.[42]

It is the same in Mesopotamia, although there the ascendancy of Anu passes to Marduk and at times to other gods. Here too there emerges clearly enough a recurrent tension between the god paramount in the theogonic pattern of ideas and the gods associated with religious life at the practical level. Of course, behind these tensions there lies a process of historical development; yet the remarkable thing is that with all these changes and contradistinctions the idea persists of a monarchical pantheon: the dignity of 'supreme godhead' can be transferred from one god to another.

In the case of Phoenicia the same thing is noticeable; and we are compelled to recognize that here again the monarchical pantheon, under the paternal rule of El, persists for centuries, despite the fact that El acquired a companion in many respects more vital and powerful than himself in the figure of Baal. Some scholars stress the point that El was already a *deus otiosus* in the period that gave rise to the Ugaritic literature and that the supplanting of El by Baal was one of the things it was intended to propagate.[43] It seems to me that to think in terms of ousting or replacement here is wrong and that we must assume that notwithstanding the great popularity of the Baal-figure El continued to be acknowledged head of the pantheon.[44] With the example of the Babylonian Anu before us we must get used to the idea that whilst gods may indeed grow old and full of years, they never actually disappear as figures with a role in a religion, unless the culture which produced them is completely destroyed. Throughout the entire period in which the culture that produced him existed El never became a *deus otiosus* to the same extent as the Sumerian Anu in the Babylonian world. Evidently, continuity in the Phoenician sphere was at no point interrupted as it was in Mesopotamia (albeit by a slow process and, even there, never completely),[45] but in spite of every change the world of men and of the gods did no more than evolve. The truth is that in polytheistic systems one can expect nothing else. In such systems were not the very gods of conquered peoples taken into the pantheon of the victors? Syncretism is surely part and parcel of polytheism.

The monarchism of the pantheon by no means presupposes the universal consent of the gods. In the world of Sumerian deities such unanimity is often far to seek; and the gods are not infrequently hostile to one another. Among the Babylonian gods, however, there is evidently a greater degree of unity,[46] and the various deities work much more together when in council,[47] although even here their co-operation leaves a good deal to be desired, and there is always uncertainty about what they are up to.[48] In Ugarit also it was not all that rare for the gods to be at loggerheads, as when even El is threatened thus by Anat:

> I'll have your grey hairs dripping with blood,
> Your hoary old beard clotted with it.[49]

On the other hand, the headship of a single god can evolve into a firmer unity in the divine world, so that it approximates to a particular form of monotheism or rather, monarchism. The chief deity is then the bearer of every divine name and likewise of every divine attribute.[50] Most remarkable is a Babylonian text in which the poet conceives of his chief god (Ninurta) as embracing all the gods: that is to say that each of his god's bodily parts is constituted by one of the principal gods: 'his eyes are Enlil and Ninlil, the iris of his eyes is Sin, Anu and Antu are his lips, his teeth are the divine heptad', and so forth.[51]

O. Eissfeldt believes that something of the same kind occurred in Phoenicia in the case of El[52]; but the evidence for this is extremely scanty and not altogether certain. One can more readily stake a claim for Egypt in the time of Ikhnaton,[53] although the companion gods of Aton certainly did not disappear. Even here, however, the predominant god kept his naturalistic associations.

All this makes it evident that on the score of unity within the pantheon there were widely divergent conceptions and that the polytheism of the ancient East hovered between two poles: the one extreme was an unintegrated collection of many gods, the other involved the recognition of an all-embracing godhead. For the latter the word 'monotheism' is hardly appropriate. Monotheism, as a form of religious belief, is not a matter of acknowledging a particular phenomenon in nature as having prior place over and above all others, but of a wholly peculiar and underived spiritual being or essence of godhead, qualitatively of a different character from anything in nature.[54] In the case, for example, of Marduk and Ninurta, (who comprehend all the powers of nature), as well as of Aton, the solar disc (who is envisaged as the bearer of all divine functions), the divinity in question is the apotheosis of the sum total of natural forces. It is more a case of nature-mysticism and a stage on the road to pantheism than of monotheism in the true sense of the word.

In saying this we have already made one essential point concerning what we now propose to consider (even though it means interrupting the flow of our argument, which is intended to outline the religions beyond Israel), namely, the relation of the unity of the divine world in the ancient East and in ancient Israel. There are in Israel elements that display a similar kind of oscillation between a divine world containing a large number of figures and a self-contained unity of the divine Being. Expressions such as: 'Yahweh, God of gods and Lord of lords',[55] 'O sons of gods, give glory to Yahweh',[56] 'God stands in the council of the gods, He judges amid the gods'[57]—and there are a lot more that could be mentioned—indicate that the notion of plurality in Israel's divine realm continued to be preserved in circles loyal to Yahwism. Yet this plurality is dominated by the one God of Israel, Yahweh, in a manner quite different from anything to be found elsewhere; for Yahweh is the one God, who requires all Israel to worship him—and him alone. None of the other gods is comparable with him (Ps. 89:6). Among the gods[58] who are admitted to exist there is none *who has a name* and therefore a claim to be mentioned, even 'next to God'. Thus Yahweh, as God of gods, is exalted so far above the other divinities that there can be no question here of a pantheon with its head or even of a council of the gods, in the sense current elsewhere, beyond the borders of Israel, although there too the notion is a familiar one (Ps. 82:1; Job 1f., *et al.*). How it was in fact understood appears from a narrative like that at 1 Kings 22:19: the conference that Yahweh is pictured as holding occurs without so much as a mention, by name, of any of the spirits that surround him (as also in Job 1:6ff.; 2:1ff.). The divine council is there for the greater glorification of Yahweh rather than to signify any limitation of his power.[59] Syncretistic groups could, however, easily tag on to these ideas and import all kinds of figures alongside Yahweh. This must have happened in the Bethel-cult, as appears from the evidence afforded by the community at Elephantine (see p. 261).

Elsewhere, on the other hand, the unity, the majesty, the match-lessness of Yahweh find such emphatic expression[60] that even these last, lingering remembrances of extra-biblical notions cease to exist. Besides all this, even in the other forms of representation, God in his oneness, his uniqueness, is so completely *other* in character, in his mode of being-the-God-of-Israel, his all-controlling, all-governing relationship to this nation, his moral and supernal qualities, his faculties standing over and above the creation, his absolute power and holiness, that for the faithful of Israel nothing in the world offers to compare with him. That is why one is forced to say that mono-theism in Israel is qualitatively and essentially something different in kind from monarchism, and even from the pantheizing monarchism of the ancient East.[61] Yahweh was a divinity utterly different in his innermost being from El, for all the latter's supreme status. What was so prominent in Yahweh was the personal aspect of the celestial being and, with that, the wholly unique mode of his relationship to men. He may indeed have borrowed certain features of El's univer-sality and wisdom, which in the first phase of 'the encounter' (the revelation to Moses) were not peculiarly his own; but in Israel these traits became uniquely profound and significant, in that they were ascribed to the deliverer-God who is near at hand, for it is only because these characteristics are acquired by Yahweh, the living God who enjoins his will upon his people, that they come to have a real and positive religious function. In the El religion they were just a very vague concept; and they meant little for the life of mankind in a religious context. But when Isaiah, who saw Yahweh as the thrice-holy One, proceeds to use and apply the ideas of the universality and wisdom of God in the life of religion, there flows out from the renewed image of godhead to the man of faith an assurance that he had not known before. It is then that the holy saviour-God, Yahweh, comes to be God almighty, God of the world, who here and now has at his beckoning and command the kings of the most mighty nations and takes their comings and goings up into the designs settled upon by decree of his holy counsel. Thus it is clear in what manner Yahweh transcends, qualitatively, the highest that the ancient East can proffer, despite every point of connexion, every parallel and even borrowing that we may postulate between Israel and the world of the ancient East.

(*b*) Gods who die and rise again are like planets in the celestial firmament of the ancient East. They are to be found in all religions outside Israel and evidently belong among the oldest elements in the divine world of the several religions. In each one they have names of their own; and all have a distinctive mythology built around them by the various peoples.

Obviously, what we have here is a very ancient and ineradicable stage of religion, which has persisted and been conserved through every development of the several religions and goes hand in hand with an agricultural way of life. All sorts of new layers of religious ideas have been superimposed on the peoples and their *modus vivendi*, but not to the extent of effacing this ancient form. The role that it plays will vary a great deal from one religion to another. In Babylon it would seem to be more or less confined to the popular cults; and in the official religion, which is both national and astral, very little is heard of it. In Egypt it persists, right through every national aspiration and all the speculations of theosophy, as one of the basic elements in Egyptian theology. In Phoenicia, where because of the system of city-states the national forms of religion are unable to gain the upper hand and the astral forms also remain apparently of secondary importance (but for a few gods who are to be met with everywhere and which are not lacking, even here), this ancient type of religion dies hardest of all: here it is the most popular element of belief, which is so popular in fact that it dominates the state religion. Of this the Baal-figure is the symbol. This is the case too with the Canaanite world, which in matters of religion is essentially on a par with Phoenicia. Hence it is this form of religion with which Israel has mostly to deal and with which Yahwism clashed most fiercely. Because Yahwism was conscious of it as a special threat, it offered the keenest possible resistance, rooting out pretty well every element that had taken hold in the sphere of religious practice and striving to wipe away every lingering recollection of it.

But before we go any further we must take the religions one by one and say something in greater detail about the ideas that they present on the subject of dying and rising gods.

That we should refer in the first place to the religion of Egypt will not seem strange to anyone who knows such a book as W. B. Kristensen's *Het Leven uit de Dood* (Life out of Death). The title, which is meant to typify the essential core of Egyptian religion, in any case speaks for itself. In Egypt there are no less than three figures which exemplify the dying and rising godhead: Min, Re and Osiris.[62]

Each of these, in his own distinctive way, stands for the principle of self-renewing life.[63] The notable thing about the Egyptian religious outlook is that it is governed by the idea of the 'duality of life and death, which constitutes not an antithesis, but more of a polarity',[62] although alongside this, in the practical sphere of daily living, the antithesis of life and death is stressed explicitly enough (see p. 45, n. 99, cf. p. 283).

This polarity governs not only the life-process in nature—yielding plant and vegetational growth—but also the cosmos and the life of men.[64] It comes out particularly in the figure of Osiris, who besides being a god-man (hero) is also the god of flooding and vegetation and god of the moon—in short, of all that dies and comes to life again.[65] It is hard to say which trait, historically speaking, is the most primitive in this god;[66] but it is undeniable that he is very closely connected with vegetation, that at any rate an extremely important function of his being is that of a vegetation-deity. To judge from the myth of Isis and Osiris, he certainly belongs to the category of dying and rising gods (even though he rises in the person of his son, Horus[67]), as is recognized by, among many others, G. van der Leeuw, who describes him as having an affinity with Adonis, Attis and Tammuz.[68] He must be accounted one of the oldest elements in the religion of Egypt. Erman would trace him back as far as to the end of the fifth millennium;[69] but this dating is uncertain. Even so, one can assume here, as also in the case of the other religions, that the dying and rising god as a type of the vegetation-deity goes back to a very remote period. He ought probably to be included among the types of god to be found already in an era prior to the emergence of states, when the life of the people was still predominantly agrarian in character.

In Tammuz, one of the most ancient gods of the Sumerian and Babylonian world, we are confronted with the oriental type of the dying and rising god. Although it would appear from Babylonian[70] and other sources[71] that through his connexion with Ishtar he is associated with life and death and through her likewise with vegetation, he cuts a somewhat elusive figure in the ancient Babylonian world. In the official religion, at any rate, he is evidently, or as near as makes no matter, 'swallowed up' by the Ishtar-figure. His functions are for the most part taken over by that goddess, who is one of a less ancient Semitic group of deities. Like Osiris, he is a hero-figure, a divine king of the primeval period.[72] His proper place is with the ancient gods of Sumeria, since his name, at any rate, is Sumerian (Dumuzi =the true son;[73] and 'Tammuz' represents the Assyrian version of this). There are extant quite a number of Sumerian songs of Tammuz; but they are very difficult to read and as yet have not been altogether satisfactorily explained,[74] so that the best Sumerologists are reluctant to bring out in translation such texts as exist only in a Sumerian version.

There is still much uncertainty as to his essential character, as is clear from the great variety of interpretations put forward.[75] In the Sumerian age, certainly, his role is that of a fertility-god;[76] and he is linked in more than one way with Inanna-Ishtar.[77] Although he was much venerated[78] and must have been one of the most popular gods, he is neither one of the three central Sumerian deities nor one of the four major astral gods of Babylon.[79] He probably ought not to be included among the deities imported into Mesopotamia from the West Semitic world,[80] at any rate in a historically accessible period.It is a possibility to be considered, because he was not originally a god first and foremost of husbandry but rather of the fertility of the herd. In the ancient stories, therefore, he is invariably the herdsman, associated, certainly, with the open country. It is a more likely supposition, however, in his case as in that of Osiris, that as a figure he goes back to a very early period of the religious development of Mesopotamia. It looks as though he has been carried over from a *vorstaatliche* period.[81]

How firmly the Tammuz-figure was implanted in the life and the mentality of those who inhabited this area appears from the fact that even in much later times the Mesopotamian world associated him, under the name of Tammuz, with vegetation. J. Pedersen,[82] basing himself on an Arabic writer of the 10th century A.D., tells us that according to the inhabitants of the Harran district Tawuz 'was slain by his master, his bones were crushed and scattered to the winds'. That is why throughout the festival in his honour the women lament for him and during that time eat no ground corn. The same fate that befell Tammuz is ascribed in the Baal-tradition of Ugarit to Mot. This name, dating from the Arabia of the medieval period, is old-Babylonian, whilst the story is of Phoenician origin, as far as one can postulate at present. Yet even in this syncretistic form the connexion with the ancient gods of fertility is plain enough. It goes to show how persistent religious ideas can be, especially when they go hand in hand with an agricultural way of life.

We have already referred in the foregoing passage to the West Semitic conception of the dying and rising god—familiar to us from the Ugaritic literature in the person of Baal; though when it comes to the texts with a bearing on this deity, there is a wide divergence of view among the experts.[83] As it seems to us, that interpretation comes closest to the meaning of the texts which sees the figure of Baal as a fertility-god.[84] According to this view the texts depict the cycle of the agricultural year in the conflict between the gods of life and death, and in particular between Baal and Mot. Just as in Egypt Isis goes in search of Osiris after his death, and in Babylon it is Ishtar who looks for Tammuz, so here Baal's spouse and sister, Anat, hunts for his corpse; and when she has found it, she destroys Mot by threshing and grinding him as corn and tossing the meal out upon the open plains.[85] After a dream of El, the revivified Baal appears and takes his revenge upon his adversaries. In the seventh year Mot succeeds in avenging himself on Baal; but even then Baal is able to vanquish him in the end.[86] The text here, having described the annual cycle of fertility, summer drought, new life in the fall of the year, evidently alludes also to the fact that after every seventh year the land lay fallow, which was seen as a very special form of contest between Mot and Baal, as the final phase in that struggle.

Besides being portrayed in this form of the conflict between Baal and Mot, the god of life and fertility was represented in Phoenician culture by the person of Adonis.[87] Lucian says that at the festivals in honour of Adonis, held within the sanctuary of Aphrodite at Byblos, the god was first mourned as being dead; but then it was given out that he was alive, after all.

In the Hittite world too we find the story of a fertility-god, upon whose expulsion the vegetation also disappears. The chief figure here is Telepinu, god of husbandry, beside whom, in another version, there is a parallel god of the weather who fulfils the same role.[88] Here again, therefore, it is not really strange, any more than in Egypt and Phoenicia, for two gods to have one particular function to discharge between them.

As we said before, this is the most important religious complex with which the oldest Hebrew tribes, and later on, the more recent, assertive Yahwistic group, found themselves having to deal, in the form of Canaanite Baalism. This (we may suppose) differed hardly at all in essentials from its Phoenician counterpart. It could well be that in Canaan, precisely because of the simpler cultural conditions which, more than in Phoenicia, were still regulated by the demands of agriculture, it played just as significant a role as in the highly urbanized coastal territories to the north. Such evidence as can be inferred from personal names of the Amarna period[89] and from the fairly numerous place-names in Palestine[90] which have 'Baal' as a constituent part points in that direction.

To the extent that the tribes ceased to be (semi-) nomadic and began instead to cultivate the soil[91] they came within the compelling orbit of Canaanite ways and customs and thus of the rites and festivals of Baalism. The process was facilitated by the fact that the name 'Baal' had originally been an appellative, with the meaning of 'Lord', 'Owner', and so could be applied to the deity whom they themselves worshipped. In Yahwistic circles, therefore, it could do very well for Yahweh himself. That this is what happened is clear from the evidence of certain personal names current among the devotees of Yahweh (Jerubbaal; Mephibaal). Consequently, the use of such names was later regarded as a very dangerous practice and as something to be abhorred; and then only names compounded with Yahweh or El were employed, whilst at a still later time the names containing the 'Baal' element were even pronounced and written as though they were in fact compounded with 'Bosheth' (meaning 'reproach' or 'shame'). It became inadmissible to use the word 'Baal' in connexion with God's relationship with men (Hos. 2:16). Episodes like the story of Baal Peor (Num. 25:1ff. being among the oldest sources; cf. Hos. 9:10) witness as much to the urge to assimilate and to its power of attraction as to the opposition which it aroused.

From the earliest times Yahwism had flung itself into the struggle with this cult of Baal. The very being of its God was wholly different in kind from that force of nature, which was glorified in the person of Baal, and disclosed itself through a specific cycle of rising and shining, of declining and rising again, as happened with the passing seasons of the year. With Yahweh nothing of this is so much as hinted at. He is the living God, not the dying and rising one; the God of the here and now, of the onward march of history, who by word and action wields control over the world (of men).[92]

Therefore Yahwism rooted out, as a matter of principle, those elements in her religious ideas which had become infected with Baalism and had to do with the fertility-ritual, with the sexual rites that were its issue and with the death and resurrection of the god. Only those elements such as the agricultural festivals were retained which could be neutralized from a religious standpoint and thus assimilated. Very possibly we have here the source of the cycle of the three festivals of the soil (spring, summer and autumn), and in particular of the feast of weeks as it is called. At a later date especially, the festivals are purified of every taint of paganism by being linked with events in the history of Israel's deliverance (Deut. 16; Lev. 23).

Perhaps the most important legacy of Baalism to Israel is the fact that as the living God, Yahweh was *also* seen as the giver of fertility. In some areas this was taken so far that, like Baal, Yahweh came to be associated with the bull (temples in the northern kingdom at Bethel and Dan; see 1 Kings 12:26ff. and cf. Ex. 32f.). Whilst this aroused a lot of opposition, he was legitimately connected with fertility in another manner (cf. Hos. 2; Ps. 67), which does not, however, mean that Yahweh is personally implicated in the course of natural processes, but rather, as we said before, that all this comes from him as the giver. The earth yields her corn at his command or through his blessing (Gen. 1:11f.; Ps. 67:7); and the gifts of fertility and fecundity are brought into being through various agencies, although Yahweh remains the ultimate donor (Hos. 2:20ff.).

Still, the Baal cult and its customs must have retained a considerable influence, at least among some sections of the populace in certain areas, especially in Northern Israel. This is evident from the way in which the prophets did battle with various religious deviations—and most evident of all in the case of Hosea and Ezekiel (Hos. 6:1–6;[93] Ezek. 8:14f.). The 'gardens of Adonis' were to be found even at Jerusalem (Isa. 17:10f.); and at a later period Megiddo still resounded with cultic elegies and lamentations for Hadad-Rimmon (Zech. 12:11). More especially in the syncretism of the Elephantine-'sect', which was certainly of North-Israelite provenance (and akin to the Bethel-cult; see p. 261ff.), one finds all sorts of elements pointing to these forms of religion.[94]

Along with the denunciations, therefore, went a wide diffusion of various elements of this type of nature-worship throughout the whole of Israel. It is not really surprising that they persisted under the monarchy, at a time when Israel was principally an agrarian people; and it is hardly likely that their influence was confined to the popular religion. Ezekiel in fact connects the cult of Tammuz even with the temple at Jerusalem.

As a third generally disseminated element in the religious worldview we mentioned (p. 33) 'the three-storeyed universe'. We need not linger for long over this subject, which is familiar enough to us from the Bible: the earth is enclosed by the heavens; and beneath it is the underworld, Sheol.[95] Across the vault of heaven move the stars in their courses, whilst the underworld is the home of the dead and of demons.

The Egyptians viewed the world in the same way, with heaven, earth and Duat (the underworld) as parts of the cosmos;[96] and so did the other peoples of the ancient East.[97] In a number of mythologies the creator-god makes the world by 'dividing' or separating heaven and earth (in Egypt the sky-goddess is uplifted from the earth by the creator; in the Babylonian world the body of the vanquished chaos-monster is cut in two. There is a reminiscence of this in the wording of the passage at Gen. 1:4ff. The act of creation as one of dividing, of separating out, indicates that the world in its original, chaotic state was envisaged as a single mass, as is also found in the Phoenician view). The one thing that really distinguishes Israel from the rest is her view of everything in heaven, on earth and in the world beneath as being subject absolutely to Yahweh and, essentially, as having been created, even though in Gen. 1:2 the *tehom* (the primal waters) are thought of as existing before the creation, and though in the oldest accounts of creation allusion is made to certain incidents in Yahweh's battle with the monsters of chaos (Amos 9:3; Isa. 27:1; Ps. 89:10f.; Isa. 51:9f.). In the (less ancient) creation story in Genesis 1 the heavenly bodies are stated to have been called into being by God on the *fourth* day, and so were held to have been created 'fifth in line', and not before. We may say, then, that the world was progressively de-divinized by Israel, in that with ever-increasing emphasis she ascribed divinity to the One Being alone, to Yahweh alone. Whatever similarity of view there may have been, it is this that fundamentally divides Israel's understanding of the world, and her outlook upon it, from that of the nations round about her.

The various religions of the ancient East severally outlined

Our purpose in handling the matters discussed in the foregoing section was to bring out some of the features shared by the religions of the ancient East. Yet in a great many ways they do differ; and each has a distinctive character of its own. It could even be said that when they differ, it is on some very fundamental points and ideas about religion. In outlining the common traits we have so far confined ourselves to the ancient religions of the soil and of husbandry, for which adequate literary sources are extant. As soon as we come to characterize in more general terms the ancient religions amid which Israel lived, we have to consider quite a number for which such sources are available only in part. In some cases, particularly when it comes to the religions of the ancient Arab world, the evidence consists of inscriptions only—and only to a very limited degree is it possible to construct a picture of this complex of religions. They vary in form from tribe to tribe and from one area to another; but however much each may differ from its fellows, these North-Arabian religious complexes between Mecca and the Euphrates are nonetheless so closely akin that they can be treated as a unit.

We shall consider first the ancient religions of land cultivation, beginning with that of Egypt.

The religion of Egypt

This is so complicated that it has been well and truly likened to a 'huge, rambling, unmanageable property with innumerable rooms'.[98] Indeed, one cannot help noticing the fact, as soon as one sets about examining this religion. The impression that one gets here is of a conglomeration of age-old agrarian elements, mingled with a variety of less ancient ones which are partly Hamitic, partly Semitic in origin. The facets of this religion are therefore most diverse; but all witness to a process of development over many thousands of years. We can trace its course through roughly three millennia; but its origins are as often as not shrouded in a very remote past. The unity in all this multiplicity is not an easy thing to uncover. Still, there are some parts of crucial importance which typify the whole and stand out by way of contrast when this religion is compared with others of the same period.

A few such features have been indicated already: the pantheon with its single head and the belief in a dying and rising god, represented primarily by the figure of Osiris. Again, one thinks immediately in this connexion of the care bestowed on the dead, with the aim of ensuring the continuance of life in the hereafter. The pyramids, the tombs of the kings, the mastabas with their celebrated grave-utensils, their 'books' or inscriptions of the dead and their wall paintings, are incontrovertible evidence of this.[99] The divinity of the kings is yet another very important aspect of this religion. Different again is the strong emphasis placed on animal-worship and the animal form assumed by many of the gods.

Most of these factors, with the exception of the last mentioned, have one thing that unites them all: both the monarchism of the pantheon, or as the case may be, the syncretistic merging together of the gods (p. 34, n. 42; cf. p. 280), and the polarity of life and death, together with the divinity attributed to the Pharoah, point to a powerful strain of monism in the life and thought of the Egyptians.

Egyptian mythology (in a fairly late and very complicated text) conceives of the cosmos as created by the sun-god: he generated himself, then formed the images or ideas of created beings, impregnated himself by masturbation and so brought forth other gods; and finally he annihilated the dragon of darkness.[100] Other myths present us with a different version; but the gist is the same. The sun-god is not only autogamous, he is autogonous as well: he is the symbol of spontaneous life, which was self-generated in him. He has at his disposal the secret life-force, which 'is the ground of all things. It is present in the solar energy; it is in the atmosphere too, as an all-pervasive vital element. It comes close to the idea of the sustaining, self-creating cosmic energy that is "life".'[101] Perhaps we should even speak here, as does J. Zandee, of a 'pantheistic conception of an all-embracing cosmic energy'.[102] There is in the world's mode of being an arcane oneness that is also life. Even though the sun must constantly overcome the darkness, the latter is not a substantive, anti-divine power which should actually be regarded as antagonistic to the life-force. J. A. Wilson[103] is certainly right in finding a connexion between the Egyptian religious understanding of life—with its marked emphasis on equilibrium, on polarity—and the natural environment in which the Egyptian had to live. If we are to say with Frankfort, who edited the book to which we have just referred,[104] that for the Egyptians the divine was immanent in nature; and if we can allow the essential character of nature, as they saw it, to be contingent upon the conditions of life that they encountered in and through their natural environment, then we can only conclude that in the representation of religious experience the prevailing 'facts of nature' have a substantial part to play. Wilson goes on to point out the uniformity of nature in Egypt, which offered mainly the contrast between desert and fertile land, night and day, but hardly at all that between rain and sunshine, summer and winter. Scarcely anywhere in the world is the general similarity between the seasons greater than in that land, where nature inclines men to a monistic view of life, in terms of which light and darkness, fecundity and barrenness, death and life, are rhythmically conjoined. It is chiefly the sun that determines this rhythm; but the Nile too, which is the source of fertility and inundates the land with her swollen waters more or less regularly every year, is a contributing factor. A constant periodicity sets its mark upon the whole of life, which itself is geared, basically, to an attitude of optimism.

The pursuit of cultivation, which along by the great rivers gave regular opportunity at an early stage for the growth and formation of the state (because men came to depend on one another over large distances for the proper control of the waterways), is also a stabilizing factor. The state with its polity, created in order to maintain unity and so to sustain life itself, is part and parcel of the monistic view of creation and is itself subsumed as a focal element within that creation. That is why the kings are held to be sons of Re and, as such, are vehicles of the vital, divine energy that keeps everything in being. Consequently, they are the link between heaven and earth. The divine kingship fits perfectly into the structure of the Egyptians' outlook on life. Here again is one of the roots of their concept of immortality: as son of Re, the Pharaoh participates in the continuous process of life. In the grave this is ensured for him by the provision of all kinds of objects and a variety of human attendants.

This sense, this feeling, that life is monistic in character sets its mark on the way in which most religious ideas are conceived and presented, even though certain doubts and questionings come to the surface in the wisdom-literature and give rise to a sometimes strident scepticism which is another case of nature being stronger than nurture.

The religion of Babylon

Although this has many allied features, its essential character is not that of the Egyptian religion. Instead of a religion formed and focused on monism, what one detects here is a basic element of dualism. The world arose out of the struggle between the powers of chaos and of order. This confrontation of opposites is there, in principle, from the very beginning of things in the figures of Apsu, the 'sweet' (fresh) water, and Tiamat, the ocean; and it is in fact going on all the time. The Babylonian creation-story, in which the battle of the gods, and specifically that of Marduk with Tiamat, plays such a major role, shows how the world order, represented by the pantheon, can maintain itself only by destroying chaos; but it is an everlasting contest, a battle renewed with every passing year, and Marduk must vanquish Tiamat over and over again.[105] One might say, therefore, that the essence of the Babylonian view, as opposed to the Egyptian, with its governing idea of uniformity, is summed up in the word 'change'. Everything arises out of conflict, has its being in conflict and ends in conflict, renewing its life only to endure the conflict over again.[106]

Here again one ought perhaps to connect this 'thinking in opposites' with the nature of the country, as indeed is done by Th. Jacobsen.[107] Compared with the Nile, the rivers of Mesopotamia are altogether more dangerous and turbulent. There can be raging storms and heavy rains, causing the rivers to overflow. The forces of nature are unbridled and hard for man to subdue. Life is a perpetual struggle. Such order as the gods and men have fashioned is under continual threat of dissolution. Only in that kind of a world could a story like that of the Great Flood have come about. Often enough there is dissension among the gods; and they can act deceitfully. Amid the forces of nature man feels puny and unsafe. The world of the gods, who personify those natural forces, is extremely diverse, frequently capricious and always hemmed round by chaos. Man himself is surrounded by a host of demons who bring all kinds of misfortune upon him. Although often regarded as the creatures of Anu, they are rather a source of chaos than of order.

The way in which the Babylonians felt about life is closely bound up with the idea of the tragic.[108] A sentence in the ancient Gilgamesh-epic says much in this connexion: 'man—his days are numbered; whatever he does, he is so much wind'.[109] Far more than in Egypt, death is felt to be an enemy; and it is inescapable, decreed for man at his creation by the gods. Life in the hereafter is envisaged as a wretched state and there is nothing here of the optimistic Egyptian outlook. The result of all this is a strong sense of insecurity, of menace, and a propensity to look on the black side of things. Religion in Babylon is not so much permeated and dominated by the idea of the dying and rising god as it is in Egypt. In Egypt Re was transformed by the figure of Osiris; but Marduk is not 'Tammuzized'. At any rate there are no texts known to us that would clearly support such a thesis.

The world of the gods is envisaged far less theriomorphically than in Egypt; in fact it is anthropomorphic, almost without exception;[110] and in Babylon the astral element is much more prominent. That is understandable enough when one considers how deeply nomadic elements had penetrated the Mesopotamian milieu. Babylonian-Assyrian culture and religion spring in fact from a fusion of the ancient Sumerian culture, which in many respects continued to flourish, with the not so ancient Semitic variety. It is difficult to disentangle these two strands;[111] but we cannot and need not pursue the problem here. We may take it on trust as evident that the astral gods—sun, moon and stars—derived from the Semitic sphere of influence round about the Syrian-Arabian desert region, even though their relative stations within the hierarchy were often different in Mesopotamia.[112]

In Babylon as elsewhere in the world beyond that of the Bible the gods are thought to be male or female. More even than in Egypt they go together in pairs and have a male or female consort, as the case may be. Each town would have one particular god as its chief deity; but there would always be temples of other gods too. According to the Babylonian religion the gods form part of a pantheon, a council,[113] which rules over and maintains the world under the direction of a chief god (in Babylon, Marduk). Man is created to be at the gods' disposal: he must serve the godhead, submit and obey, which means, first and foremost, paying due regard to the cult and the rites. This is needed to put the gods in a position to sustain the world. It enables man to keep in with the gods and to hold the demons at bay (magic).

This is why the temples, the *loci* of the cult, are of such paramount importance. They constitute the focal point of life, cosmic and mundane, the centre of the state. The deity is the supreme power in the state and is represented on earth by the head of the state, the king-priest.[114] The latter is not usually regarded, as he is in Egypt, as being of divine origin; but his mandate is divine, and with it he acquires divine authority.[115] Consequently, the state is a sacral institution. Treaties or compacts concluded by the state carry a divine guarantee. The man who goes against the state is just as much a transgressor as one who infringes the rites. The way in which Hammurabi introduces himself into his celebrated Code makes this perfectly clear. The primary laws, which deal with the violation of property-rights, (§6ff.), treat temple and palace as being on a completely equal footing. Just as the cosmos is regarded as a state, so the state can be envisaged as part of the created cosmos. A didactic poem on the creation can even picture Babylon as the first work of creation.[116]

Thus the Babylonian form of religion was a 'nationalized' one. Side by side with astral gods and gods of nature a variety of national

D

gods peopled the heavens too. Religious thought was dominated by these three basic elements of life: the forces of nature, the stars, and the power of the state. It did not, it is true, range them together in a neat and rounded system; but it posited them and identified experientially with each of them severally in the powerful and reciprocal tensions of so highly variegated a divine world.[117] In the great universe that was unfolded to the eye of the Babylonian beholder the individual felt insignificant and insecure. By faithfully discharging his religious duties and by diligently carrying out the rites he kept firm hold on the gods who were all around him.[118] The man who forfeited that stay was reduced beyond recovery to a pessimistic and enervating scepticism.[119]

The Phoenician-Canaanite religion[120]

It is generally accepted that there is so great a degree of kinship between the religion of pre-Israelite Canaan and that of ancient Phoenicia that they are to be regarded as a single religion. Naturally, there will have been local and 'provincial' variations here and there; and in this or that centre particular elements will have come to the fore. Yet this need not detract from the close affinity between the varying forms. In the religions of Egypt and Mesopotamia too there were local differences, and this is true, in fact, of all major religions.

We propose to handle the Aramaean religion separately, although it was related very closely to its Canaanite-Phoenician counterpart. It enters the light of history only at a later period. The distinction between the two forms of religion is a nice one; but it is sufficient to distinguish them and to enable us to tell them apart. What does become fairly clear in the Aramaean world is the preference for certain gods and the connexion with the ancient desert-religion of Northern Arabia.

The Phoenician-Canaanite religion is much less well documented than either of those—the Egyptian and the Mesopotamian—that have been discussed so far. Besides the Old Testament, there are a number of sources of Greek provenance[121] to which we can turn; and then there are the el-Amarna letters and, since 1929, the inscriptions discovered at Ras Shamra, in addition to the archaeological finds, which are widespread and continually mounting in number.

The two last have added enormously to our knowledge of this religion and have made available authentic material from the archives of the palace at Ugarit (on the coast of Northern Syria), belonging to the pre-Israelite period, ± 1400. (The Amarna letters are of a somewhat later date).

Some of the deities have been dealt with already: El, the head of the pantheon,[122] Baal, god of the storm and rain, of fertility and natural life—who has roughly the same role in the countries to the west as Hadad (Adad) in the more easterly situated areas and is frequently identified with him[123]—and Mot (the antagonist of Baal), god of the summer drought and of death.[124]

If the relation between Baal and Hadad is not altogether clear, the case is much the same with the three goddesses: Asherah, Astarte and Anat. These are treated in some quarters as separate beings; but they would appear, at a later period especially, to merge together, being then regarded as the great goddess of fertility. The first-mentioned, Asherah,[125] is evidently the same as Elat and may be regarded as the female counterpart to El and as mother of the gods. She is probably also the one who created all life; but this fertility-aspect of her character is less conspicuous in Phoenicia than in the world of the Old Testament, where she is seen principally as a vegetation-symbol.[126] It also appears to associate her directly with Baal and to identify her with Astarte.

In Ugarit Astarte is the goddess of fertility and the consort of Baal.[127] Whether she is the Ba'alat of Gubla (Jebel or Byblos) is uncertain, but highly likely.[128] If so, we might perhaps identify her also with the Ba'alat[129] venerated in more than one locality in Canaan, and with the Asherah who pairs with the Baal of Sidon.[130] Originally, Astarte must have been the female counterpart to Astar, the evening and morning star, and possibly a parallel to Ashtar from Moab.[131] Later she is identified with Anat.[132]

The third and most important goddess in the literature of Ugarit is Anat.[133] She functions there as the sister of Baal and avenges his death upon Mot, the god of drought and death. She is the maiden goddess, but at the same time is represented as extremely warlike. The poem named after her describes her wading up to the hips in blood.[134] She is the goddess of battle and probably represents the power of life in the struggle with death and chaos. She is certainly pictured as being clad in an ephod.[135] In a late text from Cyprus (4th century B.C.) she is identified with the Greek goddess Athene.[136] She was frequently worshipped in Egypt too. Traces of her worship are found in Canaan in place-names like Beth Anat, Anathoth.[137] She was probably venerated in the later Bethel and regarded there as a daughter of Yahweh. At any rate, the Elephantine texts link her with Yahweh (Anath-Yahu) and give her a connexion with Bethel (Anath-Bethel).

Various pictorial representations of goddesses have been found which must belong to the Phoenician culture; but only a few of these can be identified with one of the goddesses above mentioned.[138]

It would seem that the fertility aspect came more and more to dominate the Phoenician religion and that as a result Baal became, in practice and to an increasing extent, the principal god and Astarte the principal goddess. It was chiefly in this form that Israel became acquainted with the religion of Canaan.

Even so, there was a whole string of other gods, who have only become somewhat better known to us through the Ugaritic literature, having left very few positive traces of themselves in the Old Testament.

One of the gods who does appear there and turns up in Phoenicia too is Dagon. He is found quite often in Mesopotamia, and in Mari is one of the major deities. His role in Ugarit is more limited; but he is regarded there as the father of Baal. Like Baal he is probably a weather-god and at the same time a god of fertility.[139] It is highly likely that his name corresponds to the Hebrew word *dagan*, corn. In Palestine he is worshipped by the Philistines (1 Sam. 5, in Ashdod; Judges 16:23 in Gaza) who probably took over, as an indigenous god, the old deity of West-Semitic provenance.[140]

Ashtar [141] has been mentioned already. He is a male god, representing the morning and evening star; and he appears a good deal among the Arabians (of both the North and the South). After Baal's death he makes a brief attempt to seize his throne but cannot hold on to it. His secondary function, apparently, is as a god of life and death, associated with the waxing and waning of the star of Venus.[142]

The sun-deity in Ugarit, as in the Arabian world, was feminine and went by the name of Shapash—like the moon-deity Verah. The three last-mentioned gods, which are familiar enough to us in an Arabian context, had little or no place in the cultic life of Phoenicia.

Important as a deity who had his own cult of public worship was the god Resheph, with his great temple in Byblos. He was the god of the underworld and the plague, whom some identify with the Mekal found at Beth-Shan.[143] The root of the word occurs in the Old Testament in the sense of 'fire', 'pestilence'.

From theophorous names (in the el-Amarna letters) and other data we can draw a conclusion as to the incidence of the god Milk. This title was in use for various gods (El, Baal, Ashtar).[144] When it was meant to denote a particular god, this would probably have been El or Baal; but in principle this could vary from place to place and from one period to another. In Tyre the chief god was called Melkart (the god 'Milk of the city' or 'melech of the city'). Here we appear to have what is essentially a Baal-figure.[145]

The Ugaritic texts make frequent mention of the sea-god Yam. They envisage him as one of the adversaries of Baal, and thus as a deity who constitutes a danger to life.

Some of the lesser known gods of whom mention can be made are: Horon, who was worshipped in Canaan in the locality of Beth-Horon and is also known from certain Egyptian texts—but what he stood for cannot be determined with any certainty;[146] Shahar and Shalem, who appear together but also independently—they were known as the lovely and beautiful gods and represented the flush of dawn and of evening.[147] 'Shalem', as the name of a god, probably occurs in Jerusalem.[148] It was certainly regarded as propitious. Then again, El was known in primitive Jerusualem under the name El Elyon, who was thought to be head of the pantheon and treated as a creator-god (Gen. 14:18ff.). From theophorous names one can deduce that there must also have been a god Ṣedeq.[149] There would undoubtedly have been yet other gods to whom service was rendered. Ezekiel refers to the fact that Jerusalem has a hybrid cultural background: it was born of an Amorite father and a Hittite mother.

Furthermore, we encounter in Ugarit a divine overseer and artist, Koshar, usually with the sobriquet *wa-Hasis*, ('the wise').

Some claim to have found the name Yahweh (in the form 'Yw') in Ugarit; but most scholars postulate that the relevant text be given a different reading: e.g. YM (Yam) or Yr.[150]

A few further observations on the institutional side.

Our knowledge of temple-building in the Phoenician-Canaanite world is steadily increasing. It shows a considerable affinity with that of Israel at the time of Solomon, which ought not to surprise us since the Old Testament says quite clearly that Solomon's temple was built, or at any rate was embellished, with the help of Hiram of Tyre, a renowned worker in copper (1 Kings 7:13ff.). The temple which most resembles (so far) the one in Jerusalem is that discovered in Northern Syria between Aleppo and Antioch at Tell Tainat. It is not quite so old (9th century) and is smaller; but it presents the same ground-plan, with the same threefold division into forecourt, holy place and inner sanctuary, which in the main is at a higher level.[151]

The same area also yields a variety of notable objects: altars, thrones, cherubic figures, representations of this or that temple, and so forth—all of which gives us a broad picture of what there must have been in the Israelite sanctuaries at Jerusalem and elsewhere.

From Ugarit we can gather something about cultic practices.[152] Here too sheep and oxen were sacrificed; and it was stipulated that the animals must be whole and 'without blemish'. There were burnt-sacrifices and communion-sacrifices.[153] Feasts of the new moon were observed—and in the month Tishri a feast of purification, which may be a Canaanitic parallel to the Great Day of Atonement.[154] We come across various officials or cultic personages, including a high priest, priests, soothsayers, temple guardians, *Kedeshoth* (temple prostitutes) and female mourners.

We learn from an ancient Egyptian account of Wen-Amon[155] that there was current an ecstatic form of prophetism. Regal inscriptions witness to an attitude of reverence (there is some talk of 'the holy gods'[156]) and to an affectionate attachment to the godhead, specifically *vis-à-vis* the Ba'alat of Byblos.[157] The monarch declares twice over in a votive inscription that the goddess has answered his prayer. Oath-taking formulas are, of course, plentiful enough.

Excavations in the Canaanite area have brought the picture to life in more than one respect. So far as the history of religion is concerned, one of the most significant developments, certainly, is the work carried out at Nahariya (along by the coast in the north of modern Israel), where a Canaanite sanctuary has been uncovered on the top of a little hill (there were in fact two temples, one above the other, from the period between 1800 and 1550). The oldest temple consisted of a small, square-shaped chapel, in front of which was placed a round platform on which the votive offerings could be laid. All sorts of valuables were found, made of gold or silver, semi-precious stones, fascinating terracottas of animals (a little monkey, for instance), libation-vases, each with seven tiny cups into which oil could be poured, and a number of silver platters bearing a representation of the female deity worshipped there. Also discovered amid the débris was one half of a mould used for making small models of Astarte.

At a later period this sanctuary was extended, by the erection of a larger building alongside it. In view of the pictorial design and the mould, the sanctuary is thought to have been a 'high place' for Asherah of the sea.[158]

The nature of a 'high place' is well illustrated here, as a locale in the open air which usually was simply fenced round, and which lay near to a spring and a sacred tree, being furnished with a small cella.

No less important is the find comprising three temples discovered at Hazor in the course of excavations directed from 1955 onwards by Dr Yigael Yadin.[159] They carry us into a period closer to the Israelite epoch than the one previously mentioned: that is, from 1550 to 1150.

The item of most importance is a temple consisting of three parts: an open fore-portal, a great hall and an inner sanctuary. As may be seen from the bases that have been discovered, at the entrance to the portal there once stood two pillars of basalt. Portal and inner sanctuary alike were lined with sheets of basalt stone. In the inner sanctuary there was a niche on the north side, meant apparently to accommodate the image of the god. At the same spot an altar of incense was discovered too, along with, among other things, a solar disc, four small images, one male and two female deities and the figure of a bull, as well as vessels of various kinds, among them several large pots. At the entrance was stationed a lion, made of basalt.

Of the other two temples one was only small; but it yielded an exceptionally rich haul of sacred objects, including a figurine of a god in a niche and a number of small basalt steles, on one of which two arms were chiselled, uplifted towards a divine symbol (the sun and the crescent moon). Another find of interest was a tiny bronze standard with a snake-goddess. The snake in the Canaanite world was the symbol of life.

If the sanctuary at Nahariya is an outstanding example of a *bamah*, a 'high place' (of which the Old Testament has so much to say), the first of the Hazor temples, like the one at Tell-Tainat mentioned earlier, reminds us forcibly of Solomon's temple in its structure.

We may round off this brief survey of Canaanite religion with a look at a characteristic feature to which W. W. Baudissin calls our attention in his study of *Adonis und Esmun*. He points out[160] that both these gods illustrate the significance attached to *the idea of life in Phoenician religion*. It is plain that this whole religion is typified not so much by El, nor by the astral gods even, as by the predominating, and indeed, as things turned out, increasingly paramount figures of Baal and Astarte.[161] The picture of Canaanite religion reflected in the

Old Testament is accurate in this respect. The West Semitic religion was in origin an agricultural one; and above everything else it preserved, and even reinforced, its vegetative character through each phase of its growth. The prominence and strength of the orgiastic element were a direct and fully accepted consequence of this. What was important enough in the religions of Babylon and Egypt here remained central, more than anything else in the cult.

The Aramaean religion

We decided to keep this separate from the Phoenician-Canaanite religion because, as it seems to us, it has a number of independent features and because the Aramaeans as a people appeared on the cultural scene much later than Phoenicians and Canaanites. They were the latest branch of the Semitic group to play a part in ancient history (during the time of Israel's existence as a state). In the middle of the second millennium the Aramaeans are spoken of in Babylonian sources as a group of tribes, although we hear tell, it is true, of certain individual Arami within the context of East Semitic culture at a much earlier period.[162] They crop up in the Syrian-Arabian desert after the Sutaeans and the Ahlamu (to whom they were closely related); and by the start of the 13th century they have penetrated as far as Mesopotamia. Between the end of the 12th and 11th centuries they overran and occupied the territories to the west of the desert area.

In some respects more, therefore, than with the other West Semites, their religion bears the characteristic marks of the ancient desert religion of Northern Arabia and has certain East Semitic features as well. This again turns very much on the environment in which the Aramaeans settled down.

No documents of their religion—in the way of myths, ritual texts or psalms, for example—have come down to us. We have to get what we know of their religious life mainly from a few historical texts and from treaties. The former come from votive inscriptions and contain various outpourings of gratitude to the god. The treaties give us, besides the names of certain gods, various maledictions and rituals. Theophorous personal names from many different sources help to fill some of the gaps in our knowledge of the nomenclature of the gods.

One thing is clear. Hadad, the storm- and weather-god, is the chief deity—at all events in Damascus, where he is known from the names of several kings (as, for instance, in the Old Testament). He was also called Rimmon, 'the thunderer'. The name El also occurs here, as a matter of fact; and a dedicatory inscription mentions the god Melkart. In Arpad too Hadad is the principal god, and probably in Hamat. Since Hadad is a very ancient North Semitic god anyway,[163] it seems likely that the Aramaeans brought him with them from the desert, or else that he was adopted as a result of their settling in the West. Precisely what Hadad's character was it is hard to say. He seems to have been identified (as in Syria) with Baal Shamayim, the Lord of heaven, the West Semitic El, but elsewhere (in Phoenicia) he merges with the fertility god, Baal.[164] He is probably not like the West Semitic Baal, just a rain- and storm-god, as is the Babylonian Adad: cf. Rimmon in Damascus.

The question whether Hadad can be in every respect identified with Be'el Shemayin (Baal Shamayim) is difficult to resolve. Opinion is divided on this issue.[165] In the inscription of Zakir,[166] king of Hamat and La'ash (c. 800), lavish thanks are bestowed on the last-mentioned god for all that he has done; whereas the stele itself is dedicated to the god Ilu-Wer (a Hadad-figure). It is possible, however, that at the foot of the inscription these gods were named side by side; but because of the corrupt state of the text we cannot say for certain. We do not know, either, what the name Ilu-Wer signifies or from what cultural milieu it derives. Besides this god (or these gods) the inscription refers to: Shamash (borrowed from the East Semitic pantheon), Sahr (a South and West Semitic term for the moon-god), the gods of Heaven and the gods of Earth (the latter being identifiable, perhaps with the Babylonian Igigi and Anunnaki).

It is worth noting that evidently according to some texts[167] Yahu was known as the name of a god in Hamat, although at a later period. The name must surely be the same as the Hebrew Yahweh-name, which even in the Old Testament is repeatedly shortened to Yahu. The most likely explanation for this is that the city of Hamat, having had contact with Israel since the time of David, added this deity to its pantheon.[168]

It is a relevant point that Earth and Heaven, as gods in their own right, occur in the treaty concluded between a certain monarch KTK and a king of Arpad.[169] The following gods are mentioned in it: El and 'Atar (both in personal names), Hadad as deity-in-chief, Sibitti, El, Elyon, Heaven, Earth, Abyss,[170] Well-springs, Day and Night.

These names show just how composite the Arpad pantheon was. There were some very ancient gods in it, whom one finds in the

Arabian and West Semitic region: El, 'Atar, Hadad (East Semitic too). Besides them there are the Sibitti, pointing, surely, to the Babylonian milieu,[171] whilst Elyon is again West Semitic.[172] As divinities, Heaven and Earth, Well-springs, Abyss, Day and Night are difficult to pin down. Day (Umu) appears in Mesopotamia as an independent deity;[173] and Night is known there too, as Lilitu, the night-demon (taken over into the later Israel as Lilith). Heaven and Earth, Abyss and Well-springs, are invoked as witnesses in a treaty with the Hittites; but such appeals to natural forces and phenomena are also to be found elsewhere.[174] As is only to be expected, therefore, there was in this North Semitic city a divine company of a highly international complexion. That Hadad was the head and leader is in itself a significant pointer to the Aramaean character.

The gods of the other party, Barga'ayah, king of KTK, whom we should probably take—as M. Noth does—to be an Aramaean ruler, are nearly all East Semitic.[175]

The Sam'al (Zendjiri in North west Syria) inscriptions, of the 9th and and 8th centuries, reveal the following pantheon: Hadad, El, Resheph, Rakab-el, Shamash, Baal Harran (=Sin), Baal Semed and Baal Hamman.[176] Here again we find Hadad at the top; whilst there is room too for the West and South Semitic El, for the typical West Semitic Resheph and the East Semitic Shamash and Sin. Three of the gods are not otherwise known: Rakab (or Rekub)-El (=charioteer or chariot of El), Baal Semed and Baal Hamman. They are perhaps merely local gods.

From the inscriptions we learn something of the relations between gods and men. Kings are grateful to the gods for their royal office and keep in contact with them through prayer, through sacrifices, through the prophets. The gods show themselves willing and ready to hear their servants.

A good deal of emphasis is put on seers and soothsayers. Princes know that they are called to help the oppressed and to put away evil. The gods punish unrighteousness and safeguard contracts. Indeed, they are witnesses when agreements are concluded and take revenge on those who break them.

Tombs are committed to the protection of the gods. Curses are laid on all who desecrate tombs, or plunder and destroy them.[177] The most interesting epitaph—from the standpoint of the history of religion—which is known to us from the ancient West Semitic world is that of king Panammu of Sam'al, who caused to be cut into his own burial inscription his wish that his successors might always bring food and drink to his grave and, in so doing, should utter these words: 'that the death-soul (*nephesh*) of Panammu may eat with Hadad and that the death-soul of Panammu may drink with Hadad'.[178] The expectation voiced here is that through the gifts of his successors the king will live on in the grave with Hadad.[179] In the context of these ideas one can well understand Amos' protest at the spoliation of an Edomite king's grave by a Moabite chieftain (Amos 2:1f.). (For the Syrian cities at a later time, in the Hellenistic and Roman periods, see p. 65f.).

The religion of some Transjordanian peoples

Of the Ammonites, Moabites and Edomites—ethnic groups so very closely akin to Israel (cf. the narratives in Gen. 19 and 25)—we know only a little; but that little is enough to confirm the assumptions that can be made on geographical and historical grounds regarding the character of their religion. It is obvious enough that we are to see these minor peoples—living on the edge of the desert and on the borders of the civilized world—as upholding what are usually referred to as the religious ideas of Northern Arabia—but then as being so strongly affected too by their age-old contact with the rest of the Semitic (especially West Semitic) cultural sphere that their ancient Arabian religion is powerfully infused with West Semitic elements.

Something of the sort has been the case, in fact, with practically all these tribes (races) living on the dividing-line between desert and inhabited world, and even with towns in the desert oases, right up to Roman times. We may expect, then, to find here early on much the same syncretism in religion that one comes across at a later period in cities such as Palmyra, Gerasa or Petra. These places preserved in their religion the basic pattern of the old Arabian religious notions; but that pattern had been covered over with a layer, sometimes thick and sometimes thin, of elements borrowed from the culture that dominated their environment. The greater the influence of that culture, the more completely the basic 'North Arabian' pattern was obscured—sometimes to such a degree that the old names of the gods were abandoned in favour of new ones taken from other cultural milieus.

In comparing the ingredients of the religions of some of the minor centres of culture alongside the desert, one can more or less predict, by the use of geographical data, what the relative proportions of the admixture will be. For instance: the religion of Mari, a desert town close to Mesopotamia, exhibits, even at an earlier time, far fewer original features of North Semitic religion than do other North Syrian towns at a later period such as Arpad.[180]

Thus Palmyra and Petra in the Hellenistic period remained in all sorts of ways much more eastern than Baalbek or Gerasa, which were almost completely hellenized.

As for the small states in the middle of the Transjordanian region, like the territories to the west of Jordan (Canaan and Israel) they were greatly affected, culturally, first by Egypt and then by Mesopotamia.[181] The small number of *objets d'art* that have been found show at any rate that the top circles in these countries kept up with the times. Of course, this could only have been true of the very small groups that formed the entourage of kings; for the country and the people, then as now, must have been pretty poor. The chief means of existence were: agriculture (on a limited scale), trade (these lands lay along the trade-routes from Northern Syria to Arabia and probably owed their existence as independent states to that circumstance) and a little 'industry' (mining, at any rate). In the late monarchical period (7th century) Ammon would seem to have been the most prosperous of these little kingdoms. Anyway, it paid twice as much in taxes as Judah and Moab,[182] which is due, perhaps, to the fact that it commanded important posts along the caravan routes.

In the Ammonite religion we encounter a few names of gods that are known to us from elsewhere in Arabia: for example, Yerah and Allat, the former being the moon-god and the latter the great goddess whom one comes across in the Nabataean world, in Mecca and elsewhere in old Arabia.[183] Both appear in Ammonite theophorous names: Yerah-'azar, that is, 'the Moon (moon-god) helped';[184] and Allat-Tesha.[185] To these it is quite possible that we should add a third name of Arabian origin: El.[186] However, this personage occurs as a god in his own right not just in Arabia but in the West Semitic sphere particularly;[187] so that we cannot be sure from what quarter the Ammonites took this deity—whether from their own Arabian history or from the West Semitic world. Further, one can infer from the nomenclature that a god called 'Amm was worshipped;[188] but whether this theophorous element[189] should be regarded as a vestige of a particular 'tribal god' conception[190] or as offering a parallel to the god 'Amm (another name for the moon-god)[191] who is found in Southern Arabia is uncertain. No more can we decide with a sufficient degree of certainty from the theophorous element in names like Adoni-Pellet and Adoni-Nur whether Adon is used as the personal name of a god or is rather to be taken as an epithet. The same applies to the designation of a god as Molech in the Old Testament (1 Kings 11:7), which occurs also as Milkom (Jer. 49:1 and 3)—again, probably, in 2 Sam. 12:30.[192] The most likely conclusion to be drawn from these three texts is that Molech (Milkom) was the city- and state-god of Ammon, just as Chemosh was of Moab. What deity in particular is signified by this name we simply do not know.[193]

What emerges from this brief résumé is that the Ammonites retained the typical North Arabian deities Yerah and Allat (probably also 'Amm, and perhaps El), whilst at the same time adopting West Semitic elements into their religion (Adon, Melek, El perhaps). Unfortunately, we know nothing of their religious practices and nothing about their conception of the life after death, even though a few graves have been discovered. On the cultic side we can make certain assumptions with a fair degree of confidence, because in this respect the Ammonites would have been little different from the Moabites. In some ways we know even less about them; but we do know more, where the cultic aspect is concerned.

As regards the Moabites, there are at all events some direct, and a few indirect, items of evidence which permit us to say a little, at any rate, about the religious life of this people. The direct evidence is supplied by the Mesha-stone, the indirect by the Old Testament.

Moab. Only a few names of gods are reliably transmitted to us by either the Mesha-stone or the Old Testament. One such divine figure is reasonably familiar to us: Chemosh. He turns up in a number of theophorous personal names mentioned in Assyrian sources,[194] in some biblical stories and in the Mesha-inscription. There are a few other gods whose existence we may confidently deduce from the information available to us: Ashtar[195] and Baal.[196] The tribal and state-god, however, was Chemosh, cf. Num. 21:29; Jer. 48:46. The name is something of a mystery but looks as though it derives from an Arabian rather than from a West or East Semitic background. According to the Mesha-inscription he was worshipped in Dibon. He received a child-sacrifice in the shape of the first-born prince (2 Kings 3:27). It is possible—but not certain—that Ashtar-Chemosh, who is referred to in the Mesha-inscription (line 17), is the chief goddess and female consort of Chemosh.[197] Some people presume that both deities appear on the stele of Balu'a, Chemosh on the king's left and Ashtar on his right.[198] One may hazard a guess, at any rate, that on this stele—which exhibits a marked Egyptian influence—a Moabite king is depicted between two gods, whilst two divine emblems—probably the sun and the crescent moon, or sickle of Venus (?)—are visible above the king's shoulders. Assuming that the sun-symbol belongs to the god on the left and that Chemosh is rightly regarded as being akin to Nergal[199]—who was also originally a sun-god—then the left-hand god could indeed be identified as a sun-god with Chemosh. Whether the female figure on the right would then be the moon-goddess or Ashtar remains uncertain.

In general terms we may conclude—as we did in the case of the Ammonites—that the Moabite pantheon exhibits markedly Arabian features. Even so, Baal must be of West Semitic provenance. It is impossible to determine whether that is also the case with the 'fertility-goddess', of whom several figurines[200] have been found which, while exemplifying a type so far rare,[201] are nonetheless akin to some similar figures discovered in Western Palestine; nor have we yet been able to make out whether these are representations of the female (?) Ashtar.[202]

The obvious thing is to take the Mesha-inscription first and see what the evidence it provides has to tell us. It records the setting up of a sanctuary near Dibon; and in it king Mesha[203] declares that Chemosh had been angry with Moab and had (apparently) turned his back on the country, but had afterwards rescued him and the land as well. In gratitude for this, Mesha established the high place, Qerhah. Having conquered, he put to death all the inhabitants of two places, Ataroth and Nebo, which for a long time past had been part of Israel's territory. He did this to make a show or to make reparation to Chemosh[204] (this in the case of Ataroth) and (as regards Nebo) because in pronouncing it accursed he had devoted it to Ashtar Chemosh. There is mention too of his seizing some 'utensils (?) of Yahweh'[205] and of their being transferred to Chemosh's temple.

We learn a certain amount from the Bible as to the reason for Moab's recovery. 2 Kings 3 tells how the Israelites had almost conquered her chief city, when Mesha gave his firstborn son as a burnt-offering to Chemosh. This caused the god to turn his anger upon Israel (2 Kings 3:27), with the result that she had to withdraw. Apparently, this marked the beginning of Moab's restoration by Chemosh, of which Mesha speaks.

One can see that what the Moabites believed about their god offers important parallels to what the Israelites believed about theirs. The favour of the god of the country is crucial for the existence of the nation; and his anger means its downfall. The god is gratified at the destruction of the enemy; and then there is the 'ban'[206] and the mention of the high places. Yet even apart from the polytheism there are radical differences. The wrath of Chemosh, unlike that of Yahweh in the Old Testament, has no moral or religious quality about it, any more than has the ban, which is enforced upon the enemy without pity or remorse.[207] The child-sacrifice would seem to have made the god change his mind,[208] whereas in historic times this form of sacrifice had ceased to be practised in Israel.[209]

It is evident, therefore, that although the Israelite tribes shared with the Moabites the same historical background, their mental and spiritual formation had undergone a fundamental change—thanks to the distinctive character of Israel's belief about her God.

Chemosh has been said[210] to be a war-god; but even though one cannot deny to him (or for that matter to Yahweh, either, who is himself described as a 'man of war' in the Old Testament) his martial exploits, one should not simply call him a god of war any more than Yahweh is simply that. Chemosh is a national god and, as such, is directly involved with the calamities and triumphs of his people. His solar character remains, in all likelihood, the essential thing about him.

Besides Chemosh, the sources acquaint us also with the Moabite god, Baal. It is debatable whether we are to identify this Baal with Chemosh, as van Zÿl does.[211] Although associated, it is true, with a wide range of localities, the Baal-figure has been shown to be too much a god of a distinctive type for that.

The vegetation-cult of Baal-Peor,[212] with its variety of associated sexual rites, is probably of Canaanite origin and had made its way into Moab. Indeed, we read elsewhere of places in Moab where Baal was venerated (see p. 61, n. 196). The terracottas that we mentioned earlier (p 62, n. 200; Astarte-figures, perhaps?) must have some connexion with this fertility-cult. In all probability Baal-Peor was a place situated on Moabite territory but lying close to the border between Israel and Moab, where over a long period the Israelites had observed the cult of Baal.[213] It is no wonder that Moab, being mainly an agrarian country—at least to the extent that it was situated on the high plateau—chose to adopt this cult.

It is not at all unlikely[214] that from the earliest times this Baal-Peor was connected with the Balaam-story and that the sanctuary there played an important role in the procuring of oracles in Moab. In Moab, as in Edom, Ammon, and the other lands round about Israel, oracular practices must have been highly developed (cf. Jer. 27:9). The Balaam-story is material evidence of this, as is the Mesha inscription which cites twice over and word for word a command given by Chemosh.[215] This presupposes the existence of a divine oracle.

The oracular utterance in this case is intended not merely as a prediction but as something with magical implications. It amounts in fact to aiming at one's adversary a dictum charged with a curse (or blessing). Israel too discharged this kind of verbal salvoes at her opponents, which is why prophets had their part to play in warfare there as well (cf. the story of Elisha, 2 Kings 3:13ff. and 13:14ff.).[216]

When this type of magical divination involved the offering of sacrifices to put the god into a sympathetic frame of mind, according to Num. 22ff. these consisted of bulls and rams. It is worth mentioning, for that reason, that the heads of images representing these animals have been discovered in Moab.[217] These would probably not have been the only animals sacrificed among the Moabites; but they were evidently the chief ones.

The Edomites

These are third in the line of peoples with whom Israel was conscious of having a close affinity—closer even than with either the Ammonites or the Moabites, whom we have just been discussing. Edom ranks as a brother nation, not only in the Genesis narratives[218] but also in Deut. 23:8. Even if one declines to accept that there was a primitive connexion between the Esau-figure and Edom,[219] there is still no denying the fact that the two peoples were akin.[220] They were in intimate contact with each other in the Negeb and perhaps even shared a sanctuary together there.[221]

Of Edom's religion little that is substantial is known, apart from the names of a few gods; but we should note that besides the Arabian strain in them these names also show an obvious West Semitic and Aramaean influence. One might well wonder whether this very heterogeneous composition of the pantheon, built up from a North Arabian foundation, could not be said to typify the land of Edom. Through trade, apparently, the country's intellectual and spiritual life acquired a strongly international flavour. Lying on the Elanite gulf and stretching out as far as Moab and the Negeb, it had contacts with Egypt on the one side (1 Kings 11), on the other with Arabia and at the same time with Israel and the Philistines (Amos. 1:6) and Aram to the north, and then with the desert tribes of North Arabia to the east. All this might also help to explain why 'wisdom' that always had about it a distinctly international character was so intensively cultivated in Edom.[222]

The names of Edomite gods are known to us from archaeological finds that have yielded a few theophorous names, from the Old Testament and from Babylonian sources.

The principal god would seem to have been Qaus, who was still being worshipped at a later period by the Nabataeans.[223] The name occurs as the first part of a royal name in a letter to Esarhaddon, ±680,[224] and on some jar seals.[225] In Assyrian annals we find names, known to be those of kings, composed with *Salman*[226] and *Melek*;[227] and from the Old Testament come royal names with the theophorous elements: *Hadad*[228] (cf. 1 Kings 11 and Gen. 36:35f.), *Baal* (cf. Gen. 36:38f.) and *El* (cf. Gen. 36:39).

Of these Hadad is North Semitic, Salman probably Assyrian, Qaus Arabian, the rest generally West Semitic (El may also have an Arabian background). The name 'Hadad', found again in the Aramaean world and current in Edom in the earliest period, is certainly worth remarking. It could indicate that the Edomites (or an old 'top layer' among them) were related to the Aramaeans. Qaus must be a name of Arabian origin and evidently (in the later period) was that of the chief god (at any rate in the time of the Israelite monarchy). No one knows for certain how to account for it; but one might be inclined, with Wellhausen, to see in it a storm-god of some sort. This would connect him with Hadad.[229]

The religion of the North Arabian tribes

A few years ago O. Eissfeldt wrote an article entitled *Das Alte Testament im Lichte der Safatenischen Inschriften*,[230] in which he shed light on the significance for the Old Testament of the North Arabian world and of its legacy of written material. Thereby he compelled attention to this matter of Israel's relation to the Arabian world, which is so often neglected in contemporary study of the Old Testament. These inscriptions from the region to the east, south and west of the Hauran are of course only from the first six centuries of

E

our era, and so not contemporaneous with the Old Testament; but the culture of these desert areas in this period is nonetheless still akin to that of Old Testament times, when the so-called 'children of the east' lived there (cf. Jud. 6:8; Isa. 11:14; Ezek. 25:4, 10; Job 1:3). To that world belongs, for instance, the land of Kedar (Jer. 49:28ff.; Ezek. 25:4ff.). The last of the passages cited makes it clear that these 'children of the east' (eastern tribes or clans) are camel and small livestock breeders—like the Safatenes, that is, who are traders moving about in caravans and are mainly herdsmen tending small livestock. In this same area Eissfeldt, with many others, locates the original Jacob-Laban story (Gen. 29–31; see 29:1). The inscriptions are concerned with spring and summer journeys, with springs that have been tapped and are regarded as private property, with certain places where cattle are watered, with the rearing of sheep and goats, with hunting and so forth—all sorts of things, in fact, that figure in the stories of the patriarchs. When a dead person had been interred, the relatives covered the grave with a load of heavy stones, so that wild animals could do no damage to the corpse (cf. 2 Sam. 18:17 et al.).[231]

Apparitions (of important deceased members of a family) have a part in the religion. In praying to Baal Shamayim, the god of heaven, the suppliant turns towards the sky. The most frequently importuned deity is Ilat or Allat, from whom men seek to elicit compassion or help upon a journey or in battle, or fair weather. There is a 'saviour' god, 'Itha', who gives protection from enemies and cures disease. Besides these there are, for example, Ilah, the male counterpart to Ilat, the astral gods, sun, moon and Venus ('Athtar or Ashtar, a male god), Dushara, Gad-'Awidh and Shay'-ha-qaum, and various others. These names show that the pantheon is of very diverse composition, that it includes typically Arabian (Allat or Ilat, Ilah, 'Athtar; cf. also Dushara as a Nabataean god), West Semitic (Baal Shamayim) and desert gods (Arabian again, of course). To the last-mentioned group belongs Gad 'Awidh—that is, the god of fortune of (the clan) 'Awidh—a deity related to the *theoi patroioi* of the ancient Semitic nomads, from as far back as the age of the patriarchs.[232] Again, the name of Shay'-ha-qaum is interesting; for it means: '(he) who rallies and leads the clan'. He had been known already to the Nabataeans and the people of Palmyra.

Blood-sacrifices were made to certain of the gods; and circumcision was practised. There were areas of holy ground, serving as grazing-lots for camels, that had been consecrated to the deity.[233]

This is a fitting point at which to say something very briefly about the Palmyrene and Nabataean religions, for which the only evidence available comes from the first few centuries A.D.[234] Here we have two principal gods, Bel and Be'elshamin, the former being the god of heaven (in the sense of 'Lord of the starry sky'), the latter the god of heaven, meaning 'the cloudy air, the atmosphere'. Bel is proprietor, creator and ruler of the cosmos and of human destiny (cf. Marduk or Bel-Marduk, the West Semitic El); whilst Be'elshamin is the fertility- and thunder-god, akin to the West Semitic Baal or Hadad. The same sort of tension, therefore, which we found it necessary to take note of in the Phoenician and Aramaean world between the head of the pantheon and the real god of the people had in this case penetrated into the desert. From the way things went in Palmyra it is clear that because of the strong henotheistic tendency to which we referred earlier on, the diverse types of gods came to exhibit more and more kindred features.

In the Palmyra of Graeco-Roman times the worship of Bel was in official circles wholly predominant. Bel had the largest temple. He had probably taken the place of the earlier god Bol or Bolastar (that is, a fusion of Bol with 'Athtar (Ashtar), the old Arabian and West Semitic star of Venus, who was possibly the most ancient deity of the desert settlement of Palmyra-Tadmor). Bel was attended by two other gods: Yarhibol, who despite his name (which suggests the moon) was a sun-god, and Aglibol, a moon-god, who is also found accompanying Be'elshamin, as a matter of fact (really: bull-god). The two represent, in this case, sun and moon.

As well as in Palmyra, the god Be'elshamin was worshipped throughout the whole territory of the Nabataeans and in the Hauran and further to the east. In Palmyra itself he was venerated as Lord of eternity and as the merciful one. He also was attended by two gods, the selfsame Aglibol, the moon-god who was originally a bull-god, and Malakbel, a fertility and sun-god. He symbolized the sun in its various phases and in that capacity was the god of self-renewing life.

Besides the major gods there were others of lower rank: spirits, jinns, tutelary spirits of some sort (often also called Gad: that is, tutelary god), and gods of the family and of the ancestors.

The gods in Palmyra had no female partners. In enlightened Palmyra, apparently, where there was actually some expression given even to monotheistic belief, the existence of a purely sexual partner- ship had disappeared. There were goddesses, of course; but they stood by themselves or were paired off together. One finds here the three names which occur later on in Mecca: Allat (Ilat), *the* celestial goddess, Ozza (female in Mecca, male in Palmyra), a form of Venus, and Manat, goddess of destiny or fortune. Another goddess met with in Palmyra, and who is found elsewhere among the Arabians, is Rowda, a naked goddess who is a female symbol of the evening star. In addition to these, which have an Arabian background, we also find goddesses of North Semitic extraction (Astarte, Atargatis) and others originally from Babylon and Persia. Greek and Babylonian names are by no means unusual among these gods. Palmyra offers the example of a syncretistic religion which has nonetheless clearly retained its essentially Semitic character and at a deep level is governed by that circumstance, even in its modes of thought and religious ideas. This basic constituent, however, is obviously due to a crossing of Arabian with West Semitic elements.

Nabataean culture is known to us from the later—the Hellenistic—period of its existence; and its remains are scattered over Transjordania and the Negeb. Especially famous is the cultic centre of Petra, to which has been added, through the excavations carried out by N. Glueck since the nineteen-thirties, that of Jebel Tannur to the south-east of the Dead Sea.[235] Taken together, they give us a particularly fine impression of great rock sanctuaries nestling on top of the mountains. At Petra, after a heavy upward climb by way of steps, one passes two mighty columns, six to seven metres high, that serve as an entrance, like the pylons in Egypt. The actual temple, which lies behind them on the extreme summit and affords a striking view of the mountains around Petra, has an extensive forecourt, hewn out of the rock-face. On its west side is set an altar with four steps leading up to it. On the left is a rock with a trough hollowed out of it, on which the sacrificial victim was slain, so that the blood, running along the trough, could drain off into a basin by the altar. Several larger basins held water for the priestly ablutions. Around the open space there were probably rooms for the use of the priests and for stowing all the utensils required by the cult. On the square space itself lies a small platform, not quite directly opposite the altar. What its purpose was is not clear.

In the Nabataean period this imposing, open-air sanctuary was probably dedicated to Dushara (graecized as *Dusares*), that is, the god of Shara, the region in which Petra itself is situated. This Dusares was head of the Nabataean pantheon and was also thought of as 'god of our master' (i.e. the king). Alt—and others with him—puts Dusares, on account of his relationship to the Nabataean monarch, among the *theoi patroioi*. He does, in point of fact, take most of his examples from the Nabataean milieu. What Dusares' real name was we do not know for certain (possibly Aara). The Greeks identified him as a fertility-god with Dionysius. In that respect he is probably to be reckoned among the Baal-types, to which the Arabian gods generally —with names that begin with 'Du', i.e. 'that of . . .' (corresponding to the Hebrew *zeh*)—possibly belong.[236]

Shayʿ-ha-qaum, a clan-god whom we have already referred to in connexion with the Safatenes, is also a member of their pantheon, like Hobal, who was perhaps a version of Ilah (El), and other gods and goddesses such as Motabah and Manoto.

Both the first-mentioned names make it clear that in essence the Nabataean religion was of Arabian provenance—even the other names point in that direction. One finds these cultic places situated on the tops of mountains all over the West Semitic world. According to later classical reports the blood-rites of the cult would seem to have involved the use of 'a black, rectangular, unhewn stone'. This calls to mind the black stone of the Kaaba in Mecca and the custom of venerating stones, current among the Arabians in general. Such stones are often of a meteoric or vulcanite nature. They were regarded as divine; and as a dwelling-place of the deity they represented his presence. They were known as *bait* (house) and treated as '*bet' il*' (that is, house of the god), which is also used as a divine appellation (perhaps also in the name 'Bethel'?).[237]

Besides these there were other natural objects that had a part to play, especially sacred trees and springs, as well as certain sacred spots, usually fenced off by a small trench or rampart.

The Central and South Arabian world, which for the most part is rightly distinguished from the North, cannot be included within this survey of religion in Arabia; for that would take us too far afield. There are, however, a few points that should be made: (*a*) whilst there are evident differences in the spheres of history, geography and the history of religions (names of gods), the distinguishable forms of religion in Arabia present a great many kindred elements; and the Arabian world, taken as a whole, offers repeated and surprising parallels both to the ancient West Semitic and the Hebrew religion; (*b*) South Arabian inscriptions (which have yielded most important material) suggest all sorts of points of comparison with Hebrew terms,

particularly on the score of sacrificial worship;[238] and (c) in South
Arabia, especially, the religion is very much dominated by astral gods,
the moon, morning- and evening-star ('Athtar), both male, and the
sun, who is a female deity. Along with Venus as morning- and evening-
star, the moon-god is of principal importance. It is hard to say which
of the two predominates. Ryckmans would have it that Athtar comes
ahead of the moon-god, Jamme that it is the other way round.[239]
Apparently, the position changed from one period to another.[240] The
religious calendar in South Arabia is ordered by the moon; but in
addition there is an agricultural calendar which is ordered by the sun
and regulates the agrarian and economic side of life.[241] As the moon
plays a big role in respect of the religious calendar in Israel too, this is
a valuable piece of evidence for a correspondence between the religions of Israel and Arabia.

To wind up this section we shall now attempt, briefly and in general
terms, to characterize Arabian religion prior to the coming of Islam.
In this we concur, up to a point, with J. Henninger[242]—more particularly in regard to that facet which with this writer we may call the
Bedouin religion or, better still, the 'desert religion'. What underlies
and mainly informs this type of religion is a dynamistic-cum-
animistic apprehension of the world, issuing on the one hand in the
veneration of stones or other natural objects or phenomena (in
which the divine being is envisaged as being incorporated), on the
other hand in a belief in spirits (jinns) who are abroad everywhere and
make their influence for good and evil felt in a variety of ways. Thus
the poet, because he is an inspired person, is a vehicle of supernatural
wisdom and is animated by a jinn.[243] Crossing and intermingling with
this primitive way of experiencing the world is a belief in the ancestors
who after death continue to exert an influence on the life of the clan,
and a belief in divine powers tied to this or that locality. All these
manifestations of superior vital forces or divine powers are in one way
or another the object of veneration, be they sacred trees and springs
or progenitors and local divinities, ancestors worshipped at their
graves or stones smeared with blood or oil, and so forth.

This chaotic totality of dynamism, animism, ancestor-worship and
local 'powers' is still further complicated by the inclusion of some
astral gods, in particular the moon and the morning- and evening-
star; but again on the other hand it is simplified by a certain primitive,
henotheizing strain of thought in the religion, which in referring to
the godhead can use the general term *il* or *ilah*.[244] Detected in the

several forces of one kind or another is 'the divine', *il*, a term associated with various phenomena. This can be viewed as a substantive
power *per se*, or as qualifying the particular forces already mentioned.

Sacrifices were as often as not unbloody, and hardly ever involved
the immolation of human beings. The animals for sacrifice were
slaughtered by the offerer in person and were frequently prepared for
communal consumption. Sacrifice of the firstborn (animal) was
something that the Arabian nomads and herdsmen had in common
with the Hebrew tribes. Israel's paschal rites, specifically, had a
nomadic background and exemplify the type of spring ceremonies
widely practised among the Semites.[245] Then again, circumcision, the
method of divination[246] and the structure of thought and mental
outlook demonstrate the close relationship between the Israelite way
of life and that of Old Arabia.[247] Even if J. Pedersen has put a somewhat one-sided emphasis, perhaps, on this correspondence, it has
been a major and highly significant achievement on his part to direct
our attention to it; for the cohesion between Israel and the Arabian
world has been too much and too generally lost sight of. We are more
than happy, therefore, to cite a short passage from a book no longer
exactly new: Montgomery's *Arabia and the Bible*[248]: 'We come to
realize that Israel had its face turned towards those quarters we call
the Desert and that this was its nearest neighbour. With the Arabs
they were more closely related in original and ever-replenished stock,
in common religion and social formation, than with Philistia, Phoenicia or Syria, while the civilizations of Egypt and Mesopotamia were
distant and alien.'[249]

The character of Israel's religion

Despite the many tokens of an affinity with the religions all around,
it is amply clear that Israel's religion is something altogether different
from them. It is pitched in its own peculiar key, even though it is
hard to say in a word precisely what that is, since the dominant is
itself such a complex thing. Bleeker,[250] like many others, typifies this
by pointing to the 'profound fear (awe) in face of God's holiness',
Van der Leeuw[251], with the words 'Religion des Willens und des
Gehorsams' (a religion of will and obedience), Von Rad[252] (in
company with many others) by fastening upon its 'Geschichtskarak-
ter' (its essential historicism); and I have myself[253] stressed the

'fellowship or communion of the holy God with men'—thereby citing as the commanding factor here two elements that stand one toward the other in a relationship of high tension. All these pointers give prominence, of course, to one—or sometimes more than one—important aspect. Fundamentally, all that one can do to typify the whole is to name the name of Yahweh. But as our business in this chapter is not with an overall historico-religious typology but with an attempt to characterize the religion of Israel over against those of the surrounding peoples, we cannot rest content with trying to range it under a single common denominator. The relationship which it has to the other religions is too complex for that; and the characteristic traits presented by Israel's religion itself are too multifarious.

First of all a few negative observations. As with her whole life and spirit as a nation, Israel's religion was not static like the Egyptian, but dynamic, in continuous development and so not inclined to monism as the Egyptian was. It is a capital error to set Israelite monotheism on a par with a pantheizing kind of solar monarchism in whatever form—although this has often been done.[254]

Nor was Israel's religion a form of dualism like that to which the Babylonian religion was always giving rise. Israel's idea of God was essentially different from Babylon's; for though certain naturalistic features were by no means foreign to it, its fundamental *character* was not naturalistic. The world is not a battle-ground of forces personified by the gods, but is defined and determined absolutely by a single Power to whom all forces are subject. Even at the stage when what men believed about God was not monotheistic in the strict sense, Yahweh was absolute master of all the powers. Not one of the beings around him had a name. In fact, he was incomparable.

A third negative stipulation is this: more even than in Babylon and Egypt, religious belief in the Canaanite-Phoenician world especially is rooted in and fundamentally conditioned by natural and vegetative phenomena; but that is not true of Israel's religion. There life is governed neither by the caprice with which the elements (rain, wind, drought) sport with the earth (arable land, mountains, desert) nor by the sexual potentialities of man and animal (which magic art may use to further fecundity and growth), but by a divine will, operating in various ways, through the mind and spirit, the word spoken, the governance of history, the blessing conferred, or through natural channels such as rain, storm and sunshine.

This contrast is not to be taken lightly; for historically speaking, it is the factor that more than anything else governs the religion of Israel. The religion which Yahwism was forced to oppose with the greatest determination was that of the Canaanites, which was so markedly vegetative and naturalistic. It was as a result of this stand that the Israelite religion acquired a large part of its character in practice; for in the struggle it developed its own separate existence and became aware of the experience which had fallen to its lot in the Mosaic period as something of exceptional significance. It was through being obliged to define its attitude to so many different religious ideas (not only those of Canaan and Phoenicia but of Egypt, Babylon, the Arabian world and later of Persia and Greece as well) that Israel's religion became what it did become—one might even say, became fully and wholly itself.

What the encounter with the Canaanite-Phoenician religion meant is quite admirably explained by W. Baumgartner,[255] who lists as the three important points of difference involved:

(a) The fact that in Israel the crucial element of sex is absent. Whereas in the Phoenician world goddesses and gods appear side by side, the former often envisaged as naked, and even El is said to have debauched two female deities, such a thing is inconceivable in Israel. When a goddess does occasionally find a place alongside Yahweh (1 Kings 15:13 and in Elephantine), it is only a fleeting instance of syncretism. Even though sacral prostitution does occur in Israel from time to time (with the aim of stimulating vegetative growth), still there is never any question of a sacred marriage between a divine being and a human one (prince or priest); and one has to add that not only is there no female consort of the godhead in Israel, but the priestly office is never exercised by women. They are increasingly excluded from all direct contact with the holy place.

(b) The fact that magical rites intended to induce fecundity were repudiated by Yahwism; and this meant that in reality the way was barred to all forms of magic. Hostility to witchcraft of whatever sort runs right through the Old Testament. Both these elements are clearly present in Jehu's condemnation of Jezebel on the charge of being a harlot and a sorceress (2 Kings 9:22).

(c) Baumgartner mentions as a third point of importance the fact that the Israelite religion has little use for the idea of the dying and rising god. Except for a very few isolated reminiscences this finds no place in the Old Testament—a circumstance, one might add, which so far as Israel is concerned removes any thought of time as a cyclical process. The Israelite world view is governed not by the recurring cycle of the year, the beginning of which represents, as it were, the world's own coming into existence, but by a kind of thinking moulded by important events in the march of history, by the saving acts of God.

Here we touch on one of the most central elements in Israel's religious outlook on the world. Because Israel came to know Yahweh through his liberating action in history, she knew that her being and her continued existence derived from and depended on God's acts in history. Her religious ideas, therefore, were so orientated as to be neither naturalistic nor cyclical, but teleological and grounded in history.[256] It may indeed be true that Yahweh had been a pre-Israelite god—certain, too, that he was thought of as a god of mountain and sky and was akin in that respect to Hadad (or Enlil); yet Israel, at any rate, only came to know him as her God through the course of events that befell certain tribes in the Mosaic period which proved to be the decisive factor in the faith of Israel as a whole.[257] During that period they became acquainted with Yahweh as a redeeming Power, who through Moses put himself into an abiding relationship with those whom he had set free. Thus from the very start he was a saving God as well as a national one. He entered personally into fellowship with Moses on the one hand, and on the other through Moses also with the tribes; so that he is truly characterized by both the personal and the social aspect.

Both types of relation to God, the personal and the social, persist in Israel. The former finds expression in prophetism and in God's relation with the individual man of faith, the latter in all that goes with the cult in its familial and public forms. The remarkable thing about it all is that one cannot really speak of Israel as a nation without at the same time thinking of her religion. This people as a community is grounded in the relationship to Yahweh; and it is a community more of religion than of blood, however powerfully that too may be felt. The members knew themselves to be descended from the same forefathers; but the essential relationship between them was denoted by the word *rea'*, that is, not 'brother' but 'neighbour', he with whom one is in fellowship. One of the key words in a social *and* religious context is the *ḥesed*, the bond of fellowship. Finally, at both the personal and the social level the religious relationship can be regarded as one and represented by the word 'love'. The brotherhood of those who are bound together by Yahweh carries with it radical consequences of an ethical nature. A man has obligations toward the neighbour, even to the slave and to the 'stranger' living on the national territory.

In the perspective of this relationship the world is apprehended as a unity created by God which subsists not *qua* state (as with Egypt and Babylon) but *qua* community, through a reciprocal connexion with, and intrinsic relation to, its Creator. What really matters is that God's will be fulfilled in the community of the nation and of the world.

It is important to note that when it comes to interpreting the world, in contrast with the creation myths outside the Bible there is no theogony in the biblical account of the creation and that chaos (Gen. 1:2) in no way functions as an anti-divine power: God creates through his word and so fashions the world that he can find it 'very good' (Gen. 1:31). What strikes one about this view of the world is rather its optimism than its pessimism. The world is seen as a harmoniously constructed whole; and this harmony is vested absolutely in the unitive picture of God. There is no place for dualism, any more than for the tragic.[258]

The contrarieties and suffering in the world arise not from any recalcitrance on God's part but from the fact that man abrogates the bond of fellowship with God and becomes a law unto himself. This is why disobedience to God's will can be seen as, in essence, sin.

The will of God is known, seeing that he has revealed it. Just as in a particular case he makes known his will for each man individually by a priest or prophet in the *torah* (a pointing to the way), so too has he done for the community. He has given it his commandments, his desire; and in specific cases, at critical moments in history, he gives his instructions through prophet and priest. On God's side there is always good intention toward men. It is only man's obstinacy that can turn this good pleasure to wrath and evoke God's judgment.

If the relationship is broken, then there is the possibility of restoring it by carrying out the propitiatory acts which he has appointed for that purpose in the cult.

History as event, disclosure of the divine will and a personal relationship, determine the course and character of religion in Israel. They also define the idea of God, which man, however, can never completely make his own. Although there is a knowledge of God and although the Old Testament assumes some form to the Godhead, God cannot and must not be delineated by men. Yahweh will not be tied to any kind of embodiment in pictorial or representational form: *finitum non capax infiniti*. The worst of sins in Israel are: to acknowledge other gods besides Yahweh and to make an image, a 'likeness'.

Whilst the resistance to giving any form to God may have deprived art in Israel of its most important theme (the divine image) and so have had an impoverishing effect in that sphere, it did enable Israel to preserve her vision of God as the One of absolute and illimitable power. This resistance flows from the essential character of Yahwism, which explains the name Yahweh as: He who is (probably in the sense of: (the One) who is here, thus, the One who is at hand; but at the same time, the Unnameable). The ban on images, which in the world of the ancient East was an altogether *new thing*, produced a great struggle in the heart of the people of Israel, who still had recourse to the worship of images in various ways.

Yahwism took up the fight not only against images but against every form of demonism, questioning of the dead, magic and sooth-saying. It was permitted to the faithful Israelite only to ask of Jahweh regarding his will and for his help; and he was required to forgo all other kinds of religious prop. At the practical level of religious conduct Yahweh was the one and only God long before monotheism as a theory was carried to its logical conclusion.

The religion of Israel was guided much more by practical considerations than by theological ones, because it turned not on a system of belief but on a vital relationship between God and man and was therefore concerned with bringing the life of men into line with God's will. Just as Yahweh is a God of action, so does he require that men confess and honour him in what they do.

Lastly, no sketch of Israel's religion, however brief, can be complete which does not make the point that belief in the God who is at work in history involves a kind of thinking that is at bottom teleological. God's activity has an end in view; his actions are directional and their goal is his kingdom. This leads to the conviction that God is active not only in creating and regulating, but in re-creating too. The world of the ancient East, thinking as it did in cyclic terms, subsumed the renewal of the world in the annual renewing, repeated *ad infinitum*, of the life of nature, whether conceived on the agricultural basis of the alternation of summer and winter, drought and rain, life and death, or in astral terms as the rising and setting of sun and moon with the appearing and disappearing of the stars. In Israel, however, the existence of the world *in toto* was to be seen under the light of the Eternal and his purposeful activity. The whole idea of life as a cyclic process was broken through, making way for the knowledge that a new world was coming—the kingdom of God, which would bring an end to the injustice of the present structures of human society and lead on to a world in which justice prevailed.[259] At times a saviour-prince was expected, who would bring in, and rule over, that world. He was known by a variety of names and was often linked with the royal house of David. Later Jewish theology called him Messiah; yet the role which it attributed to him was not that of ruler but of servant.

Thus history is not an endless reiteration but is leading up to a renewal, set either within the framework of history itself, as a renovation of Israel and of the nations, or (later on) in a cosmic context as a re-creation of the entire world. History is not a circle but a line pointing into the future toward a goal appointed by God, or, better still, a path by which at God's behest and under his instructions man is travelling toward a new world. Life and the world acquire a goal, pointing beyond itself. It is a vision with not only a national aspect but, at any rate for the greatest among the prophets, a universal one: they know, that is, that all peoples are to have a part in the community of which Israel is the vehicle, Jerusalem the symbol and Yahweh the salvation.

In this vision, which forms the summit and climax of Israel's religion, she has quite evidently broken free from the religious ideas of the whole world around her: and through this eschatology of hers she has radically influenced the mental and spiritual life of mankind and the history of whole peoples.

At the heart and centre of these expectations is the crucial element of faith in Yahweh, the God of life, who although he cannot be known yet is known in what he does with and through history and in his communing with those who carry out his will. Indeed, speaking in terms of the history of religion, the best account we can give of Israel's religion is to describe it, with Van der Leeuw, as the religion of will and obedience. As such, it has fathered two other world religions: Christianity and Islam.

The description of Israel's religion that we have just been giving has inevitably been incomplete (the place of the cult, the kingship, wisdom literature, the sects and so many other matters have not been mentioned); and it was taken mainly from the classic period, although this has been the case with the other religions too. It is only thus in their most mature forms that these religions present themselves to us in their truest colours and may be properly compared with one another. As for the religion of Israel itself, we shall attempt in the succeeding chapters to describe the course of its development so as in some sense to lay bare its roots and in some degree to make it possible to see it, as a spiritual phenomenon, in process of formation. In that way we shall be in a position to see the extent to which, besides the form outlined above, in which the religion came to greatest maturity, there have been all kinds of other manifestations of it that were less well developed and consequently less fully characteristic. One cannot imagine one of these syncretistic or reduced versions surviving the downfall of Jerusalem in 587 on a lasting basis, as *did* happen with the classic group which bore the impress of the prophets.

CHAPTER 3

Religious Life at about the Year 1000

A T THE END of the previous chapter we offered a schematic
view of Israelite religion, which served mainly as a companion-
picture to that of the other religions of the ancient East. In this
chapter we go on to a detailed phenomenological outline, culled from
the oldest historiography that Israel has bequeathed to us. It dates
from the first years of King Solomon's reign and deals with the period
of the first two kings, Saul and David—the very time, that is, when
the great change in Israel's life and religion begins to take effect. It is
an age of transition between the time of the judges and of the later
monarchy—between a period of settlement and conquest and one of
domination and established possession.

In the Davidic period Israel enters upon a new stage in her life; but
on the score of religion her links are still very much with the earlier
period. Politically speaking, the epoch of the tribes—or one might
say, the old provincial period that had continued to preserve so much
of the ancient tribal way of life (even though the pastoral setting had
largely given place to an agricultural one)—ended with David. In a
religious context this happened somewhat later, in Solomon's time;
although David, by having the ark transferred to Jerusalem, certainly
set the scene for the new period. We may consider the Davidic period
the last and greatest heyday of the Israelite religion in its earliest
phase; and that is why we propose to use here as a source for our
phenomenological sketch the document which tells the story of his
reign.

The choice of this document, be it said, is open to objection on the
ground that it was not written by a man of the people, from the
countryside or the areas where the herdsmen lived, but by someone
from the city of Jerusalem who must have moved in court circles
there. Although he cannot be identified for certain, we must obviously
look for him among the group of people attached to Solomon and
related to the prophet Nathan; and that is why I have more than once

79

mentioned the name of Zabud in this connexion—a son of Nathan and a known friend of the king's.[1] In a case like this it is a mistake to put too much store by the techniques or conclusions of literary criticism; but one may say that in their broad features the passages that make up this work are as follows: 1 Sam. 11; 13:16–14: 46; 16:14–23; 18:1–2 Sam. 21; 1 Kings 1 and 2.

What it really amounts to is that we are offered a picture of the religion which is somewhat one-sided and gives too rosy an impression to be taken as representing what was happening in the country as a whole. Thus what we mainly get is a picture of Yahwism at the start of the first millennium, as professed by a man belonging to a culturally refined and loyal Yahwistic coterie.

There is still another objection: that a complete phenomenological outline cannot be given on the basis of this source; but this does not outweigh the advantage that we have here a literary source ready to hand which besides being fairly comprehensive is roughly dateable *and* in the main a unity.

Yahweh, the God of Israel

One is struck by the way in which the whole life of the nation is seen as being under the rule of Yahweh and of him alone. Even if one cannot say that a monotheistic way of thinking is pressed home to its strict conclusion, still it is clear enough that what the Israelite lives by is an absolute faith in Yahweh. In the affair with the men of Jabesh he takes hold of Saul, who then gathers together the people. They are so possessed with the fear of Yahweh that they march as one man to crush the Ammonites. At Gilgal Saul is proclaimed king 'before the Lord'. It is Yahweh who fights for Israel against the Philistines and gives them victory (1 Sam. 14:6ff., 12, 15, 20, 23, 45).[2] Just as the spirit of God renders Saul fit for his task, so the withdrawal of that spirit spells ruin and destruction for him. In place of Yahweh's spirit an evil spirit from among those around Yahweh comes upon him, depriving him of every shred of confidence and making him so inept at handling affairs that through anxiety and irresolution he brings about his own downfall (16:14ff.; 19:9ff.; 22ff.). Nothing goes right for him any more, especially in his moves against David, with whom Yahweh is (16:18). Because of that, David succeeds in every undertaking (18:12, 14, 28). He is Yahweh's elect (2 Sam. 3:9ff.; 5:2ff.; 6:21; 7:8ff.), who has the promise made him of a permanent kingship. Whilst Saul tries to get David out of the way, David obtains unlooked for support from Jonathan, with whom he concludes a pact in the presence of Yahweh (1 Sam. 20:8, 12ff., 23, 42). Yahweh protects David when the latter flees before Saul (ch. 23ff.) and time and again replies to his (as opposed to Saul's) questions before an oracle (30:7f.; 2 Sam. 5:19ff., *et al.*). David knows that he is dependent on Yahweh alone (1 Sam. 22:3) and looks for Yahweh to do the right thing by him (23:13; 25:39). Yahweh is just and righteous in what he does (24:16), both in his punishments (25:39; 26:10) and in the blessings he bestows (24:20ff.; 26:24f.). Yahweh controls everything (23:26; 2 Sam. 17:14), gives victory (30:23; 2 Sam. 5:19ff.) and blessings (2 Sam. 6:11ff.). For man, however, Yahweh is unapproachable; so that the consequence of any contact with the ark is death (2 Sam. 6:6ff.). He can incite to evil (1 Sam. 26:19) and does so when he wishes to punish (2 Sam. 24:1ff.—in a chapter which is by another hand and is somewhat later). Saul is overtaken by an evil spirit which proceeds from Yahweh (16:14ff.; 19:9ff.). That evil too comes from Yahweh does not seem to have been regarded as a problem: it was simply accepted as pointing to the fact that Yahweh's was an absolute authority. It did not mean that he was pictured as being demonic. Yahweh is righteous and punishes man, even David, his elect, justly. The punishment is made commensurate with the sin (cf. 2 Sam. 12:11f. and 16:22; 2 Sam. 12:9f.; 16:8ff.). He knows even the hidden transgression of David (2 Sam. 11:27).

All this serves to demonstrate that Yahweh is the God of Israel, the One with whom alone she has to do, the ground of her every hope and expectation. Consequently, Israel as a *nation* is described as the inheritance (or better still, the possession) of Yahweh (1 Sam. 26:19; 2 Sam. 14:16; 20:19; 21:3)—a term sometimes applied elsewhere in the Old Testament to the *land* of Israel. This expression implies that as a country and a people Israel is the personal property of Yahweh. There is a duly constituted and indissoluble relation between Israel and Israel's God, Yahweh;[3] and this governs the whole religious life of Israel and of the individual Israelite.

The absolute character of this relationship puts out of court all foreign gods and forms of religion, except for those given by Yahweh, and entails that Yahweh exclusively is the God of Israel and of the individual Israelite; but it has not yet come to mean that he is God 'pure and simple' or is acknowledged as 'God alone', in an absolute and universal sense.

F

That much is clear from a remark in the same document which assumes the existence of other gods outside Israel. We find it in something that the fleeing David says to Saul (1 Sam. 26:19). David is supposing here that people have incited Saul against him and want to drive him out from the community which constitutes Yahweh's inheritance, saying to him: Go hence, serve other gods. This shows that Yahweh was thought by the Israelite of the time to be tied to his own territory—and it was taken for granted that beyond the borders of Israel there were other gods besides Yahweh. The idea of a bond between the deity and his land turns up again in a still cruder form at a later period, when the non-Israelite Naaman takes a load of earth home with him from Israel to Syria, because he thinks that only on *this* soil will he be able to offer sacrifice to Israel's God in Damascus (2 Kings 5:17).

It is more than evident, therefore, that in the Israel of the early monarchy there could have been no question of monotheism in a universal sense. What did obtain at that period might well be described as 'mono-Yahwism'. Yahweh is Israel's God and demands for himself the exclusive worship of Israel; but the Israelite did not as yet carry this to its logical conclusion in a theoretical monotheism. Thus whilst on the one hand Yahweh was extolled as the Supreme, and whilst it was realized that he was sovereign not only on Sinai but also in Egypt, in Canaan, over the very stars and planets (think of ancient songs like Judges 5 and Psalm 68), yet still the existence of gods outside Israel was taken for granted. Again, even though these gods were probably held, in comparison with Yahweh, to have little or no authority (cf. the stories concerning Yahweh and Dagon in 1 Sam. 4ff., which are admittedly of a later time but probably come, all the same, from the period of the early kingship), still they are there—and they can make their presence felt (cf. 2 Kings 3:27; although in the text as it stands it is not explicitly stated that it was actually Chemosh who felt the 'great indignation').

That there could be such inconsistency in the way men thought about their god(s) shows that Israel's belief in Yahweh had still not been thought out very far on a theoretical basis. It shows too that despite Yahweh's absolute authority over his people, even here there was a degree of tension in their manner of understanding the relationship between God and 'the gods'. This tension did not fundamentally affect the worshipful esteem in which God was held, nor the relationship between the God of Israel and his people, but rather the whole area of religious conceptualizing in a broad sense. Yahweh was for a long time envisaged, and celebrated in song, as God of gods, as without peer or parallel among heavenly beings; but only much later did men come to confess him as the One Being with the right to be called divine. This inconsequence, this lack of equipoise between religious practice and the world of ideas, contained elements that could easily have had an effect on the whole subsequent development of the religion. The possibility of worshipping more than one god lay well within the purview of Israel and could have been put into practice. In point of fact, that is probably just what did happen in a good many circles. The weakness and confusion of the Israelite religion on this crucial point is surely not least to blame for the fact that the religious practices of the Canaanite cities and the neighbouring peoples held such a great attraction for Israel over such a long period. The powerful stresses and strains and the fierce struggles that resulted from this opened up new aspects as events unfolded, and prepared the way for the recognition of Yahweh's exclusiveness in a universal sense. It was to be hundreds of years before that came about.

Holy places

There were various holy places in the country, although only a few of them turn up in the story of Saul and David: those were at Gilgal (1 Sam. 11:15), Nob (1 Sam. 21:1ff.), the house of Yahweh in Jerusalem (2 Sam. 12:20), Hebron (2 Sam. 15:7ff.), the Mount of Olives (2 Sam. 15:32).

The fact that only these places are mentioned does not mean, of course, that there were no others. On the evidence of the stories in the Book of Judges, the later Books of the Kings and the prophetic writings, it is beyond question that at the outset of the monarchical period many more sanctuaries were in existence (see also Chapter 6). During that period, even if in our source they do not loom very large, they must have formed more and more the centre of religious life. It was there that the agricultural and family festivals were kept, and on particular occasions people would come there to seek the *torah* of the priest, and in special circumstances would make a personal offering in fulfilment of a vow, in order to expiate sins, or in case of sickness, and so on (the later narrative in 1 Sam. 1–3, especially, gives a very good idea of the function of a holy place).

The central sanctuary of the tribes at Shiloh, where for some time the ark was given shelter, disappeared in the struggle with the Philistines, who had probably destroyed it (Jer. 7:12; 26:6; Ps. 78:60; cf. 1 Sam 1–7) The ark later fell into the hands of the Philistines and was subsequently deposited at Kiriath-jearim (see below).

The old Benjaminite sanctuary at Gilgal was doing service as a religious centre in Saul's day (1 Sam 11:15) and was in use even in David's time (2 Sam 19:15ff). Later thrown into the shade by Bethel, it was nevertheless an important sanctuary up to the time of Amos and Hosea (Amos 4:4; 5:5; Hos. 4:15; 9:15; 12:12; cf. also 2 Kings 2:1; 4:38). It would seem that the position of Gilgal is now established as having been some ten kilometres north-east of Jericho. In 1953 some small-scale sampling excavations were carried out there by J. Muilenburg of New York,[4] who found on and within several small *tells* (artificial mounds) near Khirbet el-Mefjir sherds dating from the early and middle iron age (1200–600), as well as a few claystone walls characteristic of the old Israelite period. According to biblical testimony this was the very period when Gilgal was in existence. On the basis of Muilenburg's findings, among other things, there is a lot to be said for the thesis that Gilgal was a typical sanctuary of ancient Israel. There is no mention of a temple at Gilgal, but there is of an altar (Hos. 12:12) and of sacrifices. This could well be a characteristic mark of a primitive Yahwistic sanctuary.

Indeed it could well be regarded as having been set up there by the Yahwistic tribal groups who had fled from Egypt and were on their way into the land of Canaan as the narratives in the Book of Joshua assume (Josh. 4:19ff.).

At Nob (1 Sam. 21f.) there was a sanctuary where Ahimelech was priest and where David was succoured with the 'showbread' laid before Yahweh. Saul took his revenge by putting the entire college of priests to death, a calamity from which only one man, Abiathar, escaped. According to H. W. Hertzberg[5] this Nob is the temple city that corresponded to Gibeon[6] (cf. 1 Kings 3). In that case it must be the place now known as En-Nebi Samwil, from which one gets such a good view of Jerusalem.

The priesthood at Nob was apparently descended from the house of Eli, which ministered originally at Shiloh. It is not unlikely that after the razing of that city the priests settled at Nob and there re-erected the old sacred booth (the tabernacle).[7] That would explain why at a later time David attached such great value to the ark, which according to 1 Sam. 1–3 had originally been housed in Shiloh; and it likewise makes it understandable why he sheltered the ark in a booth (2 Sam. 6:17) and why he was minded throughout his life to maintain the booth-tradition (2 Sam. 7:6f.; 1 Kings 2:29f.). The spot in Jerusalem where this booth stood is evidently referred to in 2 Sam. 12:20 as the house of Yahweh.

As appears from 2 Sam. 15:32, on the top of the Mount of Olives was a place of prayer. Whether this indicates an ancient pre-Israelite or Israelite holy place is uncertain; but as in many instances, there is little to differentiate between them. Like the nations around them, people in Israel (as is evident at Nob and many other places) ministered to their God on high places, on mountain-tops. Dalman[8] thinks that he can locate the spot close by the Church of the Ascension on the Mount of Olives. The question of a sanctuary or an altar clearly does not arise in this case.

Hebron, the city where David was anointed king (2 Sam. 2:4; 5:3), must have had a sanctuary of Yahweh, with which Absalom, who had been born in Hebron (2 Sam. 3:3), was conscious of having some tie (at any rate he could pretend as much; 2 Sam. 15:7ff.). Ever since the time of the patriarchs there had been an old-Israelite holy place at this spot (by the terebinths of Mamre). According to tradition Abram built an altar to Yahweh there (Gen. 13:18; cf. 18:1).[9] Although there is nowhere any allusion to this sanctuary at a later period, it must still have been known during the remaining course of events. One witness to this is the fact that the holy place must have been frequented in the Herodian period, otherwise Herod would not have caused a splendid sanctuary to be erected there.[10]

These scanty data are sufficient to show that the holy places of the patriarchs were recognized and frequented by the Israelites, but that at the same time the sanctuaries deemed to be vehicles of the desert-tradition were held to be the most important (certainly by the Yahweh-worshippers in the Jerusalem of David's time, among whom was the author of these annals). This is of great significance for a proper evaluation of the Jerusalemite outlook, which had so many ties, and the ark in particular, with the ancient Yahwistic tradition. When later on Solomon's temple was set up in Jerusalem, this influence persisted. Even though non-Israelite elements from the Jebusite period were certainly adopted into the Jerusalem tradition, they are not to be regarded as dominating religious life as a whole. Leading circles in Jerusalem during David and Solomon's time are linked with the ark-tradition (Abiathar, David, J.). Granted that Abiathar was after-

wards eliminated (1 Kings 2) and that the central place was taken by
Zadok (who is often considered to be the original representative of
the Jebusite cult), still the ark was too firmly rooted in the Jerusalem
sanctuary to be regarded as of secondary importance. (One has only
to think of Psalms such as 24 and 132.)

For the religion of Israel, therefore, the fact that the ark was
transferred to Jerusalem (2 Sam. 6) is of the highest importance.[11]
That Israel's greatest king, whose dynasty was to command the throne
in Jerusalem for four hundred years, brings the ancient sanctuary of
Yahweh out of the desert[12] into the city means above all else that
Yahweh is constituted the one and only God of the new state of Israel.
It means too that the patriarchal and later syncretistic forms of El
worship drop more into the background, whilst Yahweh comes to be
the divine name *par excellence*. M. Noth has shown statistically that
the paramount role of the Yahweh-name is clearly reflected in the
nomenclature of the monarchal period.[13] This too is certainly a
result of David's action, taken at a juncture so very crucial for
Israel.[14]

It is not only the fact itself that is so important but also the course
of events, as related in 2 Sam. 6. The death of Uzzah, who had
touched the ark during its journey, made a deep impression. In
consequence the ark was laid up close by the spot where the mishap
had occurred, and the event was commemorated for all time in the
name which the place acquired. Thereupon David was at first
unwilling to have the ark in Jerusalem at all, until he saw what a
powerful source of blessing it was. The business of transporting it was
resumed, but now with more pomp and ceremony than before. The
first idea, apparently, was to carry in the ark as a palladium of war
with much festivity and show;[15] but that led to disaster. Then David
realized that the transfer must be done in far more solemn style. For
the second time, therefore, he put on the ephod—the linen apron of the
priest, worn about the loins. As soon as the procession had started,
sacrifices had to be offered. The ark was no longer conveyed on a
cart, but was carried by porters assuredly qualified for the task. The
whole thing was executed in cultic style, with the king playing a
leading part (verses 17ff.). His role in all this was no burden or
humiliation for David, but an honour (verses 20ff.).

These events had once more shown the ark to be an effective
instrument of Yahweh's, and had considerably enhanced its prestige.
The death of Uzzah, in particular, drove home the fact of the ark's

direct relation to Yahweh, as appears from David's words to Michal, when he avers that he has danced in Yahweh's presence.

As this incident suggests, the cultic dance was a not uncommon phenomenon in Israel. It is remarkable that not a single priest is mentioned in connexion with this story, and they are completely over-shadowed by the figure of David, who represents the priestly func-tionary here. The authors of the Chronicles give a quite different account of the matter (1 Chron. 13 and 15).

Evidently, therefore, David was in a position to discharge the priestly functions, as was everywhere the case with kings in the ancient East. This again becomes apparent later on, when David deliberates with Nathan about the building of a temple (2 Sam. 7). David here wants to do what all the princes of the ancient East were doing at the time. The noteworthy thing is that David consults not with the priests but with the prophet.

This story told in 2 Sam. 7 is important enough for us to linger over it a little longer. It is surely remarkable that although Nathan agrees with his plan in the first instance, he later forbids David to build a temple. At a later period a specific reason for this was sought in the person of David himself. The chronicler explains in 1 Chron. 22:8 that David was not permitted to do this because he had shed so much blood.

The cause of Nathan's behaviour is to be looked for in the fact that in David's day minds were deeply divided over the idea of building a temple. What decides the matter for Nathan is a divine utterance commanding him to deter David; and the reason is that Yahweh, as he himself says, had never dwelt in a house but had resided in a tabernacle (verse 6).

The ark that David had brought to Jerusalem and had housed in a tabernacle had always, according to tradition, been lodged in a booth of that sort.[16] It was the ancient desert-sanctuary, which had been moved from place to place as a sign of Yahweh's presence. A charac-teristic feature of Yahweh's essential being found expression in this symbol—something that would be lost, were it to be housed in a building of stone. It is best summed up, probably, in the antithesis between the static and the dynamic. A temple-house would tie Yahweh to the spot, whereas the tabernacle made it possible for him to move about wherever he wished. Just as the Rechabites refused to live in houses in order not to lose hold of the customs of the patriarchs and so become assimilated to the Canaanites, this protest against building a temple and this insistence on the tabernacle as Yahweh's dwelling-place were plainly a tilt at Canaan. The old Yahwism considered a change in the old form an evident violation of Yahweh's essential nature. He, the mighty God of Sinai, Lord of the celestial spheres, the God who interferes with the course of history and accompanies his people here and there, does not wish to bind himself permanently to Jerusalem, in the sense of becoming the God of Jerusalem. Although this expression does occur just once, and very late, in the Bible (Chronicles) and once on an inscription inside a grotto in Judah,[17] it was a formula eschewed in principle in ancient Israel—at least in consciously Yahwistic circles. Yahweh was always too exalted in majesty to be incarcerated in a city, even though it be Jerusalem (as was the case, of course, with many gods in the world beyond the Bible). This protest against 'nailing down' the person of Yahweh and turning him into a static entity is one of the most important characteristics of Yahwism and reflects the vital, self-subsistent, almighty, absolute nature of its God.

The stress laid in the same passage on the fact that Yahweh moves among the people of Israel (*hithallek be*, verse 7) shows Nathan aware that what really counts in Israel's religion is the good relationship, the communion, between God and man, and nothing else (cf. the same note as sounded by a provincial prophet like Micah, some centuries later: Micah 6:8). Yahweh does not desire a cedarwood temple or a cult splendidly performed, but to be and to move amid the nation.

Granted that there may have been quite a lot of prejudice (of a purely sociological nature) behind the opposition to setting up a temple, and for that matter behind the resistance to the introduction of the kingship or the building of cities, fundamentally and in its deepest motivation it also expressed the desire not to expose the old and tried relationship of communion to danger from all kinds of new, disintegrative factors. Each fresh period in the nation's life starts with resistance to what is new. This is usually followed by a period of accommodation, which in its turn gives rise to further tensions. The process leads on the one hand to a degree of equilibrium and on the other to an abiding confrontation of opposites.

What the relation was between king, prophet and priest during the first period of the monarchy is not altogether clear. Saul does indeed build an altar (1 Sam. 14:35), but is not, in the early version of the story, the sacrificing agent; and in the later versions, where he does act in that capacity, it is held to be a serious blunder (1 Sam. 13, cf.

15), whereas there is no criticism of similar activities on David's part. It would seem that the older standpoint prevailing in Jerusalem was not opposed to the combination of kingship with cultic functions, as was the case later on. Perhaps the influence of the Jebusite tradition was still at work, according to which the king was considered to be not just the political but also the cultic head of the city.

The priests Ahijah, Ahimelech and Abiathar had the task of consulting the oracle of God on the king's behalf or on that of his ministers, when some enterprise was afoot, be it a battle (1 Sam. 22:10, 13, 15; 2 Sam. 5:19f., 22ff.; and for Saul too, before judgment overtook him: 1 Sam. 14:18f., 36) or an expedition (1 Sam. 23:9ff., 30:7ff.; 2 Sam. 2:1f.). For this purpose the priest had an ephod (1 Sam. 14:3; 23:6ff., 30:7), the form and function of which are not altogether certain; but we ought probably to understand it as a sacred garment (a divine one, in fact) which served in some way (through the *urim* and *thummim*?) to convey instructions from God.[18] Apparently, the king enquired through the priest as intermediary (in the presence of this garment, or while the priest was wearing it?) of God's will. The interrogation was carried on by putting a particular case, to which the god would reply 'yes' or 'no': for instance, 1 Sam. 23:11f.: will Saul come?—answer: He will come (this is the Hebrew idiom for 'yes'). Another question: Will the citizens of Keilah hand me over to Saul? —answer: They will hand you over (that is, 'yes'). Thus for the oracular verdict to be given the only things needed were cultic objects that could yield the answer 'yes' or 'no'. The *urim* and *thummim* were probably 'lots' of this sort. Yahweh could also refuse to answer; but how that happened we do not know. At all events, it indicated that he was angry and had removed himself from his people (1 Sam. 14:37ff.).

The priest in person, like the king, is an unassailable figure. Saul's soldiers refuse to kill the priests at Nob (1 Sam. 22:17f.), just as on more than one occasion David declines to lay violent hands on Yahweh's anointed—that is, the king (24:5ff.; 26:9ff.; 2 Sam. 1:15f.; cf. 2 Sam. 19:21). Once anointed with holy oil, the king was made holy and was brought within the divine realm, so that he became unimpeachable. The priest was evidently in the same situation, because he lived and worked in the temple (the pre-exilic texts do not speak of his being anointed). At all events, he performed the anointing (1 Kings 1:39; cf. 1 Sam. 10:1) with the holy oil.

The cultic offering of sacrifices would not appear to have been the most important service performed by the priests in Israel—at any rate, the document with which we are concerned makes scarcely any mention of it. Such sacrifices as are referred to are offered by non-priestly persons (David, 2 Sam. 6; 23:16f.; 24:18ff.; cf. also 1 Sam. 26:19). In 1 Sam. 14:31f. the people themselves slaughter the oxen; and this is evidently understood to be a sacrifice, as Saul raises an altar for the occasion. It is clear that the people were forbidden to consume blood. Even when animals were slaughtered in the open countryside, the blood had to be offered to Yahweh—and for that the presence of an altar was apparently requisite. There is only one allusion to an offering, or rather, a 'gift', by the priest: that of the showbread (1 Sam. 21:6). Bloody sacrifices were probably still few and far between; and the real sacrificer, as was assumed even at a later time by the Levitical law, was the man who presented and slaughtered the victim, although even at this period, probably it was the priests who had to perform the blood-letting, set the victim upon the altar and apportion the pieces. Certainly this was so under the subsequent sacrificial regulations. Thus they ministered at the sanctuary; and it was for this that their presence was needed.[19]

That our document enshrines the idea of a close link between the priestly function and the holy place is plainly demonstrated by the story in 1 Sam. 21: the sacred showbread which has been set 'before God' may not be consumed by unconsecrated persons. It is given to David notwithstanding, because, as he says, he has consecrated himself before battle (by having no contact with any woman), is bearing hallowed weapons and so is holy himself (21:5). Holiness is here a property imparted by the objects to the person wearing or carrying them (cf., on the other hand, Haggai 2:12f.).

The priest, then, is to be regarded first and foremost as one who performs sacred actions at a sacred place with sacred objects (ephod, showbread). It looks as though, after the ark, the ephod was the most important sacral object, because with it communication with Yahweh was effected. Next to the ark, it was the symbol of God's presence. If it symbolized divine apparel of some sort, as may well have been the belief at the time, its existence points to two things: (a) that there was no actual image of the deity, and (b) that ancient Phoenician-Canaanite insignia were certainly employed to symbolize the godhead. Thus the Yahwism of this early period effectively excluded image-worship but had nonetheless adopted, even then, syncretistic traits. It is at least probable that Israel borrowed the ephod from the

Canaanite world; for in all likelihood, at any rate, the word is used in the Ugaritic texts to denote a god's apparel.[20]

Ahimelech of Nob, Abiathar, his son, and Zadok are all known to us as having been priests. The two last were the priests who served David—Abiathar from the time when the priests were massacred at Nob, Zadok when David came to live in Jerusalem. Their sons were, respectively, Jonathan and Ahimaaz. Abiathar was banished from Jerusalem at the beginning of Solomon's reign (1 Kings 2); whilst Zadok was put in charge of the priesthood at Jerusalem. With Nathan he was one of Solomon's supporters. It is not certain where he came from; but some people suppose that he emerged from the Jebusite priestly circle.[21] It would appear that David invested sons of theirs with the priesthood (2 Sam. 15:24ff.), as well as sons of his own (2 Sam. 8:18).

Besides several priests there were in David's entourage a number of prophets. Gad and Nathan are mentioned in this capacity. The word 'seer' is used once with reference to Zadok (2 Sam. 15:27); but the text is corrupt at that point. Gad is described as a prophet in 1 Sam. 22, where he turns up suddenly in an annalistic note (verse 5) and indicates to David where he must go. In 2 Sam. 24 Gad is also called a seer (hozeh) of David. He twice brings a message from Yahweh regarding the punishment incurred for 'numbering' the people.

Nathan plays a far more important role. He too makes a sudden appearance on the scene, in Jerusalem (1 Sam. 7); and he remains in David's company as if he were a court prophet (2 Sam. 7; 12; 1 Kings 1). There are three crucial occasions in David's life which constrain him to take action. At the king's request he delivers himself on the question of building a temple and, after having received a revelation from God, disallows it. From this we may fairly conclude that Nathan is no temple or cultic prophet; nor does he belong to the ecstatic genre. On the contrary, he is a man who, like the great prophets of a later time, is guided entirely by the revelatory word of Yahweh (2 Sam. 7:4; 12:1ff., 25).[22] Alongside the negative message from God, inhibiting the building of a temple, stands a quite different one of a positive character: namely, the promise that Yahweh will build David a house that will stand for ever.[23] The account of that divine utterance is probably a direct reaction to the end of the story in 2 Sam. 6, where we read that David parts company with Michal, so that a successor to the throne from the marriage with Saul's daughter, which for Israel as a whole would surely have been the most satisfactory solution of the dynastic issue, is no longer a possibility. David's opting for Yahweh and against Michal, as related in chapter 6, gives occasion for the word from God conveyed by Nathan. So far as the ideas and terms of expression are concerned, 7:8ff. fits neatly on to 2 Sam. 6:21f. Through Nathan David gets complete approval for his course of action and receives the promise that God will build his house and give him a dynasty that shall last 'throughout the length of days'. This message, which is echoed again in 2 Sam. 23:5,[24] was an event that made history. It proved to be the starting-point for the tradition in Israel that linked her expectations and hope of salvation with the dynasty of David (the Messianic-Davidic expectation). The manner in which Nathan intervenes in David's affairs after the king has committed adultery with Bathsheba and has caused the death of her husband, Uriah, in 2 Sam. 12, shows that Nathan is a prophet for whom the word of Yahweh (12:9) is completely paramount. Even the king is subject to it. One's thoughts can hardly turn here to anywhere other than the decalogue, the tradition of which Nathan upholds along with that of the ark. The three judgments which this prophet pronounces upon David and his house (12:10–14) come true. Still, David is pardoned (verse 13); and Nathan is allowed to call the newborn, second son of David's marriage to Bathsheba Jedidiah: that is, 'darling of Yahweh'. No wonder that the prophet gave his heart to this child, whom David named Solomon, and that he later came to look upon him as the appointed successor to the throne and at a crucial juncture took action in defence of his rights (1 Kings 1). Eventually, Nathan's son, Zabud, becomes a priest and one of the highest officials at Solomon's court; and he bears the title of 'the king's friend' (1 Kings 4:5). Whether we are to take Zadok's priestly title as a pointer to the fact that his father's position as a prophet had a background in the priesthood is a question not easy to decide.

Apart from this form of prophetism, which we know about from the activities of Nathan and Gad, we learn from later sources that there was a quite different sort: namely, the ecstatic prophetism centred around the figure of Samuel, which is described in 1 Sam. 19:18ff. and 10:5ff. Some form of prophetic ecstasy can be detected in Israel quite early on, it is true; but it was of Canaanite rather than Yahwistic origin. We shall be dealing with this in Chapter 7, where we discuss in more detail the whole complex phenomenon known in the Old Testament as prophetism.

As regards offerings: besides the gift of the showbread in the temple ritual (see note 19, p. 90; see p. 291), there is the practice of libation, which can take place anywhere 'in the sight of Yahweh', and in a special case can even consist simply of pouring out water (2 Sam. 23:16ff.).

The general term for an offering is *minchah*: that is, a gift, a present; and it can be either bloody or unbloody. In 1 Sam. 26:19, as what is in mind here is a burnt-offering (Yahweh must be able to smell the sweet odour), one should think primarily in terms of an animal sacrifice.

Other terms for an offering besides *minchah*, are *shelem* and *'olah*. The typical sin- and guilt-offerings (the *haṭṭath* and *'asham*) of a later period have as yet no separate designation, although sacrifices could certainly have a propitiatory effect. For discussion of this see further on below.

Shelem-offerings are made when Saul is proclaimed king (1 Sam. 11:15) and when the ark is deposited in Jerusalem (2 Sam. 6:17f.; cf. 24:25). They are referred to as *zebaḥ shelamim* (1 Sam. 11:15) or generally as *zebahim* (offerings) (e.g. 2 Sam. 15:12). Such offerings give opportunity for a festive meal. Yahweh and the priest are allotted certain pieces of the victim; and the devotees consume the remaining portions at a solemn meal. In this way the mutual bond of communion between Yahweh and those who partake is strengthened. It is clear that these kinds of offerings are well suited to coronation feasts (cf. also 1 Kings 1:25).

We may think of these sacrifices as taking place on other festal occasions too. In the early part of the Book of Samuel (chs. 1–3; a later source) we hear tell of the journey made annually by the faithful to the temple at Shiloh. Sacrifice and prayer had an important place in this event. We cannot be sure which of the three prescribed major festivals is in question here (see pp. 149f. and 171), although it is probably the autumn festival. Beyond this there is only the occasional allusion to a religious festival in our Saul-David narrative; and then it is to private, not to official, celebrations. David speaks of an annual feast of sacrifice kept by his family in Bethlehem at the time of the new moon (1 Sam. 20:5f.; this will certainly have been conducted on a high place of some sort); and in 1 Sam. 21:7 it says of Doeg that he was *neʿṣar* ('detained') before the face of Yahweh. Thus he will have had a 'solemn assembly' (*ʿaṣarah*) at the temple in Nob.

In the early period the *'olah*-sacrifices (2 Sam. 6:17f.; cf. 24:22ff.) or burnt-offerings are less in evidence than the *shelamim*. They are entirely consumed by fire on the altar, and are meant to honour Yahweh. They can have a propitiatory function (cf. 2 Sam. 24:22ff.).

To what extent the account of the vendetta of the Gibeonites with the house of Saul (in the section added to the story of Saul and David in 2 Sam. 21) is to be connected with the notion of sacrifice it is hard to say. The word 'sacrifice' does not occur in the story; and the human victims who are put to death are no offering in the usual sense of the term. In fact the whole transaction is juridical rather than cultic. Even so, it has a fair number of religious associations; for the matter that demanded such bloody reparation was revealed in a pronouncement made by Yahweh. Because blood-guilt for a crime lay upon Saul and his house, punishment in the guise of a famine had descended on the country. The story ends with the remark that God had mercy upon the land (verse 14). There is also mention of a propitiatory or atoning act, making it possible for the Gibeonites to bless the inheritance of Yahweh.

All this goes to show very clearly how much law and religion go together in early Israel. Offences against the law are punished by Yahweh himself, because he is the guardian of law and justice; and he is invoked whenever a treaty or agreement is concluded. In this instance the matter is primarily one of legal restitution, because justice had been abrogated by the shedding of innocent blood. The atonement spoken of in 21:3 is not so much a cultic as a juridical transaction. By the death of the seven members of Saul's family the blood-feud is applied to (the family of) the king, who killed Gibeonites during his own life-time. In that this action at the same time violated the oath sworn 'by Yahweh' when the pact with the Gibeonites was concluded (cf. Josh. 7: e.g. verse 18), Yahweh took the matter to heart and acted in such a way, by inflicting the penal famine upon Israel, that the bloodshed was duly avenged and the blood-guilt thereby removed. The bloody vengeance exacted served in this case as a deed of atonement for the Israelite community, which shared the blood-guilt consequent upon Saul's act.

Thus the sons of Saul who were executed were not a sacrifice to Yahweh. Neither Israel nor David sacrificed them; but the Gibeonites had opportunity to take revenge upon them for their own dead. The fact that this took place in Gibeah of Saul further signalizes the thoroughness of the revenge: it happened at Saul's own township. That it was done 'in the sight of Yahweh' still does not make it an act of sacrifice; but it shows that with David's co-operation (cf. verse 6f.)

the Gibeonites carried it out openly, in the presence of him who is the protector of oaths; so that Yahweh is witness that by the vengeance which the Gibeonites have taken the blood-guilt of Saul's house is removed from Israel (the word *kipper*, to atone, to wipe off, in 21:3, is indeed appropriate, therefore; the blood or the blood-guilt (= *damim*) is hereby done away with).[25]

J. Pedersen rightly asserts[26] that the blood-feud is a legal process designed to afford redress to an injured party (family, community). It gives a man the opportunity to vindicate himself, by enabling him to obtain satisfaction. 2 Sam. 21 is about the juridical restoration of the Gibeonites by the Gibeonites themselves, under the watchful eye of Yahweh, the God of justice, and with the collaboration of David who, as king, is called upon to ensure that justice takes its proper course. It would seem not altogether correct, therefore, to say that the ritual in question is quite clearly reminiscent of Canaanite practice.[27] What we have here, as Pedersen has shown, is an example of juridical thinking and behaviour typical of ancient Israel.

Other transactions belonging to the area between cult and law—or better, perhaps, to the plane in which they are contiguous—are, for instance, vows, oath-taking and the concluding of pacts or agreements. These are best discussed in association with the subject preceding.

In the story of Saul and David we read of a vow in the episode about Absalom (2 Sam. 15:7ff.), who when in foreign parts had vowed before Yahweh that he would perform a cultic act (verse 8). This he fulfilled by offering sacrifices (*shelamin*) in Hebron. It is clear from this, as from many other instances elsewhere in the Old Testament (cf., e.g., Gen. 28:20), that a vow was made to back up a petition, in order to induce Yahweh to grant it. Such a vow was something sacred. David, when he hears about it, at once agrees to Absalom's request that he should be allowed to honour it.

Oaths are sworn on a variety of occasions: upon concluding a pact or making a vow or a promise. An oath is an utterance by which the subject confirms any given statement or undertaking by calling God to witness and (or) pronouncing a curse upon himself, should the undertaking not be carried out. Oath and curse are so closely interconnected that both are used together, sometimes, as a hendiadys (for example, Num. 5:21). Along with the invocation of the name of Yahweh, the curse adds force to the oath: an uttered curse is in fact regarded as charged with power and as self-operative. The invocation of Yahweh's name in this proceeding was surety for the fulfilment of the oath or in case the curse itself should fail to ensue. That is why a promise given on oath has the force of law, even if it be given inadvertently (Lev. 5:4) or uttered on the strength of a false assumption (Josh. 9:15ff.). Oaths are usually sworn in the name of Yahweh with the formula: 'as surely as Yahweh lives'; and the curse-formula starts off: 'Thus may Yahweh do, and more also . . . if so be that' (the content of the curse is usually kept secret; cf. 1 Sam. 20:13; 2 Sam. 3:35). In 1 Sam. 30:15 an Amalekite prisoner, before declaring himself ready to conduct David to the camp of the Amalekite forces, asks of him an oath: 'swear by God that thou wilt not slay me or deliver me up'.

The word for an oath and the verb meaning 'to swear' are connected with the root of the numeral seven. Precisely what the connexion is is not evident. Seven is the perfect number. Whether the declaration was originally repeated seven times, or a curse was spoken seven times, and whether people even invoked seven gods, is no longer clear; but something of the kind it must have been.[28]

It is obvious from the Saul-David narrative what significance attaches to oaths (1 Sam. 14:24ff.). Saul requires his men to utter a curse (verse 24; it is later said to be an oath, verse 26), the purpose of which is to reinforce their promise to abstain from food during the battle. When Jonathan, who had not been present at the oath-taking, eats something all the same, the pursuit of the enemy cannot be proceeded with, because Yahweh makes no reply when questioned through the oracle (verse 36ff.). Thus it appears that the people are at fault in some way. When the casting of lots points to Jonathan as the cause, Saul swears to have him put to death; and Jonathan is ready to die. It is only because the people will not hear of that and discharge him[29] (probably by killing an animal victim on his behalf) that he escapes the consequences of the curse which Saul had constrained the people to utter.

The oath as a curse is taken with the utmost seriousness by those who swear it and by God in whose name it is sworn, even though it be uttered without thought and though not everyone may even have heard about it. Jonathan could only escape death because the possibility existed of redeeming him. Indeed, the bearing of an unmerited curse may even prove a means of blessing (2 Sam. 16:12); and so the curse evidently does not operate in a purely mechanical fashion.

The business of concluding a pact or covenant is also carried out 'before the face of Yahweh' (1 Sam. 32:17f.), and is on the same footing as the swearing of an oath (cf. 1 Sam. 20:12–17; 41–43; 23:17). With a covenant each party assumes an obligation toward the other (20:15). The pact between Jonathan and David starts from the fact that Jonathan, the crown prince, allied himself totally with David, placed him on an equal footing with himself, by giving him his clothing, his tunic and even his weapons (18:2ff.). The bond was reinforced when danger threatened David (20:12ff., 41ff.) and Jonathan saw fortune beginning to smile upon him. They undertake to remain loyal to one another and to stand by each other's families (20:42). In the end, Jonathan acknowledges David's future kingship and puts himself at David's disposal (the third covenanting; 23:17). David always stuck by this alliance (2 Sam. 1:26; 9:5ff.; 19:24ff.; 21:7). Whatever in such an association is sanctioned by an oath sworn 'by Yahweh' is fixed and final: it is rendered holy, because Yahweh stands as guarantor between the parties (1 Sam. 20:42). One might properly describe the association as an a-natural union, not constituted by any ties of blood or marriage, but as brought into being by God as agent and intermediary. In Israel as elsewhere, therefore, a covenant is not just a practical arrangement or contract, but a union forged in the presence of the deity, involving a group of persons fused into a unity, as solid as any family or fellowship of kindred.[30]

Although our document makes no direct reference to the idea of a pact or covenant in the relationship between Israel and Yahweh, it does presuppose a direct link between Yahweh and the people and country of Israel. It several times speaks of Israel and her land as an inheritance of Yahweh (1 Sam. 26:19; 2 Sam. 14:16; 20:19 and 21:3) —which implies that Israel accrues to Yahweh personally as his domain and that there is an abiding relationship between God and the nation, a relationship firmly grounded in legality. We are brought still closer to the covenant-idea when the *ḥesed Yahweh* (or *'Elohim*), his kindness, is spoken of. Because the relation to him is one of fellowship, of communion, Yahweh evinces a divine solidarity (1 Sam. 20:14 and 2 Sam. 9:3). What this means is best illustrated, apart from the texts already cited, by the words of the woman of Tekoa (2 Sam. 14:14), where she says of God that he does not take away life but ponders upon means to ensure that the exile is not banished from his presence for ever. From this way of speaking about the relationship with God we cannot fail to realize that people in

G

Israel were aware of a bond of fellowship with him which involved not merely the nation as such, but the individual person too.

In view of this it is really nothing strange to come across utterances that show how personal in character was the piety current in Israel at this period. In 1 Sam. 23:16 we read of Jonathan that he 'heartened David with God', fortified David's confidence in God. When David stands utterly alone (1 Sam. 30:6) because even his trusty followers felt so bitterly towards him that they wanted to kill him, seeing him as the cause of all their misfortune, David has but one support: Yahweh. 'David strengthened himself in Yahweh his God.' The personal aspect of the relationship is expressed clearly enough in the word 'his'. This appears again and again, even if in quite a different way, from many other instances: as when, having been notified of it by Nathan, he bows to the judgment of Yahweh, confesses his guilt and accepts God's punishment (2 Sam. 12:13–23), even though David tries by prayer and fasting to persuade Yahweh to relent and let the child live. In 2 Sam. 16:10ff. David consents, because God requires it of him, to suffer a wrong without seeking to avenge himself. The spontaneity of his religion is evident too from the manner in which he personally flings himself into the business of transferring the ark and repudiates Michal when she objects to this. At an early stage of his flight (1 Sam. 22:3) he carries his parents into safety, whilst awaiting more certain knowledge of 'what God intends for me'.

Something of the same sort, although with a greater degree of resignation, appears in the swashbuckling Joab, who having prepared his men for battle urges them on with the words: 'be strong, and let us bear ourselves bravely for our people and for the cities of our God', but then concludes with: 'The Lord do what is good in his sight'.

Despite this well-meaning personal piety, it is still quite possible to come across such a remark as: 'If Yahweh has set you against me, then let him savour an offering' (1 Sam. 26:19), which presupposes that Yahweh can intend evil, and expresses the notion that a sacrificial gift may win him over to a more favourable attitude. This is plainly disparate, of course, with the idea of a shared relationship between God and his people. As appears on several occasions (see also p. 30f.), the attitude adopted toward Yahweh, although one of trust, still contains an element of uncertainty as to how God will behave. Yahweh's power remains arbitrary; and man is totally dependent upon him. David had already had experience of this with Saul, and had seen that he who may grant a man his gracious support and his spirit can also withhold these things. He is the mighty One, who does as seems good to him. Yahweh is quite capable, therefore, of acting preposterously. There is certainly a place in the belief of ancient Israel for an apprehension of what Otto has called the numinous.[31] What may astonish even more are the words in the fierce cry of the incensed warrior to Saul: 'Then let him smell an offering!' Besides spite and anger, there is here something too of the calculating *do ut des*, of: 'give God his due and he will be good again'. Even though the supposed situation may largely account for this, it does show that this idea persists below the surface in ancient Israel. However, it is the only instance that does so; for neither David's attempt by fasting and prayer to persuade God to spare his child's life (2 Sam. 12:13ff.)[32] nor the blood-feud of the Gibeonites (2 Sam. 21; see above, p. 94) can be referred to this precise form of placation.

Some social factors

Under this head we intend to bring together a number of matters with a bearing on ancient Israel's general outlook on life—matters which do not, however, relate directly to the cultic or the political sphere. It is true, of course, that in a legal, social and family context, as well as a personal one, religion is the essential, determining factor. We are faced in particular with the issues of life and death.

Life is something given by Yahweh; and it is his alone. On the first score our source has nothing directly to say; but the second is manifest enough from various actions: for instance, when David refuses to drink the water obtained at mortal risk from the spring at Bethlehem, but pours it out before Yahweh (2 Sam. 23:16f.). He calls this water 'the blood of men who have taken their lives in their hands'. Again, man is forbidden to use the blood of animals, because it is a vehicle of life (1 Sam. 14:33ff.; see p. 90f.).

To kill a human being, unless it be in battle or in consequence of a juridical sentence, is one of the worst crimes that one can commit. It calls therefore for retribution, which can be lawfully exacted only through a blood-feud or by means of capital punishment. Although David did not personally contrive Joab's death after the murder of Abner—apparently because he was too greatly indebted to him or needed him too much—he nonetheless put a curse upon him, expressing the wish that the blood of Abner might be upon the head of Joab and of his entire family (2 Sam. 3:28ff.); and on his death-bed he charged Solomon not to let Joab escape his punishment (1 Kings 2:5f.). At the very first opportunity that presented itself Solomon fulfilled this duty in what was for Israel an extremely horrifying fashion: he had Joab struck down at the holy place of sanctuary itself—the altar (1 Kings 2:28ff.). David's son Absalom, who slew Amnon, had to flee abroad in order to evade the death penalty, but was later reprieved, when Joab and the woman of Tekoa interceded for him (2 Sam. 14); for she had first persuaded the king to absolve from the blood-feud her own son, who having murdered his brother was now in peril of falling victim to the family vendetta (which would have left her helpless and unprotected). The blood-feud was actually taken to such lengths that it obliged the family to kill the murderer within their own domestic circle.

Even the king, if he killed anyone unlawfully, did not escape being punished. The story in 2 Sam. 21 shows that the vendetta could be applied to Saul, even after his death. David, who through his orders given to Joab had been the guilty cause of Uriah's death, is punished in the loss of the child born to him and above all with the sentence pronouncing that the sword will not depart from his house.

David's adultery with Bathsheba is not directly punished with death, as the law requires; but the death of his child is clearly the penalty for this misdeed. It happened as it did because David made frank confession of his sin. Even so, he was punished for it in another way too, in that later on his son was to dishonour David's wives (2 Sam. 12:11f.; cf. 16:22). That a king should be held responsible for an act of this sort is in itself quite an exceptional thing in the world of the ancient East. It points to the fact that the ethical and religious laws of ancient Israel had a universal validity, and they applied to absolutely everyone (see p. 143). The rape of a young girl is sharply condemned, by implication at any rate, in 2 Sam. 13 ('such a thing is not done in Israel'); and the act is described as 'foolishness'—one might better say: an act of lunacy (verse 12). But the law did not exact the death penalty for this (Ex. 22:16f.; Deut. 22:28). At all events, when Absalom, brother to the girl Tamar whom Amnon had ravished, slew him, Israelite law adjudged this to be fratricide.

The soothsaying so generally recognized throughout the ancient East was severely penalized in Israel. According to 1 Sam. 28 Saul had soon made short work of the practice of interrogating the departed and other occult skills, and had removed the practitioners of the black art from his territory (1 Sam. 28:3), thereafter punishing with death

44925

those who continued with it (verses 9 and 21). This was in line with ancient Israelite law (cf. Ex. 22:18; although it is magic in particular that is mentioned there). Witches, soothsayers and mediums were all condemned. Only 'wise women' were still allowed to play some part (2 Sam. 14:2; 20:16); but whether they did anything more than offer counsel, as in the chapters just cited, and whether they had access to some secret wisdom and so resembled in certain respects the 'aged women' of the Hittite world[33] is hard to say.

At all events, soothsaying certainly persisted in Israel, despite the official prohibitions. 1 Sam. 28 tells of a woman of Endor who was a medium and was able to call up the ghost of Samuel. One reads of this kind of thing happening again later on in the time of Isaiah, of Manasseh and of Josiah (2 Kings 21:6; 23:24); so it is a fair assumption that soothsaying of this sort continued to exist in Israel and was always having to be combated (Deut. 18:10f.; Lev. 19:31; 20:6, 27).

From this it would appear that the one type of prognostication acceptable to Israel was that which came from Yahweh, either through the priest, who could ask Yahweh by means of the ephod with *urim* and *thummim* (see above, p. 89) for an oracle, or through the prophet, who in certain cases could give a definitive answer (1 Sam. 22:5). At the start of a battle, especially, the oracle of God was consulted (see p. 164); and then God could usually be relied on to give his reply. The famous message from God spoken by Balaam (in another document) puts it like this: 'Although there be no conjuration in Jacob, nor yet soothsaying in Israel, when the time comes it is told to Jacob and to Israel what God will do' (Num. 23:23). If that did not happen, it was the sign of an impending judgment (1 Sam. 14:37) or was a general indication that Yahweh had turned away from those who had asked for the oracular message (1 Sam. 28:6).

As for death, it is in store for every human being (2 Sam. 14:14); but this does not terrify the Israelite. One can descend in peace to the realm of the dead. To die a violent death is bad, of course (1 Kings 2:6); and the death of a child is a dreadful thing (2 Sam. 12:15ff.). At death man goes to Sheol, the kingdom of the dead, where he leads only a shadowy existence. The dead person lives on, in the aspect which he had previously presented during his life on earth (1 Sam. 28:14; cf. 1 Kings 2:9), as a preternatural being ('*elohim*; 1 Sam. 28:13). If bodies were not buried or were mutilated, the deceased could find no rest; and that is why people were so anxious to put their dead into a grave. It was not only an honour paid to the dead

Lincoln Christian College

man—it brought him peace in the lower world, peace in the society of his forefathers, among whom he arrived in the grave (1 Sam. 31:11ff.; 2 Sam. 21:8ff.; 2:32; 17:23; 18:17; 19:37; 1 Kings 2:10 and 34). The mourning customs observed were fasting and weeping (2 Sam. 12:21f.; 3:33ff.) and outward manifestations of mourning such as rending the clothes, putting on mourning attire and wailing (2 Sam. 3:31ff.). Some customs that existed among other peoples, such as shaving the head and slashing the skin until blood was drawn, were forbidden in Israel. By contrast with the world of the Near East— where in one way or another there was provision made for the dead, cultic worship of the dead, interrogation of the dead—Israel's attitude to the lower world was a negative one of avoiding everything that might imperil the uniqueness of Yahweh's dominion. Yahweh was the God of life, not of death, even though at a later time Yahweh's power was extended to the realm of the dead.

CHAPTER 4

The Prehistory

ALTHOUGH THE RELIGION of Israel, in origin at least, is a national rather than a world religion, it nonetheless shares certain basic features with world religions such as Christianity, Islam and Buddhism. Besides the fact that it addresses men as such and appeals to a revelation given in history, one such feature worth remarking is that it is rooted in, and draws its life-blood from, more than one layer of religious soil. It is a complex religion, not only because of its later development but also as regards its origin; and like the other religions mentioned, it has some association with a previous stage in which it rests. Buddhism admits to having its source in the Enlightenment of the Buddha; but it retains a background of Brahminism. Christianity bases itself on the divine revelation in Jesus Christ; but he came from within Israel, in the context of whose religion his life was lived. Islam took the shape it did because of the revelations vouchsafed to Mohammed; yet in their form and content these go back in many respects to the Bible. It is the same with Israel's religion, which rests on more than a single stratum. It comes to fruition through the revelation to Moses in the desert; but Israelite tradition attests that this is based in its turn on the religion of the patriarchs.

Although on the one hand there is a clear distinction drawn between these two phases of the religion, on the other hand there is an underlying continuity. The difference is chiefly apparent in this: that the Mosaic religion is associated with the name 'Yahweh' for God, whereas the theism of the patriarchs is characterized by more than one divine name. It is remarkable how long the consciousness of this dual background survived in Israel, even in the period when the ancient traditions were committed to writing, and even long after the unity of people, state, culture and religion had apparently been realized.

If anything about the religion of ancient Israel is certain, therefore, it is this: that it has more than one substratum. The very circumstance that people were conscious of this, and remained so during centuries of their history, is a cogent argument for its historical truth.[1] The process of historical memory and association tends, of course, to marshal the facts of the past in one historical plane. When it obstinately insists, therefore, in distinguishing several periods, one has every reason to take it seriously. So there is no doubt about it that Israel's religion is rooted in that of the forefathers as well as in the Mosaic religion itself.

If, then, this double character of the background, and the recognition of its historicity, does not itself run into any difficulties, it certainly raises quite a few; for it makes the history of the earliest phase of Israelite religion extremely complicated, and its reconstruction (so far, at any rate) next to impossible. What now becomes the main question is how we are to see the relationship between the two forms. Is there a certain degree of continuity here; or are we faced with two totally different forms of religion, blended or fused together?

The tradition as we have it in the Book of Exodus treats Yahweh, the God who reveals himself to Moses as a deliverer-god, as being one and the same with the God of the fathers (Ex. 3:4ff.; 6:1ff.). Yet a close comparison of the evidence from the patriarchal and Mosaic periods, respectively, discloses so many differences that one is forced to conclude that where their apprehension of God is concerned, a very real distinction must be made between them. It is not possible, the differences being what they are, to establish with sufficient certainty or in any detail what measure of agreement there may be between the two periods in question. One can only get as far as a number of vague and markedly hypothetical basic propositions.

This is the more true because, to start with, it is a matter of the utmost difficulty to say definitely, in the case either of primitive Yahwism or of the patriarchal religion, what the characteristic traits are. Present-day experts on early Israelite religion hold widely differing views on both; and the main reason for this is the lack of religio-historical material for comparison, dating from either period—a lack which makes it especially hard to assess the historical trustworthiness of the early traditions. Scarcely any reliable contemporary data are available for this purpose; and what evidence there is is insufficient. During recent decades a few important things from the period to which the patriarchs can be assigned have come to light; but for the present they are restricted almost entirely to social, juridical, cultural and historico-geographical considerations (see below; p. 115ff.).[2] In certain respects these data offer such striking parallels with the contents of the patriarchal narratives as to justify the conclusion that some fairly ancient strands of tradition must have been worked in here; but unhappily, so far as religious elements typical for the patriarchs are concerned, they yield almost nothing. When it comes to the Mosaic period, we are not even as well off as that. Up to now, *all* attempts to relate the traditional material to the study of the religion and its history have remained hypothetical—and this as much from the standpoint of a negative critique as from that of a more positive one. Thus every reconstruction of the two earliest religious periods can only be treated as hypothetical; and this is doubly true when someone tries to tackle the question of how the two periods are related.

Our aim in this chapter is not so much to devise a sketch of the patriarchal religion but in a quite tentative way, and on the basis of a critical use of the biblical and non-biblical material that is available, to specify some of the lines on which future research will have to proceed.

To begin with, we must say something in brief as to the nature of this material and its uses. We have already discussed this on a broad front in the introductory chapter.

The material offered by the Bible on the patriarchal period is embodied in a collection of songs, or rather, proverbs, about the ancient tribes (Gen. 49), in a number of separate stories (such as Gen. 34 and 38) and in some serial narratives, ascribable to various writers whose work belongs, successively, to the 10th (or 9th), the 8th and the 6th centuries.[3] These sources have been edited to form together a single, composite narrative, which proves very embarrassing to the historian in his handling of the early material; for it is a matter of the utmost delicacy to decide what ought to be ascribed to a given source and what in that source is to be regarded as an early element, and what a more recent one.

The big question is therefore: how can we sift the material so as to render it usable for historical purposes? It is only too easy to understand that when attempts are made to do this, the sifting process offers some very diverse results. Some scholars abide quite closely by the tradition and make fairly full use of the material transmitted. I am thinking, for example, of the reconstruction of the patriarchal religion put forward by F. M. Th. de Liagre Böhl,[4] M. Buber,[5] and O. Procksch.[6] B. Gemser[7] is more cautious and critical, but arrives at closely allied conclusions, especially in his account of the type of piety.[8]

Many others consider that nothing can really be known about this religion—a conclusion reflected in various books on the religion of Israel which instead of describing the patriarchal period either leave a total gap[9] or give an account of a hypothetical proto-Semitic religion.[10]

In very recent years there have been some schools of thought that fall in between. They maintain that in certain respects this period is indeed accessible. They have to be divided into those who approach the problem chiefly from an archaeological standpoint (W. F. Albright and his school) and those who (following A. Alt) attempt through the *traditionsgeschichtliche* method of enquiry* to come at the sources of the tradition in Israel, and so try more by means of a literary technique to find various fixed points for the religion of the patriarchs. There is a lively exchange of ideas between each group; and they are certainly not just polar opposites. On the contrary, someone like M. Noth, who must be reckoned among the second group, although very critical of the alacrity with which archaeologists all too often jump to conclusions on the strength of their data, works as much within the archaeological field as in that of literary tradition. Or again, a man like O. Eissfeldt, although in a way that is in some sense different, has always worked in both camps simultaneously. To this is added in his case a special concern with the actual historical course of the religion.

In point of fact, all three schools of research—the archaeological, the literary and the 'history of religion' school—need one another very much, if reliable new ground is to be broken in the historical study of religion. Compared with one or two generations ago, much has been achieved already. If 'stormy progress' is perhaps a somewhat heavily charged expression for what has taken place so far, it is quite certain that we stand on the threshold of a new phase in the study of the prehistory of Israel's religion.

It is impossible, of course, in this brief survey to give an overall picture, even in outline, of the different standpoints and conclusions, to date, of the several lines of investigation. What is more important is to present the material itself, biblical and extra-biblical alike.

First of all, then, the biblical material; because up to now, at any rate, it is the only literary evidence that has come down to us—

* *See Chapter* 1, *note* 9.

granting, of course, that in view of the later redactions of the tradition it cannot have direct relevance as a historical document when we are trying to construct a historical account of the patriarchal period.

In any survey of this that is arranged according to the various redactions (sources), first in turn comes the Yahwist(J). He has already placed the traditions concerning the three patriarchs within a settled historical and genealogical scheme, in which Abraham plays the principal role. Abraham is the lineal ancestor and ideal pattern of the future people of Israel. In the promise made to him Israel's high destiny is also given (Gen. 12:1ff.). Yahweh constrains him to leave his territory in Upper Mesopotamia (in accordance with the purpose of Yahweh, who scatters mankind over the world; this motif in 10:25 and 11:1-9) and journey to the land that he is to show him; and Yahweh undertakes to make of him a great nation—for which reason Abraham stands under Yahweh's personal protection, looking forward to a blessed future in which all the races on the face of the earth will have their part (12:1-3). This promise is the *Leitmotiv* of the Yahwistic account of history and outlook upon it, which begins at this point.

There are evidently two motifs worked in together here, which J represents as governing Israel's history: the promise of the progeny (the 'seed') and that regarding the land of Canaan and its occupation. Alt insists that they are distinct in origin and must be kept apart.[11] The Genesis stories return again and again to the motif of the acquisition of the country; and in the first chapters (12-13) it is even the main theme. From chapter 15 onwards, the 'progeny' motif begins to assume the chief role in the story; and all the rest of the story of the patriarchs looks to be woven around it.[12]

When we look closely at the tradition, it seems as if it contains more than one Abraham-figure. On the one hand he is called Abram (a name of North East Semitic structure), on the other Abraham (which is formed with a word so far known to derive from the Arabic only). Abram is on the one hand a figure who roves about between Shechem and Hebron; but on the other he is a nomad who (like Isaac) inhabits the Negeb, where his relation with the Philistines and the Ishmaelites is a prominent feature of the narrative. There is as a matter of fact yet a third, quite different, Abraham-type: that of the warrior of Hebron (Gen. 14). The fact that he is here referred to as a Hebrew (verse 13) raises the question whether the thought here is not indeed of some ancient memory of the Ḥabiru.[13] Thus three sectors in the country, certainly, had their own version of an Abraham-figure.

This many-sided picture presented by the figure of Abraham prompts one to ask certain questions of an ethnic nature about the ancient patriarchs. The recent finds in Mesopotamia, by turning the spotlight on to the connexions the patriarchs had with Northern Mesopotamia, have pushed consideration of their relations with the South Semitic world quite into the background. At an earlier juncture, it is true, this aspect was given unduly one-sided emphasis (by Wellhausen and others); but it is hardly right to range over against this a new set of prejudices. In figures like Cain (Arabic: 'the smith') and the Kenites, Esau and the Edomites (Gen. 36), Hagar and the Ishmaelites, in the very marked prominence that the stories of Abraham and Isaac give to places in Southern Palestine, in the relations that existed with Egypt and the like, all kinds of elements are preserved which show that the provenance of the Hebrew tribes out of which Israel arose is bound up not only with the North-east but with the South (South-east). There were always contacts and relations with tribes coming from the South. Palestine has always been a country penetrated by nomads from both the North-east and the South-east. Since the narratives themselves provide a clear pointer in that direction, which, after all, backs up the general rule, we ought not to disregard the South Semitic strain in the forerunners of the later tribes of Israel.[14]

Returning to the Yahwist's narrative, we see him relating how Abr(ah)am obeys the word of Yahweh and travels to Canaan, where in the heart of that country near the town of Shechem Yahweh appears to him under an ancient and sacred oracle-tree (the terebinth of Moreh) and promises him that he will give the land to his posterity. Abr(ah)am builds an altar there, as he does later on between Bethel and Ai.

The stories that now follow—about Abr(ah)am's journey to Egypt, Sarai's abduction (12:10–20), together with the parting of Abram and Lot (13)—have more to do with the traditional history than with the history of religion. This chapter 13 again mentions the altar between Bethel and Ai and the building of an altar by the terebinths of Mamre near Hebron, which incident provides a transition to the next set of narratives dealing with the story of Abraham. Genesis 14, the value of which as historiography is sharply contested, gives us the remarkable story (not itself part of the Yahwistic account of Abraham) of Abraham as a man of war and deliverer of the cities of the East and, in the same connexion, of his meeting with the king of Salem, Melchizedek, the priest of El Elyon. Abraham is blessed by him in the name of the Creator-god, El Elyon, and gives him tithes of all his possessions, thereby acknowledging El Elyon of Salem as his God. From a religio-historical viewpoint this chapter is extremely important, in that it recognizes a relationship between Abraham and the world of Canaanite religion. Here again Abraham is called a Hebrew (verse 13).

From chapter 15 onwards, the collection of stories is supplemented with Elohistic and priestly passages. In chapter 15 the Yahwist and the Elohist are at one in telling us how in answer to Abraham's question Yahweh promises him a great posterity and makes a covenant with him, ratified in a remarkable and ancient sacrificial ceremony.[15] Verse 6, which extols the faith of Abraham, is from a later hand than JE. The important thing about this story, which must be reckoned among the most ancient traditions regarding Abraham, is first of all that Yahweh appears as the patriarch's partner in a covenant, but also that a new theme (that of Abraham's childlessness) is introduced at this point (see p. 107, note 12).

In chapter 16 Abraham, because the promise in chapter 15 has not been fulfilled, at Sarai's request and in accordance with legal custom in the ancient East, takes to wife his female slave, Hagar.[16] The name Ishmael reflects the notion that from the patriarchal period on there were close ties between the ancient Hebrew and Arabian tribes.

After chapter 17 (P; the covenant of circumcision) comes the celebrated account of Sodom and Gomorrah, which did not originally form part of the story of Abraham (but was perhaps introduced through a tradition connected with Lot).[17] His intercession for Sodom (18:22ff.) endows the patriarch with prophetic traits, even in the J narrative.[18] It is indeed arguable that this is already implied, in J's case, in the whole relationship of Abram to his God (the God of Abram). One thinks of the opening words of Gen. 12. This would then be of a piece with the character of Abraham's *theos patroios*, who according to Alt functions as essentially a revelational deity.

After the birth of Isaac (ch. 21, heavily edited by E) there follows at the end of this chapter the planting by Abraham of a sacred tamarisk at Beersheba, when he invoked the name of the El ʿOlam, the unchanging God.[19] Whether this name may be regarded as a parallel of an epithet given to El in Ugarit—namely: *ab šnm* ('the father of the years'?)—is uncertain.[20]

In chapter 22 comes the story of the offering of Isaac at Moriah. This forms just a part of the Yahwist's main narrative; but E has worked it up into a new and powerful whole. When one compares this story, which is integral to the 'childlessness-posterity' motif, with the tragic fate that befalls the son in the *Dan'el* epic (he is slain by command of the jealous Anat)[21], then it is clear that the Abraham story is in a certain sense a parallel and is yet entirely different, offering its own distinctive view of the situation, with a profound significance wholly consonant with the Israelite religion. The point is that Yahweh here is not only honoured as the giver of all things, with a rightful claim upon them, but once more appears as the One who seeks, not the death of man but his wellbeing. This element typifies, therefore, the Yahwist's view of events.

With chapter 24 the Yahwistic account of Abraham ends. Here we have the remarkable oath-taking of Abraham's servant, who touches his master's hip[22]—but above all, the persistent talk on the servant's part about the God of Abraham.

From a lot of the features already mentioned it is plain that the Yahwistic narrator has worked his own views into his version of the Abrahamic story: the use of the Yahweh-name, the typical vein of piety (the obedience of the ancestral father, Yahweh as the saving God), possibly also the framework of the narrative as a whole, and in particular the arrangement of the material under the programmatic viewpoint of Gen. 12:1-3, the whole view of Abraham as at once the historical and the spiritual father of Israel and, with that, the exposé of Israel as a nation brought into being by the call of God and by obedience to his word.

Yet at the same time a variety of ancient features have been incorporated: these are, alongside the *theos patroios*, the God of Abraham, the El-types which are mentioned; the fact that the oracular terebinth at Shechem and the sacred terebinth at Beersheba, as well as the sacred stone at Bethel and the *teraphim*, are all included. The worship of El, at any rate, dates from before the Yahwist's time. By the earliest period of the kingship it had been pushed into the background, although it certainly still existed under the judges and continued into the final period before the monarchy.[23] Again, the non-occurrence of the Baal-name and the generally very good relations between patriarchs and Canaanites could be taken to indicate that the Yahwist has preserved the atmosphere of the old patriarchal stories.[24]

Quite the most significant fact that emerges from all this, however, is that a writer like the Yahwist, who does accept Yahweh as the God of prehistory as also of the patriarchal period, yet makes so much play with the El religion of the different sanctuaries.

Setting the data provided by E and P in the Abraham-story side by side with those of J, it is safe to say that E has not added much of his own. He has given some elements greater prominence: for instance, the prophetic character of the patriarch (in the E passages of chapter 15 and in chapter 20). He also stresses the contrast between the old inhabitants of the area and the patriarchs (cf. 20:11 and probably 19:30ff.). Hagar's son, Ishmael, is blessed, therefore, despite his mother's being of non-Hebrew origin, because he is a son of Abraham's (21:13). E is adept at signalizing the special significance of Abraham as both the 'chosen man' and the 'obedient man' (this in chs. 22 and 15). Thus his contribution is in the theological field particularly—at all events, where the story of Abraham is concerned.

P adds mainly certain historical and theological emphases: Abraham's background in the world of Northern Mesopotamia, his genealogy, the stress on the great age of Abraham and Sarai when Isaac is born, and especially on the covenant-idea, symbolized by circumcision (ch. 17). By the change of name from 'Abram' to 'Abraham' P harmonizes the two traditions regarding the name (17:5). For the rest, he emphasizes that Yahweh reveals himself to Abraham under the name of El Shaddai (17:1); and in Ex. 6:2 he returns to this theme. He draws a clear distinction, then, between the Yahwistic and pre-Yahwistic revelations. P here exhibits one of the early priestly traditions, which among priestly writers (including, for example, Ezekiel) are by no means an isolated case. El Shaddai must be one of the old Hebrew ways of designating the god. One finds it in the Old Testament most frequently in the Book of Job, where the name is in regular use among the principal, non-Israelite personages in this document. Although the explanation of the name is uncertain, one's first inclination is to think in terms of the powerful mountain-god.[25] This would account not only for the protective character of El Shaddai (for instance, Ps. 91:1) but also his fearsome aspect (Ps. 68:15; Ezek. 1:24; 10:5; Isa. 13:6; Ruth 1:20f.). The final part of the Abraham-story in P tells how the cave of Machpelah was obtained as a burial-place for the patriarchal family and the patriarch's first acquisition of estate. The story shows that around 550 there was an already ancient tradition about the cave of Machpelah near Hebron.

Isaac. Although Isaac evidently represents a distinctively Southern type of tribe, which is later absorbed into Northern tribal groups, in the tradition as now assembled the Isaac-stories hardly have any longer a role to play in their own right. They in fact constitute a bridge between the story of Abraham and that of Jacob. One could say that the figure of Isaac is retained because he is father to Esau and Jacob—and they are both essential to the Jacob-story. As regards the God of Isaac: the 'god of Abram, your father' first appears to him at Beersheba, the centre of the territory which he inhabitated. Yet Isaac's own God is later spoken of as *paḥad Yiṣḥaq* (Gen. 31:42), which according to the most likely interpretation means[26] the 'one affianced with Isaac'.

Jacob is the second major patriarchal figure. He too has a double affiliation. On the one side it is with Esau, whose name (like Se'ir) means originally 'hairy' and whose habitation is Southern Jordania (the name 'Edom' must be secondary in this connexion;[27] Edom, the red country, is the area later occupied by the Esau-group). It would appear that Esau, the hunter, as opposed to Jacob who is a herdsman, belongs initially to a region further to the North and was an older rival to the Jacob-tribes. In the tradition two elements, that of the hunter, Esau, and that of the tribal founder, Edom, are combined.[28]

On the other hand Jacob is connected with the North-east, the land of Laban. We may understand the Jacob figure to be a second and later wave of North-east Semitic semi-nomads invading the West Semitic world. In view of the North East Semitic (Noth: proto-Aramaic) nomenclature, the name 'Jacob' points plainly in this direction.[29] These traditions, transmitted by J, and more especially by E, in the form of various stories based on ancient sagas, certainly preserve important historical memories and associations. The Jacob-group fended for itself effectively in the centre of East and West Jordania. Bethel and Peniel, in particular, play a major role in the tradition. To the south of Jordania the migrants were unable to push forward, because there Esau was too strong for them; so they sheered away to the West, towards Central Palestine.

There is yet a third peculiar thing about this Jacob-figure: namely, that he is also the figure of Israel. Here the question arises as to whether the two names do not point to what were originally two figures, unified in the tradition. It does indeed seem clear from the Merneptah stele that there existed in Central Palestine a group of settlers who are regarded as a powerful element in the population. Might not this Israel-group have been an initially independent tribal group which around 1220, or even earlier, already had a quite considerable standing in Palestine? It is possible that the Jacob-group was still in East Jordania at that period and was only pushed up after the expulsion of Israel by the Pharaoh, assuming the name of Israel at that juncture. This hybrid Jacob-Israel group would then later still be combined with succeeding groups, the Joseph-tribes, who joined with the older Jacob-groups in Central Palestine and so came to be known as the 'younger' Jacob-group.

According to J's account Jacob is the younger of the twins born to Isaac; but by a trick he succeeds in obtaining his father's blessing. He has to flee, however, in order to escape the vengeance of Esau (Gen. 25ff.). On his flight to Haran the God of his father Abraham and the God of Isaac appears to him and repeats the promises previously given to Abraham (Gen. 28:10ff.). In Haran he marries Leah and Rachel, daughters of Laban, and has twelve children (29f.). Differences between Jacob and Laban cause Jacob, despite Laban's attempt to stop him, to go back. Jacob appeals to the God of his father Abraham and to the *Paḥad Yiṣḥaq* (31:42). The same narrative —possibly in a section that should be ascribed to E—makes mention of the God of Abraham and the God of Nahor and tells how Jacob swears an oath by the *Paḥad Yiṣḥaq* (31:53). Right at the beginning of the story Jacob speaks of 'the God of my father' (verse 5). At his encounter with Esau (Gen. 32f.) Jacob again calls upon the God of his father Abraham and the God of his father Isaac (verse 9). At the Jabbok he wrestles with the deity and for that reason calls the place Peniel (countenance of God). Behind this struggle as J depicts it there probably lurks a piece of mythology in which the tutelary gods of Jacob (Israel) and Esau (Seʿir) (cf. 33:10) wage a battle over access to the country to the south of the Jabbok. Jacob has to present Esau with a conciliatory gift (32:14ff.; 33) and—having with difficulty held his own in the struggle (it is here that he gets the name 'Israel')—turns westward via Succoth to Shechem. At Shechem (and this is again an E-fragment) Jacob erects an altar which he calls: *El is the God of Israel*. In this way the relationship between Jacob-Israel and El is constituted at Shechem. The fact that this was the place where Abram also set up his first altar clearly demonstrates that in the primitive

H

Hebrew tradition Shechem plays an important role. The connexion with Shechem mentioned at 33:20 must belong to the second phase in the history of the Jacob-tribes, when they have settled down in Canaan and have assumed the Israel-name. A third phase is that which tells of the struggle for Shechem in Gen. 34, which follows directly upon the E-tradition of 33:20.

This record of the battle between the tribes of Simeon and Levi for Shechem probably stood on its own originally and was only later interpolated into the patriarchal history. Its place is certainly within the later period, but before that which sees the Joseph-tribes, Ephraim, Manasseh and Benjamin, established in this area; for in Gen. 34 it is held to be the domicile of the tribes of Simeon and Levi. It is not easy to determine what this conflict was about. One gets the impression from Gen. 34 that it was started in requital of some offence against the ritual and moral code of the Hebrew tribes; but in Gen. 49:5-7 it seems rather to be regarded as a simple act of violence.

In chapter 35 E carries the tradition forward when he relates that at Shechem Jacob makes his people put away all alien gods and amulets and then buries them. After that, Jacob proceeds to Bethel, where God had revealed himself to him (on this point E, in chapter 28:17ff., offers his own tradition alongside J) and there he establishes an altar for El Bethel. This is a remarkable name, which certainly appertains as an old divine appellation to the deity worshipped at Bethel since ancient times, and must be considered as one of the pre-Israelite-Yahwistic styles of designating the god. In Israel the godhead is not normally called after a place. This piece of evidence suggests two things: (a) how important Bethel was to the early Hebrew tribes, and for the Jacob-group in particular, and (b) that in this case pre-Israelite-Canaanite forms of venerating the god were incorporated into the religion of the tribes and apparently persisted for a very long time.

In the Joseph-story we shall instance only Gen. 46:3, where the 'god of the father' reveals himself once again.

As for Gen. 49 (the early collection of proverbs about the tribes), we turn our attention to verses 10 and 24. Shiloh, in verse 10, is possibly the name of the place where the ruler of Judah is expected.[30] That would indicate that this text comes from the later period of the judges (before 1050), when Shiloh was the centre of the religion of the tribes of Israel. The proverbs must, generally speaking, be a reminiscence of that period, when the tribes still formed separate, independent units. Next to Judah, Joseph (Ephraim and Manasseh) was the most important of the tribes, as appears from the close of Gen. 49. In verses 24f. there is a description of Joseph which for the history of religion is of exceptional interest:

24 His bow remained stout, and his strong hands supple, through the strength of the Bull of Jacob[31] through the name (?) of the shepherd, the Stone of Israel

25 through the God of your father who will help you, and with Shaddai, who will bless you.

In these formulas we again find the 'ab(b)ir Ya'aqob, the God of the father and Shaddai, besides shepherd and stone of Israel, both of which, however, are conjectural.

There is no build-up of substantial data from the P-texts. On a few occasions P does use the name El Shaddai (cf. 28:3; 35:11). Other elements from P (e.g., the emphatic injunction laid upon Jacob by Isaac not to take a wife from among the women of Canaan) derive from the later priestly theology.

When the evidence is compared with what was said about Abraham, one has to admit that the results obtained from the stories of Jacob's life do not differ so very much from those we get from the life of Abraham.

The chief differences are that in the figure of Abraham a prophetic element emerged, which is not the case with Jacob; the further religious elements bearing on the god of the father and on El are similar—but the first receives more emphasis than the second, whereas with Abraham it is rather the other way round. All this is probably to be accounted for by the way the data have been edited, as the Abraham-figure has been 'written up' more than the traditions regarding Jacob.

There is no need for us here to discuss the Joseph-narrative, which in any case is orientated quite differently and is less a compilation of traditions than a novelette, written under Egyptian literary influences.

Finally, let us briefly survey the non-biblical material from the patriarchal period (between 1700 and 1220), which can be taken to parallel the biblical data, in so far as it clearly demonstrates that the biblical evidences of that time stand in some relation to it. We remarked earlier that what this mainly involves are geographical, juridical and cultural elements, and only now and again evidences of a religious kind. It is naturally impossible to bring under discussion all the data that have been adduced. We must leave on one side the data with a bearing on particular historical questions: those, for example, that concerns the relationship of Ḥabiru and Hebrews, the kings named in Gen. 14 and the princes of the ancient East,[32] Hebrews and Hyksos. We must likewise pass over a variety of Egyptian and North Semitic names that have come to light and whose roots connect them with certain names of the patriarchal period. These are to be found in H. H. Rowley (see above, note 32). None of the persons actually mentioned there has any historical connexion with the figures of the patriarchs; but from the incidence of such almost homonymous names or of names with the same construction one may of course conclude that the names mentioned in the biblical stories of the patriarchs were certainly current during the period in which the said patriarchs were supposed to have lived. This is of special importance historically where it concerns (as on more than one occasion it does) names known in the Israelite world only from this particular period, which later on ceased to be in use. This was the case with the names Abram and Jacob (Isaac and Abraham do not recur in the Israelite world, even later on; whereas Joseph, for instance, certainly does, although for the first two names no source outside the Bible has so far yielded any parallel). The two facts, that these names were used exclusively in the patriarchal period and were also current beyond Israel at that period, constitute when taken together a solid argument for the antiquity of the tradition, at least as far as the actual names are concerned. Thus they were certainly borrowed in Israel from very ancient traditions that must go back to the period they purport to represent.[33]

The finds consisting of the Nuzu-texts, which belong to the region of Assyria and to the 15th century, as well as the Mari-texts of the 18th century, have a special claim to be regarded as important. They do not help directly, it is true, to establish a date or dates for the patriarchs; but they do show that the patriarchs came from the kind of milieu that the stories about them would suggest. Because of the correspondence that they present, the Mari-data must have first claim. They not only provide the same kinds of names as the patriarchal ones, but also have many words whose roots occur nowhere else but in the Hebrew.[34] In the religious sphere the significant thing is a form of prophetism having important features in common with the prophetism of Israel.[35] Noth has stressed the parallel between the concluding of a covenant in Mari and in the Old Testament (Gen. 15).[36] Parrot, in his article in *La Bible et l'Orient*, points to related cultic elements of Mari and ancient Israel, which would however appear to be fairly common in the ancient West Semitic milieu. As regards the patriarchal period itself, it is interesting that the Mari-texts also present us with the phenomenon of a father-god.[37] Apart from these kindred elements in the religious field, one finds in Mari all sorts of parallel juridical phenomena reminiscent of the ancient Israelite world: for instance, the privilege accorded in both (and so far as we know, nowhere else) to the firstborn, who acquire two-thirds of the inheritance;[38] or the existence in both social milieus of a form of marriage according to which the woman continued to live with the parents,[39] and other institutions of a similar kind.

Consequently, it has been established that the patriarchal narratives point in the main, and quite properly, to Northern Mesopotamia as the background to the life of the patriarchs.

Also interesting in a juridical context are the relations between data from Genesis and from the texts discovered at Nuzu, east of the Tigris and south-east of Nineveh.[40] The texts found between 1925 and 1931 enable us to catch a glimpse of social and legal life in an Assyrian town of the 15th century, and thus in a world quite substantially remote in time and place from that in which the patriarchs are usually located. Here we have contracts making over possessions to an adopted slave (this reminds one of Gen. 15:1ff.), or in the case of a marriage contract laying it down that should the wife have no children, she is to give her husband a slave for wife and also that she will not drive away any children that the slave may eventually produce (cf. Gen. 16 and 21:9ff.); again, a tablet in which a man surrenders to another party his right to inherit in exchange for three sheep (cf. Gen. 25:29ff.); then a text describing a case of adoption and stipulating that should the adoptive father afterwards have another son, the latter shall enjoy equal rights of inheritance with the adoptive son, and shall moreover acquire rights in the gods of his father (cf., especially, Gen. 31, the story of the *teraphim* of Laban).

This is an obvious selection from a wider range of cases serving to show that (not in a historical sense, but in substance) there is a close affinity between the family law of the group of Hebrews living in Canaan and of this urban population of Central Assyria at the middle of the second millennium. The fact that these legal institutions, which at a later time disappear from Israel, find their closest parallels here obliges one to conclude that the conditions of patriarchal life as the Genesis narratives represent them do have their historic basis in the same type of social and legal relationships.

Having admitted this, however,[41] Noth quite fairly adds the comment that none of it justifies our giving a precise historical setting to the patriarchal record; so that even now it is not possible to localize the biblical traditions or their backgrounds in time and space. Still, it can certainly no longer be argued, as J. Wellhausen felt himself obliged to insist in his *Prolegomena*, that the stories of the patriarchs have no value as history at all, but for historiographical purposes can only be cited as testifying to the outlook of a later epoch whose ideas were here projected back into the distant past.[42]

On a broad view of the evidence from within and outside the Bible one may accept the following conclusions as justifiable working hypotheses.

The patriarchal period is unstable and complex, so far as the people and their religion are concerned.

The background of the early Hebrew tribes is provided mainly by the 'East Canaanite' or (with M. Noth) the 'proto-Aramaean' world —but also, even though it be to a less important extent, by the South Semitic world as well. If the world of Northern Arabia has in the past been wrongly regarded as *the* background to early Israel, people have now, as a result of the historic finds in the North-east, swung to the other extreme and have pretty well completely ignored Northern Arabia as a part of the early Israelite background. We have to allow, however, for the fact of ethnic, social and religious connexions here.

Of relations with the North East Semitic world various examples have been worked into what has been said already. As for contacts with the South Semitic groups we may bring together, in summary form, the following essential points: (*a*) the places where the 'southerly' Abraham and Isaac lived, as well as (*b*) their names (Abraham, from *Ab+raham*, otherwise known only from the Arabic *ruham* =crowd; *Yiṣḥaq*, a name composed with a West Semitic verb, known only in Hebrew, Ugaritic and Arabic) point to connexions with the South; (*c*) the name of the *theos patroios* of Isaac is *paḥad Yiṣḥaq*, which with C. van Arendonck[43] we may best understand as 'the one akin' to Isaac (after the signification of the stem in Arabic); (*d*) relations with Esau, whose name derives from an Arabic root,[44] and Lot,[45] both of whom are recognized as kindred; (*e*) relations with Ishmaelites, Edomites and Kenites—also with Hagar, a name later found in South and North Arabian nomenclature; various names in the prehistory of the Old Testament, such as Cain, Lamech, *et al.*;[46] (*f*) the occurrence of early Hebrew religious terms paralleled only in the Arabic langugae or culture: e.g., *ḥag*, feast, *kohen*, priest, institutions like the curse,[47] the vendetta,[48] circumcision;[49] (*g*) finally, in the course of history the land of Canaan-Israel-Palestine has always been exposed, apart from Egypt in the South-west and the states to the North, especially to the North-east (Aramaeans, etc.), the South and the South-east (North Arabian tribes such as Midianites, Kenites, Edomites, Nabataeans, Arabs after Mohammed). It is to be expected that the situation would have been the same in the patriarchal period, that at that time groups from the desert region to the South must always have been trying to penetrate into the North. That is certainly what the stories of the patriarchs suggest; and for the later premonarchical period it is a generally admitted fact.[50]

Clearly, the Abraham-figure with its contacts with both North and South (these would even now appear to be the most primitive) embraces the two elements. As we have said already, he becomes the ideal type of Israel, the one in whose ideal image Israel's whole structure, religious and historical, is summed up; whereas in Isaac and Jacob, respectively, the southerly and northerly relations each find their own expression and so as tradition make a more reliable impression.[51]

As a tentative picture of how the religion may be thought to have developed we may propose the following:

With Alt and many after him we have in my view to recognize as the oldest typical element of the religion of the patriarchal age a belief in the *theos patroios*, the god of the ancestor. In one way or another this figure evidently acquires a personal relation to a specific deity, who is called after him. This personal bond involves for the patriarch or ancestor something that at a later time is comparable with the prophetic relationship (as happens in J and especially in E).

The deity speaks to him and through him to his community. The features that most typify the god are his personal character and his relation to the family of the individual to whom he has disclosed himself.

That this god would be linked from the outset with some major divine figure known already from elsewhere seems unlikely. When and if that happens, it means that a second phase in the process of development has already been reached.

Just as in the case of Abraham a relationship with the deity who enters into a binding association with him—the god of Abraham—is presupposed, so is it with Isaac: the *paḥad Yiṣḥaq*. This figure is regarded—and the case with Abraham is different here—as being somehow akin to the Isaac-clan. Different again is the case of the *'abbir Ya'aqob*, who had perhaps the typical character of a fertility-god.[52] Whether other such types existed but have been wholly lost to memory one cannot say. Those we have mentioned are the only divinities belonging to the oldest Hebrew clans to have been preserved. There is a close affinity between these types and the god of Nahor, also referred to in Genesis (Gen. 31:53). It is probable that, when at a later time the gods of the fathers are pictured as being repudiated, the initial thought is of this type of god.[53]

It is hard to say to what extent the *teraphim* are to be linked directly with this most frequently occurring father-god type among the earliest Hebrew tribes. Certainly, they belong to the same religious climate; but they are not so much gods as divine symbols, a means by which oracles might be received.[54]

In the period when the clan was wandering hither and thither this god-type—the personal god in a direct relation with the head of the family—was best suited to the social conditions: it is, as it were, the incorporation of the community relationship between God and man. This type of god belongs with the clan and moves with it, is 'at home' with it. It does not at all make for an accurate characterization to say that therefore such a personal and family deity is a specifically 'migratory god'.[55]

B. Gemser (*op. cit.*, p. 20) maintains over against A. Alt that these figures of the 'god of the fathers', who were known to various tribal groups under a variety of names, were viewed even in the patriarchal period as a unified entity; but such a thesis is difficult to verify. The story in Genesis 31 (verses 42 and 53) gives no support to the idea, any more than does the instance of Abed-rapsas (of Syria, in the 4th century A.D.), to whom appeared the god of one of his forefathers, the god of Archesilaos. In this latter case, indeed, the name of the deity is not passed down to Abed-rapsas. That even in the patriarchal age family members and descendants would have invoked the god of a (fore)father may surely be regarded as likely. The question is, however, whether the genealogical relation of the Abrahamic tribal group(s) and of the Isaac-Jacob-Israel groups was in fact so close originally that they invoked each other's 'father-god', as the later tradition postulates. Against this, besides the admittedly late provenance of the genealogical liaison between the tribes, stands the fact that in any case this type of god is linked with more than one patriarchal name.

When the old Hebrew tribal groups found their areas for pasturage in Canaan and were able to settle more and more into the country, they began gradually to adapt themselves to the religious practices of the land that they were learning to regard as their own. To the extent that agriculture made headway among them, the religious customs and ideas of the country of their adoption also came to play a bigger role. They took over the sacred stone-worship at Bethel and the sacred trees at Shechem, Mamre and Beersheba. It is notable that nothing is said about Baal-worship in these periods, whilst it certainly is about more than one form of El-worship, to which the patriarchs conformed. The question arises at this point as to whether the absence of the Baal-cult is not owing more to the hostility felt toward it by those who compiled the narratives than to a total absence of the cult in the historical circumstances as they actually occurred.

At all events the sources that have reached us certainly connect the patriarchs in Canaan with El: the El Elyon of Jerusalem (Gen. 14), the El Ro'i in the South (Gen. 16:13), the god of Be'er Lahai Roi—the place to which Ishmael and Isaac (see 24:62 and 25:11) both belong[56]—the El Bethel (Gen. 28), the El 'Olam (Gen. 21:34), the El Shaddai (Gen. 17, P).

One may agree with Eissfeldt that in this second phase the religion of the early Hebrew clans was accommodated to that of the great gods, and in particular to the chief god El of the Canaanites: El who was head of the pantheon, creator-god, the god of wisdom. It was, we may suppose, precisely at the stage when life in Canaan was still semi-nomadic that El would have priority over Baal, who is a vegetation-deity, the farmers' rather than the shepherds' god. The association of the patriarchal god with El reinforced certain paternal elements already present in El and rendered El—a figure set in the high and lofty place and therefore somewhat remote from men—a deity both nearer and more prone to take a hand in life's affairs, whilst by the same token the *theos patroios* aforementioned acquired features of greater universality. Thus it was possible for an El-type to emerge which was proper to, and characteristic of, the Israelite tribes. How far this El, who was worshipped in different places under different names (aspects), was consciously envisaged as a 'great god' is a matter of guess-work. Eissfeldt makes much of this idea, whereas others—Alt, for example—are opposed to it. However, we may take it that despite all the variations that existed the Els acknowledged in Canaan were not seen as purely local divine beings but rather represented a great god. Thus too the idea of the oneness of the *theoi patroioi*, whatever name they went by and with whatever El they might be associated (the possibilities here are indeed numerous), would gradually have sprung up and have led to an awareness that a single *theos patroios* was to be deemed head of the tribal group collectively and was to be addressed as El—whether he were then worshipped as El Elyon, as El 'Olam, as El Shaddai (as El or Baal Berith?) or as El Bethel. Yet it is not unlikely that even at this stage behind the various El-revelations various types of gods continued to exist to this or that degree, the one enshrining more the memory of the El Abraham, the *paḥad Yiṣḥaq* or the *'abbir Ya'aqob*, the other conserving the idea of the god as covenant-protector or as residing at a particular spot, or of the deity's omnipotence or permanence.

The question whether this form of El-religion continued to maintain a measure of independence as over against the Canaanite form of religion is as difficult to answer as the question to what extent the worship of other gods came to be associated with this El-religion (cf. the sacred stone at Bethel and the sacred trees at Shechem, Mamre and Beersheba). From Genesis 14 one gathers the impression that in Jerusalem the possibility was afforded of a complete identification of the god of Abraham with the god of Jerusalem (if this chapter is in fact usable as a source for the history of that early period). On the other hand the Elohist, in Gen. 35:1ff., puts forward the idea that when the people entered the land the 'strange gods' were done away with; but this notion owes more to the Elohistic theology than to any recollection of what actually occurred.

The distinctive thing about this form of religion was not so much a tendency to monotheism (it was at most strongly monarchistic) but, as we have already remarked, the religious climate that came about as a result of a particular strain in it: that of the *theos patroios* type. This made possible a more immediate relationship between El and the social group than was the case with the El figure elsewhere in Canaan;[57] because there the vegetative form of the religion (Baal) was much in evidence among the farming community; and in the towns the state religion, besides being highly official, contained a powerful element of the ceremonious and the traditional. Here one has to remember that the manner in which the connexion came to be made between *theos patroios* and El was bound to give rise to a more or less deviant form of the religion, and also that in certain groups or areas belief in the god of the father(s) would have achieved and kept a marked ascendancy over the El-religion. Indeed it was by no means every clan that came into intimate contact with the culture of the towns. Then too, besides the links created between 'father-god' and El-religion, one has to bear in mind those which at a later time and in particular circumstances formed a connexion with the vegetative Baal-religion.

Finally, we may postulate that more than one form of this El-religion will have continued to exert an influence on the later course of events. Even though Yahwism, once it had achieved its sudden breakthrough at a later stage, was able to press forward with so much vigour, it had all the same to adjust itself to certain already developed forms of religion. It is simply impossible to assume a *tabula rasa* in religion and to begin to construct without adapting to something already in existence. To give an example: if it is right to connect the Jacob-tribes in the patriarchal period initially with a more vegetative form of 'father-religion'—the *'abbir Ya'aqob*—then there is nothing odd in supposing that this form is still an effective influence in the later Northern Israel and had helped to bring into being the cults of Bethel and Dan, which adopted the bull-calf as a symbol of the divine. Despite the later El-religion with which this *'abbir Ya'aqob* becomes associated, even despite the connexion with the Yahweh-religion, the vegetative element must have preserved its ancient title down the centuries. Whereas in the North this religious form was revived (or maintained), in the South there was apparently little call for a combination of Yahweh with the bull. This was because in the South the patriarchal form of religion continued to be dominated much more by the family type of the *theos patroios*. Looked at in this way, the later contrasts between North and South in the religious sphere are seen to have had roots that went really deep.

CHAPTER 5

Yahweh

WHAT UNDERLIES THE Old Testament as a whole—and the writings of the prophets in particular—is the primary conviction that Israel's encounter with Yahweh took place in the desert (e.g. Hos. 2, 13:4ff.; Jer. 2:1ff.; Ezek. 20; cf. Amos 2:10ff, 5:25). The E and P authors of the Pentateuch, to whom we referred earlier, also start from the same idea. Only J, who sees Yahweh as the God of human kind from the very beginning of the world and the worship of Yahweh as having been instituted by Enoch (the representative of mankind) in the primeval age (Gen. 4:26),[1] passes over this belief. Evidently, his outlook is informed more by considerations of theology than of history and is in line with a mode of thinking which postulates the absolute and universal character of the Yahweh-revelation as holding good for the world *in toto*.

Testimony to the fact that the 'desert period' was the time of Israel's encounter with Yahweh runs through many writings that exist quite independently of one another, which shows that this was something so deeply rooted in the consciousness of Israel as to justify our regarding it as the most settled and basic tradition about the origin of Israel's religion in the Old Testament. Such unanimity can only point to one inference: it obliges us to recognize that there must be some foundation here of historical fact.

This conclusion is given added force when we consider that it may be thought very extraordinary for a people to derive its religion from experiences undergone not in their own but in an alien country; so that the only real explanation of this unusual phenomenon must lie in the historical background to it.

Then again, it is remarkable that the Yahweh-name is nowhere to be found in Canaan, Phoenicia, the North-west Semitic or North Arabian world, but in Israel alone, and then not in patriarchal times but from the desert period on. Still, this is a merely negative asseveration; and to deploy arguments *e silentio* is a dangerous proceeding.

124

Theoretically, one must leave open the possibility that the name will be found somewhere outside of Israel, and likewise that the name 'Moses' will turn up again here or there. Yet remarkably enough, the more we come to learn about the ancient East, the more diffident are the claims to have discovered the divine name in other places. Time and again people have supposed that they could point to the existence of the name in the Assyrian-Babylonian, Phoenician and Arabian worlds. So far, however, this has proved to be wrong; and the various identifications have had to be retracted.

One of the oldest hypotheses regarding the occurrence of the name 'Yahweh' outside Israel—that is, among the tribe so closely linked with the Moses- and desert-tradition: the Kenites—is still much in favour; yet however attractive and plausible it may be, it can never be finally substantiated.

In support of this hypothesis one can adduce, for example, the fact that prehistory connects Cain (originally, indeed, the tribal father of the Kenites) with the name 'Yahweh'. Not only in the past but even today, therefore, there is a persistent chorus of opinion ready to associate Yahweh with the Kenites. We cite here—as examples only —B. D. Eerdmans,[2] W. Vischer[3] and H. H. Rowley[4]—perhaps an astounding assortment of names to find harnessed together.

Besides this more or less speculative contention, the fact that in very early evidential documents Yahweh is repeatedly associated with Sinai or with Se'ir constitutes a more solid ground of argument. He is even described as *zeh Sinai* (Judges 5:5; Psalm 68:9): that is, the Lord of Sinai. Epithets in this form are known in the ancient East only from the Arabian side. It is one of the customary terms in the desert religions to indicate that the deity is connected with a particular spot.[5] Sinai occurs as the name of a region, of a desert area and of a mountain or range of mountains. Perhaps the name was initially that of a region, and Sinai *qua* mountain denotes the Sinaitic range. As a region, Sinai is equated in Deut. 33:2 with Se'ir; whilst in Judges 5:4 Yahweh is also associated with Se'ir, in a passage where Edom is used as a parallel. As Se'ir is the country east of the Dead Sea and on both sides of the Arabah, Sinai would then be located either west or east of the gulf of 'Akaba. Both views have their champions. The majority favour what is nowadays known as the Sinaitic peninsula;[6] others, such as, for instance, M. Noth, who on the strength of Numbers 33 locates it to the south-east of the gulf of 'Akaba,[7] point in an easterly direction. A few think in terms of the north-western part of the Sinai peninsula; but the mountains there are hardly awe-inspiring and the distance from Palestine is short (cf. Numbers 33 and 1 Kings 19:8). Both the epithet *zeh Sinai* and the name 'Sinai' clearly point, therefore, to the North Arabian world and to a sojourn on the part of Israel in the Sinai desert.

The Yahweh-revelation (in association with the journey through the desert and the exodus from Egypt) is evidently connected with the Sinai history, not only in the tradition of J and E and of the later historiographers but also in the settled belief of the poets responsible for the earliest songs of victory such as Judges 5 and Psalm 68:8f.[8] Admittedly, these songs do not link Sinai with the events of the exodus, as J and E do; but they do present *zeh Sinai* as the God who fights for and with Israel (cf. with this, Ex. 15:21).

This matter (of the Sinai traditions and the deliverance, and the connexion between them) has recently been the subject of persisting discussion. To be specific: there is a group of scholars, including G. von Rad[9] and M. Noth,[10] who would sever completely the link between the two traditions. They are of the opinion that the former has no place in the historical account of the exodus from Egypt and was not originally connected with it. The question is of the utmost importance for the history of Israel's religion; and we must look somewhat further into it at this point.

The theory propounded by M. Noth and G. Von Rad is that in origin the Sinai tradition forms no part of the main block of the Pentateuchal tradition which tells of the deliverance from Egypt, the desert journeying and the trek into the land of Canaan. It must originally have been distinct and separate from the historical record and have been based on cultic motifs. Its basic material consisted of the *Festlegende* of the covenant-renewal festival (cf. Deut. 31:10ff.) celebrated each autumn in combination with the feast of tabernacles.[11] The manner in which this feast, which reflects the events of the Sinai story, was celebrated must have had a determining influence also on the way the Sinaitic revelation came to be represented. Noth, whilst not disguising the fact that he has some important reservations to make,[12] endorses this view of the matter. On its historical side this interpretation, which has attracted a large following, is given a basis by von Rad's discovery (in the book cited[9]) of what according to him is a very ancient 'historic creed', to be found in Deut. 26:5b–9. According to von Rad this 'creed', although transmitted only in the deuteronomic writings, is much older even than the oldest traditions assembled by

J and E and emerged in early times at the sanctuary of Gilgal. Because this (putative) ancient creed makes mention of the patriarchs, the exodus and the entry into the country but says nothing about Sinai, he concludes that the Sinai tradition did not belong originally with the story of the exodus and entry.

All this might be convincing enough, if it could be shown that Deut. 26:5bff. is indeed very ancient. But the contrary is true; for in style this passage is typically deuteronomic. As it stands, it is not early, and furthermore can hardly be described as a 'creed', being quite evidently a formulary for the offering of the firstfruits of the land (as the context roundly emphasizes), in which the offerer extols Yahweh as the giver of all good gifts, as giver of the land and its produce. This set form of words is evidently based on a theological standpoint that is deuteronomic; and it is as clearly a pointed thrust at Baalism (cf., for instance, the notions of the syncretistic Israelite as described and censured by Hosea in chapter 2). There is not a single reason, therefore, for taking Deut. 26:5bff. as an ancient cultic formulary derived from the temple at Gilgal, any more than it is right to treat these verses as summarizing the entire history of exodus and entry and to make that a basis for a historical analysis of the tradition by 'disentangling' the oldest compilations of J and E.

So far as the early compilations of tradition in Exodus are concerned, the Sinai tradition with its mountain of God and revelation by Yahweh is an indispensable element. Chapter 3 is already a preparation for the account in chapter 19. In the earliest prophets too, in Hosea, at all events, we find both elements: the law-giving on Sinai and the exodus tradition (2; 4:2; 8:1 and 13; 13:4f.). One must allow that the events subsequent to the Sinai story (as they are given in Exodus 32–34) do form a fresh cycle of tradition; but chapters 19 to 24, complex though they are, and despite the fact of their having been edited and re-edited many times, are integral to the account of deliverance from Egypt and journey in the desert. The story of the liberation from Egypt in J and E leads up to Exodus 19 as the climax of events. One cannot conceive of any other point rounding off the story of the deliverance, even Exodus 15; although there was a time when J. Pedersen felt it necessary to argue in favour of this.[13] One can state with equal emphasis that anyway in the oldest collections of traditions regarding events in Egypt and the desert the Sinai tradition is an integral part of the whole:[14] this whole certainly cannot be dislocated from a literary standpoint by conclusions based on a

THE RELIGION OF ANCIENT ISRAEL

supposedly ancient creed. The question attaching closely to this, of course, is whether—granting the integral cohesion of the narrative in the oldest tradition—we have here facts that are *historically* accurate.

To this we may reply that two things are certain: namely, that Israel acquired her belief in Yahweh in the desert; and that, independently of the early traditions assembled by J and E, other yet more ancient sources (we have already instanced them: Judges 5 and Psalm 68) connect Yahweh and Sinai so closely together that they even refer to him as Lord of Sinai. This being so, must we not then say that it is to a high degree probable that the Sinai tradition is part and parcel of the desert tradition? The idea that these two, although coming from the same period and belonging of necessity to more or less the same setting, are yet entirely separate and unconnected is beset with a host of difficulties. Could there really have been two mutually independent groups of Hebrew tribes, one of which experienced the liberation from Egypt and the other the revelation of Yahweh? Or did this second group not experience a single revelation but become familiar just with certain cultic ceremonies at Sinai and simply take over the Yahweh-name from the surrounding alien tribes; or did it indeed receive its own peculiar Sinaitic revelation but without any recollection of that event, beyond the conservation of a solitary priest or prophet? Would not such a group necessarily amount to a 'double' of the Kenite clans? It would be simpler, surely, to revert to the old theory, which postulates that the groups that had fled out of Egypt into the Sinai desert took over Yahweh-worship from the Kenites living there. As to the first group: if this had not been at Sinai and so did not know Yahweh, did they then *not* ascribe their deliverance to a deity? Or has the divine name which they used at first been lost? And did this group start using the name 'Yahweh' later on? Did 'Yahweh', then, come into circulation not only to denote the 'God of Sinai' but in some other fashion also? Where and when did that happen? Not after the desert period, surely? To divide out the elements of the tradition among more than one group is to make of the whole record of the exodus and the sojourn in the desert (not to mention the later period) an insoluble riddle. Whence arises Israel's intense feeling for her saviour-God, Yahweh, if it does not rest on a historical experience that was the determining source of her whole existence, religious and social? Not, surely, from a *post hoc* theological interpretation or from some cultic ceremony? All things considered, one can hardly avoid reaching the conclusion that there is only one adequate solution to the problem—that which insists upon an integral connexion between the Sinai-Yahweh record and the account of the liberation from Egypt, the journeying in the desert and the entry into Canaan. In other words, one has to accept the main features of the tradition on this score as being historically correct. There is one point, however, that still needs a little clarification. We said (on p. 124ff.) that Israel acquired her belief in Yahweh in the desert, and not later. This thesis calls for further explanation. The argument that Israel's belief was formed in the pre-Canaanite period is strengthened when one considers that the conflict between Israel's religion and that of the Canaanites could never have raged with such intensity, had the belief in Yahweh not already been formed *before* Israel made contact with the other religion. If the tribes of Israel who made the desert journey and had entered the land of Canaan had possessed nothing but the vestiges of an Egyptian religion or the rudiments of a desert religion or even of a religion of the fathers, in its encounter with the Canaanites their religion would never have persisted or have developed so potently in a distinctive form as was in fact the case. The elements of the Egyptian or the desert religion would certainly have been mixed with Canaanite ideas and customs, and this would hold also for the religion of the patriarchs. One can see in the religious development of the tribes who had obtained a firm footing in Canaan and had adapted themselves to the El-religion of the Canaanites how much they were inclined to purely syncretistic forms. The religious type of the *theos patroios* did not command sufficient characteristic features of its own ever to grow into a distinctive religion *per se*, even though it was able to give a personalistic character to the syncretistic religion, once that had been formed.

Without Yahweh, who had a character all his own, the tribal groups emerging from the desert could never have stood their ground, spiritually speaking, against the (in every cultural respect) vastly superior Canaanites. Horace's celebrated tag, *Graecia capta Romam cepit*,[15] which, one may say, is generally true enough in history, in the case of the Israelite tribes and Canaan simply does not apply. Only one reason can be adduced for that: the peculiar religious character that marked the Israelite tribes coming out of the desert; and that character was determined wholly by the relationship of those tribes to the particular God whom they had encountered and who governed their lives.

It is not for nothing that so many, not only on the more con-

I

servative side but in those critical circles where one would not expect it, are committed to the view that besides the 'father' form and the Canaanite El-religion, a third element must have entered into the picture: namely, Yahwism.[16] This Yahwism Israel brought with her into the contest; even though, in consequence of the tensions that developed with the Canaanite religion, it did then proceed to assume many of the forms that were to characterize it in later times. If, therefore, there is every reason to admit that at a definite time—in the desert period, that is to say—and after the liberation of certain tribal groups from Egypt, Yahweh did establish a relationship with them, then we are faced with the question: who is this Yahweh? It is a question that has been answered in so many different ways that we must pronounce it impossible to consider all these viewpoints and opinions here. Many people have based an interpretation of Yahweh's essential nature on their explanation of the name itself; but because the possible derivations are so many, this procedure presents an exceptional number of problems. Here, as elsewhere, etymology lands us in major difficulties. The simplest interpretation starts from the Hebrew and considers one form or another of the verb *hayah*, that is, 'to be' or 'to become', thus rendering the name as: He is or will be, or as: He causes to be, He creates. The first interpretation is prompted by Exodus 3:14; and our friend E, of course, is responsible for it. It has an underlying basis that is deep enough; but as it stands it is not entirely clear, because in this instance the mode of Yahweh's being is not so far closely defined.[17] This Hebrew explanation tells us nothing, however, as to the original meaning of the name; just as when, on the basis of the Hebrew, 'Jacob' is said to signify 'light-heeled', 'deceiver', that really says nothing about the original meaning of this name and others of the kind. The same applies to the attempt to explain the name as: He who causes to be, who creates.[18] Etymology does not, therefore, shed any certain light here. Equally uncertain are interpretations through the Arabic, which yield such meanings as: He falls, or: He causes to fall.[19] These are in line with the view which holds Yahweh to be a storm- and thunder-god.[20]

If then we have to discard any kind of etymological explanation as the way in to a definition of Yahweh's essential being, we must try and approach the matter by a different route: that is, we must ascertain what the functions are that are ascribed to him and what the relation is in which he stands toward those who serve him. Now this again presents problems, when we realize just how many facets his disclosure has, and that ever more and more have been added, in the course of the centuries, to his being. He is god of a people, of history, of war, god of nature, personal god, god of the heavens, god of life, redeemer-god, creator, sustainer, judge, and so forth. He would not merely *seem* to have assumed into himself every conceivable element of the divine—he has really done so!

Still, by comparing the Yahweh-figure with El, by attending to certain pointers and to activities associated particularly with him, we can say a few things about the most characteristic and primary features of his being, even though we surely cannot plumb the final mystery of this or get right through to what the tribes of Israel (or Moses) experienced in the desert.

When we study the life of those tribes, from the standpoint of religion, on opposite sides of the dividing-line constituted in this case by the desert period, we are bound to conclude that there is a big change. In the patriarchal period the leading of the *theos patroios*, in various guises and under a multiplicity of names, is the central element; whereas the tribes arriving in Canaan fit in quite easily and naturally with the El-religions of the various sanctuaries. There is a prevailing atmosphere of contentedness and a hopeful outlook on the future. The religion would appear to be one buoyed up by the sure sense of a fatherly godhead, his nearness and his guidance, and to have gone along very well with the belief in a god of wisdom, El, governing the world. There is no question of priests or of divine symbols, and hardly a mention of sacrifices. Particular revelations are given through voices, visions and dreams. There is room for certain elements of a religious, but secondary, nature, for *teraphim*, for sacred trees and stones.

As we saw earlier on, after the desert period we have a central divine symbol: the ark. There is a priesthood, there are sacrifices, there are cultic channels through which Yahweh reveals himself. But this is not yet the most important difference. All these things could have been taken over from Canaan. It is after the desert period, however, that everything centres upon a God: Yahweh.

If this God has to be typified in one word, that word must be: Power; or, still better, perhaps: Force. Everything about and around Yahweh feels the effect of this. He as it were electrifies his environment. N. Söderblom in *Das Werden des Gottesglaubens*, P. Volz in *Das Dämonische in Jahwe*, even J. Pedersen in his *Israel* have each in their own way stressed that element of the ineluctable operation of force;[21] and though on this or that point one might wish to criticize their view of things, they have pointed clearly enough to what the central element is.

To illustrate this thesis we may refer to the Song of Deborah, one of the most ancient literary strands in the Old Testament, a lyric composed under the vital impact of a great event: the victory won by the hard-pressed Israelites over superior enemy forces.[22]

In his splendid literary analysis of this Song G. Gerleman has shown just how the impressionist poet has worked into it his own immediate impressions, not setting out to give a rounded and unified picture but bringing to life, one after another, the different facets of what had taken place. The language of the Deborah-lyric, with its impressionism, its lack of the logical reflex, is deeply rooted in the turn of mind of early Israel, with its characteristic nationalism, its religious outlook on life and its emotional fervour.

M. Buber has rightly maintained[23] that as typifying early Israelite belief in and about Yahweh this Song is a principal source for the oldest form of Israel's religion on Canaanite soil. It shows how for the lyric poet the whole of life derives from Yahweh and depends on him. For the poet he is still the God who has his dwelling in Se'ir, but at the same time the God who rules the heavens, the atmosphere (verse 4) and the starry sky (verse 20). The mountains shake, the earth trembles when he rises up to do battle. Yahweh is here the God of heroic strength; and he is served therefore by heroic men (verse 9), who are said to be helpmates of God (verse 23). Yahweh is a fighter,[24] but not primarily a war-god like the classical Ares or Mars. He is the God who works righteousness (verse 11) and with a mighty hand expedites justice by assisting the oppressed against their enemies.

Here, of course, there is a direct link between Yahweh and Israel. The piety that marks early Israel is indeed strongly tinged with nationalism. Yahweh's enemies are one and the same, therefore, with the enemies of Israel. The fact that he dwells in Edom, on the other hand, puts a certain distance between him and the Israelite tribes. He is not a national god *simpliciter*, to be simply identified with the nation or with the 'soul' of the nation, as J. Pedersen is too much inclined to argue. Yahweh is too much himself, too free of Israel, for that.

This oneness of nation and religion is indissolubly connected in Israel's consciousness with her particular historical experience: Yahweh had revealed himself as Israel's God in her deliverance from Egypt. This again creates an unbreakable bond between history and religion.

Notice the multiplicity of ideas about Yahweh that find expression in this Song. Out of Yahweh there comes forth power ('force'). He is so to speak the embodiment of power, that sets in motion the heaven and the earth and the constellations themselves; and so the loyal and true of heart resort to him, freely offering themselves (verse 9) and coming to his aid. They are 'inspired' (even though the word 'spirit' is not used in Judges 5), they receive strength from Yahweh to perform mighty acts: spirit is also strength. Spirit (*ruah*) plays no part in the story of the patriarchs;[25] but in the experiences of Yahweh described in Judges and the Books of Samuel it comes again and again, as inspiration, powerful in its effects, proceeding from God himself. Another concept absent from the patriarchal record is that of God's holiness—although even there (in Gen. 28:10ff., according to E) there is certainly a strain of dread in the respect felt for God. This is sporadic, however;[26] whereas the Yahwistic religion and mentality are informed and wholly dominated by the sense of holiness. Everything having to do with Yahweh is charged with this holiness, which symbolizes an ambit of power and a kind of majesty above and beyond all that appertains to the realm of men and of the world. However close the relation between Yahweh and Israel may be, there is always this strong sense of an unbridgeable distance between him and man.

The conclusion is not to be avoided that in the Yahweh-religion a wholly new form of belief in God was manifested, in the period separating the patriarchs from the judges. It consequently gave rise to a powerful hostility toward the Canaanite religion, of a kind which one is hard put to it to detect in the relation between the religion of Canaan and that of the patriarchs. This last was able to make itself at home with the temples—of the El-religion, at least—and, as becomes evident in the later course of events, to assimilate various rites and symbols of Baalism too. Yahwism, however, cannot come to terms with the religion of Canaan and at all events clashes fiercely with one side of it in particular: Baalism. Although the text is obscure on this point, it is nonetheless probable that there is already an allusion to it in the Song of Deborah (Judges 5:8).[27]

That the patriarchal period exhibits no conflict of this sort may be due also to the social character of tribal life at the time, which was still typically semi-nomadic. As a way of life it was able to persist in the shadow of the cities; and so too with its religion: belief in the guiding divinity of tribe or family, which continued alongside the recognition of the 'High God', El. But Yahwism cannot so easily permit the combination—least of all with Baal. Not with El, certainly, because of Yahweh's own absolutism: for that reason, the only way to acknowledge El was to identify him with Yahweh and to allow Yahweh to appear as El. With Baal, however, even this was impossible; because the vegetative traits in Baal, his dying and uprising, especially, as well as his sexual relations, were an affront to the essential being, the absoluteness and majesty, of Yahweh. He could of course take over certain features of Baal: for instance, that of the giver of earth's fertility; but identification with Baal he could not tolerate. Because, as a matter of experience, the Baal-figure was by nature so essentially and totally other than Yahweh, the antithesis between the two types of theistic belief was bound to emerge.[28]

The question may be asked as to whether we can comprehend the conflict between Yahweh and Baal purely in terms of the social context and background. J. Pedersen does in fact offer to explain the struggle between them as arising out of the contrast between the nomadic desert-god and the agrarian god of the cultivable soil. Although there is an element of truth here, it is hardly permissible to see Yahweh as a type of the desert-god, pure and simple. As we noted when discussing the Song of Deborah just now, in his essential character he differs from the type of the desert-god too much for that. His being utterly transcends the type in question. In his control of nature in all its ramifications, and of history too; of the course of events not only in the desert but also beyond it outside his own personal domicile; in his rescuing the oppressed; in his relationship with the nation and with individuals, his support of justice, and so on.

Belief in Yahweh embraces completely novel elements which, taken together, give to his divine being a character that is likewise entirely new. The conflict between Yahweh and Baal was inevitable, therefore; and in that unequal struggle Yahweh was to be the victor, despite the fact that those whose faith was placed in him were so much feebler, culturally and politically speaking, than their adversaries and despite the powerful attraction which for a variety of reasons Baalism exercised. That triumph of his was due to his basic character, which set him, spiritually, above every notion of God that the surrounding world had to offer. It was not political factors that made him the unique and universal One; for from the very start, but even more at the finish, when Israel's downfall was complete, the political situation was loaded against it.

When we ask how it was that the Israelite tribes came to know the essential nature of Yahweh, as that is manifested in the story of events, tradition supplies the answer: through Moses. The united voice of this tradition, from the earliest compilation up to the very latest period, is quite striking. Not only J and E but the prophet Hosea also (12:14) speak of him or point to him as the man who plays the leading role in the release of the tribes from bondage in Egypt as also in the matter of God's revelation of himself.

For years the authority of this tradition has been under attack by attrition. A fair number of scholars, even of an earlier generation, men like Kuenen and Wellhausen, were denying that Moses played any significant role;[29] although many others of their school claimed for him an important place in the process of establishing Israel's religion. We may cite as earlier examples: Smend,[30] Marti,[31] Budde,[32] and as more recent ones: A. Lods,[33] Oesterley-Robinson[34] and R. H. Pfeiffer.[35] From the Netherlands one ought to mention here B. D. Eerdmans, who in his *Religion of Israel*[36] argued not only for the historicity of the Moses-figure but also for the Mosaic origin of the decalogue; although like the others—and even more emphatically, perhaps, than some of them—he denied that it was Moses who gave monotheism to Israel.

With critical but more 'right-wing' scholars, such as A. Dillmann, R. Kittel, E. Sellin and P. Volz[37]—and especially with the school of Albright,[38] which leans to the traditional standpoint—the significance of Moses' achievement for the religion of Israel is an established fact; and many of them still view him, if not as the man who taught monotheism, at any rate as the founder of Israel's religion.

On the Jewish side opinion is unanimous in crediting Moses with both accomplishments.[39] Of recent years a lot of books on Moses have appeared, from this quarter especially. There has been a Roman Catholic work about Moses too, in which the author deals with Moses in a historical setting and presents him, albeit with some reserve, in a traditional light.[40] He ascribes not only the decalogue but also the so-called book of the covenant (Ex. 21ff.) to Moses.[41]

Keenest champion of the traditional view of Moses and of Israelite monotheism is Y. Kaufmann in his book (published in modern Hebrew) on the *Religion of Israel*, which is now available, in part, in an English version.[42] Kaufmann accepts the monotheism of Moses' religion as an established fact, and makes that his starting-point.

Diametrically opposed to this view is that of M. Noth, who declares that there can be no question of Moses' having founded the religion.[43] He might seem to be harking back here to Wellhausen's position; but in fact he is not. Wellhausen, in seeking a basis for constructing his historical account of Israel's religion, worked to a scheme grounded upon evolutionary principles[44] (which could not allow any distinctive character of its own to Israelite religion prior to the prophetic period); whilst Noth's construction rests upon inferences which in turn are based on his method of enquiry: namely, that of the *Traditionsgeschichte* school. Noth admits the distinctive nature, in certain respects, of even the patriarchs' religion, and sees it as evidently determining, in principle, the character of Israel's religion; whereas for Wellhausen what the patriarchs believed was neither here nor there.

Even so, Wellhausen ascribes a more considerable role to Moses than does Noth. Wellhausen says that Moses' close association with the ark, which can be described as the historical element with probably the best credentials in the whole account of Moses, should be taken to indicate just how great his influence was; and Wellhausen adds: 'without a guiding mind the forming of a nation under the aegis of Yahweh cannot have got under way. It was he who first introduced the Torah . . .'. His successors (i.e., the prophets) were then able to build upon what he had accomplished.[45] Noth is less assured of Moses' importance; and for him it is in any case smaller. Although Moses would *appear* to have had an original connexion with the Sinai tradition, an analysis of the tradition and its history, Noth argues, rules out any such possibility. All that may properly be ascribed to Moses is the role which, within certain circles, he played in the area to the south-east of the Jordan, 'perhaps even apropos of their gradual move over to their later West Jordanian habitats, for which the change of grazing-lands had been a preparation'.[46] Thereafter Moses would have been launched in the role of a leader-figure within one of the themes which Noth distinguishes in the traditions: that is, the trek into the land of Canaan; and later still, Moses must have been allotted the 'great leader' role in the account of how the nation had been liberated.

It is worth noticing that when the *traditionsgeschichtliche* method is brought to bear, the personalities (Abraham, Moses, Joshua) slowly fade, or almost fade, from the historical record; and places, the sanctuaries especially, assume a major role. It would seem that for the type of thinking engendered by this method there is hardly a place any more for the handing down of history via the memories of an ethnic group, for a transmission by word of mouth from one generation to another. 'Folk tradition', in fact, is simply out of the running. It would seem that concrete evidence attaches only to sanctuaries, in virtue of monuments (tombs, such as that of Moses![47]), the names of places and persons. This drastic limitation of what is historically reliable tradition might appear to make for a more solid grounding of historical knowledge. But because its norms of selection are so stringent, pronouncing all kinds of things to be secondary and unsure and then ruling them all out, it leads to such an impoverishment of the materials for constructing the history of a given period that it threatens to lead us as far (or further) astray from the historical picture of events as a viewpoint that puts more trust in tradition for its version of what took place—even when that tradition has been embroidered with various later additions. The former procedure is a case of under-exposure, the latter of over-exposure. Both can yield a distorted image of what really occurred.

If I frankly admit the lack of much to be desiderated sources outside the Bible that might serve to confirm the biblical data respecting just that very period of exodus, desert wanderings and entry which is so crucial for the history and religion of Israel; and if I likewise fully recognize the fact that even the earliest compilations of tradition carry later accretions that fill in, embellish and simplify the picture (by putting data from different periods all on one historical level), I still feel obliged, in the interests of sound and scholarly enquiry, to plead for an approach to tradition that will take the general framework within which its data are marshalled just as seriously as its smaller-scale components. The general scheme in which the tradition sets things *is* an exceptionally valuable piece of historical evidence, after all. We may well argue for a somewhat greater degree of confidence in the whole picture and in the cohesion of the several parts over against the atomizing tendency of the *traditionsgeschichtliche* method, if only on the basis of recognizing the relative trustworthiness that 'the popular memory' must be allowed to derive from the oral transmission from father to son of important events in the nation's life. Certainly, it will always involve a gradual process of combining this, that and the other in a variety of forms, by which the picture of history will be modified to some extent, through being added to, embellished and so romanticized. But popular memory will not so readily distort it that the passage of a century or two is going to render all but unrecognizable happenings which have left such a deep impression in the mind of large groups of people. It occurs to me also that as various new discoveries have confirmed quite ancient traditions in the Old Testament (indeed, have discredited some important ones too), we must weigh, evaluate or disqualify the traditional material only with the very greatest exercise of caution.

In this connexion it strikes me that we ought to put more store by the fact that the length of time separating the oldest body of tradition (J) from the events of the Mosaic period is less than three hundred years, which is nothing like the span between J and the patriarchal age. Moses lived probably between 1250 and 1200. The oldest compilation can be dated between 950 and 900. If its material springs from oral tradition stemming from 1000, or thereabouts, the gap that this had to bridge amounts to scarcely two centuries and thus constitutes a span that may be bridged by a few transmitting individuals.

We have leave, therefore, to ascribe a relatively high degree of historical value to the tradition, where the main ingredients of the story are concerned. It looks very probable, in the present case, that these main features include not only the deliverance from Egypt and the entry into Canaan but also the Sinaitic Yahweh-revelation and the person of Moses. Particularly in the Semitic world with its marked attachment to traditions, it is hardly possible to conceive of the creation of a binding link between a people and a deity without the intervention of a religious personality, equipped also to give a powerful lead. It is difficult to imagine a God like Yahweh, the Lord of Sinai and the God of Israel, with all the complexities of his nature, being taken over by Israel 'as a matter of course' from a desert people such as the Kenites. Whether he was initially a Kenite deity or no, the forming of the bond with Yahweh demands the presence of an intermediary figure. On this point one may draw support from the tradition, which is equally persuaded of the matter, and also from the impression that Moses made on posterity, which assessed him in the role of the charismatic figure who was indeed active in the desert as the intermediary of Yahweh. Perhaps one might be allowed to refer at this juncture to something that Karl Jaspers submits for our consideration in treating of a number of historical themes: that when as a historian one is presenting an account of some major figure, it is quite in order to make use of the response which that figure has elicited, the effect that he has had on succeeding generations.[48]

Moses has gone down to history, at all events, as Israel's great

prophet; and that is a datum not to be ignored. It is scarcely conceivable that within the short space of two hundred years tradition
would have created the figure of Moses, in all the many functions that
accrue to him, out of absolutely nothing. One is at a loss to understand the tradition as J presents it, unless Moses did in fact play an
important role.

We propose now to sketch, in brief outline, the picture that the
earliest compiler of tradition, J, has given of him.

When the Israelites were under restraint in Egypt and the very
infants (boys) were all in danger of their lives (Ex. 1:8–10, 22), Moses
was born. Saved, through a trick of his mother's, at the behest of the
Pharaoh's daughter, he later on put his life in jeopardy by standing
up for a Hebrew, and had to flee to Midian. There he was taken up
by a priest and afterwards married this man's daughter, Zipporah
(Ex. 2:1–22). When the Pharaoh who had been after Moses' blood
was dead, he returned at the instance of Yahweh to Egypt (Ex. 2:30;
4:19, 20a) and on the way was symbolically circumcised by Zipporah
(Ex. 4:24–26). In Egypt he was commanded to go to the Pharaoh and
ask him to give the people leave to hold a feast in honour of Yahweh
in the desert. This he was later required, under the threat of various
penalties, to repeat. As the Pharaoh paid no attention, Egypt was
visited with a number of plagues (probably seven), of which the worst
was the destruction of the firstborn (chapters 7 to 11, where it is
impossible to distinguish with any certainty what each of the several
authors has contributed, although a variety of hands can be recognized). In order to escape the impending doom Israel was required to
slaughter a lamb and smear its blood upon the door-posts. This
became the basis of the observance of the Passover feast (Ex. 11:4–8;
12:21–23). After having let the Israelites go, the Pharaoh thought
better of it, pursued them and, in so doing, perished in the Red Sea
(Ex. 12:29–39; 13:20; 14:5f., 9f., 13f., 21, 23, 26ff.). They set out by
way of the desert of Shur, Marah, Elim and Rephidim, where they
fought with the Amalekites (end of ch. 15, beginning of chs. 16 and
17), to arrive subsequently in the neighbourhood of Sinai and to
undergo the experience of Yahweh's revelation, to receive his law
when the covenant was made (chs. 19 and 24, 32 and 34 *passim*). The
rest of J's narrative is to be found in specific sections (from Num.
10:29 on to ch. 14; ch. 16:21–25). Of particular interest from a
religio-historical standpoint is the part played in the story by Kadesh
(cf. Num. 13:26 and ch. 20).

The next task is to offer some answer to the question as to which elements in the tradition are historical in character. Hardly anyone to speak of would have doubts as to three of the principal elements, which are the liberating of Hebrew tribes or groups from Egypt, a journey through the desert, and the fact that, after setbacks, they won through to Canaan, either from the South or the East, or by a number of routes. This last question, being purely a matter for the historian, in a historico-religious context is neither here nor there.

The issues that especially concern us are the Yahweh-revelation and the role of the Moses-figure. As regards the former, we have already given it as our opinion that there is an integral connexion between the revelation and the exodus-wilderness tradition. It was during the period spent in the desert that Yahweh came to be the God of the Israelite tribes.

For determining the relation of the appearance and activity of Moses to history, the relevant factors are as follows: (a) his name, which despite the doubts expressed by some is certainly of Egyptian origin. [49] Admittedly, this derivation has been objected to, because the Egyptian word is not spelt in the same way as the Hebrew; but the objection can hardly stand, for in the transcription of the el-Amarna letters such spellings as the Hebrew would yield also occur in the case of Egyptian names. The Egyptian name here means 'child'; whilst the derivation from the Hebrew in Exodus 2:10 must be treated as popular etymology, as has already turned out to be the case with other names (Jacob, etc.); (b) his connexion with the Kenites. His father-in-law, brother-in-law and wife are all specifically named, albeit more than one name occurs for the first of these (Reuel and Jethro), which means that there is more than one tradition involved here. Even Noth acknowledges this datum as an element with a genuinely historical basis. [50] J's compilation recognizes (Ex. 4:24ff.) that Moses' circumcision was a symbolic act carried out by Zipporah, and so evidently sees it as deriving from the Kenites; whereas the E tradition (Ex. 18) represents the system of administering justice as being taken from the Midianites. According to the tradition, there-fore, the Kenites-Midianites (names that are sometimes transposed in the traditions) made their own contribution to the life of the Hebrew tribes who had fled out of Egypt. Somewhere in a tradition of this sort, since it certainly could not have been thought up at a later time, when Moses was universally held to be the great founder of Israel's religion, and since it is not told just to embellish the story, there must lie an ancient kernel of history; (c) along with Noth[51] we can surely recognize in the tomb-tradition associated with Transjordan a core of history.

If these three elements rest on a historical foundation, then the *framework* of the Moses-story, which in every version of the tradition, from first to last, connects him with Egypt, the desert and Transjordan must surely have some grounding in history.

The frame within which the story of Moses' career is set would then parallel completely the scheme of things in the account of the Hebrew tribes who, fleeing out of Egypt, came through the desert via Transjordan and turned up again in Canaan. We may take this parallel structure as confirmation of the fact that a direct link does exist between Moses and the Hebrews who escaped from Egypt.

On the question of what precise, historical place Moses occupied in the whole course of events it is difficult to make firm assertions. One thing is clear: that for J, E and later traditions Moses is to be associated first and foremost with the Yahweh-revelation (Ex. 3:19). He gave Yahweh to Israel. This particularly strong relationship with the Divine Being of Sinai points to the charismatic nature of Moses' activity. This was, and always remained, the most central element of the tradition. In the earliest reference made to him outside of J and E's compilations he is called a prophet (Hos. 12:14); and in Deuteronomy he is remembered in the same role (Deut. 18:15; 34:10f.; cf. also Num. 11:24ff.; 12:6f.). In Exodus 33:7ff. he is associated with the tabernacle of revelation,[52] which likewise has a prophetic character.

As prophet too he fits into the framework of Israel's early history. Indeed, the further one goes into the history of Israel, the more obvious becomes the extent to which charismatic figures appear as leaders of the nation. In the Song of Deborah (see also the related account in Judges 4) that prophetess is the real guiding light, enthusing the people by her call to action (cf. verse 12ff.) and rousing them to deeds of heroism;[53] and vice versa, the leaders who deliver the nation in the period of the judges are charismatics.

Moses gives every appearance of having been such a charismatic leader (see note 48, p. 138), who in response to Yahweh's summons addressed himself to his brethren in Egypt and gave them the incentive to set themselves free from Egypt, perhaps first of all to hold a feast for Yahweh in the desert, as the tradition says. From the very start he was bent on forging a link between his people and Yahweh.

That is not only the first point but also the high point, the climax, of
the story of the liberation; and therefore, as we pointed out before,
that climax occurs not in Exodus 15 but in Exodus 19, 20 and 24 and
related passages. The compilation takes in the deliverance from
Egypt, lets the story develop without interruption as far as what
happened at Sinai, thereupon presenting only certain quite dis-
jointed traditions, until in the stories centred upon Transjordan some
degree of coherence is restored.

It we now proceed to the last question: what, at the level of fact, is
there in the story of Israel to which we can point as dating from the
time of Moses, then we would think it permissible to refer to the ark
and to the decalogue (if only, perhaps, in a very brief form); whilst
we must pronounce it altogether uncertain whether, in addition to
these, we ought also to mention the cult or particular elements of it.
If that were to be the case, then one would have to keep in mind,
besides Sinai, a second place which played its part at this period:
namely Kadesh.

So far as the first-mentioned items, the ark and the decalogue, are
concerned, discussion has now reached the point where various
scholars, without departing at all from the rules and standards of
critical investigation, have concluded, despite the refusal of many
others to do so, that these two elements are best relegated to the
desert period. It is impossible to mention all their names here or to
summarize the discussion, however briefly. For the issues concerning
the ark one should read the concise but detailed article by E. Kutsch
in the recent *R.G.G.*;[54] and for those raised by the decalogue see the
detailed articles by L. Köhler[55] and J. J. Stamm[56] on the literature
from 1930 to 1960.

In disagreement with a number of Jewish scholars, O. Eissfeldt,[57]
in particular,[58] has fixed the provenance of the ark as belonging to the
period before the settlement in Canaan. It seems to me that Eissfeldt[59] is right in taking the transfer of the ark to indicate that David's
purpose was to connect the desert tradition, as an ancient national
tradition incorporated in the ark, with Jerusalem.[60] At the close of
the period of the judges, then, this must have been what it stood for;
and that tradition could have survived nowhere else but in ancient
Shiloh, which even before Saul's time had been destroyed. It therefore has very ancient credentials (see further pp. 146 and 151).

Where the decalogue is concerned, both Köhler and Stamm, after
having amply discussed and reflected upon recent literature—which

has quite often contested the idea of a Mosaic provenance—have given it as their firm opinion that the ethical decalogue at any rate (Ex. 20) in its basic form contains nothing that would contravene its having been drawn up in the time of Moses.[61] Stamm is prepared to accept the 'Mosaïcity' of the decalogue as a fact, rather than ascribe it to some unknown author or other of a later period.[62] But he has to admit that proof direct and positive of the fact cannot be provided.[63]

This standpoint seems to me to be right. One must always bear in mind that with the data available to us there is no proving anything to be historical fact; but there is not a single argument to hand which proves the opposite. Some of the arguments in favour of an early provenance are: that a succession of terms plainly reminiscent of the ethical decalogue turns up in Hosea (4:2) and Jeremiah (7:9). This shows that the decalogue is pre-prophetic (the typical contemporary ethic of the prophets is to be found much more in a passage like Jer. 7:3ff.; and it is far more socially oriented). The fact that after the adultery with Bathsheba David accepts Nathan's sentence of punishment and knows that he is worthy of death (2 Sam. 12) shows that he bows before a law that has absolute authority, to which even the king is subject, and which demands the death of those who transgress it (something that for the rest of the Eastern world was quite unthinkable). There is one final but important consideration to be extracted from the researches of A. Alt, who in his book on law in Israel[64] has shown that there must be a correspondence between apodictic (divine) law in Israel and the requirements of the decalogue. Most of the reasons for exacting the extreme penalty in Israelite law are based on violations of the normative standards laid down in the ethical decalogue (Ex. 20; Deut. 5). In other words, it would appear to enshrine the elements forming a basis for the entire penal code of Israel.

Now the question is whether we are to think of a summary of this sort as having been drawn up at the start of events, or no. A. Alt and many others with him are sure that it was not. Alt believes, that is, that the decalogue is a later summary of major offences in law, which in the course of time and because God had so decreed came to carry the death penalty.[65] The decalogue, in his view, is concerned with 'extreme instances of wrongdoing' and positively (in the second series) with protecting the Israelite's basic personal rights. The latter point is clear enough; but the former, as stipulated, is far from clear. Alt views the decalogue too much from the standpoint of legal history and too much as a text constructed on fixed, purely juridical lines. The fourth, fifth and tenth commandments, and the introductory sentence in particular, argue against that. These are no juridical pronouncements. The decalogue has much more the look of an 'ideal legislation', giving a 'programme of principles' and a summary of normative rules for national existence than a batch of strictly juridical requirements. The fact that its injunctions cover the whole of life—religion, family, society, property, legal conduct (ninth commandment)—confirms this. The ancient East was not unfamiliar with a diversity of such programmes legislating for reform. They were drawn up by this or that princely ruler at the outset of his reign (cf. that of Lipit Ishtar, *A.N.E.T.* 159, Urukagina of Lagash, and of Hammurabi; see W. von Soden; *Herrscher im alten Orient* (1954), 12 and 48) and thereby ushered in a new age. The same is true of the Reform of Josiah, which Deuteronomy inaugurates. More forcefully even than all these documents the decalogue gives the impression of a desire to institute a new beginning—for instance, in its opening words, which relate it at once to the new Yahweh-revelation.

To sum up: we may say that while it is not possible to give a definite answer to the question as to the origin of the decalogue—an answer, that is, backed by direct historical documentation—it makes most sense, having regard to the way things stand at this moment, to regard it as being the earliest summary of legally embodied principles giving direction to the life of the new Yahwistic community in all its internal relations, religious and social.

The form that introduces the 'Ten Sayings' as a divine utterance, the fundamentally religious point of departure that goes along with this, as well as the fact that the remaining contents centre on the practical ordering of the community and its mode of life, are typical elements well suited to the establishing of a clan-community on a religious basis.[66]

On this view, for anyone prepared on other grounds to believe that the God of Sinai would need to be introduced by a prophetic figure, the conclusion is really inescapable that the tradition here must be right, in principle, when it associates the decalogue with the figure of Moses. A succinct set of rules governing conduct, such as is given here, would work extremely well in the historical situation in which the Hebrew groups who had fled from Egypt found themselves. They gathered around Moses at Sinai in order to meet with Yahweh who had delivered them, and to receive at Moses' hand the basic law of

Yahweh for their new way of life. Thus out of the refugee groups there
arose a Yahweh-league.[67]

As for the question whether the process that brought this socio-
religious community into being was conditioned *ab initio* by the
covenant and the outlook which it engendered, that is something
which we can only touch upon briefly here. It is a very complex
problem which is of more significance to theology than as a religio-
historical issue.

The fact is that all traditions, particularly the deuteronomic
(Ex. 24:3ff.) but also the older J (Ex. 24:12–15a and 34:10a and 27f.)
and E (Ex. 24:9–11), as well as the more recent P, in one way or
another employ the notion of a covenant in this connexion.[68] Among
the earliest prophets (8th century), apart from Hosea, the term is not
in use; but it is with those of the 7th century (Jeremiah and Ezekiel),
who had been influenced by Deuteronomy.

As the ancient Semitic world made repeated use of the covenant
concept to indicate the idea of community or shared connexion (such
a connexion exists by virtue of blood-relationship or the marriage
bond or by virtue of a covenant) it is quite possible that the relation
between Yahweh and the new religious community was at once
viewed in that light (the covenant-theology is at all events ancient, as
is evident from J). We have to take fully into account, therefore, the
possibility that this notion goes back to the actual foundation of the
Yahweh-community.

The issue is whether the words of the decalogue may be taken in
evidence as demonstrating this point, as the American professor,
G. E. Mendenhall, contends in an article that has enjoyed a good deal
of acclaim.[69] He believes that especially the introductory words of the
decalogue (Ex. 20:1f.) are demonstrably so closely akin to those
found in the Hittite treaties that the decalogue must be characterized
as a formal deed of covenant and furthermore that it must be ascribed
to the same period as the Hittite treaties. Both conclusions are questionable. It would seem to me more correct to look for parallels to the
decalogue among codes of law rather than treaties or contracts. This
is true, for a start, of the opening formula, which is better compared
with the beginning of the Codex Hammurabi and with that of Lipit-
Ishtar (apropos of the 'self-styling' adopted by the code-giver) than
with that of the treaties in question. This line of argument does not
get us as far as many people have supposed.

Besides the possibility that the covenant-idea belongs with the

K

desert period, there is another one that is still open: namely, that it developed out of the later Yahweh amphictyony which came about in the land of Canaan (see the next chapter). The covenant made between Yahweh and the tribes in Shechem was a *berith*, a reciprocal connexion by covenant or treaty under Yahweh's protection and in his honour. The covenant-idea, therefore, could have had its beginning in the Shechem amphictyony, where Yahweh became the God of the covenant. The formulation was then transferred from the relationship in which the tribal groups had placed themselves toward Yahweh to that of Yahweh to the national community itself. It was preserved in North Israelite theology (Hosea) and given a central place in the deuteronomic system.

Yet another matter relating to the decalogue, and indeed to the new community *in toto*, concerns the significance and function of the ark. Its character has been much disputed; and no doubt the fact that its function changed with the passage of time has something to do with this. The various facets which the ark presents, as throne, foot-stool, divine symbol, palladium of war and depository for the tablets of stone, may best be regarded as historically interconnected. In the course of time the ark was successively all these things. The earliest function of the ark (the Hebrew name for it, *'aron*, meant originally 'chest') was perhaps indeed that of a chest, containing the law. Deuteronomy has in that case (Deut. 10:2f.) put the oldest tradition to the forefront. One can think of this in various ways: either that the ark was the socle or pediment on which the stele of the law was set as a 'testimony', when the people stayed for a time at a given spot, and that the stele was stowed inside it when they moved on; or, as was often the case with contracts, treaties and even official correspondence,[70] that the tablet existed in duplicate (there is a tradition regarding two tablets), the official exemplar being kept in the ark (chest),[71] the other being on public display.[72]

That the ark as the container of the divine 'Ten Sayings' later on became itself a symbol of Yahweh is not strange, when one remembers that, generally speaking, the *cella* became the sanctuary, because it was the place where the divine image(s) stood. Furthermore, one can no more distinguish between law and lawgiver than one can separate the divine image from the deity. At the close of the Codex Hammurabi (rev. XXV) we notice how the king assumes that whoever reads his law will be filled with reverence for him and will utter a blessing for him too. The identification of the symbol with what it symbolized was taken pretty far in the ancient East[73] (see also p. 151).

We conclude, then, that the core of the Exodus-tradition offers a coherent and very fair picture of what took place among the refugees from Egypt. We have found the most important constituent items which offer solid ground, historically, to be: the connexion of Israel's God, Yahweh, with Sinai, the figure of Moses as prophet of Yahweh, the decalogue and the ark. These elements, taken together, make a fair whole, fitting admirably into the historical situation and extremely well suited to help explain the course taken by Israelite religion in its later history; for these are the very elements which later turn out to be the central spiritual pillars of support, bearing up the whole life of Israel. Not one of them could have been taken over from Canaan; nor can they be satisfactorily accounted for in terms of what transpired later on. Thus they are the constant factors in the whole religion of ancient Israel, governing its structure from the beginning right up to a late period. They give to Israelite religion a character which distinguishes it fundamentally from that of the Canaanites, and so confer upon the Yahwistic group the religious self-awareness that prevents its members from assimilating themselves to the Canaanite world.

For a historical understanding of the further development of Israel and her relation to Canaan, and especially for any understanding of her spiritual genius in that context, one cannot brush aside the four basic elements to which we have referred.[74] They provide a firm point of departure for the history of the nation as also of its religion in the desert period, which helps sufficiently to explain conditions during the periods that follow.

A final matter in connexion with the decalogue has still to be briefly considered: namely, that of the two different and distinct decalogues, the cultic and the ethical. This may serve at the same time to carry us on to the third point, mentioned on p. 142 regarding the Mosaic period but not so far discussed, the question of the cult.

Besides the ethical decalogue of Exodus 20 and Deut. 5, there is a cultic one, found in Exodus 20:23; 23:13–19; 34:14–26.[75] The point to notice is that in Exodus 34 the cultic decalogue is held to be the law given on Sinai (this is the J tradition), whereas Exodus 20 says that it was the ethical one. We cannot discuss here the literary and critical complexities of the problem.[76] The question has often enough been asked: which of these two is the most ancient and which is most likely to be of Mosaic origin? As many and various answers have been advanced in favour of the ethical decalogue as against it. The viewpoint propounded by H. H. Rowley[77] is an interesting one: that the cultic decalogue of Moses was taken over by Hebrew tribal groups from the Kenites, and that the ethical decalogue was given later on by Moses himself.

It may of course be asked whether both decalogues do not perhaps go back to a single core or nucleus which was later amplified in two directions. It is at all events remarkable that in both decalogues the first two prohibitions, which are mutually independent so far as their form is concerned, do occur in the same order of sequence. The oldest core of the decalogue would then have comprised the first two sayings which both versions have in common (Ex. 20:3 and 4a; cf. Ex. 20:23 and, with that, Ex. 34:14, 17), with an opening and closing sentence, which means in effect: 'I am Yahweh your God, who brought you out of Egypt, the house of bondage. You shall have no other gods before me; you shall make for yourselves no image, for I, Yahweh, your God, am a jealous God.'

These primitive sayings would then, in the next instance, have been amplified, both ethically and cultically, possibly by Moses himself or by others. If we may think of Moses in this connexion, then the most probable occasion would be the period of the sojourn in Kadesh, which was the focal point for the tribes over a long time (Num. 13:26; 20; Deut. 1:19). It was an oasis, probably in the North-west part of the Sinai peninsula, situated just to the west of the present Israeli-Egyptian border ('Ain Qedeirat), although some (A. Musil, for example[78]) locate it near Petra. This place, which in Gen. 14:7 is identified with 'En Mishpat (that is 'source of law') (cf. also Num. 20:13), could have been the place where near by a sacred stream the tribes dispensed justice. In that case the organization of the tribes could have taken place here, in the manner described in Exodus 18. The idea that we are to think here of legislation given in the form of the ethical decalogue is at any rate not to be swept lightly aside.[79] The decalogue would then have to be envisaged as ten short sayings formulated rather in the style of the sixth to ninth commandments as they still appear, and intended to serve as a basis for the administration of justice.

On the other side, the original prohibitions would be elaborated with a cultic reference. It is scarcely possible to think of this as happening prior to the settlement in Canaan.[80] If it did, one's thoughts would naturally turn once again to Kadesh. It is more plausible, however, to envisage the cultic decalogue, as passed down in Exodus 23 and 34, as having been drawn up on Canaanite soil after the occupation there, when the tribes had adopted an agricultural way of life. The arrangement of the three major feasts, the stress on going up to the sanctuary and the business of offering the firstlings, all suggest an agrarian period,[81] and therefore one subsequent to the settlement in Canaan.

What further ideas one should entertain as to how the cult was regulated in the desert period is quite uncertain. Admittedly, in Exodus 25ff. the Old Testament does give a detailed account; but this is all the work of the late priestly writer, P. He was quite likely able to make use of some ancient sources for this purpose; but it is unlikely that these really derive from very early material. Anyway, in the time of the kings there are critical voices, as we know, ready to deny that the regulation of the cult has anything to do with the desert tradition (Amos 5:25 and Jer. 7:22). The tradition lying behind these utterances obviously assumes the ethical decalogue (see, e.g., Jer. 7:23 and 9) to have been the basis of the covenant among the tribes in the desert.

There is a lot to be said for the above-mentioned supposition that most of the cultic development came about in the settled land and that previously ancient traditional rites had been in use. We have in mind here various sacrifices, such as burnt sacrifices and immolations, lustration ceremonies, especially at the time of the spring festival of sacrifice, new-moon days, and so forth.

These rites survived in part from the early Hebrew period; but they came partly from the Kenites, who were Moses' kindred by marriage. Sometimes the rites will have acquired a fresh content and meaning, as was surely the case at an early stage with the spring festival. On the night of the vernal full moon it had been from the very earliest times the practice of the herd-tending clans to make preparations, in festal style, for the trek to new pasture-lands, by means of sacrifices and a ritual of purification.[82] The nocturnal festival at the time of the full moon gave occasion for stories to be told. One would assume that it was regular practice among the Yahwistic groups to rehearse the events connected with the exodus, and that this tradition came more and more to dominate the feast, giving rise eventually to the Passover festival of Israel. Thus this became the earliest core of the collected stories of the exodus.

In Canaan it afterwards came to be linked with the first annual festival of autumn, the feast of Massoth, which was observed in the agrarian territory at about the same time. Despite the fact that the two festivals were celebrated more and more as a single event, the tradition does clearly differentiate them.

This locating of the story of the exodus in the period of the old pastoral festival helped to preserve in the tradition a number of features originally associated with the rites of the ancient feast. Thus the practice of slaughtering a lamb and spreading its blood upon the door of the tent gave rise to the tradition which describes how the Israelites were preserved on the night when the firstborn of the Egyptians were smitten with death. In the settled land the important item of the eating of unleavened bread, taken from the feast of Massoth, came to be affixed to the Paschal legends.

Thus this herdsmen's festival, which retained throughout its further development a markedly family character, until in the deuteronomic period it became a temple observance, was gradually assimilated to the genius of Israel and historicized.

In that way other ritual usages also changed their character, sometimes gradually, sometimes through deliberate tampering with them. To the former category, perhaps, belongs circumcision,[83] which was at first probably unknown to the tribes and was introduced at a particular moment, only gradually finding general acceptance. It formed part of the Kenite rites for males and for initiation into the tribe, and was intended to ward off demons (cf. Ex. 4:24ff.). Once adopted by the Yahwistic groups, circumcision became in effect a rite of religious initiation into the community of Yahweh; and then the demonic and sexual aspects of the original rites faded into the background.

To the second group of customs which were deliberately introduced belongs, probably, the institution of the Sabbath.[84] So far, evidence for this had been found in Israel alone; and we may take it to be a religious institution peculiar to that people. It is not clear what background it had in the ancient Semitic world. Eerdmans thought in terms of a day on which the Kenites were forbidden to work (to kindle fire; Ex. 35:3). Others point to the days marking the phases of the moon, which were not observed, however, at set intervals of seven days, and yet others to marketing-days. However that may be, it is clear that from the moment the decalogue came into being the Sabbath as a rest-day consecrated to Yahweh acquires in Israel a special character of its own, and, if the decalogue is indeed Mosaic, is to be regarded as a day deliberately brought in by Moses. The week as a period of seven days takes its origin from this: on each seventh day work was interrupted by a day sacred to Yahweh. From a very early time, therefore, the hallowing consisted in the actual suspension of work: by thus refraining from work people made the seventh day into the day of Yahweh. Letting the land lie fallow in the seventh year was an action closely related to this. Thus to stop work (cf. that the word for a 'solemn assembly', 'aṣarah, means the same thing) as a gesture of sanctification to Yahweh implies that man entrusts and commits everything to Yahweh, who takes charge of it and to whom it all belongs (in this connexion cf. Ex. 34:24 and Deut. 11:10ff.).

The ark, as that which carries the divine symbol of the words of Yahweh, is a most important cultic element. As the most primitive Yahwistic symbol, it quickly filled the place occupied in the religions outside the Bible by the divine image as representative of the deity. It also acquired a significance analogous to the *cella* and the image (or the last by itself) in the other religions. It was carried in battle as a palladium, and betokened the presence of Yahweh; and later on it was regarded either as his footstool or his throne. That in the initial stages it was connected with the performance of cultic actions is unlikely.[85] In later times the ark as a divine symbol came to be addressed as though it were Yahweh himself (Num. 10:35; cf. further above, pp. 142 and 146; also Chapter 3, p. 83ff.).

It is impossible, then, to say with any precision what the belief regarding Yahweh was during the desert period, or to give a fully corroborated historical picture of Moses and of what he did and experienced after his call by Yahweh. In summary form, at least, we can offer the following reconstruction with a fairly high degree of probability.

A Hebrew, a refugee from Egypt, went into the desert, where he established a liaison with the Kenites. There he experienced a call from Yahweh, the God of Sinai, to incite the Hebrew groups under the yoke of Egypt to leave the country. During their flight they had a marvellous escape from the Pharaoh's vengeance at the Red Sea and subsequently made their way to the place where Moses had been charged by Yahweh with his task. Here the Hebrew tribal groups formed a bond with Yahweh and received his law. After a protracted stay in Kadesh, during which they lived in the desert, tending their herds, and received from Moses a basic code of laws, they succeeded in getting through to the country east of Jordan and combining with the kindred tribes in the East and later with those in the West Jordanian territories. We need not pause here over the question of the extent to which certain tribal groups were able to force their way from Kadesh right through the territory of other desert tribes (such as the Amalekites) and reach the land of Canaan by the southern route. We shall have to accept the tradition that Moses was not with the liberated tribes on the last stage of their journey as being historical fact.

Yahweh, the God of Sinai, whose call inspired and took possession of Moses, was perhaps already known to the Kenites; but the call of Moses and the liberation of the Hebrew groups that was its outcome meant that his essential Being as God of Israel was disclosed in a manner wholly new. The original natural functions appropriate to Yahweh as a God of mountain, wind and storm, by which he set bounds to the surrounding atmosphere and controlled the life of the tribes who lived near Sinai, remained, even when he became the God of Israel. They continued even when Moses and the tribes, having heard his call and known his deliverance and newly received the law at his hand, had come to apprehend his Being in a new way. What men had so far experienced of his Being in many and various modes, in all its serenity, unapproachable majesty, wildness and exalted pride, was a terrible power and command over the forces of nature, to bless and to destroy. Now, however, the call had come personally to Moses in the midst of history, and there had been the liberating experience of deliverance from a now remote Egypt. Yahweh had established a bond of fellowship and communion, which he had seen fit to bestow upon a people who were at first strange and foreign to his territory. In conjunction with this he had made known his will to them. Through all this his Being was illuminated and made new. His personal, inspiring, redeeming aspect, and the fact of his instituting a shared fellowship and community, as well as his role in the course of events involving a world far beyond Sinai, do not nullify that substratum which links Yahweh with the natural world. Rather, the two elements interpenetrate and reinforce each other. In this way Yahweh became the God who governs both nature and history, the God of thunder, portending good for his own and death for his adversaries, the ruler of the mountains, and also of the sea and the desert, and even of great civilized states. He is the Mighty One, at whose command and service stand the heavenly hosts, who in battle goes before his faithful followers. He is the One who is far off, unattainable, and is Might incalculable; who yet for those bound under covenant to him is at hand, dealing with them according to the rules which they have been given. These regulations are governed by the exclusive nature of the tie binding him with the liberated tribes. He is the *El qanna'* : the God jealous of his rights. It is this exclusiveness of the life-giving Lord that controls the relation between Yahweh and the refugee multitudes (later the people of Israel). From this tribal group, therefore, as they are appended in Canaan to the brother-tribes already settled there, inevitably comes a powerful resistance to the process of assimilation; for those who have come out of Egypt are conscious of being called, no matter what the circumstances, to fulfil that service to Yahweh which he has laid upon them. It was evidently this which imbued this group with a hostile and militant attitude to the Canaanites which was not displayed by the earlier clans who had found their way into the country during the patriarchal period.

CHAPTER 6

The Victory of Yahwism

IT IS BARELY conceivable that the ancient Hebrew tribes would have developed into a single entity if there had not been some powerful factor contributing to bring that unity about. Neither the early Phoenician and Palestinian city-states in the centuries before the rise of Israel (the Amarna period) nor the later Syrian and Phoenician states in the time of the Israelite kings, nor yet the small clan-states and the tribes of Transjordan and the Negeb, ever achieved a greater unity than that attained in Canaan and Transjordania by the tribes of the Hebrews. It was not imposed from outside, but was born of the cohesion of the tribes themselves—not, however, without the cementing influence of a religious motif. Social and political factors alone will not serve to explain the unity and exclusive solidarity of the tribes among themselves or the self-generating and unfolding opposition to the Canaanites and their culture.

The spiritual growth of Israel in general, and her religious growth in particular, have often been explained in terms of the opposition that was bound to develop between a religious community emerging from the desert and an agrarian-cum-urban culture. But it is impossible to make these sociological factors the basis for explaining the peculiar and unique spiritual genius of Israel, its history, or how it came into being. It is plain enough that for centuries desert tribes had settled on the fringe of the cultivated land and gradually availed themselves of its products, first in the agrarian, and later in the urban, sector. Social groups once so different were thus quietly and peaceably assimilated.[1] We can see for ourselves this process coming about in the case of states like Ammon and Moab; and we may assume its having happened time and again, when the Ḥabiru or Ipri settled in Canaan or Ugarit, or even with the evolution of a town such as Shechem. It seems to me very likely that Täubler[2] is right in assuming that, for instance, the community of that town in the pre-Israelite period was based on a covenant-relationship between an old-

Canaanite and a more recent Hivite population, who together worshipped the Baal-Berith as chief god of the city. He was the patron of the city-community. In the same way—as would appear from Judges 9—groups from the tribes of Israel (even after their acceptance of Yahweh) later on still agreed upon some communal arrangement with Shechem, which apparently began with both sides accepting the *connubium* and ended with advances being made to the Baal-Berith (Judges 8:29ff. and 9).

The generally current routine was for a socially and culturally inferior group which had found its way into the area of cultivation to be assimilated to the old, culturally superior community already living in the country. This was the pattern followed again and again in the Near East, in Canaan and also among the tribes of Israel. The only group that could hope to evade what was a wellnigh predestined pattern of historical development was one which could really command, or was impelled by, a principle of its own—a principle which, however great the cultural lag might be, gave it enough spiritual backing to overcome the imminent danger of disintegration and to remain homogeneous. The less well developed group, in other words, had to be characterized and conditioned by a positive spiritual force—like, for example, the Arabs who under the impetus of Islam not only succeeded in bringing down the Byzantine and Sassanid empire but in keeping it permanently subject. It is undeniable that the real power of this Arab movement lay not in the Arabs' military aptitude but in the Islamic religion, which infused the religio-military state and community created by Mohammed with a strong and mounting aggressive inclination.[3]

What I would think to be wrong with various attempts to explain the religion of Israel on historical lines is that they are based almost exclusively on the social antitheses and do not sufficiently expose the nature of the spiritual resources of the groups involved. Yet in the case of Israel's history, which was so largely determined by religion, this is absolutely necessary.

It is here not just a matter of the clash between a desert religion and culture and an agrarian-urban civilization, but of the struggle between the Mosaic groups with their Yahwistic desert religion and its very specific attributes[4] and the Baalism of the Canaanite civilization. This it was that set the Israelites in the country on the march.

Over a long period already Hebrew tribal groups had been settling in the land of Canaan. They were engaged in changing over from a semi-nomadic to an agrarian existence. They assimilated themselves partly by seeking to join in the El-religion and by frequenting its temples. Anyone who did not conform in this way continued to cling to the customs of his forefathers and shut himself off from the culture, as was done at a later time by the Rechabites, when they returned as an organized group to the desert areas.

The most recent historiography on Israel in the writings of A. Alt and M. Noth lays particular stress on the Hebrew tribes' slow and peaceful penetration of the settled land. In the process of occupation acts of war are recognized by Noth to be the exception, not the rule, and this, not merely in patriarchal times but also in the period which, on the strength of the biblical tradition (especially of the Book of Joshua), is generally regarded as that of the conquest. The activity of an important figure like Joshua, as the Old Testament portrays it,[5] is emphatically denied. His part in history is limited to the fact that it was he who prompted the Shechem-amphictyony (Josh. 24).

The question that must be asked at this point is whether this way of expounding the history of the period following the entry by the Yahwistic groups, which even Noth wholeheartedly admits,[6] is the right one, and whether full justice is being done here to the evidences of tradition.

The method of *Traditionsgeschichte* sifts these to their source in relation to the tribe- and local or temple-traditions. For an overall Israelite figure like Joshua there is hardly a place, although Noth is prepared to grant him one, when it comes to the institution of the Shechem amphictyony. But at all events we cannot allow him to have been the conqueror of the land; and major conquests in the Centre, North and South are equally unacceptable. We have to recognize the relative justice of this view and of its point of departure, which is based entirely on tribal history.

There is one observation to be made about this, however: that far too little attention is paid here to the historico-religious factors involved: namely, the peculiar spiritual *élan* of the new Israelite groups pouring in, who were highly charged with Yahwistic ideas. These groups thereby brought new inspiration to the members of the old, established tribes (such as Reuben, Simeon, Levi, Judah, Issachar and Zebulun,[7] in so far as they still existed) and still more to those of the younger Joseph tribes, stimulating them to a much more conscious and independent attitude and even in certain cases to belligerency[8]—as, for instance, the fight led by Deborah and Barak at

THE VICTORY OF YAHWISM

a later time so powerfully demonstrated. Touched off by the prophetess, Deborah, this aggressiveness set the tribes of Central Palestine ablaze (Judges 5:14f.) and led to a victory of the volunteer forces of the Central Palestinian tribes over a strong concentration of Canaanite troops from the North. What is important about this event, which must surely have taken place before 1100, is that it illustrates the manifestation of a new *élan* among the various tribes and a willingness to act together under the leadership of a prophetess inspired by Yahweh.

Even though this event may have happened only when the process (started by the numerous Yahwistic groups) of imbuing the tribes with Yahwism and consolidating them was nearly completed, it is nonetheless clear that it depended entirely on the spirit stirred to life by the Yahwistic bands, which was thoroughly religious, and Yahwistic into the bargain. The opening part of the Song of Deborah makes the connexion between the role assumed by Deborah and Yahweh, who came out of Sinai, too evident for there to be any doubt that the same spirit is expressed here as inspired the groups liberated from Egypt, who were the covenanted allies of the Sinaitic Yahweh. The space of two lifetimes separates their entry into the country (soon after 1200) from the fight with Sisera (*c.* 1120).

So we can expect to find a more militant attitude among the old Hebrew tribes after the arrival of the Yahwistic groups[9] and under their influence than had been displayed previously. It was mainly from the central point at Gilgal, which they founded and which afterwards became one of Yahwism's principal holy places (see p. 84), that they obtained a firm foothold particularly in Central and Southern Palestine, so following in the earlier tracks of the old tribes. The so-called Joseph-tribes and Judah came to be sturdy supporters of Yahwism. If the names of Joshua and Caleb, which turn up, albeit in variable fashion, in the tradition, have any claim to historical recognition, then they must have been the leaders of the Yahwistic groups after the death of Moses (the former, Joshua, was a Hebrew, an Ephraimite, the other a figure from among the Kenizzites, a group akin to the Edomites—and Kenites?). Whilst the first pressed on with the group of Hebrew tribes toward Central Palestine, the second group fought its way through to Southern Palestine, where two cities, Hebron and Kiriath Sepher, were taken. Joshua, it seems, made himself especially useful by bringing the tribes into an alliance. M. Noth regards the setting up of this amphictyony at Shechem as

Joshua's work.[10] As elaborated in a late tradition, the story of this is told in Joshua 24.

How far all this entitles us to recognize the historicity of the conquest-stories as these are related in the Book of Joshua is a leading question which is not all that easily answered. It is quite certain, on the one hand, that this account of events[11] was put together by late-deuteronomic writers after 600 and that, *qua* history, it is altogether too smoothly schematized and in the form now presented to us no longer reflects how things really stood; but on the other hand there are particular points with respect to which the picture of developments outlined here cannot be simply dismissed. If the excavations at Jericho and Ai have given us grounds for concluding that these cities were not razed by the tribes (and that the tradition here must therefore have incorporated elements from a quite different period and worked them up in typical fashion for theological purposes), those at Lachish and, in particular, at Hazor have served to corroborate what is said to have happened in the period immediately after the entry of the Joshua-group. It is a fact that Lachish, the conquest of which the biblical tradition ascribes to Joshua, was sacked at that time, which *may* point to the accuracy of the biblical tradition.[12] As regards Hazor: not only has the fact of the city's destruction in this very period become a certainty, but also a small layer of Israelite domestic occupation has been uncovered,[13] which warrants the conclusion that at any rate this item of information from the Book of Joshua tallies with the archaeological evidence. Nothing is known, so far, with regard to other towns; and for the present we cannot be sure what really happened in the case of the victories ascribed to Joshua. When one compares the results of the conquest as given in Judges 1 with the stories in the Book of Joshua, one is inclined to doubt the historical truth of the latter and to insist on first having some factual confirmation (especially now that archaeology has given the lie to the account of the conquest of Ai and perhaps also of Jericho).

On the other hand, not everything has yet been said about the assumption, so much in vogue at the present time, that the 'Occupation' involved scarcely any warlike activities. This theory begs a number of questions and ought to be discarded, if the evidence of Hazor can be regarded as sufficiently certain. Theoretically, there would be nothing strange about the supposition that after a stay in the country lasting for several centuries the position of the early Hebrew tribes with their allies had become so strong that they now constituted a danger to certain cities which found themselves in a some-what isolated situation. As far back as the Amarna-period the small city-states of Palestine had soon been plunged into dangers and difficulties by the attacks of bands of Ḥabiru and the like. They then appealed to Egypt and asked for miltary assistance—sometimes only a few score or so of men.[14] This is a clear pointer to the military weakness of the Canaanite cities. When in the 12th century Egyptian support came to an end, most of these places, however sturdy their walls, were isolated politically and economically, and probably made a poor military showing. It would appear that Shechem, for example, was gradually obliged to open its gates to the Central-Palestinian tribes. Even if it is hard to put a date to the story of Jerubbaal and Abimelech, it cannot be all that far away from the events celebrated in the Song of Deborah, and may possibly be pinned down to about the year 1100. If, then, it is correct that in this period when the balance of power held by the Canaanite cities was passing to the Israelite tribes who were occupying more and more of the agricultural area and establishing village settlements of their own, the Yahwistic groups had begun to influence the tribes, we may very well believe that when the right moment came the change in the mental outlook of the Israelite tribes, which was its consequence, did indeed give rise to an entirely new situation.

One of the first symptoms of the change was the centralization of the tribes, under Yahwistic leadership, in an amphictyony. This gave Yahwism the chance to make its influence effective in the realm of organization through the co-ordination of forces in the cultic and legal sphere, and so upon religion and the life of society. In this way Yahwism was able thoroughly to permeate the nation's life. As one surveys the rapid advance of Yahwism, which within the space of a century came in large measure to dominate the spiritual life of the tribes, it is hard to imagine its succeeding without some such organi-zation.

Yahwism imparted to the life of the tribes a new content and meaning. From now on it was to be controlled by Yahweh and the *torah* (that is, the 'directive' which he had given). As has been said so often already, the spiritual temper that distinguishes Yahwism is quite different from what one finds in the patriarchal, father-god and El-religions. The points of contrast and opposition between the Canaanites and the tribes of Israel, which up to the end of the patriarchal period were primarily on the social plane, now acquire a religious dimension. Things were forbidden to the Israelite groups, and enjoined upon them, that had hardly been matters for regulation before.

The new spirit of Yahwism was manifested with especial power whenever charismatic figures appeared who were inspired by the *ruaḥ Yahweh*, the spirit of Yahweh, as happened with Deborah and certain of the judges. This 'enspiriting', which caused women and men to act in the power of Yahweh and in the service of the tribes, enabling them to perform great feats of deliverance, can be seen as characteristic of Yahwism. The tradition tells how this activating power also led to the conflict with non-Yahwistic religious influences (Baal-worship; see Judges 6; cf. the polemic at Judges 5:8, aimed at 'strange gods'). This must surely be right: where the spirit of Yahweh ruled, and where the charismatic individual, activated and inspired by the *ruaḥ*, went forth to meet the foe, there was no room for other gods. One can fully accept, therefore, from a historical standpoint, that such a mentality should stipulate Yahweh's sole right to the kingly title and could reject the earthly status of a king (Judges 8:22f. and 9:8ff.). In the further course of events (the Samuel period, 1 Sam. 8) it appears how strongly this idea persisted, even at a later time. Evidently, not only the religion of the Canaanite world was repudiated, but also the kingship which was inextricably connected with it.[15]

On many scores Yahwism engendered a total antipathy to the religion of Canaan. Stringent laws were made against taking part in the cults of strange gods (Ex. 22:20; 23:13, cf. Num. 25:4), against sorcery (Ex. 22:18). Certain laws were aimed directly at the Canaanite forms of cult (Ex. 23:18ff.; cf., e.g., p. 149, note 81); and all kinds of laws relating to cleanliness, which we know from a later period (Deut. 14; Lev. 11ff.), must have had their basis in those: for instance, the law prohibiting the eating of snakes and pigs, as well as certain mourning customs, and so forth. The exclusive character of Yahweh, which in all the ancient injunctions was posited as the primary norm to be honoured without qualification, was enough in itself to make such a radical divide between the tribes and groups committed to the worship of Yahweh on the one hand and the polytheistic Canaanites on the other that the Yahwistic tribes found themselves in enduring opposition to their neighbours.

To the extent that these tribes were loyal to the amphictyony which Yahwism had instituted, a permanent spiritual gulf appeared where formerly the cleavage between sections of the population had been

The Mount of Moses (Jebel Musa) in the Sinai range

*Ikhnaton with his consort an[d]
children beneath the rays [of]
Aton, symbol of the sun*

◄*Steles and masseboth in a
temple at Byblos*

Byblos, lying by the sea. In the background, the Lebanon; in the foreground, the temple complex.

◀ *Ivory figure of a cherub from the royal palace in Samaria (8th century)*

Temple of Beʿelshamin at Palmyra (see p. 67)

alestinian amulets in the form of figurines of Astarte (see p. 54)

Temple ruins at Hazor with the 'holy of holies' in the foreground (see p. 55)

The wadi es-Siq gives access to Petra (see p. 68)

The rock tombs in front of the entrance to the wadi es-Siq

The forecourt of the temple at Petra
(see p. 68)

◀ The two steles at the entrance to the temple at Petra

Goddess on a lion. Egyptian, Ne
Kingdom

Sacrificer standing before the god El, fro.
Ras Shamra. The god is bearded an
wears a lofty crown, with horns

Stele of Balu'a (king of Moab between
Chemosh and Ashtar?) (see p. 61)

Objects—a small statue of a god and
a row of steles at a Canaanite temple in
Hazor (see p. 55)

Mount Tabor, rising above the plain of Jezreel.

On the summit of Mount Nebo ▶

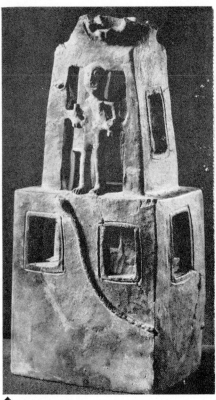

Clay altar of incense (?) in the form of a miniature chapel (Beth Shan, 11th cent., $\frac{1}{2}$m high). Notice the snake as a sacred animal. (Canaanite) (see p. 55)

Bronze figurine of a bull from Hazor (Canaanite) (see p. 55)

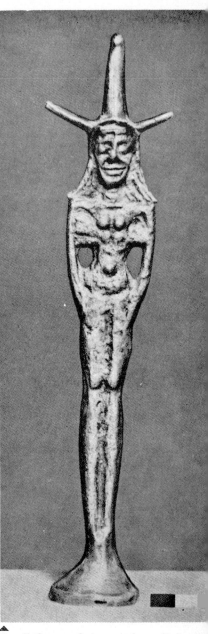

Small figure of Astarte from Nahariya. Cast from an excavated mould. (Canaanite) (see p. 54)

Horned altar from Megiddo, Rockefeller Museum, Jerusalem. For incense-offerings? (Canaanite)

◀ *Six-winged cherub-figure from Tell Halaf (cf. Isa. 6.2) (see p. 54)*

Large altar of burnt-offerings at Megiddo (9 m long, 2 m high, flight of steps on east side) (Canaanite) ▼

The Mount of Olive
(see p. 85

Site excavated by J. A. Kelso a
Bethel, 195.

Amid the ruins of Lachisꜩ

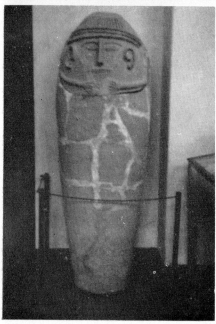

Clay sarcophagus resembling a humar
figure, Rockefeller Museum, Jerusalem
(15th–12th century, Canaanite)

*Votive offerings c
water and fire. Mura
from the palace o
Zimrilim at Mar
(18th century*

◄ *Animal sacrifice.
Mural from the palac
of Zimrilim at Mari
(18th century)*

Samaritan Torah-scroll (*see p. 265*)

◀ *Temple excavated at Shechem, 1957, with altar and fragment of a massaba*

Lilith, female night-demon (cf. Isa. 34.14) (see p. 58)

almost entirely of a social nature. According to Albright, even the archaeological evidence bears this out; for nowhere in the Israelite layers of excavated towns (Bethel, Gibeah, Mizpah, Shiloh) have figurines of Astarte or amulets been found, except in Tell Beit Mirsim, which has yielded a few (five) amulets from the period between 1200 and 920. This is to be explained by the fact that there, on the edge of Israelite territory, contact with non-Israelites was much more frequent.[16]

Thus Yahwism in the ascendant made a breach, spiritually speaking, in the centuries-old relationship between the world of Canaanite culture and the tribes of Israel, except where the latter were not inclined to surrender their rapport with the culture for Yahwism. We must recognize that despite the generally rapid and fairly well-rooted progress of Yahwism among the tribes, it did meet with resistance in some places. This must have been quite palpable in the centre part of the country, around Shechem, where on the one hand the amphictyony at first chose to be centred and where, on the other hand, the process of assimilation had already gone a long way. Very few details regarding this development are any longer available. But on the basis of the earlier and later history of a few temple-localities it is possible to make some general observations about the way things went there. We can assume that ancient sacred places with El- and Baal-sanctuaries, like Bethel, Shechem, Dan, Tabor, Beersheba and Hebron (in the case of some of these, such as Bethel, Dan, Shechem and Beersheba, we know from the prophetic writings that in the later Israelite world they were branded as centres of pagan cults), conformed only in part, or only outwardly, to the Yahweh-cult; but they will have maintained their ancient cultic forms (and perhaps also names) for a long time.

Whilst Yahwism, therefore, was making its influence profoundly felt, we must suppose that a quite far-reaching process of assimilation was also taking place. In some degree this must be the case where the Baal-name came into use to denote Yahweh. One is reminded here, for instance, of Saul's family and the names Ishbaal and Mephibaal, like Jerubbaal,[17] and so on. It might perhaps be worth taking the trouble to study not only the historical relations of the Israelite personal names but also their geographical connexions, in the hope of learning more about the trends in the various tribes, whether to Yahwism or to a greater or less degree of assimilation. Again, assimilation will have been a more powerful factor in the life of the people

L

than with the new sanctuaries, the groups of officials ranged around
the amphictyony, the descendants of the Yahwistic bands and the
religious leaders. One has only to think here of the stories in Judges
17–21, which give us a picture of what was happening among 'the
people'. There is nothing really odd, therefore, about making
allowance for an undercurrent in Israel's religion which one might
describe as 'folk-' or 'popular' religion; but it would be wrong to
think of it too much as a uniform entity.

Besides these two Yahwistic 'stances' there was evidently a third,
which was not so common and belongs rather among the exceptions:
namely, the attitude of aggressive Yahwism. As later on with figures
like Elijah, so in early Israel too violent things were done, apparently,
to protect the Yahwistic tradition and to extend it by main force; and
counter-movements were harshly knocked on the head. It would
seem to me that traditional data such as we find in Exodus 32:27ff.
(cf. Deut. 33:8ff.) may well conceal some early elements.

Although the description of the violent behaviour of the Levites in
Exodus 32 may have an etiological conclusion, the tradition is so
remarkable in itself that it could scarcely have arisen at a late period.
It has, moreover, a noteworthy parallel in the story in Genesis 34
(cf. p. 114 of Chapter 4).[18] It is very possible that the emphasis placed
by this narrative on the offence committed against ritual and morality
by the Shechemites is related to the continuing influence of elements
transferred from the Levites in a later cultic sense to the earlier
Levites (as an ancient tribe). At all events, this trait reinforces the
rightness of the assumption that from the very start the Levites were
the champion protectors of the Yahwistic tradition, as they still were
in the time of the kings (1 Kings 12:31).

In this connexion it is relevant to consider the fact that in the
'novelette' of Judges 19–21[19] the man who proved able to induce the
allied tribes to act in order to punish Benjamin was a Levite, resident
in Ephraim and party to a serious sexual misdemeanour in Gibeah of
the Benjaminites. Finally, one may point to the late Midrash on P in
Numbers 25:6ff.,[20] where Phinehas the priest (who is thus to be
regarded as one of the Levites) acts in the role of avenger on behalf of
the abrogated law—and where we probably catch an echo of the old
notion of the Levites' function.

If, as seems most likely, the word 'Levite' (which has its parallels in
the North Arabian and North Mesopotamian world) signifies: (one)
covenanted (to God), or devoted to God,[21] then on the strength of

that we can further postulate that in this early Yahwistic period there existed a group of men who had consecrated themselves wholly to the cult of Yahweh and should be regarded, in accord with the tradition, as Moses' most zealous supporters. There is little to be said for the hypothesis, which some have advanced on the grounds that the term occurs later in the North Arabian world, that they derived from an ancient non-Israelite (Kenite) priestly milieu.

These circles of the conscious champions of Yahwism, gathered around Moses, at a later time provided the people who upheld and taught the religious law (Deut. 33:8). Militant Yahwists of this sort were not in the first instance aggressive toward the world outside, but found a target for their zeal among their own people.

Yet this did help to make the tribes conscious, prepared and united, so that they were ready, as occasion required, to fight for their existence in the conviction that in so doing they were fighting the 'wars of Yahweh'. Although one has to be careful about the idea of a 'holy war', it is undeniable that there is some justification for using the term of Israel's activities after the desert period. Certainly, there is no theory of the holy war to be found in Israel—not at any rate prior to the final period of her history, in the Qumran document: 'the war of the Children of Light and the Children of Darkness'. In the very oldest, the desert, period the waging of a holy war is not in the foreground of the picture, but it is incontrovertibly there; cf. the battle with Amalek (Ex. 17:8ff.; cf. verse 16).

The term which justifies our speaking of a holy war, namely, 'wars of Yahweh', first appears in connexion with a battle against Moab, at the outset of the entry into the country (Num. 21:14). From this it appears that a document was known which went by the name of 'the book of the wars of Yahweh'.[22] The one expression that does occur is 'wars of the Lord'—and then solely in 1 Sam. 18:17 and 25:28.[23] It was in use, therefore, in David's time.

Obviously, in that period, at least, men were convinced that the battle waged by Israel was the Lord's battle. The term 'book of the wars of Yahweh' certainly comes from the time when the ancient songs of war were being collected; but as is evident from the Song of Deborah, the idea that the wars of Israel are Yahweh's wars must be older than that. The ancient notion is taken up into the context of the Yahweh-amphictyony.[24] Under the influence of the Yahwistic groups from the desert not only was a sense of the need for self-preservation strongly developed, but the conviction arose that Yahweh was himself fighting for the tribes. To an ever-increasing degree Yahweh was hailed as a 'man of war'.[25] Before battle was joined he would be entreated for an oracle. The augurers would hurl curses at the enemy (cf., e.g., the behaviour of Balaam; Num. 22–24) and the warriors be regaled with songs of victory for Yahweh (cf. Judges 5:12; and for a later period, Psalm 20). Weapons would be hallowed and the men 'devoted' (1 Sam. 21:5) by abstinence from sexual acts. Yahweh himself went in the forefront of battle (Judges 5; 4:14; 1 Sam. 4ff.). With the cry: 'for Yahweh and for . . .' (cf. Judges 7:18) men would fling themselves into the fight. This was the teru'ah, the war-cry for Yahweh.[26] At a later time the men would sing, turn and turn about, songs such as Psalm 2 (which one can well imagine to have been a battle-song). The battle would proceed entirely 'in the name of Yahweh'; and so he would give victory or would bring about defeat (Judges 7:22; 1 Sam. 14:6ff.). Terror of Yahweh would overtake the enemy. In the case of really critical or perilous enterprises vows would be made and, after the battle, the spoils given to Yahweh and destroyed as a sacrifice or donated to the sanctuary (curse, Hebrew: herem[27]). Such a 'curse' is found in Moab as well as in Israel.

It is hard to maintain that these were totally defensive wars. As against von Rad, Brekelmans is right, in my view, to insist that there were also offensive operations. Then as now, it was difficult to draw the line between defensive and offensive warfare. Especially evident is the aggressive character of the war with Amalek in 1 Sam. 15:2f.; cf. also Ex. 17:16b and Num. 24:18ff.).

Not all wars were holy wars. There were profane expeditions too (1 Sam. 21:5), apparently for plunder or simply conquest. Wars were holy more especially when it was a question of warding off an actual threat to the life of the nation. But we have the stories of the life of Samson to demonstrate that popular tales did not always distinguish between the two sorts of warfare. Taken as a whole, Samson's feats of heroism were seen in fact as the actions of a Nazirite, of a man consecrated to Yahweh.

The triumphs achieved in these wars were regarded as the ṣidqoth Yahweh that is, 'the righteous acts of Yahweh', or better: the acts through which Yahweh 'did justice by his people'. Perhaps the best translation would be: 'the Lord's beneficent or saving acts'. The way in which these saving acts of Yahweh were celebrated in song is well illustrated by the Song of Deborah and by a psalm like Psalm 68, which comes from the period of the judges or earliest kings and is a song of triumph after a battle in the area of Bashan.

A lot of these and similar conceptions and rites relating to war are to be found among other peoples as well. In the desert period Yahweh had presented the aspect of the powerful, celestial mountain-god and then that of the liberator of the tribal groups in the hour of their need. In that capacity he had bound the tribes to him. But now through their later experiences of battle and victory, their conception of Yahweh was confirmed and deepened. His might and his faithfulness in times of difficulty had turned out to be proof against every trial. It is rightly thought that this must have been the period when the figures of the cherubim were fitted to the ark—cherubim that had been taken over from the conceptual world of the Canaanites.[28] At the same time, however, they are proof of the significance which Israel had come to attach to her conception of Yahweh. The symbols of these powerful mythological creatures were made over to him as evidence of his own Mightiness. The word *Şeba'oth*, 'the Lord of Hosts', also perhaps became current in this period.

Alongside or athwart this line of development—which resulted from the course taken by political and military events—we can perceive yet another: that is, we see Yahweh taking over some quite different traits from certain deities well known in Canaan, in particular, from El and Baal. Having regard to the situation, it is not at all odd that Yahweh should have absorbed the former of these. Indeed, the old tribes who accepted Yahwism had already combined their belief in the God of the Fathers with notions of El which they encountered in the land of Canaan. When they accepted Yahweh, a second fusion occurred: the traits of the father-god and of El were attached to Yahweh, so that he could become the wise creator-God and assume the names of El, Elohim and Elyon (see also p. 170).

It was in this period between the entry of the Yahwistic tribes and the early monarchy, and above all in the latter part of it, when the transfer to agrarianism was in progress, that Yahwism was confronted with the ancient East's stories of creation, the flood and the heroes, in their Canaanite guise. The Hebrews now grew familiar with mythology and its primeval dragon-figures, the Leviathan (Isa. 27:1) and/or Rahab, the sea-dragon (Isa. 51:9; Psalm 89:11), of whom the prophet Amos relates that this snaky monster was held fast by Yahweh at the bottom of the sea (Amos 9:3). When these and such-like mythological ideas came to be linked with Yahweh, he assumed the role of El as the dragon-slayer and likewise creator of the world. These two went hand in hand in the ancient Semitic creation-myths, which were at one and the same time theogonies and cosmogonies.

At a later time many of these mythological conceptions were repudiated, as is clear from, for example, the creation story in Gen. 1, where only a very few mythical features have been retained. Even so, they lived on in the imagination of Israel right up to the time immediately before the exile; and among the poets they persisted much longer still, as Isaiah 51 and 27 show. A variety of such ideas remained part of the traditional heritage down to the latest period, as is clear from some of the apocryphal books in which these and similar figures recur.

Such conceptions were not always embraced indiscriminately, but were sometimes made to fit into the scheme of Yahwistic belief by being sifted and recast—as witness the celebrated chapters 2–11 of Genesis, which O. Eissfeldt in his *The Old Testament. An Introduction* calls the lay-source (L), and R. H. Pfeiffer in his *Introduction* calls the Seïritic (Edomite) source. Following J. Hempel I have myself, in my *Literatuur van Oud-Israël*, designated this J3. Whereas other authors date it at the time of David, I have long felt obliged to assign it to the 8th century. It is indeed possibly better to think in terms of the period of transition from a semi-nomadic to an agrarian way of life. The ideal place to live is the oasis at the rivers (Gen. 2f.), where the garden of God is; the semi-nomadic herdsman in his primitive existence is seen as living more in fellowship with Yahweh than the tiller of the soil (Gen. 4:3f.); the real desert nomad is the man accursed (Cain; Gen. 4:11ff.). Cities are dens of sin and pride (Gen. 11)—the fratricidal Cain is the first builder of cities (Gen. 4:17). The narratives, so far as social milieu is concerned, come from the circle of those who had gone over from a pastoral to an agricultural life and for whom the city was still something totally alien. Taking sociological tendencies as a reliable basis, one can then set their origin in the period between the judges and the first kings, even though the fixed, written form of the stories must still be dated somewhat later, in the early part of David's reign, when ancient fragmented traditions were first brought together (not only these thirteen chapters, but also the 'book of the wars of Yahweh' and the 'book of the song').

From a close comparison of these stories with the mythological data and saga-material of the ancient East it is clear how Yahwism arrived at its standpoint over against the literature and the world view

of the ancient East. What happened was that Yahwism incorporated
a variety of early-Eastern elements when it had purged them of all
sorts of ideas that were incompatible with itself; and then by making
use of the remainder and of its own tradition it built up its own view
and outlook on the world.[29]

This is not the place to go more deeply into this question; but one
example may be given here by way of illustration. A number of stories
emanating from the ancient East (the Accadian Gilgamesh-epic,
which must already have been known to the Canaanites at around
1400, on the evidence of a find at Megiddo in A.D. 1954; and, of the
same period, the likewise Accadian myth of Adapa, discovered with
the el-Amarna tablets in Egypt) tell how the gods barred to men the
way to permanent life. In the Gilgamesh epic it says that the gods
kept life for themselves and prepared death for men. The one man,
Gilgamesh, who had obtained a herb which could rejuvenate a human
being (and so give him continuing life) was deprived of it before he
could return to his native city by a snake which ate it up just at the
moment when he was taking a bath; and the Adapa-myth relates that
King Adapa, the favourite of Ea, at the behest of his divine master
who had given him false information (whether of set purpose or not
is unclear), refused the food and drink of life offered him by the sky-
god Anu, in the belief that it was the food of death.

Whereas in the Babylonian world death is the fate to which man is
destined by the gods, in the biblical story of Gen. 2f. things are quite
different. There Yahweh, the Lord of life, gives man access to the
garden of Eden—that is, the divine garden where stand the trees of
life and of the knowledge of good and evil (i.e. the tree of divine
knowledge). Man is not to eat of this, because he must allow God the
honour which is his due, must let God be the arbiter of his destiny
and not wish to arrogate to himself command over good and evil. Of
the tree of life, however, he may eat, signifying that so long as he is in
the garden of Eden, life is his as an abiding gift. However, once he had
tasted of the forbidden tree of divine knowledge (the serpent!), his
punishment was to be cut off from the tree of life and cast out of
paradise. Thus the message of the story is that through his disobedience man has forfeited access to the tree of life, which could
have given him life of an enduring character, even though he was
himself but a fragile creature made of the dust of the earth.

Here we can see being brought into play all sorts of elements closely
related to ideas current in the world of the ancient East. Also,

however, in the Yahwistic narrative of Gen. 2 and 3 an entirely new attitude and outlook are to be read between the lines. The deity here is not unwilling to give abiding life to man. Here are no gods divided against one another and bent on leading man astray or fooling him with their counsels. Here rather is a man who was himself disobedient toward his God and so lost the vital opportunities which God gave him. On the other hand, the biblical story does include a number of features that in one form or another are to be found outside the Bible, such as the tree of life, the serpent, the divine garden—to mention but a few. Yet though this and that pictorial image may have been the same, with them Israel constructed a world view that was in essence quite different from anything beyond her borders. For this Yahwism was solely responsible, in that in the person of Yahweh it had provided Israel with her own completely new conception of God and therewith a fresh point of departure for her religious thinking.

The same thing happened with this story as with many others: with those of the flood, the primeval ancestor and the titans (Gen. 6:1–4). Each in turn was applied by Yahwism to its own beliefs about God. That it took centuries of reflection before writers were able to state in concise yet profound terms and in the language and thought-forms of their day their own distinctively Israelite view of the problems touched upon is only to be expected.

It is a remarkable thing that so few of the Baal-myths appear in these narratives. Apparently, they were at too great a remove from authentic Yahwism for it to feel under any obligation to state its standpoint and outlook in regard to them with any degree of emphasis. Yahweh, the God of Israel, the God of life, was so remote from the dying and rising nature-god that the only way for him to make an opposing stand was to turn persistently away.

It is all the more remarkable because in Israel's religious experience at the practical level it was precisely Baal-worship that was, or rather became, Yahwism's major competitor. The more the social status of the nation moved toward agrarianism, the larger the role assumed by Baal, his cult, rites, symbols and ideas. In the patriarchal period, as long as the tribes were semi-nomadic, this was much less true. But once they had entered the agricultural sector, the Israelites had all kinds of reasons for observing the religious ceremonies bound up with normal agrarian practices. These customs, ritual and practical, were not so easy to disentangle, because they formed a real unity. If you adopted those in the one category, you were at once embroiled with the other sort too. That is why the period of social transition which came about after the Yahwistic groups had entered the country was such a critical one. Yahwism had still to be got across to the old tribes; and there it was immediately confronted with an almost invincible rival in Baalism, with all the allure that went with social progress. The customary practices of this religion, which were meant to further the forces of growth and to overcome the dangers that threaten to hinder these, comprised a medley of magical rites, libations, sacrifices and sexual activities that were held to be indispensable, if vegetational life were to flourish as it should. Thus Baalism could actually claim to be regarded as a vitally necessary factor in the agrarian milieu.

It is easy to understand that in such circumstances Yahwism found itself up against an almost invincible competitor. Baalism could be obstructed, and in many places forced into retreat; but it could not really be overthrown. Even the downfall of the state and the resurgence of Yahwism could not altogether put a stop to its influence. The colony of Yeb-Syene (p. 261) in Egypt is evidence of its ability to survive even outside its own country. In the period of the judges, and again of the kings, it was always reasserting itself. No wonder that Yahwism was so radically hostile that it strove totally to obliterate the very name of Baal. Its use in theophorous names was done away with in accordance with the requirement stated in the Book of the Covenant (a collection dating from the time of the judges or the early kings) that the names of other gods must not 'enter the mouth' (Ex. 23:13). Hence the practice in a later period of replacing the Baal-name in theophorous names (see p. 42) with the word *bosheth* (shame) and of re-interpreting composite theophorous names which included those of other gods. The effects of this still linger on in various ways in contemporary Judaism.

One consequence of the conflict with Baalism was that very stringent sexual laws were laid down in Israel (Lev. 18:20) and that women were banned from the official cult. The existence of *qedeshoth* (women who practised sacred prostitution) resulted in Israel's excluding women from the sanctuary. In strict Yahwistic circles the only role which they continued to play was that of prophetess (Deborah; Huldah, 2 Kings 22:14).

If the primary means of combating Baalism was to rebut unacceptable practices, the second, and perhaps still more effective, method was to adopt from Baalism elements that were acceptable to

Yahwism: for example, rain-rites (possibly in 1 Kings 18:34ff.,[30] and
at a later time on the last day of the feast of tabernacles; cf. John
7:37[31]) and the idea of fertility, so that Yahweh becomes himself the
Lord of the soil and giver of wine, oil and fruits (cf. Hos. 2:7ff., 13f.,
17ff.; 14:6ff.; Deut. 26:1ff.). Since then, Yahweh has been the God
who causes the pastures to 'drop fatness' and the fields to rejoice, as
the psalms say (Psalms 65:10ff.; 104). Canaanite psalms, such as
Psalm 29, were taken over and used to enhance the honour and glory
of Yahweh.

In that way the struggle with Baalism actually contributed to
enrich men's picture of Yahweh, by making him Lord over the powers
of living nature.

Thus Yahweh gradually assumed a number of the characteristics of
El and of Baal; but he also acquired a variety of titles under which
those gods were venerated: the title of Melek, king, which had
belonged first of all to El, was now employed as an epithet for
Yahweh, who was thereby honoured as Lord of all gods in heaven
and on earth.[32] For a time he was even worshipped as Baal (Lord, or
Master); but this encountered too many syncretistic tendencies and
so later on fell into disuse. The title 'Adon (Lord) was also brought
into use, but—probably for the same reasons—was not widely current.
Later on, of course, it became increasingly the custom to avoid
uttering the divine name, Yahweh, and to use the title 'Adonai' (my
Lord, plural) in its place—so much so in fact that wherever in the
Hebrew text of the Old Testament the tetragrammaton (YHWH)
occurred, that form of address was 'read in'.

Thus Yahweh turns out to be the winner in this competition of the
gods; and as a result of the struggle with El and Baal for the soul of
the people of Israel he acquires the rank of king and comes to be seen
as head of the divine world. Other gods become his servants; and
messengers come at his command. The idea emerges of a divine
'royal household', with Yahweh as absolute ruler. This notion is in
many respects not unlike that of the Canaanite pantheon. The
difference is that, as the Israelites conceived it, Yahweh is the *absolute*
ruler; and none of the gods around him is to be likened with him (see
Psalms 29:1; 82; 89:6–8), none of them even has a name. In the
Canaanite world the gods are self-subsistent beings, each with his own
name and nature, often at odds with the principal deity, El. Not in
Israel, however (see p. 33ff.). These powers belong to Yahweh as his
servants; but they have no real say. The forces around Yahweh are

described as the *Ṣeba'oth*, the (heavenly) host. They may be associated with the stars, but are also preternatural beings 'moving up and down' upon or beneath the earth (cf. the addition to the second commandment in the decalogue, Ex. 20:4).[33] The world around Yahweh is certainly inhabited, therefore, but not in a fashion that detracts from the uniqueness of his Being and his relationship to Israel.

All this obviously meant that the cult itself would undergo an entirely new development. Here again we see the same process of attraction and repulsion at work, even if it did not happen everywhere in precisely the same way. In some centres the contrast predominated, in others the assimilation. In places where the Yahwistic cult had been newly instituted the worship of Yahweh was a sober affair and conformed to the regulations which had prevailed in the desert. In other places on the other hand, where the old tribes had already formed a connexion with this or that temple in the patriarchal period, many of the ancient ceremonies already adopted were maintained, or people continued to take up with other rites. For this reason there was from the beginning a diversity of cultic institutions among the tribes of Israel; and this became a source of tension and contradictions which persisted right into the latest period.

We may regard the so-called cultic decalogue as the oldest cultic legislation within the period after the Yahwistic religion had begun to take effect (Ex. 34; 20:23; 23:12–23; see p. 147).[34] These laws were given with an agrarian community in view, as one can see from the way the festal seasons were distributed (Ex. 34:18, 21–23- and 23:14–17) so that they occurred at three points in the year. They comprised a double spring-festival at the beginning and end of the corn harvest and an autumn festival at the close of the fruit-gathering season. Each feast involved a donation to the sanctuary (the firstfruits). A few other laws related to ritual: leavened bread was not to be brought together with an animal sacrifice, the sacrificial fat was not to be left overnight and a kid was not to be boiled in its mother's milk (see p. 149, note 81). Such rules were probably intended to oppose or counteract sacrificial practices among the Canaanites. This negative spirit is most powerfully evident in the primary commandments, which must be taken to include those injunctions that forbid the Israelites to have gods of gold or silver (or, in general, gods cast in any mould) 'beside Yahweh'; see Exodus 20:23 and its parallels: Exodus 34:14 and 27 (see p. 147f.).

We cannot be sure whether the commandment concerning altars (Exodus 20:24 and 34:13) is really part of this series. Perhaps it stood on its own. In Exodus 34 it no longer appears as a separate, positive injunction, as it does in Exodus 20:24. The most primitive formulation of it evidently required an altar of earth; but alongside this in the text as we now have it altars of unhewn stone are at any rate permitted. Any fashioning of the stones with a chisel would desecrate them. What the background is to this idea we cannot be sure. The fact that in the service of Yahweh only earth or rough stone, a natural product, was to be used apparently enshrines a basic determination to oppose the use, in a cultic context, of everything that had been fabricated or in any way worked upon by an artificer, in order to ensure that nothing would appear on an altar which might be suggestive of a divine symbol.

A similar attitude of total reaction is apparent from a command which in the text of Exodus 20 is directly associated with this: namely, that no steps are to be built up to an altar, 'that your shame be not visible thereon'. Opposition to the sexual aspects of the Canaanite religion was carried to such lengths that in the religion of Israel everything that could so much as prompt a thought of sex was banished from the cult.

Such laws more than amply illustrate how fiercely opposed to Canaanite influences the temper of Yahwism was in the very *earliest* period. That these laws do indeed date from those early times is plain enough from a comparison with the later period, when Israelite temples actually had altars with steps.[35]

Altars of earth and of unhewn stone are best envisaged as belonging to the time when agriculture was getting under way. The word 'earth' suggests life on the arable land. Blocks of stone for building an altar must have been only too plentiful there, as they are in Palestine today.

The law goes on to say that wherever Yahweh visits the people, wherever he causes his name to be spoken, such altars are to be built. Clearly, the reference here is not to already existing sanctuaries but to new holy places that were set up after Yahweh had given proof of his presence there. Thus there must have existed in early Israel various holy places of an unsuspected Yahwistic origin; and so there were further instances of revelations being received from Yahweh. That much, indeed, is clear from the stories of the judges. People would then honour Yahweh by building him an altar on which sacrificial victims would be burnt or shared offerings made, leading on to a communal meal. From this (cf. again Judges 6 and 13) we may fairly conclude that the altar was the earliest focus of the cult of Yahwism. This should teach us to use caution in reconstructing the cult of Israel. We ought not to attach too much importance to the temple worship in the early Yahwistic period, and certainly should not postulate an essential connexion between Yahweh-revelation and temple-cult. On the contrary, he can, and does, reveal himself where he will.

Thus the cultic decalogue provides a classic example of the way in which Yahwism conducted itself in the agrarian territory. On the one hand, it adapted itself completely to the new circumstances; on the other, it took a fundamental stand against Canaanite religious influences. In the cultic sphere Yahwism would seem to have gone its own way entirely, so conserving the sobriety of the desert period and at the same time suiting its formal worship to the new conditions of life.

Although in the original form of Yahwism there was at first no question of temples, and though Yahweh was more often worshipped at an altar in the open, where it was still possible for anyone to organize sacrifices and sacrificial feasts, a number of fixed sanctuaries soon came into use. We can attribute that to the influence of the rest of the tribes who had settled in the country earlier on. They had already established a connexion with certain temples and had probably built their own sanctuaries, conforming pretty much in that respect to the forms of religious life found in Canaan. At all events, there is already some reference in the cultic decalogue to the house of Yahweh (Ex. 23:19; 34:26).

We really know nothing about how the Israelite temples were built and appointed. Only with regard to Solomon's temple has enough information been handed down to give us a rough idea of what it was like (Chapter 7).[36] One thing, of course, is certain: that as with the Canaanites, so here we have to distinguish between urban temples with their subsidiary buildings and the 'high places' scattered around the countryside, which were much simpler and often consisted chiefly of a consecrated space with a sacred tree and/or spring. It is unlikely that prior to the period of the monarchy the Israelites had any temple buildings of their own, comparable with those of the Canaanites. Some of the latter we know, because they have been excavated. One thinks here specifically of Shechem, Lachish, Megiddo, Hazor, Beth-Shan and Tirzah—and beyond Israel's borders in particular of

Byblos. At these places different types of temple would appear to have alternated with one another; and from that we can infer that a very ancient tradition of temple-building already existed among the Canaanites.

In Israel, however, there were hardly any cities before David's time. Only in the era of David and Solomon was any determined effort made to construct walled cities; and we can assume that as regards the building of sanctuaries it was the same.

How far the tribes, once they were committed to Yahweh, proceeded to utilize Canaanite sanctuaries it is difficult to say. The practice may have been relatively sporadic and confined mainly to those instances where the use of such holy places was hallowed by patriarchal tradition. It would seem, however, from a story like that of Baal Pe'or (Num. 25) that even sanctuaries which were encountered later excited the Israelites' interest.

The story told in Judges 17f. gives us a glimpse of religious life beyond the Yahwistic centres, showing how people sought to obtain Yahweh's blessing by making private cultic arrangements of their own. Although this story presents certain problems from a critical-cum-literary standpoint,[37] we can regard it as being in the main a unity and as of considerable historical value. It offers a remarkable picture of clan religion in the mountain fastnesses of Ephraim during the period before the kings. The story is told in what may be termed a legend about the founding of the sanctuary at Dan, even though it has been marred by the addition of various elements disparaging to Dan, which are the work of some critical editor of a later time.[38] What we in fact have here is a double sanctuary-legend: first, one about the founding of a chapel by the Ephraimite, Micah, for which a costly ephod and teraphim had been purchased, and then, conjoined with that, one about the founding of the chapel in Dan. The ephod in this case, as in Judges 8:27, was probably an article of 'divine' apparel (cf. p. 91, note 20), taking the place of the divine image[39] and symbolizing the deity. It would have been kept in a consecrated place. With the ephod there went the teraphim which was probably a mask (cf. p. 120) serving to enable the priest to obtain the oracle from the god who was present in the ephod-symbol. These two cultic objects belong together, therefore. When Micah took into his service a Levite, to whom was allotted this special oracular function, he was assured of Yahweh's help. With a Levite at one's service success is assured. By giving out oracles he can deter one from misguided ventures and pass on directions from the god. When Danites, on their way to reconnoitre in the North, enter Micah's sanctuary in order to consult the oracle, they get a favourable reply. On their later journey of conquest they succeed in persuading the Levite to go with them and to take along the sacred objects. With these a sanctuary is set up in Dan, with the Levite in charge. The Danites claim for this Levite the distinction of being a descendant of Moses. He is himself held to be the ancestor of the priesthood there, which served the tribe right up to the captivity of Northern Israel (734), although under Jeroboam I the worship in this temple altered, of course, in character (the calf-worship was then introduced) and importance (it became a state sanctuary). Jeroboam's decision and arrangement hastened still further the process of assimilation.

The story shows that each tribe (or part of one) could apparently set up its own sanctuary. There Yahweh would be venerated; and Levites were in demand as priests, because they were regarded as descendants of Moses. Even at this early period the Levites had spread throughout the country. Although the man in this story is said to be 'of the the family of Judah', he can still be a Levite, which established that being a Levite at that early period denoted a particular religious status. The chief cultic elements at the sanctuary are ephod and teraphim; so that as in the later Davidic history, here too the provision of oracles seems to have been the most typical activity of the priesthood (see p. 89f.). Naturally enough, at sanctuaries for a larger community a place for sacrifices, and thus an altar, would certainly have been provided.

In this connexion we have to reckon, anyway, with four kinds of holy place:

(a) The private house-chapels (or small, independent chapels). Besides the account given of Micah, the story of Gideon also gives us reason to suppose that these existed (Judges 6:25ff.). Just as Micah's chapel may be put to public use, so may that of Gideon in Ophrah. The fact that David's house has a teraphim (1 Sam. 19) raises the question whether every family did not perhaps possess a small domestic chapel of its own, even if there were not always a god or a priest in it. They may have existed ever since patriarchal times (Gen. 31) and have been kept going in the Yahwistic period. Yahweh's name was associated with Micah's inquiring of the oracle. The teraphim was a general phenomenon in the ancient East, as we can see from the patriarchal narratives; but the ephod was a cultic object borrowed, apparently, from the Canaanite world. A Yahweh-chapel like Micah's seems therefore to be a typical instance of syncretism. The account of this adventure would appear to show that under certain conditions the transition was easily made from a purely private cultic institution to one of a semi-public, and then of an official, character.

(b) The ancient temple-sanctuaries of El, which had been accepted already in the patriarchal age and which Israel evidently shared with the Canaanites. Among them were Shechem, Bethel, Hebron, Beersheba, Mahanaim (Peniel). From the earliest period right up to the time of the conquest of Jerusalem they were in constant use; and for all Israelites until the deuteronomic reform (which declared the temple in Jerusalem to be the only legitimate sanctuary) they were authorized centres of cultic worship, even if there were often a good deal of criticism of the cultic practices carried on in them.

(c) The ancient open sanctuaries of the countryside, the high places, the *bamoth*. They were to be found on hill and mountain tops, and among the Canaanites must have been a feature of many, if not all, of their towns and villages. Their typical features were sacred trees, springs and stones (the stones were later given a special cultic style as 'erected stones' (*masseboth*) and the trees as 'sacred poles' (*'asherim*), symbolizing respectively the male and the female deity). We can well imagine that all this offered the possibility of making sacrifices on an altar. The criticism voiced later on by the prophets makes it clear that to an increasing extent Israel adopted the habit of using such high places from the Canaanites. The process must have been in full swing by the time of the judges and may even be of an earlier date, as far back as the patriarchal period. Yahwism was obviously unable to put a stop to it, despite the special connexion which the *bamoth* and their symbols had with the cult of Baal. The *'asherah*, which represented the female deity, Astarte, was one of the most compelling reasons why things developed as they did.

On the other hand, it is not impossible that at some of these high places the cult practised conformed much more closely to Yahwism. This we can assume, for example, in the case of the sanctuary at Nob (see p. 84f.), which was put to use by the Israelite priests from the former Yahweh sanctuary at Shiloh—and likewise of the holy place on Tabor, the mountain top on the plain of Jezreel, where there had once been a very ancient Canaanite cultic centre which the tribes thereabouts had already begun to use, probably, in the time of Deborah and Barak (Judges 4:6, 12ff.; Deut. 33:19; Hos. 5:1). Some commentators associate Psalm 68 with this place.[40]

(d) Finally, there were the Yahwistic sanctuaries, either set up by the Israelites when they founded a new settlement, of which Gilgal is a case in point, or else established on the ruins of a former Canaanite town, as at Shiloh and possibly Nob. Shiloh, where Eli and his sons discharged their priestly office, was probably devastated before the period of the monarchy by the Philistines. To judge from the critical attitude of the prophets, Gilgal too was much affected by Canaanite traditions (Amos 4:4; Hos. 9:15).

The holy places grew more and more influential. They were the centres not only of cult, but of law and justice; for here the *torah* (divine oracle, often indicating what had to be done) was dispensed and the tradition gathered together. To them would come the neighbouring tribes, tribal groups or families to keep the three great agricultural festivals, bring in the firstfruits and offer sacrifices. In later times, at least, there were rooms set aside for sacrificial meals (1 Sam. 9:12f., 22), where particular groups would come together. Naturally enough, the major temples especially became centres of cultural and religious life. Here armies would assemble before going into battle, and the people gather to elect a king (1 Sam. 11:13). Through this combination of cult and politico-social life the sanctuary acquired enormous influence; and in that the holy places had conserved or taken over many of the ancient traditions of Canaan, a considerable, if often unnoticed, adaptation of Yahwism to Canaanite culture and religion was thus facilitated. No wonder, then, that Yahwism strove, with the support of stringent cultic laws, to maintain as much as it could of its distinctive character.

For service in the temple there were various ministers: priests for ministering especially at the altar, Levites more for the imparting of oracles. Even prophets (for whom see Chapter 8) would for the most part have set up at the temples and formed close ties with them.

All this suggests, on the basis of the available evidence which is positive enough, that the temples did not all have precisely the same function, although the foremost of them must have had special facilities for every cultic purpose. It is very likely, however, that some sanctuaries were used more for pilgrimages, mourning ceremonies or in case of sickness, whilst others would be celebrated for the giving of oracles, administration of justice, and so forth.

Lastly, a word or so about a group who were not directly included

M

among the temple-ministers: the Nazirites. Nazirites[41] were men consecrated to Yahweh. They are most familiar to us from the period of the judges and the stories of Samson and Samuel. In Amos 2:11f. they are mentioned side by side with the prophets and, like them, were evidently regarded as charismatic figures (cf. Judges 13:25; 14:6, 19; 15:14), even if in their case the working of the spirit showed itself more in deeds of warlike prowess and the impulse to liberate and deliver than in uttering the divine word. Although the origins of the Nazirate are obscure, it is highly possible that it emerged during the period of the judges, when men had to fight time and time again for their very existence as a people. They were solemnly 'devoted', but devoted first and foremost to the skills of the warrior and to the pursuit of holy war. They had to let their hair grow (cf. also Judges 5:1) and abstain from wine, which indicates that they were of an essentially anti-Canaanite mind and purpose. A man could be consecrated a Nazirite by the elders (Samson and Samuel) or could make a vow for himself (and for a shorter period). The institution remained in existence until the latest period and was subject to very precise official regulations (Num. 6). It seems that the Nazirites possessed a high degree of holiness; for like the high priests they were forbidden, in the later law, to touch a dead person, even the closest blood-relative. One may wonder whether the Nazirate is perhaps a rank or an order which ought to be understood as somewhat akin to that of the primitive Levites as Moses' nearest helpers (see p. 163), but as having arisen in a later period (the time of the judges). If so, they must have taken over the Levites' original function, as these became more and more drawn into the institutionalized sector of cultic life. Once the kingship had been introduced, the Nazirate lost its original significance as a charismatic order of warriors, because permanent mercenary forces and a military command were formed. Thus its character was changed and its value restricted to the personal sphere.

CHAPTER 7

New Forms of Life, State and Religion

As in the realm of history proper, so in that of the history of religion, with the arrival of the kingship a new age begins to dawn for Israel. Thus it is that the Davidic dynasty can be held to have introduced the second major period of Yahwism. The reign of Saul was too unstable and too brief for us to make much capital out of it from a historico-religious standpoint. Even David's time cannot be said to have decided the issue in this respect. Rather, it is a moment of transition between one era and another. The new forms of government begin to make their mark, without as yet bringing about any profound changes in the pattern of life. There are cities built, for example; and various forms of organization develop in the wake of the growing unity of the state. Yet none of these has any immediate consequence in the religious or spiritual sphere. Religious life goes on in the old ways. An internationalizing process, religious influences from abroad, a royal temple-cult—none of these as yet comes into the picture. They do so only later—only *after* David, who certainly brought the kingship to its zenith, but even so was not responsible for any radical structural and spiritual modifications in the life of the nation. No doubt he prepared the ground for them; but it was only after his time that they became really effective. David's position as king was based on his personal qualities as a leader, and amounted to little more than the rule of a judge, although of a permanent kind. It had not so far reached the stage of being what the ancient East understood by an absolute monarchy.

With Solomon things were different. One can barely conceive what a sudden change took place in Israel under his administration. Within a generation semi-nomadic and agrarian Israelites became the citizens of a powerful modern state. Yet more cities were constructed. Jerusalem became a real capital city, with resplendent buildings and strong walls. Towns like Hazor, Megiddo, Gezer (which are specifically mentioned in 1 Kings 9:15, and which all, when excavated,

proved to have their Solomonic gates still in a fair state of preservation) were expanded into great fortresses. But besides these there
were certainly others, restored from a condition of ruin or raised on
virgin soil. So rapid was the progress made that in 701 Sennacherib,
referring to Judah alone, could speak of forty-six walled cities and
innumerable villages round about. Urban civilization unfolded and
exhibited its own distinctive culture, which adopted many customs
and ideas from the Canaanites and from further afield. The kingship
brought in its train not only a royal household but a good many
officials also. To meet the demands of the time a military machine was
built up, with horses and chariots and a standing army. There was a
joint venture in gold-mining and a system for regulating taxation.
Industry and commerce (including foreign trade) expanded. Science
and art made swift headway. In fact the word 'explosion' better
describes this rapid upsurge of culture than 'development'. One can
only stand amazed at the forward-looking mentality of Solomon,
who must have had an enormous interest in, and concern for, matters
cultural and economic and who, as an enlightened despot, superin-
tended the development of it all. Yet we must also be amazed at the
capacity of the people of Israel to adapt themselves, even if there were
many circles that could have felt none of the effects of all this, except
as something alien to their outlook and experience. These were people
of the countryside, the desert areas, and partly even of the city too. In
this brief heyday, which came to a head in a matter of a few decades,
the spiritual and intellectual life of Israel was greatly enriched, and its
cultural life also, in the spheres of art and speculative thought.
Thrown now into contact with the international scene, Israel was
fetched out of her isolation. On her religion the effect was revolutionary. She became acquainted with the wisdom literature and so
learned to appreciate the element of a common humanity and the
heritage of humane and universal thought. Yahweh was at last seen
as the Lord of all mankind. The old Yahwist author can envisage him
as God from the beginning, from before Israel existed. On the model
of the Jebusite El-Elyon theology, the creation-idea is likewise taken
up into the pattern of belief about Yahweh, so that the universe is
thought of as depending on him. He becomes the God of wisdom and
providence. A view of life and the world such as the Yahwist (J,
writing at about 900) evinces would be out of the question, apart from
this development. Authors like the one responsible for the Saul-
David-Solomon story—and the Yahwist—would be unthinkable

without the influence of the wisdom literature.[1] The humane and universal strands which were the product of Israel's encounter with the great world of culture are an enormous good and a great gain.

The monarchy grew along with the state and became the predominant centre and focus of it. It was absolutized by means of various traditions and ceremonies taken from the Canaanites, Egyptians and Phoenicians; and it was given an aura of religion. Jebusite traditions, especially, were at work here. Without going along with the theory propounded by those who believe that the kingship in Israel was thought to be divine,[2] we can see clearly enough that the notions of kingship prevailing in the Canaanite cities and in neighbouring states, where the king was regarded either as a divine figure (Egypt) or as a substitute for the deity (Babylon), had a profound influence on the monarchal system which the Israelites took over from those nations. Psalms 2 and 110[3] are incontrovertible witness to the conviction in Israel that on his accession the king was adopted as a son of God (Psalm 2:7). This is what made him, as Psalm 110 says, the priest *par excellence*. The Jebusite rite of Melchizedek (cf. Gen. 14) provided the foundation for this idea. By his anointing the king was consecrated to this sonship of God, which made him the servant-in-chief of Yahweh (he sat at the right hand of Yahweh; Psalms 110:1, 4). In battle he could be assured of God's strength. All enemies are 'made his footstool' (Psalms 2:8f., 10f.; 110:1, 5ff.). Again, he is the great dispenser of justice, rescuing the poor and bringing peace and prosperity (Psalm 72)—which is what the ancient East in general sees as the ideal (prologue and epilogue to the Code of Hammurabi). Consequently he is the true judge; and anyone may appeal to him. As adjudicator in obscure and difficult cases he has the wisdom of an angel, as the woman of Tekoa says to David (2 Sam. 14) and as is evident from the incidents related in the life of Solomon (1 Kings 3). Furthermore, he is the great sage (1 Kings 4:29; 10). He it is who brings rest, peace and blessing upon the land. The wellbeing of the economy and of the soil derives from him (Psalm 72). Thus the anointed king can even be described as the vital breath of his people (Lam. 4:20). One comes across such ideas outside the Bible too. They show that the kingship was generally regarded as a divine office, although in Israel (and here the peculiar Israelite-Yahwistic element comes out) the bearer of that office is himself never divinized in the sense of receiving the honours due to a god. The king's person was not sacrosanct, but remained subject to the law of Yahweh and so to the criticism of the men of God, the prophets. In certain instances he is still chosen by the people. This limitation of authority applied also to the state. The state as such was not sacralized; nor was it considered to have been instituted by God 'from the creation of the world'. Yahweh did not identify himself with it and therefore, as we remarked earlier, was never called God of Jerusalem.

Despite these qualifications it is nonetheless clear that when the kingship was instituted an entirely new element entered the life of the nation: one infused with enough authority to bring about the unity of the tribes and so, acting as a catalyst, calculated to enhance enormously the whole process of their development.

The significance which the king acquired as intermediary between Yahweh and Israel comes out again in the cultic functions which he discharged. We saw earlier on (in Chapter 3) that the king as the representative of the nation made sacrifices to God. But his cultic function went further than that; for he also acted as God's representative with the people, as an ordained priest (Psalm 110:4). The king came to be, in principle, the high priest of the state.[4] Not only did he have the temple built; he also carried out all the ceremonies at its opening (1 Kings 8:5, 14, 22, 54ff.). The one thing he never did was to give the *torah*, the divine directives. As the state came to govern every aspect of life, the king's religious function grew to be very important.

In the rapidly changing world of the time the need soon arose for a temple, a royal, one might better say, a state sanctuary (kingship and state in fact coincide here). This Solomon therefore proceeded to set up in Jerusalem, fairly soon after his accession, in the fourth year of his reign, although it took seven years for the building to be completed. The later historian who came from deuteronomic circles described this fourth year as the 480th year after the exodus from Egypt. Thus he regarded it as a quite extraordinary date (12×40 years after the deliverance) and as the start of a new era.

It is a remarkable thing that Solomon was able to found the temple without the least further scruple being voiced. When we compare that with the situation in David's time (2 Sam. 7), it becomes clear that the passage of a generation had left behind it a very different state of affairs. The wishes of the now absolute monarch were final, in religious as in other matters. We can be sure that there were still scruples enough in certain circles, but they no longer had opportunity to make their objections heard. One can see, however, from the way things went afterwards (the later emergence of the Rechabites), that there must have been continued resistance, underground, to these changes in the pattern of the nation's life.

Through the building of the temple Jerusalem became the religious as well as the political centre of things. David had laid the ground for this when he brought in the ark; but only now was his action fully 'honoured in the observance'. The founding of the temple did not mean the abolition of the other ancient sanctuaries, which continued just the same. Numerically speaking, it meant simply that one more sanctuary was added to the rest. But in fact a completely new situation had been created in Israel. This temple was potentially able to outstrip all others, because it bore the title 'royal'. It would one day thrust every other temple aside; but three centuries were to elapse before that actually happened.

It was not very long before people in the capital city of Jerusalem began to see their temple in a quite special light. The high hill on which it had been set up, now known as Zion, was not merely regarded as holy but also as a place to be compared with the divine mountain of old-Canaanite mythology, in the far North. The author of Psalm 48 extends this honour also to the city of Jerusalem. It is described as the incomparable city, the city of God, the dwelling-place of Yahweh, Lord of hosts. Part of the explanation for this idea of exclusiveness (the full impact of which was not felt, apparently, till after the partitioning of the kingdom; see verse 11) must be the stresses and strains that developed between Israel and Judah and between the temples outside Jerusalem, primarily those in the North (Shechem and Bethel), and that of the city itself. More especially after the breach between the two kingdoms Jerusalem bolstered its position by claiming a unique, indeed absolute, status for its temple. The royal sanctuary, which despite its youth could, after all, produce the most ancient credentials (the ark), became for many people, and for the Jerusalem priestly circles in particular, the sanctuary of Yahweh *kat' exochen*. Naturally enough, this was a standpoint fiercely contested by the other sanctuaries in both North and South. It is even questionable whether in this uncompromising form it was shared by every loyally Yahwistic Israelite in Judah and Jerusalem themselves. We may infer from the utterances of the prophets Micah and Isaiah that they, at any rate, did not take this view.[5]

As regards the temple and its construction we are provided with quite detailed information in 1 Kings 6 and 8 and in Ezekiel 40ff.; and now that excavation has brought to light a number of important data which are valuable for making structural comparisons, we can form a fairly good idea of what the sanctuary was like.[6]

It was raised on the hill to the north of the old city of David (Jebus), where Solomon's palace was also erected. As a shrine, it gave a powerful impression of Israel's ideas. It was a building of about 30 metres in length, 15 metres high and 10 broad (the size, in other words, of a small village church), divided up into three apartments: an entrance-hall or vestibule, the holy place and the holy of holies. This last room was cuboid (10 metres along each side) and was situated (as was the case also with Syrian temples of a much later date) higher up than the holy place, so that it could be reached only by a flight of stairs. Inside it was the ark, flanked by two mighty figures of cherubim. Within the holy place stood an altar of incense, a table with showbread on it and, on either side, five candle-sticks with seven branches. In the forecourt were the altar of sacrifice, the bronze sea (as a cosmic symbol) and ten 'lavers' to hold the water needed for purifying the priests. At the entrance to the temple there towered two pillars, known as Jachin and Boaz. Albright considers them to have been great candelabras; but Galling is surely right in regarding them as *maṣṣeboth* to mark the entrance to the temple, like those discovered in the course of excavations at Shechem. Their function, apparently, was wholly ornamental; and in all probability they were put there only because they were a customary feature of a temple in the ancient East. In point of fact, the Book of Kings makes it clear that the temple was built with the assistance of Phoenicians; and excavation has revealed that an architectural style of the same type was current in Northern Syria (Phoenicia). One temple, at any rate, has been found there, in Tainat, with the same tripartite structure, although it is of a somewhat later date (9th century). The lavish ornamentation of the temple walls with cherubim figures and palms again points to the activity of foreign architects.

This temple was reckoned to be the house of Yahweh, where he dwelt amid his people, although the deuteronomic theology of a later time was more cautious with its terms of expression, declaring that Yahweh had caused his *name* to dwell there. In this way the tension between, on the one hand, the temple and the heavens as Yahwe's 'locale' and, on the other, Sinai as his dwelling-place, was overcome. It was now stipulated that Yahweh was indeed there but that in his person he far transcended the temple.

We know little about the priestly and sacrificial ministry in the temple. At the beginning of Solomon's reign, after Abiathar's banishment, Zadok became head of the priestly college. He was possibly an offshoot of the Jebusite priesthood (see p. 91). Then again, one of Nathan's sons is mentioned in a priestly capacity (1 Kings 4:5). Certain princes too must have acquired priestly functions (2 Sam. 8:18). As the laws on sacrifice date, in the form in which we now have them, from the time of the second temple, we cannot go into them here. It is likely that as in the earlier period (see p. 149) burnt-offerings and peace-offerings were the principal kinds of sacrifice, the other special task of the priests was to attend to the oracle-ministry (for instance, in time of war for victory; Psalm 20f.), that they assisted in drafting laws, said prayers for the sick and in cases of recovery, carried out purificatory rites, and so on. It must surely have meant, as it did elsewhere in the ancient East, that the priests were the custodians of contracts, that in principle the sciences and medicine, as well as the stock of common lore and education, were their responsibility. That is why the temples required so many annexes. Certain functions were gradually detached from the priesthood, among them that of the wise man and perhaps also of the medical practitioner.

The priests, certainly with a high priest at their head, were aided by various functionaries. Guilds of singers were formed, according to the Book of Chronicles, by David. In Solomon's temple, at any rate, there would have been temple servants, Levites, responsible for the songs (psalms) and the music. Amos ascribes to David the invention of new musical instruments (Amos 6:5); and we may surely concur with the tradition in crediting David with the composition of psalms (cf., for example, his celebrated elegy in 2 Sam. 1).

One thing in particular, the pursuit of various forms of knowledge, gave opportunity for men to familiarize themselves with the skills and the wisdom of other lands; and to judge from the wide range of Egyptian influences that can be demonstrated on the basis of literary evidence, the Israelites seized it with enthusiasm. The result was that before long city life in Solomon's day had become a very different affair from the simple ways of primitive Yahwism. The most questionable outcome of this, so far as Yahwism is concerned, was that because of his political relations and his espousal of so many foreign princesses the king was obliged to make all sorts of concessions to the religions which these ladies brought with them from home. Solomon apparently made no bones about establishing, outside Jerusalem, various shrines and sanctuaries for other gods, for the benefit of these foreign women (1 Kings 11:6ff.; cf. 2 Kings 23:13). There was yet another reason for Solomon's policy of toleration: the fact that numerous towns in Canaan and in territories outside Palestine had contrived to get themselves annexed to the state of Israel. These would have gone on practising their own religions; so that Israel in fact became a 'pluralistic' state, even if Yahwism was still the only religion officially recognized. Thus, because she had developed in the political sphere with such incredible speed, Israel's religious structure suddenly became extraordinarily complex. With the arrival of the kingship, therefore, came a complete change not only in the social structure of the nation (the building of towns, political and military organization, a class of officials, industry, trade, economic life, social modifications) but in the religious structure too. For the second time Yahwism was tried in the fire. It will appear what a big, even if not totally decisive, influence the kingship exercised on the further development of, religious life.

After Solomon there began the second phase of the period now under discussion. A new turn of events was precipitated when the kingdom was split up and the North broke away from Judah and Jerusalem. Internally, three forces were at work which to some extent assisted one another: the will of the North, under the leadership of Shechem, to free itself from political domination by Jerusalem and Judah, the social antagonism felt by the overburdened mass of subjects in consequence of the forced labour system—a hostility fostered by the man in charge of the corvée, Jeroboam—and the critical attitude in prophetic circles, who, with Ahijah as their mouthpiece, attacked the social and religious measures adopted by Solomon.

After the breach between them the two small kingdoms of Israel and Judah were extremely weak. All the annexed territories had broken away, even the Philistine towns and the minor states beyond the Jordan. For the history of religion the rift had important consequences in that it severely limited Jerusalem's sphere of influence, even though in theory (on the basis of Nathan's promise in 2 Sam. 7, which had signalized the house of David as a dynasty enjoying Yahweh's protection in perpetuity) it persisted with its claim to be the national capital and the holy city. Above all, Jeroboam I promoted as a counter-move two ancient shrines in the North to the rank of state sanctuaries: Bethel on the southern frontier, and Dan on the northern. Still more relevant in this respect was the fact that he put the image of a bull in these temples as a symbol of Yahweh[7] (1 Kings 12:28), thereby giving a powerful fillip to syncretism.

Taking into consideration all the arguments for and against the view that the bull was a Yahweh-symbol, I believe that in virtue of the text just cited (which, as in Ex. 32:8, is best rendered as: 'This is your God, who led you out of Egypt') we are forced to conclude that Jeroboam did indeed erect the bull-figure as a symbol of Yahweh, although we are certainly not entitled to speak here of a Yahweh image, as Yahweh was envisaged anthropomorphically. The bull-figure, which must have represented Yahweh, could be used by Jeroboam the more readily because it enabled him to find a link withthe pre-Yahwistic religion of the patriarchs, which in the '*abbir Ya'aqob* probably also had something that stood for a bull as symbol of the god of Jacob (see pp. 115, 129, 123). Thus it is not strange that this figure should be set up in Bethel, which was, after all, the holy city of Jacob. Jerusalem could boast of possessing the ark, the desert-sanctuary itself, in its temple. Nevertheless by doing what he did Jeroboam I had resorted to a symbol more ancient than anything Jerusalem could show, and by using this symbol from the patriarchal age, which was the oldest to be found among the tribes of Israel, he set out to make the cult of Yahweh in Bethel more venerable than the one at Jerusalem; for he too was a devoted champion of the cult (witness the fact that he was designated by a prophet from Shiloh, 1 Kings 11; and that his son was named Abijah, 1 Kings 14). Now the bull was not only a symbol for Baal, but for a great number and variety of gods.[8] The '*abbir Ya'aqob* which was revered among the tribes of early Israel in Bethel was in origin probably an El-symbol. Indeed, El was constantly referred to as a bull in the Ugaritic world (see p. 120, note 52); but in the West Semitic area, on the other hand, it was usually the storm and fertility god who was envisaged in this way. It is highly possible, therefore, that in the later period the bull served especially as a Baal symbol.[9]

Thus, in a period when Baalism was finding new opportunities of one sort or another this bull symbol helped increasingly to obliterate the distinction between Yahweh and Baal. From the terms of Jeroboam's inaugural declaration it looks as though that was not what he intended. He wanted his people to hold to Yahweh, the deliverer-God, who had rescued them from Egypt; but because things took the course they did, Jeroboam's experiment evolved in the direction of a Yahweh-Baal syncretism.

The bull was introduced in Dan as well as in Bethel; and as a symbol it spread even more widely in the North. According to Hos. 8:4ff. (cf. 13:2) this form of cult later appeared in Samaria too;[10] and that is likely enough, when we remember that Samaria was a royal city and that it was precisely the royal (state) temples in the North that were the typical centres of the cult. Sacrifices were offered to this bull; and it was kissed as a divine symbol (Hos. 13:2).

There was an immediate outburst of protest at this cult, as we can see from the stories in 1 Kings 13f., where we read, among other things, that a curse was pronounced upon the altar at Bethel (13:2) which went echoing down the centuries (2 Kings 23:15ff.). From the prophetic side, therefore, opposition started to come at once. We may suppose that Northern Israelites who were loyal to Yahweh continued to recognize Jerusalem as a centre of pilgrimage; although some would perhaps still have carried on the cult for a long time in Gilgal or elsewhere, until syncretism got the upper hand there as well (cf. Amos 5:4; Hos. 4:15; 9:15; 12:12). The deuteronomist who put together the Book of Kings used a stereotyped expression for the cultic measures taken by Jeroboam: 'the sins of Jeroboam'—sometimes called 'the way of Jeroboam'. The same man distinguishes sharply between the calf-worship and that conducted at the high places—which he also condemns, after the founding of the temple at Jerusalem. Still, he takes unusually strong exception to the former and to all who support it, threatening them repeatedly with the direst judgment and destruction. However we choose to explain this cult, for the people of Jeroboam's time it could only have been an experience steeped in syncretism. The religious policy of this king, therefore, left the door wide open for a movement calculated to reconcile the Yahweh-cult with the religion of Baal. That is clear enough from what has come to light at Yeb-Syene in Egypt regarding the religious ideas of the descendants of the Bethel-cult community there. The cult had become a pure mixture of Yahwism and Baalism (see p. 261).

Jeroboam's action is yet another illustration of the fact that the kingship profoundly affected the course of religion and its development in Israel. That is plain also from subsequent events. Even if they did not have the last word, through their religious policies the kings very largely determined what influences were to be effective in the national life; for by their decisions they exercised not only a direct but an indirect influence. The latter led in a direction contrary to what

NEW FORMS OF LIFE, STATE AND RELIGION 189

they intended, because they were perpetually arousing antagonism in strictly Yahwistic circles.

This comes out very clearly indeed during the reign of Ahab. This prince of the house of Omri was married to a Tyrian princess, Jezebel, who made a strong bid to propagate the religion of Baal in Israel. As A. Alt has shown,[11] the position would seem to be that just as Jerusalem was 'David's city', so Omri's newly founded capital, Samaria, is to be regarded as in every sense 'the king's city', and the Baal-cult was able to develop there to the full (cf. 2 Kings 10). In the remainder of Israel that was not the case, since the state sanctuaries, as well as the rest, continued to develop along their own lines. Officially, they were and remained Yahwistic sanctuaries. Even king Ahab gave his children theophorous names, in which the name of Yahweh appeared. Jezebel, however, tried her hardest to make a way in for the Baal-cult, as is witnessed by the fact that even on Mount Carmel a further place of sacrifice to Baal was set up.[12]

Such was the resistance to this policy which Jezebel was prosecuting and which Ahab did nothing to oppose, that in consequence Yahweh's own prophets suffered a number of persecutions (1 Kings 18:13f.). This led eventually to a fierce conflict, the issue of which was decided by a contest on Mount Carmel, when Yahweh revealed himself as the living God (1 Kings 18).[13] The man who assumed leadership of the resistance was a herdsman from Transjordan, Elijah,[14] who travelled the country as a prophet and directed his public utterances against Ahab and his house. Elijah attacked the gross breach of justice and law which the king had winked at when Jezebel, the Phoenician princess who was evidently accustomed to a completely authoritarian type of monarchy, encroached upon the personal rights of Naboth, a farmer of Jezreel, and because the man refused to entertain her demands, caused him to be unlawfully put to death (1 Kings 21). Elijah announced the downfall of the house of Ahab; and after the victory by contest on Carmel, he saw to it that the old, harsh laws against idolatry, which had been operative in Israel from ancient times, were applied to the priests of Baal.[15] Galling rightly stresses the point that in this respect Elijah and his disciples turn out to constitute a link connecting the earlier laws of the Yahweh-amphictyony (Ex. 22:20)[16] with the later requirements of the Book of Deuteronomy (Deut. 13).

In this situation it is only natural that Elijah, whose name reflects his own programme of affirming that Yahweh is God, and who according to the tradition formulated Israel's most primitive creed in the words: Yahweh, he is God (1 Kings 18:39), should have been so greatly threatened by Jezebel that he was obliged to flee the country. Through the medium of another prophet, Elisha, who received his instructions from Elijah, he was apparently still able to exert a fair amount of influence (1 Kings 19:15ff.); but his public role within the country itself was at an end. He made his withdrawal by fleeing to Horeb, where tradition accords him a revelation which set the Yahweh-revelation in an entirely new light. Yahweh made himself known to Elijah not as the God of storm, earthquake and fire, but in an 'audible, rarefied stillness' (1 Kings 19:12). From then on his duty was to consist only in calling this person or that to fulfil theirs. Since this event is described as happening at Horeb, the mountain of Moses, it looks as though what is being presented here is the blue-print of a new or substitute version, now accorded to Elijah, of the Mosaic revelation. The occurrences in Exodus 19:16–19 and 20:18 are in diametrical contrast to those in 1 Kings 19. What is also remarkable is that the tradition here assigns to Elijah a revelation running clean contrary to his own behaviour, which had much more in common with the old-style Israelite Yahwism. It is difficult, therefore, to view this as genuinely typifying Elijah's line of activity, and easier to see it as a subtle form of criticism. Could it perhaps be an account, dressed up in the form of a legend, of a spiritual discovery that came his way after his flight from Jezebel and in the solitude of the desert? And could the moral of the story be that the silent battle for Yahweh, waged wherever men look to him in prayer for everything, is in the end more agreeable with Yahweh's nature and more conducive to his glory than force can ever be? Or might the story have been written by admirers of Elijah, whose only purpose was to show that the way of Elijah, the way of force, was not Yahweh's way; and could this state-ment, then, have come perhaps from the circle of loyal Yahwists (of whom the record says that there were 7000 remaining in the land) who had chosen a different way, which was one of patient waiting and of passive resistance? It is difficult to answer such questions with any certainty; but it can at least be said that for later generations the figure of Elijah was above all associated with the oracle of God and the contest by ordeal with the prophets of Baal, and not so much with the new revelation at Horeb which had been ascribed to him. On the other hand, it is clear that in prophets like Hosea (who was evidently troubled by the cruel behaviour of Jehu at Jezreel, Hos. 1:4) and

Isaiah (who appealed for quietness and confidence, Isa. 30:15) we find the same spiritual insight as is expressed in 1 Kings 19. Even without this splendid chapter, which certainly reveals the spirit of prophetic piety surrounding Elijah, he is a major religious figure. He has justly been called the forerunner of the great prophets, Amos, Isaiah and the rest. He was in fact the first major prophet under the monarchy. The Jewish tradition of later centuries was to speak of him side by side, even, with Moses, Indeed, that was already the case in Malachi 4:4f. and in the tradition of the primitive Christian church (Mark 9:6). Small wonder that he was singled out as the figure destined to usher in the messianic age.

With Elijah we stand, from a historical viewpoint, on the threshold of a new era. His creed ought not perhaps to be called in a theoretical sense monotheistic; but it sets the divinity of Yahweh so sharply over against Baal's that it does present monotheism as being, for Israel, the only right and proper thing. With Elijah comes a revival of militant Yahwism. The pugnacious spirit of earlier generations is re-awakened and with it a hostility toward false gods and toward injustice; and—last but not least—the religious revolt which he led eliminated the monarchy, at any rate in principle, as a *decisive* factor in the evolution of Israel's religion. From this moment on, the prophets resume the place in Israelite religion that is their due. Over against the rule of prince and priest imposed 'from the top', there is room once again for the voice of the individual man whom Yahweh has called. The old powers that Yahweh had released in those whom he had called through the 'enspiriting' of Moses, Deborah and Gideon were once more free to operate through this revolt against usurped authority, temporal and spiritual. The effects of their presence were felt anew in the succession of great prophets given to Israel between 750 and 500. But before this could become a reality the people of Israel were to undergo a great number of terrible and frightening experiences. This was true especially in the North, although the South too was to have its share.

The first of these was the bloody revolution made by Jehu. After that came the exhausting wars with the Syrians and the rising threat of Assyria as a great power. The further course of events on the political front, however, is something that we cannot pursue here.

So far as Jehu's insurgence is concerned, there is a connexion between Elijah's religious revolt and Jehu's bloody revolution. Prophetic circles nevertheless give every appearance of having viewed

Jehu's actions with some reserve (cf. what we said concerning 1 Kings 19; also Hos. 1:4)—despite the fact that they were behind his revolt (1 Kings 19:16; 2 Kings 9:1ff.; notice that neither Elijah nor Elisha personally anoints Jehu). Jehu's accomplice in the ruthless deeds that he committed in Samaria came from a quite different quarter: he was a Rechabite, Jonathan ben Rechab. This man had founded a socio-religious sect which was in such fierce opposition to Baalism that it would countenance only a desert way of life and eschewed absolutely everything to do with towns and agriculture. The members of the sect lived in tents, refusing to cultivate either the soil or the grape (cf. Jer. 35). Their belief was that only in this completely reactionary way could original Yahwism be put into practice. They therefore made themselves a living witness, so to speak, to the integral relationship between Yahwism and the desert period. That Jehu acted not just against king Joram of the house of Omri and his mother, Jezebel, is clear from the fact that with the aid of Jonadab (Jonathan) he caused all the priests of Baal in Samaria to be killed, destroyed the *masseboth* of Baal's temple, laid waste the whole sanctuary and installed cesspools on the site. He associated himself with the official religion, which meant that he left intact the bull-cult of Bethel and Dan (2 Kings 10:29). He wiped out the centre of the Baal religion; and the political measures designed to protect and propagate it were rescinded. Nevertheless, it went on quietly exercising an influence through the officially approved syncretism.

For politics, and even for the politics of religion, the work of the prophet Elisha, about which quite a lot of stories and legends have survived, would appear to have had little direct significance. He was an altogether different sort of figure from Elijah, and of importance more for the history of prophetism internally. He best finds a place, therefore, along with Micaiah ben Imlah, in the next chapter, where before outlining the activities of the major prophets we intend to start with a general survey of prophetism and its history.

For the first hundred years after Solomon, apart from the reign of Athaliah the daughter of Ahab and Jezebel, religious life in Judah under the guidance of the kings proceeded more or less on traditional lines. There is little that one can mention of a spectacular nature, apart from the plundering of the temple treasures by Shishak, the first Egyptian king of the 22nd dynasty (922), and the marriage contracted between a daughter of Ahab and Jezebel, Athaliah, and Joram, a son of Jehoshaphat, which had unhappy consequences for Judah. Joram evidently followed the religious policy of Ahab (2 Kings 8:18). After the death of her husband and her son, Joram's wife exterminated the whole house of David. Only one member of it escaped. This was Jehoash, who was saved by the high priest of the temple in Jerusalem and put on the throne seven years later, when Athaliah was caught unawares and killed (2 Kings 11). By a solemn deed of covenant king and people were bound to Yahweh and to each other, after which the whole cult of Baal was eliminated there as well. The story shows that at an extremely crucial moment the temple priesthood was able to intervene in the political affairs of Judah and so saved the house of David from being totally destroyed. This was in fact due particularly to the personal initiative of one of the princesses, Jehosheba, who was married to the high priest, Jehoiada. It was during Jehoash's reign that notice was given to restore the ruined temple (2 Kings 12).

Israel was seriously weakened by the wars with Syria; but after 800, during the reign of Jeroboam II, things began to improve once more. Judah also at that time enjoyed a period of recovery under king Uzziah. The economic growth which this brought in its train quickly led to a recurrence of social stresses and strains, as we can see from the preaching of the prophets in the 8th century. In the forties of that century there was added to the unrest in society further disturbance of a political kind. After 800 B.C. conditions within the West Semitic world were stabilized; but in the second half of the century a new threat arose from a quite different quarter: the East. For a long time the Assyrian kings had left the West in peace; but now, truly ravenous for land and power, they hurled themselves upon the territories of Syria and Palestine. Assyrian imperialism, threatening both Israel and Judah with destruction, had sprung to life.[17] The forces of religion alone remained steadfast and laid the ground for a new future for Israel. The period of political eclipse was also that of her religious prime. It marks the beginning of a new epoch in the history of her religion.

N

CHAPTER 8

The Great Prophets

I**T IS PERHAPS** a good thing to start with some explanatory comment on the heading to this chapter and to offer some justification for the view that the arrival on the scene of the classical prophets marks the beginning of a new era in the religion of Israel.

If this period was generally seen in the 19th century as one of the foremost, if not *the* foremost, in the whole story of Israel's religion, so that accounts of that religion very often took it as the point at which to begin, the case is altered now, and has been for a considerable number of decades. The earlier custom was to point to the classical or great prophets, or 'writing prophets', or however one may care to describe them, as the real founders of Israelite religion, in that with them the genius of Israel first began to extricate itself from the powerful clutches of the primitive or half-civilized Eastern world and to raise itself up to the heights of a rational and ethical religion. Before their time there had been a primitive folk-religion, and nothing more. This one-sided and thus erroneous view of Israel's religion, and with that, also of the prophets, is now a thing of the past.

Since those days there has been a gradual tendency, not to say a growing fashion, to regard the prophets not as the creators of Israel's religion but instead as products of it who were not distinguishable from their religious associates and contemporaries except in their individual qualities, their spiritual verve and their enthused speaking and writing.

For some, indeed, the prophets are the reactionaries of their time, great in stature, certainly, and yet very much a kind of *laudatores temporis acti*, who out of a compulsive religious motivation, if not out of sheer fanaticism, want to preserve the old *mores* (J. Pedersen).

Others again adjudge them to be, for their time, moderns, thoroughly steeped in the religion of their day with its markedly cultic orientation, but occupying a distinctive place within it, because of the tremendous stress they lay on the importance of a religio-ethical

194

attitude to life, or because they see the political situation of their country with such piercing clarity, or because they proclaim that there is no real prospect for Israel as a state and that the future alone holds the promise of good for the community of faithful Israelites.

All these understandings of the matter have some truth in them; for the prophets do look to the very foundations of Yahwism, familiar to them from ancient tradition. Then again, they are men of their time, nurtured upon the prevailing religious tradition; they are indeed impelled by a high sense of their responsibility in the political sphere; they are attuned to the need for a personal faith; and they do turn an expectant eye toward the future. But it is not possible, in their case, to isolate any one of these things from the total complex of their proclamation, which is what it is because they have received a personal call from Yahweh and because they are conscious of their responsibility for the entire nation. That is why they are at once reactionary and revolutionary, and are focused as much upon the present as the future. They are for a Yahweh-cult 'in spirit and in truth' but are averse to the sacrificial cult of the day. They address themselves to the heart while making the nation as such the goal of their message. They are opposed to political chicanery and the show of militant power, because they want to see Israel become God's peculiar people. In sorrow and anguish they pronounce judgment upon the state as they know it; but they look to the rebirth of Israel as the true theocratic state. They are men of their own time, and of early Israel too, whilst also being men of the future. Because their standpoint is one of total loyalty to God, they have something to say to every age. They led their own nation forward to a new religious awareness, exhibiting the relationship of Yahweh to his people, with all its spiritual, moral and even political implications, as something holy, unique, and enduring for ever. Religion as the service of Yahweh accepts his active role in history as his saving activity by which he delivered the nation from its servitude and bound it to himself. No service of Yahweh is 'the real thing', therefore, unless it is actualized in absolute trust and heartfelt obedience to God's will in the here and now, and unless the life of this present time is lived in the assurance of God's good grace for today and for the future, which nothing, not even total ruin, is able to take away from men.

This summary attempt to paraphrase what the prophets believed and proclaimed reveals just how much the Yahwism that they professed was given a new religious and ethical dimension through their spiritual experiences and struggles. They gave it a new profundity which made it a religion capable of embracing past, present and future, time and eternity, the life of the individual, of the nation, and indeed of many nations: a religion, therefore, that in many of its features was universal, because it bore the marks of what is common to all mankind. Of course, not all these elements are immediately evident or equally prominent; nor are they present to the same degree in each of the prophets. There is a variety of emphasis; but pretty well all of them are to be found together, when it comes to the greatest of the prophetic figures: Isaiah, Jeremiah and Deutero-Isaiah. Prophetism taken as a whole does have the general trend outlined above; and I am firmly convinced that it has to be seen as a spiritual movement, with one prophet adopting what another has said and carrying it further on his own lines.

In all this, prophetism is a perfectly legitimate interpretation of Yahwistic belief despite every contemporary contradiction. In every respect conscious of the links binding it to the old Yahwistic tradition, which it has imbibed, so to speak, with its mother's milk, it has at the same time contrived to learn from what more recent periods, like that of David and Solomon, had assimilated in the way of spiritual values (but rejecting what would not fit, or would fit no longer, into the framework of beliefs about Yahweh in its own day). Finally it has absorbed into this the experience of God and of life culled personally by each prophet in times of great and imminent danger, of bitter distress and disappointment and, above all, of shortcomings and guiltiness on the part of the nation. In the prophets' struggle Yahwism came to new life; and in their preaching it attained the highest reaches of spiritual development to which it was ever to aspire throughout the whole of ancient Israel's existence as a nation. This came about in a period of political eclipse, social uncertainty, cultural break-up and deprivation of every cultic symbol, including the temple and the ark. Between this spiritual deepening and the outward disintegration of life in all its aspects there is an undeniable connexion. The renewal comes to birth in and at a time of total disintegration, out of the vital resources and reserves of power in Yahwism or, to borrow a term from the Old Testament, of the Spirit of Yahweh alone.

It is difficult to say precisely what is old and what is new about this movement, because what is new is often only a matter of a special emphasis. There are some things that stand out clearly enough: old, of course, is the stress laid on the exclusive recognition of Yahweh, his demands, his law and righteousness, and the sure bond uniting Yahweh and nation. The more universal and humane elements are not altogether new (cf. even in J, for example; Gen. 12:3). Nevertheless the way in which they are now accentuated gives them a wholly new value for the religious life. It is the same with the prophets' strictures on the cult when this is divorced from obedience to Yahweh's will (cf. 1 Sam. 15), and also with their insistence on the heart of man as the vital core of his religious life. What is new is the universal and radical note in their proclamation of judgment. In earlier times such condemnation had been reserved for particular persons and for specific acts which they had committed (cf. Elijah's pronouncement of judgment upon the house of Ahab).[1] This is bound to go along with a deepened consciousness of sin, which sees it as seated in the will (Isaiah). New also is the theme of confident trust and faith and the exhortation to 'be still' (Isaiah), although a kindred notion is present, as we have already pointed out, in the story of Elijah (see p. 190).

Hand in hand with this radical preaching of judgment goes the most typical feature of prophetism: the expectation *in the future* of well-being and salvation after the judgment. This is to be in the kingdom which Yahweh establishes through his Messiah, the prince anointed by him with his Spirit (eschatology). With the proclamation of this message history is seen no longer as a straight line issuing in Yahweh's day of salvation (*Yom Yahweh*), which is to make Israel a power finally triumphant over every foe, as both cult and popular belief envisaged (see Amos 5:18ff.), but as a broken line the continuation of which will be drawn, after the break, by Yahweh himself. From then on, therefore, it is Yahweh alone who can give salvation to the people. The unconditional manner in which all hope is placed in Yahweh, and in Yahweh alone, is the distinctive mark of the whole prophetic world of ideas, although it is expressed with particular clarity by Isaiah, Ezekiel and Deutero-Isaiah.

There are all sorts of elements, then, which are new—either because of the emphatically radical note with which they are imbued, or because of the place they now assume within the scheme of things, or because they come into it as newly discovered consequences of old belief and so in effect alter the countenance presented by Yahweh in Israel.

This process of renewal turned out to be, historically, of the greatest importance in two distinct respects. The first and principal

one was the way in which the prophets' proclamation about Yahweh
took effect in Israel: in the efforts made, both in their days and
afterwards, to reform and to restore, in the assumption of their
writings into the canon, in the later apocalyptic movements of which
they were the ultimate source, and in the revival of various 'sects' in
early Judaism, which is something not unrelated to this. It was
important in the second place because the prophets' eschatological
message of judgment and salvation was the reason why Israel with-
stood the crisis that came upon her existence as a nation, and why
through her fifty years of exile she was able to maintain her faith and,
on her return, to build once more her national existence, in the sure
conviction that she had a spiritual task to perform in this world which
was peculiarly her own. After the exile the same influence helped to
give a new form to Israel's belief, not merely in a theological context
but also in the areas of religion, cult and politics—although so far as
the latter are concerned, the paths indicated by the prophets were
fairly soon exchanged for other ways more in keeping with the earlier
ritual, religious and nationalistic ideas of the period before the exile.

Thus prophetism had more influence over the future than upon its
own times. In a sense, those who argue that the prophets had little
significance for their own day, because despite their preaching the
religious life of the people went its own way, are right. They did, of
course, gather a few disciples around them, but their ideas found
little direct response in the cultic, political, social or economic
spheres. We may, however, suppose that after their prediction of
judgment had come true the first time in the destruction of the
Northern kingdom (722), their call to repentance was taken more
seriously in the South. It is certain that, whatever else may be thought
about the origin of Deuteronomy and the forces leading to the
Deuteronomic Reform of 621, we are bound to acknowledge here the
influence of the prophetic preaching of the 8th century. Indeed, even
Hezekiah's Reform must be traced back to it. And even if from time
to time their words were so much wasted breath, these men, without
holding any official position, were frequently consulted by the kings
of their time and asked to provide an oracle.

Furthermore, the gathering together of the disciples whom they had
collected around them proved to be very important for Israel's
religion, because in the circles which they constituted spirituality and
obedience at the personal level came to stand above every tie with the
official cult and with the state. In this way groups emerged which led

a religious life of their own and formed an *ecclesiola in ecclesia* (not over against the nation and the state, but yet independently of them). These were the '*anawim* (the humble) or '*aniyyim* (the poor). They were active even in the time of Isaiah (14:32) (perhaps even before; one recalls the 7000 who had not bowed the knee to Baal in Elijah's day); and they are mentioned many times in the psalms. We ought not to describe this type of piety as simply and solely 'individualistic', although naturally enough it had a strongly personal vein running through it. We are not to regard the prophets, therefore, as exercising a calamitous influence on society and the nation, as does A. Causse, when he accuses them of being a force for dissolution, undermining the solidarity of the national community.[2] According to him the prophets with their ethical preaching broke down the primal, mystical union between God, nation and individual and encouraged individualism. One must surely object at this point; for neither the prophets themselves nor their followers contracted out of their national community as, for instance, the Rechabites did. It was not a religious individualism that the prophets advocated. If they demanded personal involvement, it meant that they called upon their disciples to join battle along with them for the spiritual life of the nation and its renewal. Of course the prophets helped to further the cause of a consciously personal religion, not at the expense of the nation at large, but in order to build it up. Equally, the groups which the prophets created became power-centres for renewing the life of the nation.

Thus they played their part in breaking down the overbearing influence of the official cult and its ministers as well as the nationalistic religiosity that rested its case on the saving events of Israel's past history (false prophets; Amos 3:2f.; 9:7f.). Every faithful individual once more had his immediate task in the service of Yahweh and was under obligation to carry out God's will. That is why the prophets declared the primary demands of morality and religion to be the primary commands of Yahweh (Hos. 4:1ff.; Isa. 1:10f.; Micah 6:8; Jer. 7:5ff.) and put them above 'worship and sacrifice'. That is also why, from Amos to Ezekiel, the prophets set themselves against the idea that Israel as such, as a nation, would be saved, and could be certain of her salvation, as the 'false prophets' thought (Jer. 28). In this way too they made a powerful contribution to the inward renewal of Yahwism.

Before we go on to give a historical outline of the part played by individual Old Testament prophets, we ought first to say something in general about the forms in which prophetism manifested itself, in Israel and elsewhere, from the earliest period onwards. We have said hardly anything about this so far, because we wanted to leave open the possibility of looking at Israelite prophetism as a whole in relation to prophetism in the rest of the ancient East.

If prophetism was formerly regarded, until quite recent times, as a typical, and almost exclusively, Israelite phenomenon, things have been very different in this regard since the discovery that a form of conveying divine messages existed in Mari around 1700 which is in many respects kindred to that of Israel. It is true with regard to the West Semitic world that the activity there of ecstatics had long been known from an Egyptian text of about 1100. This, however, provides only one parallel to the behaviour of one particular type of Israelite prophet, namely, the ecstatics of Samuel's day, but not to the activity of the classical prophets. The Mari letters, however, have confronted us with further forms of prophetic behaviour and style, which, on the surface at least, agree remarkably closely with what we know of the classical prophets themselves. In this way prophetism was revealed to be a more recent continuation of a very ancient form of religious activity.

Even so, the occurrence of prophetism there cannot be used to explain every aspect of prophetism in Israel. Specialists in Arabic studies have justly called attention to noteworthy phenomena which occur in the Arabian world (from a much later time than the Bible, it is true) and afford some typical parallels with biblical narratives.

Finally, we can point to Egyptian examples of prophetic utterances which also in some respects remind one of the Bible.

Prophetism in Israel is a highly complicated phenomenon with many facets, which are revealed with especial clarity when one sets out to trace the lines of its historical evolution. It goes back to the very oldest times in Israel's history, was affected by different tendencies in different periods, and provides parallels with many phenomena in other parts of the Near East, most of which go back to a time long before the people of Israel were even in existence. We ought first to examine the principal phenomena of prophetism outside the Bible.

In Egypt's case the issue of prophetism barely arises. Some Egyptologists are inclined to deny all but completely that it was present there at all. A. de Buck,[3] for instance, declines to allow a prophetic character to the book of wisdom of Nefer-rohu (or according to

Morenz,[4] better 'Neferti'), which has elsewhere[5] been identified as prophecy, although he does admit that this document presents a scheme of successive eras of disaster and prosperity, somewhat akin to certain of the eschatological ideas current among the Israelite prophets. However, what we have here is rather a case of wisdom literature than of prophecy. This literature does of course have a quasi-prophetic form of prediction; but its contents are really borrowed from history, and its calculated purpose is not so much to foretell the future as to admonish or extol the monarch.

One can probably best agree with Morenz (op. cit.) when he says that these texts express the idea that the wise man is aware of a plan in history, determined long in advance; so that in view of this one can say that there was in Egypt an awareness of the feasibility of 'prior knowledge', by which events were known in advance. Yet this is of a different order from prophetic proclamation as known in the Semitic world, based as that is upon revelational experience. The only other real parallel to the utterances of the Israelite prophets is the picture of social chaos which we find in these writings (including Ipuwer's) and which is reminiscent of the accounts given of this by some of the prophets (cf. e.g., Isa. 3:4f. and Micah 7:2ff.). Since, however, in both cases such descriptions are founded on past or current experiences, we can scarcely establish a direct literary connexion between them.[6]

More to the point are the parallels provided by the Mari-letters.[7] Here we have three types of prophet. The first is represented by a person actually mentioned by name—Malik-Dagan; the second by people known as *muḫḫum* (that is, 'ecstatic priest'); and the third by a man who is presented as an *apilum* (that is, 'answerer') and is possibly also a priest. This the first man was not, apparently, even though the message that he conveyed was disclosed to him in the temple.

Thus all these divine instructions would appear to have a cultic background. Moreover, they have this in common: that the prophetic figures concerned did not pass on their message to the king in response to any request from him, but because they were directed to do so by the god. The cases in question, which all come from the time of Zimrilim of Mari (c. 1700), are as follows. In the first one that we referred to, concerning Malik-Dagan, a certain governor writes to the king of Mari to explain that the man had come to him with a message from Dagan which he had received in a dream. In this dream he was constrained to go the temple of Dagan. There the god had addressed him, ordering him to go to the king and to say that the king should send envoys to the temple to inform the god how matters stood concerning the (apparently insurgent) tribe of Benjaminites. If the king were to do as he had been told, Dagan undertook to help him deal with the Benjaminite sheiks. The governor brings this divine message to the king, asking him to look into the truth of the matter and to act in accordance with the prophetic instruction. He apologizes for not sending the man in person, because the latter had to offer a sacrifice of an animal to Dagan. It would seem, however, that in order to keep a hold on the man, and to make sure that he would return (and thus that he was an honest messenger), he had retained part of his clothing. In other words, the man was of humble extraction.

Here, then, the divine message is evidently received in a dream, not by a priestly figure but by an ordinary man. It is a challenge to seek out the deity; and it includes the promise that the god will help the king against his enemies. The whole thing has very much the character of an admonition with a promise attached and the object, in this case, is a political one.

A second letter tells how a *muḫḫum* priest of Dagan came to the governor and said, 'The god has sent me. Write at once to the king that human sacrifice be made to the death-spirit of *Yahdullim*.' The governor leaves it to the king to decide what to do about this divine injunction. What we have here is a demand by the god that human sacrifice be offered to the spirit of the king's father, probably to quieten it and render it favourably disposed.

A third letter is also concerned with the activity of a *muḫḫum* priest who makes a strongly worded demand for the building of a new city gate. As only fragments of the letter have been preserved, it is not clear which deity had sent him.

A fragment of yet a fourth letter mentions the visit of a man, evidently connected with the temple of Dagan, who in the god's name demands an animal sacrifice on the 14th day of the subsequent month.

A fifth letter has to do with an oracle, of the god Adad, which reminds Zimrilim of the benefits which Adad bestowed on him 'by nurturing him in his bosom', setting him on his father's throne and giving him a palace. But now Adad is laying claim to a particular site (for a temple?). Should the king not concede it, the god will take everything away from him; but if, instead, the king is obedient, then he will be able to have everything he wishes. The god promises, among other things, that 'I will give him throne upon throne, house upon house, land upon land, city upon city; also will I give him the country from sunrise to sunset'. Those who carry the message in this case are called 'answerers'. They are probably oracular priests who have discourse with the god and give him an answer when he has made some pronouncement or other. Here again we have the god making a demand of the king, with a promise added as an inducement to fulfil it. This 'prophecy' reminds one for a moment of Nathan's in 2 Sam. 7.

The prophecies all have to do with cultic matters, apart from the first one, which involves issues of a politico-military nature. The *muḥḥum* priests belong to the shrine of Dagan, the *apilum* priest to Adad's sanctuary. Malik-Dagan is probably an ordinary man, whose dream is treated seriously, albeit with some reservation, as a message from the god. Mari had not only cultic prophets but non-cultic ones too, it seems; although the temple was in some way associated even with their revelations. All the prophecies strike a note of warning, of demand, urgency and promise. By way of contrast with the predictive oracles, where it is man (the king) who turns in the first place to the deity (this frequently happens in the Mari-letters too;[8] but we have not thought it necessary to go into it here), in the case of these prophecies it is the god who takes the initiative and by means of this or that individual addresses himself to the king.

Particularly significant where its relation to Israelite prophecy is concerned is the way in which the prophets in Mari deliver their message. They do so with the words 'Therefore has the god sent me'; and the deity sends them by saying 'Go now, I have sent thee, thus shalt thou speak.' This terminology is very akin to that employed by the Israelite prophets when they appear on the scene. They too are conscious of themselves as the servant-messengers of God.[9]

If prophecy as we find it in Mari has numerous points of connexion with ecstatic prophetism (the *muḥḥum* priests are people who go 'out of their mind', like the *nabi'*[10] in Israel), it is the same also in the Phoenician milieu. The sole example known to us from a literary source occurs in the travels of Wen-Amon (*c.* 1100), who relates how, when in the harbour at Byblos, he ran into trouble with the king, who was unwilling to receive him, and on twenty-nine consecutive days ordered him to leave. On the very night when he intended to comply, something happened which changed the king's mind and induced him to receive the Egyptian after all. This was the intervention of an ecstatic prophet. The story runs as follows: 'As he (the king) was sacrificing to his gods, the god seized upon one of his young men and threw him into a frenzy, and the youth said: Let the god come ashore, fetch the messenger whom he has with him. It is Amon who has sent him; he it is who made him come. Whilst the frenzied man was raving that night, I found a ship ready to take me to Egypt . . .'

The behaviour of this ecstatic is genuinely prophetic, because the message delivered in this case contains a divine command. As sometimes happened also with the prophetic messages in the Mari-letters, it goes against the king's will, and is spontaneously received from the god. Here again, perhaps, there is a cultic background to this activity.

From the period of the monarchy the peoples around Israel have left us an example of a message, this time one given by a god to Mesha. According to the celebrated Mesha inscription he is instructed by Chemosh to take Nebo in a battle with Israel (c. 850). The inscription says (line 14), 'And Chemosh spoke: Go, take Nebo from Israel.' Even though there is no mention here of a prophet, and indeed no prophet appears, the form of this divine utterance is clearly reminiscent of the prophetic form.

In an inscription of Zakir, king of Hamath, we read in line 12, 'Be'el-shemayin (to whom the king had addressed himself) (spoke) to me by seers and (soothsayers?)'.[11] So far as we can tell from the text, there follows only the promise of a victory, which thus tends to suggest an oracle. It is given by the god, therefore, in response to the king's prayer.

This would suggest that *ḥozeh* ('seer', or rather 'visionary') is the title of an oracular priest in the West Semitic world. Since the *ro'eh* and the *ḥozeh* (the seer and the visionary) have a place in Israelite prophetism too, and some quite specific instances of prophetic revelation received in this way are given in the Old Testament (Amos 7, 8, 9; Jer. 1), we would like to single out a few examples of the activity of such visionaries that have come down to us in the literature of Arabia. They are, of course, from a much more recent period, but are still important enough for us to take notice of them. The reader will find them in A. Guillaume's book *Prophecy and Divination*,[12] where they are taken from a 10th century A.D. collection of colourful old stories and anecdotes. It tells us, for example, about a Bedouin who was well known to be a soothsayer and was invited, in connexion with the expected birth of a child, to make a prediction.

He promptly obliged; and when later on it had all come true, he was asked how he arrived at his predictions. He replied,[13] 'All we do is take note of omens, study the flight of birds, and from what we see reach our predictions. You began by asking me what I had been called for. When I looked around the room, my eye was caught by a water-cooler with pitchers in it. I thought to myself: something that is carried, and said: an unborn child. When you asked me about its sex, I looked around me again, and above the water-cooler I noticed a cock sparrow and said: a boy, and so on.' Such persons are known as 'soothsayers' or 'knowing ones'.[14] Then again we have the words *kahin* and *ḥazi*,[15] which resemble the Hebrew *kohen* and *ḥozeh*. Like the prophet in Israel, the *kahin*-seer of the Arabic world is called 'the man of God'. The *kahin* is the man who through personal inspiration and on the basis of dreams and omens foretells what will happen, clothing his prophecies, in virtue of their ecstatic background, in short rhythmic sentences.[16] He is not necessarily connected with a sanctuary. Inspiration was regarded as material to the role he had to perform. Closely associated with this *kahin* is the singer, *sha'ir*, who emboldened the clan, and discouraged the enemy, with his song. Alongside him stands the *katib*, who speaks the decisive word and flings curses at the foe during battle.[17] These functions are distinct, of course; but they are found in conjunction.

In the earlier prophecy of Israel these elements of prophetism are clearly prominent, especially in the case of Deborah; but in the later prophets also we find those elements occurring together which in the Arabic milieu often appear separately.

Taking the extra-biblical phenomena as a basis, we must now move on to a consideration of prophetism in Israel.

Viewed in the context of the history of religion, prophetism is a particular form of divination—although it is not to be equated with soothsaying. In the Greek world the *mantis* must be distinguished from the *prophētēs*, in that the role of the former is to descry the secret or mystery, whereas the latter passes on, announces, a message.[18] In Israel the difference between divination and prophecy is much the same, or even greater. The mantic art—which in Israel is very much curtailed—seeks to discover what the god has secretly determined. That can only be done through the *torah* of the priest with the aid of the *urim* and *thummim* and the ephod, or again by means of the teraphim. All other forms of mantic activity are forbidden. Prophecy does not so much seek knowledge of what the present or the near future may conceal as issue a call to action in view of such revelations as are received. In fact, this is not only the case with Israelite prophecy but for the most part is true of the rest of the ancient East as well. Right from the start prophecy contains an element of warning, demand or preaching, or again, in another aspect, an element of intention to influence things here and now or in the future, with a blessing or a curse. Prophecy does not simply communicate or inform, but seeks to effect something, to exert an influence upon this, that and the other. The prophet intervenes in life's affairs, and this lies in the very nature of his call, and is the whole point of his receiving a message. Nevertheless, prophetism does include a mantic element.

The behaviour of the various prophets of Mari, who all approach the king with a demand of some sort, and likewise of the ecstatic in the Wen-Amon story, illustrates the same point. By its very nature prophecy stands somewhere between soothsaying and magic, and has something of both in it. It differs from magic in addressing itself to people whom it attempts to influence because it has been instructed by God to do so. We find this in the case of Mohammed and his call: in the second revelation which he receives he gets the order: 'Stand up and give warning' (cf. Sura 74 of the Koran, line 2).

This aspect is brought out in the Hebrew terminology too, which uses the word *nabi'* to denote a prophet and so stamps upon him the character of 'one who has been called'. He is posted at this or that spot in order to pass on whatever it may be that God is saying. Consequently, he is alone in being described as a 'man of God', and so as one who is wholly taken by Yahweh into his service. Within the Old Testament it is *only* prophets or men regarded as charismatic figures (David, for example, in the later literature; Neh. 12:24, 36; 2 Chron. 8:14) who are so designated. It is a very distinctive thing about the religion of Israel that it takes the prophet, and not the priest, as being more especially the 'man of God'. The value-judgment which this implies is so thoroughly characteristic of Yahwism that we may take it as a confirmation of the fact that the figure of the prophet is in principle central to this religion. Indeed, even from a historical standpoint we must regard this as typifying Yahwism. Only the king, who can be referred to as 'son of God', bears a more honorific title, although that is not Israelite in origin, having been adopted, and was used merely in a symbolic sense.

As we remarked earlier on, there are other terms that denote the prophet: *ro'eh* or *ḥozeh*, seer or visionary. There is little difference between the two.[19] They show that there must originally have been people with a primarily mantic function, whose business it was to descry what hidden factor 'lay behind things' or what was to come. It is in the later Arabian stories, as recounted above, that we again come across this form of 'prophecy'. In the Old Testament all the terms are more or less interchangeable, although 1 Sam. 9:9 suggests that in early times the word 'seer' was normally used to denote figures who were known to be 'men of God' and to whom one went for counsel and advice. Prophetism completely assimilated this 'seer's' function; and we find this method of receiving a revelation by 'seeing' turning up again among the major prophets: for instance, in Jer. 1, where the prophet sees an almond branch (*shaqed*=watcher) and by that means obtains a divine communication regarding Yahweh's being *shoqed*, being *watchful* over his word.

That prophetism in Israel, despite its affinity with the earlier ecstatics and the soothsayer-seers, should have acquired a quite distinctive character in the persons of the 'writing prophets' is all of a piece with Israel's belief about God and with the manner in which her religion developed as a result of that. Prophetism in the Mesopotamian area never meant anything more than the delivery of messages of a cultic nature; in the Phoenician world it was limited to the counselling of princes; in Egypt it resolved itself entirely into the pursuit of wisdom, and in Arabia never went beyond soothsaying or a kind of bellicose ecstasy. Whichever of these religions we consider, in each case the explanation lies essentially with the religious and cultural milieu to which the prophetism was assimilated. In Israel, however, its power and authority were such that it became the dominant factor in the religion as a whole. That prophetism should come to be so strong lies in the very nature of the Israelite religion itself. The necessary conditions, which were ideal for the purpose, were there, comprising a relationship between Yahweh and each and every man sharing in the covenant and a personal moral responsibility placed by him on every individual. It is the essential character of Israel's God, the very nature of his being, which decides both his relationship to his people and, at the same time, that of men to him and to their fellows. This likewise determines the quality, the function and the behaviour exhibited by those chosen to represent him. These ministers are neither greater nor higher than their Lord, but, as his representatives, they do reflect, in and through their activity, the nature of him who has called them to their task. It is by their preaching in particular that they express most strikingly and eloquently this 'likeness' of God; and their work takes its special character from the fact that they have but one aim: to teach men to know Yahweh, to bring them anew into fellowship with him. Above all, their role is essentially a religious one: Israel must become the people of Yahweh, as Yahweh is to be Israel's God.

There is an unmistakable continuity, therefore, in the work of the prophets, which runs through the whole course of events from Moses to Joel and Malachi. Thus the idea that the prophetic ministry bears the stamp of reaction is not really so very strange. Nevertheless, it is only half the story, and is too categorical. The truth is that the prophets' desire is to get back to the recovery or re-establishment of the close fellowship between the people and Yahweh (Hos. 2; Jer. 2; Ezek. 16) as that had been experienced in the earliest period of the nation's life. That is why they are for ever harking back in their preaching to the desert period.

The history of prophetism from Moses onward is certainly not one of continuous evolution, and, except in the period 750 to 500, the men of God make only an intermittent appearance on the scene. Not only are there great gaps in the sequence of events, but the notion that there was a gradual development 'from lower to higher' is really out of court too, although no one can deny that with the later prophets the religion of Israel did reach its highest form. Yet there were from time to time all sorts of external pressures and continual regressions, retarding and sometimes calamitous in their effects. The intensely ecstatic manifestations in one form or another, the ever-increasing encroachment of cultic practices, the shift towards a type of religious sentiment with national-political overtones, the popular piety that tended to superstition and magic, were all factors that between them had a large influence on prophetic activity in Israel. Thus the figures to whom one can point as having played a role comparable with that of Moses or of the later prophets are relatively few. The only names that spring to mind are those of Deborah, Samuel and Elijah. It is curious to note, beside this main line, so to speak, the branches and sidetracks on the route taken by prophetism.

Balaam, whom some recognize as having a historical background but to whose person it is difficult to give any real shape, is a singular personality; but that is something we cannot go into more deeply here. [20] Of course, the description of the spiritual endowment ascribed to him in the earliest lyrics (Num. 24) is still of interest and importance.

> The oracle of the man with the open (?) eye,
> The oracle of him who hears the words of God,
> and has the knowledge of the Most High,
> who beholds the face of Shaddai,
> down-sunken with uncovered eyes (24:15ff. and 4.ff).

In the claim it makes the account given here of this soothsayer's gifts goes beyond anything else known to us in the history of prophecy: namely, that he has acquaintance with Elyon, God as the Most High. Further, he is depicted as lying prostrate, with uncovered, unshut eye. The prophetic faculty is evidently portrayed here as it was usually envisaged among the ecstatics. The language employed here is veiled and mysterious, which again indicates that the thought-world is that of ecstatic prophetism. The prophet's 'falling' can only be in line with what we are told about the ecstatics (for instance, 1 Sam. 19:24, where the same verb, *naphal*=to fall, to lie down, is used).

This type of prophetism, which we must come back to later on, is quite different from that which is presented to us in a figure like Deborah (see p. 157). In the world of early Israel she constitutes a high point and shows how a person inspired by the Spirit of Yahweh acts. Her activities are more in the manner of the early Arabian enthusiasts than of the Canaanite type of ecstatics. Deborah's role has a close affinity to that of the charismatic judges and is well nigh inseparable from it. The prophet in early Israel is to be seen essentially as one who, being activated by the Spirit of Yahweh, intervenes in the nation's life, so triggering off, as it were, forces with a liberating effect. This activating force, with its religious and national reference, is totally absent from the sphere of the later ecstatic prophetism.

Another who went to work in the spirit of Deborah and the charismatic judges was Samuel. He is one of the bridge-figures between the period of the judges and that of the kings; and there is no doubt that he had a prophetic streak in him, even though he is only once referred to as a prophet (1 Sam. 3:20; also, however, as a seer, 1 Sam. 9, cf. especially verse 9; both verses are taken from a document with Elohistic affinities, which comes from a North-Israelite quarter and from the Elijah-Elisha milieu). Again, in chapters 3, 12(D) and 15 we get a picture of his activities in the prophetic vein. Hence he too is called a 'man of God'. On a historical view it is hard to place him, and

O

to size him up fairly and accurately, because his overall activity combines so many different elements.[21] Later tradition envisages him as a priest and Levite. Then again, he is depicted as a judge and as the leader of groups of ecstatic prophets. It is quite evident in the later literature that he was much looked up to by all sorts of factions and that they all sought to link him with their own particular group. Just how highly he is esteemed is apparent from Jer. 15:1, where the prophet mentions him in company with Moses. Thus he was a man of great consequence; and it is not at all strange that he should be credited with a special status, whether as leader of the Yahweh-amphictyony (Wildberger, Weiser *et al.*) or as covenantal intermediary (Newman). According to M. Noth the figures of the minor judges, in particular, who are mentioned in Judges 10:1ff. and 12:8ff. were leaders of the Yahweh-amphictyony. Because of the way in which various mutually independent traditions speak of him, we may be sure that Samuel was not merely a judge in that sense and that his significance lay in his personal charismatic, or more precisely prophetic, role.

As a Nazirite attached to the sanctuary at Shiloh, he was called to be a prophet at one of the most critical periods in the history of his people; and right through the collapse of the amphictyony, which had its sanctuary in Shiloh, he succeeded by his personal activity as a judge in holding together the tribes of Israel. Despite many objections on his part, in the end he was the man who gave the nation its first king. In virtue of his personal authority he was able, as sole leader, to sustain for some time the Yahweh alliance. It is perhaps not going too far, therefore, if in company with Newman, and in line with early Israelite tradition and with no less a person than Jeremiah, we describe him as, side by side with Moses, a covenantal mediator. In all kinds of ways he bears the marks of a spiritual leader who acts with complete authority, who selects and rejects the king, puts obedience to the prophetic word above the cult, discharges the duties of a judge, even helps to set Israel's defences in order once more. To do so, he clings fast to the ancient and iron laws of the holy war, including the *ḥerem*, applying it at any rate to the Amalekites.

Historically speaking, it is unlikely that he had any direct link with the ecstatic prophets. His own activities were too different in kind for that; and like Deborah and the charismatic judges (whose functions he combined, as Moses had done before him), he belonged to a quite different category of prophets. Later prophetic circles, being very much under the influence of the ecstatics, evidently established the connexion in order to give this form of prophecy the cover of Samuel's authority. The connexion which the (more recent) sources continue is still in point of fact a quite external and incidental one (1 Sam. 10:5f., 19:18ff.).

Here we must add a brief word about ecstatic prophetism. It made its way in under Canaanite influence, although the tribes of Israel had grown up with a form of prophetism in which seeing, scrutinizing (of omens) and hearing played the chief part. Ecstatic prophetism as it appears in the narratives just cited (especially in 19:23f.) bears a very close resemblance to that which Wen-Amon describes in the account of his travels and which was to be found at Byblos. In Israel the ecstatics appear very much in groups. They come together, it would seem, in order to perform certain mystical exercises and thereby attain a state of being mentally 'possessed', leading into a kind of trance in which the subject experiences visions or voices. To judge by the description given in 1 Sam. 10, instruments of music (and probably ecstatic dances) were important preliminaries. Although ecstasy was in origin something foreign to Yahwism, it was not absolutely forbidden; and right down to the final period of prophetism it maintained its influence (there is probably an allusion to it even in Zech. 13:1ff.; but it is roundly rejected there). Because these ecstatics made so much of the Spirit of God and referred to it so often (1 Sam. 10 and 19), the major prophets reacted against this and seldom, if ever, mentioned the working of the Spirit. Yet we do find ecstatic elements in some prophets who are regarded as men loyal to Yahweh; and they are even present in one of the classical prophetic figures. Elijah's 'running' is often explained in these terms (1 Kings 18:46); and it is certainly a possibility in the case of Elisha, when he makes use of a zither-player to put him into a sort of trance (2 Kings 3:15). But the traces are evident above all in the case of Ezekiel, of whom we are told that, among a variety of other things, he was taken up by the Spirit of God, and so on. Wherever prophets are seen as 'madmen' (2 Kings 9:11; Hos. 9:7), the explanation would appear to lie with elements of this sort.[22]

In line with typically Israelite prophetism is the role fulfilled by Nathan, although he is not actually described anywhere as 'seer' or 'visionary'. With him prophetism takes a turn in the direction of court-prophecy. Nathan is the prophet who receives the word of Yahweh (2 Sam. 7:4) and utters it (2 Sam. 12), and does not scruple to admonish the king and to judge him on the basis of the ancient laws of the covenant, given by God. He is a champion of the old traditions (2 Sam. 7:6 and chap. 12) and concerns himself with the royal succession (1 Kings 1; remember also in this connexion 2 Sam. 12:25). Through his prophetic message regarding the permanent rule of the house of David he was not only the man who prepared the way for the hereditary kingship in Judah but also the one who laid the foundation for the politico-Messianic expectation linked with the Davidic dynasty. The prophets, including the later ones, never relinquished this element of political influence over the king. In this respect, even when their actual mode of procedure changed, the original function which they had in the Yahweh-league or the amphictyonic alliance remained operative.

Along with Nathan, and active in the same vein, we have the figures of Gad, who was known as both seer and prophet (1 Sam. 22:5; 2 Sam. 24), and later of Ahijah (1 Kings 11:29ff.; 14:1ff.) and of Shemaiah (1 Kings 12:22ff.). These prophets, although up to a point closely associated with the monarchy, are still free in their activity.

Eventually, however, the political and cultic relationship binding the prophets to king and temple took effect; and one gets a prophetism one-sidedly focused upon cult and politics. In origin and essence it was independent of the cult, but certainly with no anti-cultic bias; and time and again it was related to it (Samuel). After the monarchy had developed, however, and its religious significance had also increased (see p. 181ff.), the danger threatened that prophetism too would be drawn into the sphere of the religious kingship. Then the prophet ran the risk of losing his position as a spiritual leader and becoming a servant of crown and altar. This form of prophetism became prominent during the middle period of the kingship, and principally in the Northern kingdom during the time of Ahab.

A very clear illustration of this is to be found in 1 Kings 22, where we have the band of prophets led by Zedekiah, whose name shows that he was a Yahweh-prophet, as indeed may also be true of the others, a group of men about four hundred strong. At the instance of the king of Judah, Jehoshaphat, who is represented as a prince loyal to Yahweh, these men are consulted by Ahab before the start of a battle with the Aramaeans for a town in Transjordan. They all predict, partly by performing various symbolic actions, a successful outcome to the battle. From Jehoshaphat's attitude it is plain that he mistrusts this unanimity; and so it is fair to conclude that the linking of the prophets with officialdom had not as yet made such rapid strides in Judah, and that the prophets there were still accustomed to speak the word of God on the basis of their personal spiritual experiences. Even in Israel, however, there was still one man among the acknowledged prophets of Yahweh who understood his prophetic vocation in the spirit of Yahwism, but because of his messages of ill portent had been dismissed from his office by the king. This man was Micaiah ben Imlah. When at Jehoshaphat's request he had been summoned to appear, he delivered as a message from Yahweh a prediction of disaster. As a result of this he again incurred the wrath of the king, and of his fellow-prophets, and was thrown into prison.

This story will certainly have had a historical background; and it shows that even in Northern Israel there were prophets who did not toe the line. Indeed, there were yet others who took an opposing stand. In 1 Kings 18 we read of a hundred prophets who had gone into hiding. When the military rebellion under Jehu broke out, therefore, the prophets supported it. Jehu's anointing is ascribed to a prophet, who must have been sent by Elisha (2 Kings 9); and Jehu is in any case the man who eradicated the cult of Baal.

Evidently, then, the Yahweh-prophets in Northern Israel were split into two camps, one group proceeding on the old lines, whilst another was given over entirely to the king's service and spoke in accents calculated to further the cause of a one-sidedly nationalistic religion.[23] Prominent among them would have been those who were the official cult-prophets at the state temples. This development is mainly at the root of the later opposition between the false prophets, as they were called, and the great prophets of the Old Testament, although we cannot without qualification regard *all* nationalist or cultic prophets as traitors to the ideal implicit in Yahwistic prophetism.[24]

At any rate, there were also not a few in a centre position: men who sought both to serve the king's interest and to discharge faithfully the office of a prophet of Yahweh. Elisha, although he came to be associated with the revolutionary Yahweh-prophets, was apparently more a prophet belonging to the centre group. He exhibits, of course, certain ecstatic traits (2 Kings 3:15); but it is difficult to say how far he was the ecstatic prophets' leader. He was connected, certainly, with the group-prophets; but whether these were a direct continuation of the earlier ecstatic groups is not crystal clear from the Old Testament. It is possible, of course; but then they had abandoned a good many of their forms of ecstasy. At all events, what is known of them from the Elisha-stories cannot any more be said to point strongly in that direction. Elisha seems to have been at the head of the prophetic group in Gilgal, the ancient Yahweh-sanctuary (2 Kings 2:4; 4:38ff.; 6:1ff.) and to have frequented yet other holy places (Bethel, Carmel, Samaria; 2 Kings 2:23ff.). Although critical, he remained loyal to the house of Ahab (2 Kings 3), although he was reputed to have helped in bringing about its downfall (2 Kings 9). The great number of stories and legends about him show that the people held him in exceptionally high esteem. He is credited with every function associated with the prophetic office, including various sorts of miraculous cure and resuscitations of the dead. The story-cycles about him which have been preserved are important for the very reason that they give us a picture of the kind of ideas popularly associated with a prophet. The prophet is called and is impelled by the Spirit of God (1 Kings 19:19ff.; 2 Kings 2); he is the central personage in a circle of 'sons of the prophets' (2 Kings 2ff.); he serves as oracle-giver to the kings (2 Kings 3:6ff.), but also as their critic (2 Kings 3:13); he is the mighty leader in prayer (2 Kings 4:33ff.), the miracle-worker (2 Kings 4:1ff., 8ff.; 6:1ff.), the healer (2 Kings 4ff.), the seer (2 Kings 6:12, 15, 32; 8:10); he performs symbolic actions (2 Kings 13:14ff.); he is the proclaimer of good (2 Kings 7:1ff.) and evil (2 Kings 8:7ff.) tidings; even after his death he still performs marvels (2 Kings 13:20ff.).

Such, then, is the figure cut by the prophet as man of God in the popular esteem. Despite all the magic and the fondness for the miraculous which are to be found in them, these story-sequences do demonstrate that as one who brings the word of God the Israelite prophet is not only a spokesman but a man who makes his mark on people's lives. A figure such as Elisha reminds one in many respects of late-Jewish hassidism, where one finds pious rabbis credited with all kinds of miracles. If it be asked whether we ought not to ascribe this development via ecstatic prophetism to the influence of Canaanite magical practices, one is inclined—albeit somewhat hesitantly—to answer in the affirmative.

This concludes our account of the course taken by prophetism prior to the appearance on the scene of the great prophets. We must look at their life and preaching, relating these to religio-historical developments that occurred in their day; but we shall be able to discuss these things only in quite summary fashion. It simply is not possible here to go deeply into their lives and characters or their work, as that would mean launching on a new book. The data known about them are first-class and so multifarious that we can describe the period in which they lived as the best documented in the entire history of ancient Israel. Of course, there are still a lot of open questions, even here; because it is not always consistently easy to understand the prophetic writings and to give precise dates to their constituent parts.

The history of the 8th and 7th centuries confronts us with a number of great men, of whom the Assyrian world-conquerors, from Tiglath-Pileser to Ashurbanipal, form one group and the prophets of the Old Testament the other. The clash of these two parties, which involved a struggle of matter with spirit, of naked force with religion, for the soul of the people of Israel, proved to be an issue of significance for the history of the world. That is how the prophets themselves felt and understood it, and also how it was put in so many words, not very long ago, by a distinguished Assyriologist, when he set over against the pitiless caprice and naked violence of the Assyrians the vision of the blessed prophets with their message of a God-given world of righteousness, peace and true humanity.[25]

During this period Israel as a nation fell to pieces, not without guilt on her part, for in spite of the spiritual guidance provided by the prophets she committed one act of wilfulness after another. Yet she was to return, even as a nation, to new life, thanks to the forces awakened by the prophets. Whereas, to use Kraus's[26] words, 'the Assyrian state and its doctrine of domination were swept away by the same mindless and soulless violence as had brought them into being'; so that 'Xenophon, on his way through the Tigris valley two hundred years later, could no longer imagine that he was at the heart of the old Assyrian empire'. The remarkable thing about all this is that whereas Israel had to thank for her downfall the near-sighted, nationalistic prophets of weal who went running after kings and warriors, she owed her rebirth to the clear-sighted prophets of woe, who had been pilloried as traitors and blasphemers (Jer. 26 and 37f.).

The prelude to this struggle occurred during the reign of the important king of Northern Israel, Jeroboam II (c. 792–750) and of his colleague in Judah, Uzziah (c. 790–740), both of whom ruled very successfully and brought their countries to a condition of great economic and political prosperity. This material prosperity caused profound changes within the social structure and threatened the very existence of the socially weaker sectors.

Religious life (regarding which see below) was outwardly just as prosperous. The temples at Bethel and Gilgal seemed to be flourishing (Amos 4:4f.; 5:21ff.). Men's hopes were high; and it was thought that the Day of Yahweh was just around the corner, when Yahweh would cause Israel to triumph completely over her adversaries (Amos 5:18ff.).

In opposition to both, there appeared Amos, a countryman from Tekoa in Judah. He went into action against the shallow, luxurious style of living of Northern Israel, so steeped in injustice (Amos 2:6ff.; 4:1ff.) that it had become a reproach to faith in Yahweh, and against the cult of sacrifice with its outward show. He was so outraged by the manner of life in Northern Israel that he became convinced of Israel's impending destruction because it had become totally unworthy to be the people of Yahweh (Amos 3–6). He foresaw, therefore, her being carried off into exile beyond Damascus. It is a remarkable thing that Amos would seem to be alluding here to possible intervention by the Assyrians, who so long as Jeroboam was alive, and for years after his death, had made no incursions into the West. That is not to say that in their predictions the prophets had always got hold of exactly the right idea. Amos, for example, had foretold (7:11) that Jeroboam would die by the sword, although he did not (see 2 Kings 14:29). Thus Amos apparently expected the catastrophe to happen sooner than it did.

The particularly interesting point here is that there was no political reason for Amos's prophecy of woe. This is especially evident from the visions through which he received his call (7:1–9; 8:1–3; 9:1ff.). They show that only gradually did the conviction grow within him that the religious life of Israel called out for judgment. Thus he first of all foretold the destruction of the sanctuaries (7:8f.; 8:3; 9:1ff.). The cult was magnificently well developed (5:23; 8:3); but this could not save it from destruction, because the cause of true religion, which consists in justice and righteousness, was not being advanced thereby (5:24). He did not reject all sacrificial worship in principle, although he was quite sure that it had formed no part of primitive Yahwism (5:25). He certainly accepted Zion, the Jerusalem temple, for instance, and thus apparently the cult there. The prophet based his own life entirely on the salvation-tradition of early Yahwism (3:1ff.); and that was his yardstick for the political, cultic and social life of his day.

Accordingly, the Northern kingdom was bound to pay the consequences (7:9 and 10ff.). Even its kings was not to be left in peace. We cannot maintain, as has often been done, that his real standpoint was that of Rechabite sectarianism, with its nomadic ideal; but we can say that his thinking was basically both agrarian and Judean. Zion is the place where Yahweh dwells (1:2); and the prophet entertained high hopes of the house of David (9:11f.). But fundamentally, his whole thought-world was grounded solely in Yahweh, in his will and his actions. The purely religio-ethical character of Amos's prophesying is therefore an established fact. There was nothing entirely novel about his contribution in this respect, as often used to be believed. What he actually did was to get back to the original insights of the very earliest Yahwism.

Amos's preaching must have made a deep impression—certainly in the South, and more particularly on the youthful Isaiah, whose earliest preaching strikes many a note reminiscent of Amos: the approach of the Day of Yahweh (Isa. 26ff.), the judgment upon the violation of justice and on the merely outward service paid to Yahweh (Isa. 1:10ff.; 3ff.). And yet, as is clear from a number of things (see p. 222ff.), there is at once a profound difference, in that the message of judgment which Amos had addressed to the Northern kingdom Isaiah now applies to Judah and to Jerusalem itself.

Amos's prophecies were in all probability soon committed to writing and were thus able to reach a good many people. To the extent that these prophecies had obviously begun to be fulfilled, which was fairly quickly, the spiritual forces which controlled and produced that fulfilment began to take effect.

More particularly, conditions in the West Semitic world before very long started to change. A relatively peaceful situation was shattered by the completely unexpected political growth of Assyria which now, led by that insatiable imperialist, Tiglath-Pileser, set about conquering the world. It started in 741, when he brought his armies into the West, taking Arpad and, later on, Hamath (738), and finally subjugating the whole of the West Semitic world. This policy was continued for more than a century by Shalmaneser IV, Sargon, Sennacherib, Esarhaddon and Ashurbanipal. After Northern Syria, it was soon the turn of Aram and Phoenicia. The federation of Syro-Palestinian states was no longer able to stand up to the Assyrian colossus. Israel fell in 734, but was preserved as a 'rump state' until in 722, after her last monarch's breach of trust, Samaria was overrun and the whole of Northern Israel was carried off into exile. At the first assault by Assyria Judah contrived to take shelter by putting herself under the protection of the Assyrian king; but she had to surrender her sovereignty and pay the king heavily in tribute-moneys. For the time being she was spared; although in 701 it was touch and go whether Jerusalem would suffer the same fate as Samaria.

Our information about the religious life of the period comes from what is said in the collections comprising the prophecies of Amos and Hosea, which describe conditions in the Northern kingdom, and those of Isaiah and Micah, which do the same for the Southern state.

As for the criticisms voiced by Amos, we have dealt with those already. The scene depicted by the countryman from Judah really pales in comparison with that presented afterwards by Hosea. According to him the whole life of religion in Israel had sunk down into Baal-worship and all the immoral practices which that involved (1–3; 4:11ff.). Measured against the law of God, the whole religious life stood condemned. There was not a commandment in the decalogue that was not being infringed (4:1ff.); and this was even the case with the ministers of the cult (4:4ff.; 9:7ff.). It was not to be wondered at, therefore, if the people no longer knew anything of God and his service (4:4ff.). At the high places idolatry and Baalism were being perpetrated in worse and worse syncretistic forms (4:11ff.). Like Amos, Hosea condemned Bethel and Gilgal (4:15f.; 10:4ff.; 12:12) and along with them Mizpah, Tabor and Samaria (5:1ff.; 8:5ff.).

He too spoke out against the sacrificial rites (6:6; 8:11) and even the days of penitence and mourning (6:1ff.), because he feared that there was no real change of heart behind such penitence, and that the expectations of nature-religion with its cyclical notions of dying and rising again played some part in it all. The picture painted by the prophets, particularly Hosea, who was a Northerner himself, is not a very cheerful one. The question is whether it is painted in too vivid colours. There is little reason to suppose so, however, when one thinks of the colony of descendants of people who had had their religious centre at Bethel living in Southern Egypt during the 5th century. Alongside Yahweh they even worshipped goddesses (see p. 261f.). It is possible that the reference in Amos 8:14 is not to the 'guilt' of Samaria but to the worship of Asham-Bethel, who among later deities turns up alongside Yahweh in Elephantine. The official religion in Northern Israel had apparently gone a long way towards being assimilated to Baalism. What Jeroboam had created, despite its fairly innocent-looking beginnings, proved calamitous for the development of Yahwism in the North.

We can, of course, assume that, as with Hosea and even earlier with the 7000 in Elijah's day, during the last period of Northern Israel's existence there were still people who loyally supported Yahweh. Many of them would have been carried off with their compatriots. Others perhaps fled to Judah. At all events, it would appear from certain specific theological influences noticeable later on in the South that some of the religious ideas belonging to the prophets of Northern Israel penetrated to the South and were preserved there. Among them we may reckon the prophecies of Hosea, which were collected and probably readapted in Judah and had a considerable influence on the thinking of the prophet Jeremiah. It was above all the positive side of Hosea's preaching which made this deep impression, as is clear from a comparison of Jer. 2:2f. with Hosea 2. With Hosea the loving-kindness of Yahweh is very much to the fore (2:13ff.; 11:14). Consequently, he apparently maintained a belief in the restoration of Israel, and forcefully proclaimed that after judgment would come salvation (2:14). He proved in fact to be the first to announce an eschatological message.

So far as religion in Judah is concerned, developments there were much less unfavourable to Yahwism than in the North. At all events, no major deviations from the traditional line occurred in Jerusalem. Uzziah's reign, which lasted for more than half a century, was a quiet one, in religious as in other matters. He promoted the cause of Yahwism throughout the country—not only in Jerusalem but also at the high places beyond the city. From the Book of Amos we learn that the only exception to this was Beersheba (5:5; 8:14). It is a pity that the meaning of 8:14, which states literally: 'as surely as the Derek of Beersheba lives', is not clear. Whether 'Derek' is a deity with a status independent of Yahweh, or whether a different word is to be read here, is uncertain.[27] Amos had no complaint at all to make about Jerusalem. Isaiah, on the other hand, certainly had. Even his accusations were only occasionally levelled at idolatrous rites or other serious religious excesses (in 2:6 and 8:19, certainly; also 31:7), but they did go much deeper. He contended against the lack of inwardness in public worship, the grudging attitude to Yahweh, the injustice, the lip-service, the unbelief.

It was not until after 732, during the period when under the

influence of the Assyrians Ahaz started going in for foreign cults, that
things got worse. Coming to Damascus to do honour to his great
suzerain, Tiglath-Pileser, he saw there an altar (probably built for the
Assyrians' sun-worship). He had a copy of it made and set up in the
temple at Jerusalem on the site of the Yahweh-altar which he caused
to be removed (2 Kings 16:10ff.). The Chronicler even says that he
put an end to the whole cult of Yahweh (2 Chron. 28:22ff. and 29).
The question is whether this change of cult imposed by the Assyrians
had much effect on the religious life of the people of Judah. Ahaz also
introduced the barbaric West Semitic child-sacrifices. However, soon
after Ahaz was dead, Hezekiah carried out important reforms which
brought to an end all the abuses that had crept in (see below).

In the 8th century Judah continued to escape the strangle-hold of
the Assyrian, partly thanks to her remote position in the mountains,
partly because of her limited political importance and partly through
her political manoeuvrings which, temporarily at any rate, paid off.
When Tiglath-Pileser broke through to the West and the Syro-
Palestinian states, with Rezin of Damascus and Pekah of Israel at
their head, knocked together some sort of alliance in order to try and
hold the Assyrian in check, Judah kept out of it and offered her sub-
mission to Tiglath-Pileser, so that the worst consequences were
avoided. This policy, of course, hastened the take-over of power and
really amounted to a betrayal of the common West Semitic cause.
Consequently, in 734 Judah was threatened by both the aforementioned princes, but was rescued from her difficulties by Tiglath-
Pileser's rapid advance. Naturally, Judah, like the other states, was
forced to recognize the authority of Tiglath-Pileser—but the king and
country were spared; whereas Israel lost a great part of her territory,
and Damascus was taken a few years afterwards (732) and its population sent into exile.

Later on, Hezekiah more than once joined with rebellious movements abroad (after the death of Sargon in 705 with the cities of
Philistia near Egypt, and also with the Babylonian Merodach Baladan). As he discovered to his cost, the consequences of this were
grievous; for in 701 Sennacherib overran the whole of Judah and
menaced Jerusalem. Hezekiah was able to prevent the worst by
paying heavy tribute-moneys and so buying off Sennacherib, who
moreover was apparently forced by an epidemic in his army to withdraw sooner than he had intended.[28] This was felt to be a miracle
wrought by God and gave rise to a belief among the people of Judah

and Jerusalem that the city could never go under, because it was the place where Yahweh dwelt in his temple on Zion.

The policies of Ahaz, which were based on fear, and those of Hezekiah, which were calculated and wilful, were hotly condemned by Isaiah. To the petty politics of the kings in his day (which were essentially 'short-term') he opposed the claims of a conscious attitude of faith, in foreign as in home affairs (a long-term policy). Israel (Judah) as Yahweh's people had to show that she was accomplishing his will. For Isaiah one thing is sure: it is that Yahweh reigns and that even the unexpected inroads made by the Assyrians do not simply happen but are Yahweh's own doing. Isaiah sees them as executing the sentence passed by Yahweh on his people, intended to bring the nation back to its God. Isaiah's proclamation and his whole approach to life must be seen from that viewpoint, which is through and through a religious one, utterly indifferent to every consideration of power politics. He did not come to this standpoint of uncompromising faith through experience or reflection upon the events of history, but because of a vision that he had when he was called to be a prophet (Isa. 6). This vision governed his whole outlook and remained a permanent influence in his life. It came to him in the year that Uzziah died (usually thought to be in or just before 740), when things still looked peaceful enough in the West Semitic world. As we said before, it is not unlikely that Amos's preaching had made a deep impression on Isaiah; but for the rest his whole career was based on this one inward experience, which he set down for us in one of his writings that has survived.

He saw a manifestation of Yahweh, who disclosed himself to Isaiah as far exceeding the temple in magnitude and in splendour far surpassing the more exalted of the seraphs about his throne, who were unable to gaze upon his person. These angels of light sang of the being of God with the words:

> Holy, holy, holy is Yahweh Sebaoth
> The whole earth is full of his glory.

First and foremost Isaiah understood this song to mean that God is not only the holy One in the temple or amid the heavenly hosts, but equally so upon the earth, where he is both present and active. From that moment Isaiah's belief was governed entirely by his sense of the holiness and majesty (glory) of Yahweh. In speaking of Yahweh he employs only such terms as: the Holy One of Israel, the King, the

Lord, Yahweh Sebaoth (that is, Yahweh of hosts; i.e. the God who is master of all the powers). From then on Yahweh became the sole object of his hopes and expectations: he feared no one but Yahweh Sebaoth, and him alone (8:13). He it is with whom Israel and Judah have to do; and from him they will receive the judgment due. For Judah it will be a sentence of annihilation (6:8ff.). Thus we see that although influenced by Amos, Isaiah arrived at a form of proclamation which was all his own; and whereas the former had seen Northern Israel alone as the guilty party, Isaiah felt constrained to make his own people of Judah the target of his denunciation.

His criticism was directed at the unrighteousness of the people's leaders, the oppression of the poor and simple, even in the countryside, the pride, frivolity and extravagance, the merely outward conformity in things religious, and sometimes even a kind of defection, issuing in idolatry and magic. Judah, he says, has wandered altogether from the way pointed out to her by Yahweh and must suffer a judgment that will involve not only the land of Judah but Jerusalem too in punishment. Although he does not, in so many words, speak of the destruction of the temple, as his disciple Micah was to do, there is no reason for supposing that in the case of the sanctuary on Zion he made any exception (Isa. 8:13ff.).[29] Still, after the birth of his eldest son Isaiah is able to declare that a remnant will be spared; and for that reason he calls his son *Shear Yashub*, that is, 'a remnant returns' (or 'repents'). Time and again he comes back to this expectation (14:32). The only thing for Israel to do is to put her destiny in Yahweh's hands, to rely upon him (7:8f.). His whole life is regulated by the notion that only a quiet reliance upon God will provide strength enough to see a man through the brutish times being experienced by his nation (30:15). For these are times that God himself has called into being. There would be no Assyrian, were it not for him. God whistled for him, and he came (7:18ff.). Thus the non-sensicality of things in this world has sense and purpose in the will of God. All that Judah can do is to perceive and endure God's judgment, and make it the means of her renewal. Because Isaiah's experience led him to understand his day and age as a process of judgment and sifting in which Yahweh was actively engaged, it was possible for him on the one hand to call upon the troubled king Ahaz not to be afraid but to trust in God (ch. 7), and on the other to oppose recourse to military measures and a show of force. We can no more say that he was against the cult on principle than that he was fundamentally anti-militarist. If he was against the cult of his day (ch. 1), that was because it was being run by men disloyal to the commands of Yahweh.

Again, when in Hezekiah's time political collusion with this and that anti-Assyrian interest starts up, Isaiah takes the same attitude as in Ahaz's day: the nation will not be saved by small-time politics, by alliances with untrustworthy foreign powers, but only by entering upon a firm and close relationship with the Potentate of Potentates. Chapters 28–31 (and the beginning of ch. 1) are those which contain the prophetic sayings from the period around 701. As against the scoffers of his time, who jeer at him, Isaiah declares that only one thing offers the possibility of survival, and that is faith: 'he that has faith is not moved' (i.e. he stands his ground; 28:16). Thus to the precarious line taken in the politics of the time Isaiah opposes the solid policy of reliance upon God, which puts all its hope in him alone whose judgment must be undergone but whose mercy alone can save.

Isaiah did not, therefore, live as a man without hope. On the contrary, during the siege of Jerusalem in 701 he upheld his king, Hezekiah, in the hope of salvation to be wrought by Yahweh. That in those days Isaiah saw the Assyrian not only as the scourge of God but also as a godless instrument which would one day suffer punishment at Yahweh's hand is clear from what he says at 10:5ff. (see chs. 36ff.). That in later days he hoped for Jerusalem to be preserved is not due, therefore, to the idea that because it was the city of the temple it could not be taken, but to his belief that somewhere or other Assyria would be made to recognize the might of Yahweh. For Isaiah the fate of Jerusalem remained an open question. For him Yahweh is a God of wisdom whose purposes are beyond man's reckoning and whose actions are wonderfully strange (chs. 28f.). This is one reason why in the Book of Isaiah we sometimes get passages full of hope and expectation interwoven with prophecies of woe, and without any bridge between them! Even if they did not flow from the prophet's pen in this precise sequence (and were brought together in this fashion by the collectors), still he did utter them both (for the most part) within a definite period.

Notwithstanding the doubts or denials of some scholars, especially during the 19th century, we are entitled to regard Isaiah as the author of the great prophecies of salvation, set down in chapters 9:1ff., 11:1ff. and 2:1ff., which comprise what are known as his 'eschatological expectations'. In chapter 9 he announces that Israel and

Judah, however hard the judgment that falls upon them, will one day be restored. He foresees and lyricizes over the birth of a royal child, whom he describes as wonderful counsellor, godlike hero, everlasting father, prince of peace, whose dominion shall have no end. Again in chapter 11 he speaks of hopefully awaiting a king of the stem of Jesse (the house of David, as now reigning, will itself come to ruin), who will be guided entirely by the Spirit of God; and with this Isaiah joins a description of the new paradise on earth. In chapter 2 mount Zion, the mountain of the temple, is pictured as the place where all the nations are to receive their directives from God, so that there will be peace on earth. Like Hosea, Isaiah cherished quite definite hopes of a saving deliverance; yet he did not, like Hosea, restrict these to his own people but saw them in a universal context as applying to the whole world. We may regard him, therefore, as the one who really laid the foundations of a universal eschatological (ultimate) hope. This expectancy with regard to the end was to mean an enormous amount to Israel, especially when about a century after Isaiah's death Judah went right under. It kept the people of Israel going during the exile; and it formed a basis on which the expectations of Deutero-Isaiah could be built. Even at a later time it remained a source of strength, especially to the various movements of renewal that arose in Judaism; and its influence has continued to spread far beyond the Jewish world, in Christianity as well.

Isaiah has often been called a utopian or a quietist; but anyone who thinks this has seen only one side of him. His faith was proof against the harshest trials and tribulations of his age and even held out when in 701 it really looked as though all were lost. This faith of his was at the same time a source of strength, because it was never without hope.

Micah's preaching was in entirely the same spirit as Isaiah's; and his prophesying had much in common with that of Amos. As with Amos, protest at injustice and oppression was a prominent feature in his case; and like Isaiah he pronounced judgment on Northern Israel as well as on Judah and Jerusalem. He was even the first to foretell, in no uncertain tones, the destruction of Zion, the temple-mountain (3:12), a prophecy which struck deep into the hearts of Judah's inhabitants. A century later the 'elders of the land' in Jerusalem were still aware that Micah had spoken it, and there was a moment when this saved Jeremiah's life (Jer. 26).

Like Amos, Micah was a countryman. He came from the West,

from the borderland between ancient Philistia and Jerusalem; and
like the peasant from Tekoa he was not afraid to speak plainly about
facts. His prophesying was aimed not only against injustice but
against various forms of image-worship and oracular utterance. He
evidently looked on this as Baal-worship, because he regarded them
as having been introduced by Omri and Ahab (6:16). He vigorously
attacked the leaders of the people because they did not act candidly
and were open to corruption. The same applies to the prophets and
seers of the time and similarly to the priests, who all behaved like so
many money-grubbers, doing their job not to help people and to serve
God but in order to benefit themselves.

We find in him the same hostility to the sacrificial cult as with the
others (6:6ff.). For the true service of Yahweh he has a very brief
prescription, which applies to every person and which Yahweh has
made quite plainly recognizable. It comprises three imperatives: to
do justly, to show a heartfelt solidarity with others and to walk
humbly with God (6:8).

Micah, like Isaiah, is convinced that having executed judgment on
his people, Yahweh will bring in a new age of salvation. Here too, in
almost the very terms used by Isaiah, the promise is given of the
significance that the restoration of Jerusalem as the city of God will
have for the world (Micah 4:1ff.; cf. Isa. 2:1ff.). The passage is
generally, and rightly, held to be Isaianic. Whether Micah had himself already taken it over from Isaiah or whether someone appended
it to his prophecies at a later time will always remain conjectural. He
also shares with Isaiah the expectation of a Messianic king of the
house of Jesse; but he mentions Bethlehem Ephrathah as the place
from which the ruler of the new kingdom is to come, and not Jerusalem or the house of David.

Isaiah and Micah were many times in their lives disappointed in
their people and their people's rulers; but there were also things in
their experience that must have given them hope. One thing, at least,
they will have followed with close attention: what is known as the
Reformation of Hezekiah (2 Kings 18:3ff.). This king was very much
under Isaiah's influence and consulted him time and again. Hezekiah's
Reformation was in all probability an attempt (subsequent to the
destruction of Samaria; Hezekiah began to reign, perhaps, in 720) to
set the people, religiously speaking, on a fresh course. It is not, as
some investigators have strongly contended, to be explained purely in
terms of political considerations. The report of it incorporated in the

P

Book of Kings gives no indication at all that there is any question
here of an anti-Assyrian move. There is not even a reference to his
doing away with the altar that Ahaz had set up. He might well have
done so, but his work was much more fundamental, and it can only
have assumed this radical character under the influence of the critical
standpoint of the prophets of his day, who opened his eyes to the
danger of the 'high place' cults. Their strictures on image-worship
would in any case be aimed mainly at what was happening on the
bamoth. The high places, therefore, of which there were probably a
goodly number, were thoroughly dealt with. In 1953, in the neighbourhood of Jerusalem, some tumuli were excavated (there were
several more which had not yet been attended to), which according to
Dr Yeivin[30] are so many *bamoth*, consecrated in the 7th century in
Josiah's time. The sherds discovered there dated partly from the
8th century too; so that we may reckon with the possibility that these
high places, or others like them, could have been there in Hezekiah's
day. It is possible, then, that there were examples of such natural
sanctuaries up and down the land, and that these are the point of the
reference at 2 Kings 18:4. It does not follow that a complete centralization of the cult in Jerusalem was what Hezekiah was really after
and that he destroyed, for example, even the ancient sanctuaries at
Beersheba and Hebron. He probably did, however, 'clean them up',
as he did most thoroughly in Jerusalem itself, where he broke in
pieces a very ancient relic, the Nehushtan, a serpent-symbol which
tradition associated with Moses, because votive offerings were being
made to it. All this amply demonstrates the basic character of
Hezekiah's Reformation, which was more than just an anti-Assyrian
gesture. It may certainly have some connexion with that; for as we
have already pointed out, he twice allowed himself to be persuaded to
such a policy. Hezekiah's Reformation has often been linked with the
so-called deuteronomic Reform which was so successful in Josiah's
time. They probably do constitute parallel movements, but are not
actually identical, if by that one means that the core of Deuteronomy
might legitimately be ascribed to Hezekiah. So far as we can make
out from the evidence available to us, his Reformation lacked too
many of the typical features marking the Deuteronomic movement
for that (centralization of the cult).

Finally, in regard to events in the 8th century, we must make some
reference to the measures taken by Sargon, after the Israelites had
been deported, to keep the country under his control. He brought in

people from Babylon and its environs and from Northern Syria in order to populate the area. To them was assigned an Israelite priest, whose job was to carry on the cult of 'the god of the land' and instruct the new inhabitants in it. Besides Yahweh they worshipped various other gods, among them Sakkuth and Nergal; so that among the new inhabitants of Northern Israel, who were later to be known as Samaritans, a highly syncretistic religion must have prevailed (at any rate during the earliest stage of their existence). The old syncretism of Bethel received a further admixture of Babylonian and Syrian religions in a variety of forms (see 2 Kings 17:24ff.).

CHAPTER 9

Reformation and Downfall

THE 7TH CENTURY was for a large part a period of political weakness and religious decadence. After 701 Hezekiah was completely under the heel of Assyria; and his son, Manasseh, remained so during the whole course of his long reign of fifty-five years (*c*. 693–639). So also did his successor Amon, who after only two years was done to death. Nor, so far as the domestic affairs of Judah were concerned, did the first years of Josiah (638–609) bring anything new, although the decline of Assyria as a world power had already begun in the last years of the famous Ashurbanipal (d. 631).

During this period religious life in Judah was in a state of profound decadence. The picture that the Book of Kings gives of it (2 Kings 21 and 23) is similar to that which Zephaniah (1:4–9) and Jeremiah (2) give. Their accounts make clear the considerable extent to which syncretism had got the upper hand. Zephaniah speaks of the cult of the star-gods which took place, after the Assyrian style, with incense-offerings and libations on the housetops. He speaks too of the joint worship of Milkom, god of the Ammonites, and Yahweh, of the cult of Baal, and even of a hankering after Philistine rites (leaping across the threshold; cf. 1 Sam. 5:5). The Book of Kings gives the same picture, only adding that soothsaying, witchcraft, conjuring up of the dead and the invoking of spirits were increasing hand over fist, and that the king took the lead in offering child-sacrifice, as Ahaz had done before him. It would seem that this early-Canaanite custom, which had been observed by Jephthah, the Israelite from Trans-jordania (Judges 11), and by Mesha (2 Kings 3) in Moab, still applied in times of dire emergency. In 6:7 Micah broaches in no uncertain fashion the question as to whether child-sacrifices are a religious obligation. However, he categorically rejects them. This shows that among the people of the 8th century it was still a live issue. For many of them one of the reasons why child-sacrifice was considered accept-able even in Israel would have been the commandment to give the

228

firstborn to Yahweh, which in Exodus 22:29 is stated unconditionally and applied to children. The priest Ezekiel recognizes that this commandment is ambiguous and sees it as a test provided by God (20:25f.). The official implementation of it proves that a religious impulse lay behind all these forms of sacral practice. In true polytheistic style, therefore, as many gods as possible were evidently 'fitted in' , and all sorts of secondary forms of religious activity tried out, so as to obtain spiritual support. At the same time it shows that the whole belief in and about Yahweh was plunged in mortal crisis. Thus little of the work of the great 8th century prophets, on the surface at any rate, survived. Of course, this syncretistic development must in large measure be ascribed to the pressure of the Assyrians, who wherever they established their authority obliged the vanquished people to signify their recognition of the fact by importing Assyrian gods. It is also, however, partly to be explained by the uncertainty that had arisen because Yahweh had not rescued his people from foreign domination. The explanation put forward by the classical prophets that this was a sign of the divine judgment did not appeal to many people.

Over against this there stands the fact that there must have been, albeit as an undercurrent, a powerful movement within Judah which remained loyal to Yahwism. The prophets had their disciples; and in many parts of the nation the content of their preaching was preserved, as witnessed by the 'elders' spoken of in Jer. 26, who after a hundred years are still familiar with Micah's prophecy. This was true not only in the country at large but even in court circles as well. If it be the case, as must in all probability be allowed, that Zephaniah was a prince of the blood (Hezekiah was his great-great-grandfather; see 1:1; cf. that he was the one prophet to assail the princes; 1:8), then Yahwism would seem to have had its supporters even at the court in Jerusalem. Zephaniah's preaching is clearly a follow-up on the lines of the classical prophets. Like Amos he proclaims the Day of Yahweh. His expectations of salvation to come remind one repeatedly of Isaiah (2:3; 3:12f.). He probably lived in the first part of Josiah's reign; for the influence of Deuteronomy is as yet in no way apparent.

We have now made explicit mention of a document that is another of the witnesses to this undercurrent and which proved to be the occasion for rehabilitating the old Yahwism, albeit in new forms, suited to their time.

Deuteronomy, or the oldest core of the book, at any rate, probably dates from the sombre period of the reign of Manasseh. As to the precise quarter from which it originated—and as to when—there are differing opinions;[1] but basically it is hard to deny that it must have come from some circle or other in Jerusalem, where even as early as Hezekiah's day (see p. 225) reformist tendencies had been present. The influences apparent in Deuteronomy may be partly attributable to the classical prophets of the South; but some are just as likely to have emanated from groups of loyal Yahwists who had fled to Judah from Northern Israel: for instance, the emphasis on the covenant-idea and the promises made to the fathers, which had probably been heavily accented in North-Israelite theology (the covenant-idea might well remind one of Hosea, for example, as being the first prophet to allude to it). We may assume that among the priests in Jerusalem there would have been people who gave their backing to a prophet like Isaiah, and that the same would have been true of some of the high officials, 'princes', and wise men. One sees this in Jeremiah's time and may suppose that it was also the case a century earlier.

The programme of reform embodied in Deuteronomy (12–26) must be ascribed to men from these various sectors, under some sort of priestly direction, whose sole aim was to rehabilitate religion and repair the spiritual life of the nation. They set out in the book the idea that the rites practised at the high places must disappear along with Baalism and other forms of religion, and that the only sanctuary should be the temple at Jerusalem (12). They adopted a position fiercely opposed to idolatry (13), heavily underlined the laws concerning ritual and ceremony (14ff.), and in particular laid down rules for the festivals. They insisted upon the freedom of the Israelites and that there should be an unsullied administration of justice (15:12ff.; 16:18ff.; 17:8ff.; 19:14ff.). They set out the rights and duties of the king (17), who was bound by the requirements of the law.

The rights and duties of the priests, of the Levites (including those from the rural sanctuaries that had been closed down), were determined, and the activities of the prophets put on a tight rein (13; 18). Various sorts of oracular utterance were forbidden (18). The laws having to do with war, the private citizen and punishment were properly ordered. Israel as the people of Yahweh were brought under the law of Yahweh. The chosen people (the whole book is constructed on the basis of Israel's election, attested as both the gracious act and the task of Yahweh) must be a 'clean' people, living as a credit to God, and must demonstrate their fidelity to him in brotherly fellowship with one another and in purity of religion. The book is a noble attempt to apply the ancient religious and moral standards to the circumstances of the time (one can see it, in its oldest form, as a reissue of the so-called book of the Covenant of Exodus 21–23) and to prepare the ground for a new style of life on the part of the nation.

After it had been edited, the document was brought by its authors or their supporters to the temple and was there deposited as a consecrated gift in the offerings-chest,[2] in the hope that it would eventually see the light of day and so have its effect. That is just what did happen. When the temple was restored in 621, during the reign of Josiah, the book was discovered and was hailed as Yahwism's book of law, with official status (2 Kings 22f.). This occurred during the solemn renewal of the covenant between Yahweh and the nation in the restored temple, with the king acting as intermediary (2 Kings 23). The Passover feast of early Israel was linked with the feast of Maṣṣoth so as to constitute the chief festival, which had to be celebrated at Jerusalem in the temple. Deut. 16 prescribes that the three religious feasts should thenceforward be held only in Jerusalem as the centre of the nation and its religion. This was certainly a move to prevent their observance both in people's homes and at the rural sanctuaries, and was thus a move against syncretistic influences (especially Baalism). We have to understand the provisions of Deut. 26:1–11 in the same light.

It was a Reformation which very thoroughly purified religious life. Every object devoted to alien gods was removed from the temple and burnt in the valley of the Kidron, to the south-east of the city, whether it pertained to the cult of Baal or to Asherah and the star-gods of Assyria. The priests who looked after these cults, in Jerusalem and at the high places, were dismissed. An end was made of the sexual-agricultural rites (2 Kings 23:7) and of child-sacrifices. The holy places which Solomon had had fitted up outside Jerusalem for his wives and which were still in existence were destroyed.

Foreign religions were not the only target. The worship at the high places, which was so much inclined to syncretism, was dealt with too. In accordance with the expressed intention of Deuteronomy they were abolished and the sites defiled (see above, p. 230). The priests who had been connected with the high places and the worship there were not given opportunity to carry out the cult in the temple at Jerusalem; but they did share in the temple revenues.

Josiah went still further in that he pressed home the Deuteronomic iconoclasm in the old Northern Kingdom too, at Bethel, which after the destruction of Samaria had been taken over and used by foreigners (see p. 227). Here he resorted to more violent measures, killing the priests, desecrating the tombs near the temple and burning the bones on the old altar. This was the worst that could be inflicted on the dead, and the worst desecration of a holy place as well.

Josiah evidently regarded himself by that time as master of the former Samarian territories. This was feasible, because after the death of Ashurbanipal the Assyrian state disintegrated (Nineveh was taken and destroyed as early as 612). Josiah's hope was that he could reconstitute the former Davidic kingdom. There was not only a religious purpose but also a national-political one behind his Reformation. Because of Egypt's interference in the politics of Northern Syria and Palestine Josiah was never able to realize this dream of his. He perished at Megiddo in 609, in the battle with Necho, when his reforms had had only twelve years in which to become effective. No wonder that they never showed to full advantage or had any real and profound effect on religion and the national life.

It seems that after Josiah's death, when his sons Jehoiakim and Zedekiah were on the throne, the Deuteronomic law was as good as forgotten. In the second half of his public ministry Jeremiah is full of complaints about this abuse and the evil in the religious and moral sphere. In the field of social justice there is a good example in Jer. 34, where we read how at a difficult period king Zedekiah had compacted with the people to put Deut. 15:12ff., which deals with the setting free of slaves, into real operation and had sealed this with a solemn act of sacrifice (34:18ff.). Nevertheless, when it came to carrying out the decision, in practice nothing came of it, so that Jeremiah was obliged to utter a sharp condemnation. He speaks again in similar terms (in Jehoiakim's time: 26; 7; 11) about the habit of burning sacrifices for Baal and of running after other gods.

Jeremiah put himself heart and soul behind the Deuteronomic Reform and stood by it also later on, when it was clear that people were not being faithful to it (11). We gain the impression that the prophet had at first had his reservations about such a sudden change on the part of the nation. This is if we take chapter 3:21–4:4 as referring to the people's acts of contrition at the time of the Reformation. Here, as so often elsewhere, Jeremiah stresses the necessity for a change of heart (4:4). This he continues to do to the end of his life. The word rings out again in his famous prophecy: 'I will put my law in their inmost part and will write it upon their hearts' (31:33).

The Deuteronomic Reformation was a grand attempt, by means of an all-embracing religious law sponsored by the state, not merely to bring about cultic reform but also to achieve the ethico-social and spiritual renewal of a nation. Yet in none of those three areas was it successful: not on the first score, because the political situation was against it; nor on the second, because the nation was insufficiently prepared for it; nor yet on the third, because a spiritual transformation cannot, in the end, be organized from the top. Jeremiah's reservations were justified. That in spite of them he supported the effort at reform is only what one might expect of a prophet who has put before him a programme of reform which had kept so closely to the prophetic line and even gave expression to a great many of his own ideas.

We ought, of course, to add to what is said above about the Deuteronomic Reformers and their approach that they did not simply wish to impose the law on the people 'from the top'; for they used preaching as a means of elucidating what was being introduced, and tried to bring it home to the hearts of the people. In particular the introductory chapters (1–11), and perhaps also the closing ones (29–31), are most likely to be borrowings from preaching-sessions held among the people or in the temple, when Deuteronomy was being brought in as a new covenant-law. These homilies speak plainly of a demand for heartfelt repentance and the imperative need of love toward God. In Jer. 11:1–8 we probably have two surviving sermons which the prophet himself gave at that time to support the newly imported law.

Deuteronomy sets out to remake Israel (Judah), which it holds to be the chosen people of God, as a holy nation, consecrated to Yahweh, a nation which out of love fulfils the commandments of the one Lord (Deut. 5–7; cf. Ex. 19:5f.). To sum it up in more technical language: Deuteronomy endeavours to bring into being the theocratic nation-state of Israel, where whoever happens to be king at the time is not more than his subjects, being subject with them to the law of Yahweh (Deut. 17:14ff.). All the ideals of the old Yahweh-Federation are recurrent here, but are now brought together in a single body of state law. Even if they were in error, historically speaking, the Deuteronomists were altogether right in principle when they declared that the book of the law was really nothing more than an interpretation (Deut. 1:5), or, as we would do better to say, an application of the law of Moses. With this comprehensive statute-book which was considered as essentially the word of the one God, Yahweh, who makes his name to dwell in Jerusalem, Israel's religion and her existence as a nation moved into a new phase of their history. It is true, of course, that the Deuteronomic law functioned as the state law only for a brief period (621–609); for after Josiah it was just trampled over, apparently without there being any question of abolishing it; cf. what was said above (p. 232) regarding Deut. 15:12ff.

Of special relevance in this respect are the disclosures, dating from the year 592, which Ezekiel makes in chapter 8 of his book. There he describes how a variety of strange cults have penetrated even as far as the sacred precincts of the temple.[3] Among them are: sacrificial worship at the altar of an unspecified deity, with a portrayal of it, in relief, constructed at the entrance of a doorway (the picture is represented as arousing the jealousy of Yahweh); the carrying about of incense in a dark room, with the images of all kinds of monsters depicted on the wall (Egyptian ceremonies spring to mind at this point; some scholars believe that we can actually name Osiris as intended here); mourning for the ancient Mesopotamian god, Tammuz; and the practice of a form of sun-cult, possibly inspired by Egyptian models. This sample-list of cults shows that syncretism was once more in full flower and that gods and forms of worship were being borrowed from North and South.

But despite the official neglect into which the law fell, it did eventually recover its prestige and authority. Particularly in face of the threatened destruction of Jerusalem in 587, and thereafter, its value came to be better understood in certain quarters. The Deuteronomic spirit, therefore, did have an effect. Even the Deuteronomists' literary style was taken up and maintained in the writings which appeared after the exile (the great Deuteronomic historical work that we have in the books from Deuteronomy to 2 Kings).[4] Israel's whole outlook on history came under the influence of the Deuteronomic viewpoint. This work and this viewpoint were later canonized in the Torah and the former prophets. In that way the Deuteronomic tradition became a powerful force in later Jewish life. It is worth noting, for example, that of all the books of the Old Testament so far found to have been in use among the Qumran sect, next to those Isaiah and the Psalms, most are copies of the Book of Deuteronomy.[5]

With Deuteronomy, in fact, the process of forming the canon of sacred books of the Old Testament begins. As we said, around the book are grouped the historical writings of the Old Testament; so that very soon a great historical work emerges, extending from Genesis 2 to 2 Kings 25. Deuteronomy provided a powerful impetus in the direction of making the Yahwistic religion, which began as a prophetic religion and later developed very markedly in a priestly and cultic direction, into a religion of the Law, of the book of the Law, and finally of the Book.

The Deuteronomic Reformation, therefore, brief as its hey-day may have been, did prove to be an enduring influence on the evolution of Israel's religion, the extent of which is incalculable.

We must now return to Jeremiah and his contemporaries. This man, who came of a priestly family and lived at Anathoth, was called to be a prophet in 627. As we can see, for instance, from the beginning of chapter 2 of his book, he felt the impact of Hosea's prophecies; and he was consequently one of the few prophets to cherish hopes of salvation for the Northern kingdom (30f.). He uttered most of the prophecies in chapters 2-6 prior to the Deuteronomic Reformation in 621. After it he remained silent for a considerable time—in fact, during the rest of Josiah's reign. He was waiting, apparently, to see what the outcome of Josiah's Reform would be. Not until after the king's death in 609 did he again break silence. More especially in the time of Jehoiakim a persistent note of judgment was sounded in his preaching, as exemplified mainly in chapters 7-20. Most of his remaining prophecies came after the first fall of Jerusalem (597) during the reign of Zedekiah. A striking feature of his book is the number of personal lamentations and outpourings (confessions) which it contains. They mark the prophet out as an extremely sensitive person upon whom the task of criticism lay heavily.

He was obliged to utter a message of judgment, which for him was difficult enough in itself. In addition to this, however, he was again and again involved in fierce conflict with his nation (26), with the kings (36; 22), with the prophets of his day (23; 27-29) and even with his family (11:18-12:6). He felt himself in consequence to be utterly forsaken, being even without wife and children (16). No wonder, then, that it often became just too hard for this lonely man and that he indulged in passionate outbursts of complaint (8:18ff.; 9:1ff.; 15:10ff.; 18:19ff.; 20:7ff.). This prophet more than any other expresses the personal struggle and the suffering which his office brought upon him. Things became so bad at one time that he accused Yahweh of unfaithfulness (15:18); and Yahweh had to constrain him to change his attitude, since he could otherwise have no further use for him (15:19f.).

Another notable thing about Jeremiah is his frequent use of symbolic actions (13; 19; 27f.; 32).

He is called upon not only to condemn but also to awaken new hope (to break down and to build up; ch. 1). His preaching is affected as much by that of Amos, the prophet of justice, with his call to repentance and warning of judgment, as by that of Hosea, the prophet of love, who spoke of both judgment and salvation. We may say that with Jeremiah the call to repentance was to the fore, especially in the first period (3:12ff.; 4:1ff.; 31:15ff.); so that his declarations of judgment to come were often conditional. Later on, in the second period of his public ministry, things were different: then the irrevocable nature of the judgment was given much more prominence. It was again Jeremiah who, like Micah, foretold the destruction of the temple (26:7); but this nearly cost him his life, and would have done so, had not certain elders of the land remembered Micah and had Jeremiah not had friends and protectors among the most senior officials. Himself a priest's son, he was not opposed to the temple and cult as such; and he recognized that as the temple-city Jerusalem was a holy place (7; 31; 32). He also pronounced in favour of the Deuteronomic policy of centralizing the cult. Yet he knew very well how dangerous the cult could be, because it could be practised 'with a disobedient heart' (7). He declares emphatically, like Amos, that in the earliest period of Yahwism what Yahweh had required was not sacrifices but obedience (7:22).

With the priests, the prophets and the men of war, he was frequently at loggerheads, in particular with the prophets who spoke only fair words. Jeremiah reproached them with uttering only the promptings of their own hearts (23:9ff.), and not what Yahweh was saying to them. Perhaps the truth was that they repeated what they sang in their psalms of Zion (cf. Psalm 48): that Jerusalem could never be destroyed, and that in so doing they were merely conforming to the cultic tradition of their day or were drawing the wrong conclusions from it. But in their pious 'wishful dreaming', which they gave out as prophecies, Jeremiah saw great danger for the nation (14:13ff.); and he predicted their downfall (14:28f.). Especially toward the end of Jerusalem's existence he had a difficult time with them and with the military. The latter branded him as a traitor (37), because he was saying publicly that keeping faith with Nebuchadnezzar and, after a revolt, agreeing to submit to him once more, offered the sole remaining possibility for national existence. It was probably in order to clear him of the charge of treason that Jeremiah's companion and scribe wrote a detailed account of his last years before and after the destruction of the city (36–45). After the city's capture in 587 he was, to begin with, released in company with a few of the inhabitants; and he was able to attach himself to the Judean governor, Gedaliah. After that man's murder, carried out by a handful of Judean fanatics led by prince Ishmael, those who were left fled, in opposition to Jeremiah's warnings, to Egypt, compelling him to go with them.

Just like Isaiah and other prophets, Jeremiah expected that after the judgment would come the restoration of Jerusalem. In chapter 32 he describes how at God's behest he redeemed a field that had belonged to a cousin of his; and this he took as corroborating his belief in the restoration. He expected that the renovation would come about under the leadership of a Messianic prince, 'the righteous offshoot' of the house of David (23:5). This expectation was grounded, for Jeremiah, in the faithfulness of Yahweh, who had once chosen Israel and would not discard her (31:35ff.). On this Israel's whole religion, and Jeremiah's faith, was based, even in face of ruin and destruction. It would come to pass as and when the new age should dawn, in which the governing factor would not be an external law, but each man would of his own accord do God's will from his heart (31:31ff.). This eschatological hope has a relatively minor place among Jeremiah's prophetic utterances; but it should be recognized as lying at the root of his whole life as a man of faith. It enabled him to keep going when every earthly prop—indeed, every external religious support—had gone, and when the temple really did fall in ruins, as he had foretold. The destruction of the temple did not mean for him, as it did for so many, the loss of an assured faith; for he was convinced of God's enduring faithfulness. With the ruin of the temple, the city and the state many others felt the ground giving way under their feet; and they feared that Israel was now finished for good, because to their way of thinking it had become evident that God had rejected Israel. It was a problem that weighed heavily on a lot of people (33:23ff.; a later pericope), especially during the exile. The notion is repeatedly touched upon in Deutero-Isaiah. Yet Jeremiah was sure of the opposite (31:35ff., in view of which 33:19ff. and 23ff. could also be ascribed to him).

A word or two more about the prophecies against the nations, which have been brought together in chapters 46–51 of the Book of Jeremiah (partly supplemented with more recent material). Most of the prophetic books contain such prophecies (Amos, Isaiah, Zephaniah, Ezekiel). They demonstrate that the prophets were certain of the universality of Yahweh's lordship and activity. He was also arbiter of the destiny of the peoples beyond Israel.

The wiping out of Jerusalem was felt as a crushing blow both by people at the time and by their posterity; and this finds its deepest outlet in the Lamentations, which tradition ascribed, understandably enough, to Jeremiah himself. It has more often, and with more justice, been thought that the third individual lament was the work of a poet writing with an eye to Jeremiah, whose prophetic career had been one perpetual process of suffering for and with his nation, and one continuing struggle against it. This lyrical piece may indeed have been inspired by the figure of the prophet.

The names of three prophets of this period ought just to be mentioned. It is a notable fact that just as at the time of the downfall of the Northern kingdom four important prophetic figures emerged, so now in this period when the destruction of Jerusalem was imminent, there arose so many outstanding men of God; whereas throughout the seventy years of the intervening period not a single great man appeared on the scene.

Besides Zephaniah and Jeremiah one should mention Nahum, Habakkuk and Ezekiel. Ezekiel is considered in connexion with the ensuing period of the exile because he was of such paramount significance during that time and indeed after it.

Nahum may be just briefly referred to here, because a short prophetic writing of his has survived, comprising a psalm and a few lyrics on the theme of the destruction of Nineveh. The fall of Nineveh is here greeted with such joy in the second chapter, and in the third with such great delight, as to give rise to the idea that Nahum must be the one and only prophet to appear in writing in the Old Testament who is of the same calibre as the false prophets.

It is very much a question whether this is indeed so; because the fall of Nineveh was hailed with joy not only by the prophets of salvation but certainly by all the people of Judah, including the prophets of woe. Even if it were no longer the case that all the enemies of Israel were regarded as enemies of Yahweh, still the classical prophets of doom could also, from time to time, write with a measure of gratification of the approaching discomfiture of enemy nations, particularly when it came to the tyrannical Assyrian, upon whom Isaiah had already pronounced sentence! The contrast between false and true prophets did not lie in a different way of thinking about the enemy but in their divergent assessments of the situation in which Jerusalem and their own nation found themselves.

Habakkuk is a peculiar figure, in so far as he appears to have operated as a temple prophet (2:1f.). His prophecies probably date from the years (between 606 and 600) just before and just after the Chaldeans (Nebuchadnezzar) made their appearance. After complaining of injustice and lawlessness in Judah (1:2–4), he points to the Chaldeans (Babylonians) as the people destined to assume future world power. His account of their activities does not arouse much confidence in the future. In 1:12ff. there follows a complaint addressed to God concerning their inhuman behaviour, which must have been written after the Babylonians had seized power over the West Semitic world.

In 2:1ff. he describes how he awaits a word from God and how he is told to proclaim it for all clearly to understand. The message promises safe-keeping to the righteous man who lives in faith and trust; but the proud will perish in the judgment that is so soon to come. Then come several expostulations over the sins of the time.

In Habakkuk, therefore, we are dealing with a cultic prophet who nevertheless prophesies calamity.[6] Although he does not know precisely when it will come, it will surely descend upon the nation (2:3f.). There is a considerable vagueness about his prophesying, which we might perhaps call a trait symptomatic of cultic oracular utterances, where (as in the Greek world) each man just has to know how the shoe is pinching him. This vagueness explains why there is such wide disagreement among commentators today as to what the correct interpretation is. It also probably accounts for the fact that this prophetic book later became a favourite document with apocalyptic groups and sectarians who wanted to attach to these predictions this or that interpretation of what was taking place in their own day, as was the case with the sectaries of Qumran. Among the scrolls from the Judean desert one of theirs has been found which is a 'commentary' on Habakkuk in which his prophecies are applied to persons of the second or first century before Christ, but so vaguely that we can no longer tell to whom reference is being made.

CHAPTER 10

Regeneration and Recovery

THE PERIOD FOLLOWING upon the destruction of the temple at Jerusalem, with the banishment of the people of Judah, their return and the building of the temple, constitutes an episode of exceptional importance in the history of Israel. It was an ordeal by fire, testing her spiritual vitality and her very being as a nation, which she came through in a quite remarkable way. That is so, even from a historical viewpoint. M. Noth[1] is right in saying that Israel had in common with all the Syrio-Palestinian peoples the experience of losing political independence and of seeing the leading citizens partly scattered and deported. Not one of these nations, however, maintained its distinctive character and way of life through it all as successfully as did Israel, whose *Einmaligkeit darin eine greifbare Wirkung hatte* (i.e. her singularity was in that respect palpably effective). Only, of course, we must bear in mind that Israel here is actually Judah, which rightly came to regard herself as representing Israel. There had been no recovery or restitution for the exiled people of Northern Israel. (Judah, Judean, or Jew in the Old Testament always tended to become more and more a geographical concept with a secular connotation, and had as yet no religious implications).

All this could not happen without some price having to be paid. In the first place, it was only a relatively small number of people who, as soon as Cyrus had issued his edict authorizing the restoration of the temple (538; Ezra 6:3ff.), decided to go back to their former homeland (only in or about 521 did some forty thousand return with Zerubbabel). We can tell at once from Deutero-Isaiah that he found little enthusiasm for his summons to faith and to a decision to return. But still, it happened; and the restoration was able to go ahead. It did prove possible to pick up once more the threads of the nation's spiritual life.

For this Israel had to thank, more than anything else, the work and preaching of the prophets, the pre-exilic prophets of woe, who gave her the assurance that after the judgment had descended she would be restored and that Yahweh had not abandoned his people. Above all, Israel owed this to two men of God who had themselves experienced the exile and in that situation had provided the people with new spiritual strength: Ezekiel and Deutero-Isaiah.

The most remarkable aspect of the whole story is that both these men, but especially the latter, made what was a period of eclipse into one of the culminating points, spiritually speaking, in the history of Israel's religion. This period of political annihilation brought with it a rebirth of Yahwism realized in the life of Deutero-Isaiah and imparted by him to his co-religionists. Although we must not think of the company of faithful people around him as being all that numerous, there is no gainsaying that it did exist and that it preserved his message and carried it on. It was the regenerating impact of his utterances which, in many respects, continued to affect Israel's religion up to a considerably later period and bred new life in the spiritual sphere. One need think only of the influence which his preaching had on the Qumran sect and on the first Christians.

The political nadir proved to be a moment of spiritual climax in which Yahwism acquired not only (as already with Isaiah and Jeremiah) a totally religious (Yahweh is all in all) and thoroughly human character (with Isaiah it was a question of the will, with Jeremiah, of the heart), but also a fully universal reference (this was already the case, in principle, with Isaiah). Yahweh, the creator of light and darkness, for whom the world's nations are as a layer of dust in the balances, not only has the peoples at his beck and call but is the One upon whose righteous law and instruction they wait.

The man without a homeland thus became the man whose faith was vested in a God at once universal and personal, Yahweh, and in that faith his people should be the first to share. Because the universal features of Yahweh's nature took such a prominent place, Yahwism with him assumed a new aspect. Still, this man remained 'in heart and reins' both Israelite and 'Zionist'; and his God was none other than the God of Israel. Yet the very fact that this God of a nation, this God of persons, this God of salvation, embraced the whole of mankind proved to be of supreme significance for the future course of Israel's religion, and even more, for that of more than one of the other world religions. This was the great discovery made by the prophet of the diaspora.

It is important to note, on the other hand, how little of this broad

Q

vision is actually incorporated in the religious thought of that time. The universal traits in the picture which Yahweh now presented were the very ones to fade away when the hope of Zion's restoration had been fulfilled, the temple had been rebuilt and the forms of religion current in an earlier period had become normative again as a result. What all this achieved, however, was little more than the reconstitution of the earlier conditions. As is to be expected in matters religious, the restorers clung to the old as hard as they could, not only where the foundations and construction of the actual temple complex were concerned[2] but also as regards the arrangements prescribed for religious and cultic practices. Although certain corrections were made to the cultic laws, in view of the criticisms voiced by earlier prophets,[3] we cannot speak here of renewal, but only of restoration. Clearly, not all those who restored the temple, even of those who returned, let alone of the Judeans who had stayed behind in Palestine, were followers of Deutero-Isaiah. The prophet was certainly no opponent of the restoration (in 44:28 he himself proclaims that a new temple is to be built), any more than Jeremiah, a century before, had been against the Deuteronomic Reformation; yet for both of them the renewal of religious activity was too profound and too inward a matter for the case to be met merely by this or that external alteration (for Jeremiah see p. 235f. and for Deutero-Isaiah, 42:1ff.; 43:22ff.; 44:1ff.; 51:1, 7; 54:12f.; 55:1ff., 6ff.).

This was more or less the attitude of the exilic prophet to the restoration. As the above-cited passages make clear, he certainly expected more than that, and hoped for a change of direction, a new *élan* within the new Yahweh-community, which should involve not only the Jewish nation but the whole world of nations in its aspirations.

The restrictive provisions regarding ritual and the fact that the entire religion was centred on the temple soon led to protests, which would appear to have come from the circle of Deutero-Isaiah's disciples and have consequently been preserved in the appendages to his book. Isa. 56:1ff., for instance, registers a protest at the exclusion of certain groups from the cult, and 66:1f. establishes in a prophetic manner (recalling the early-Israelite period, but yet by its inclusion of the creation-motif speaking with an accent wholly new) the fundamental irrelevance of the temple. In his preaching on the restitution of Zion Deutero-Isaiah invariably made a point of the fact that the glorious thing about the liberation was the open demonstration that

Yahweh was king over his people, that his majesty and mercy dwelt in the midst of Israel.

It is wrong, therefore, to see the two principal elements from this period as lying each directly in line of contact with the other: the transforming, regenerative proclamation of Deutero-Isaiah pointing to a new path for Yahwism, and the movement of restoration centred around the new temple, harking back to the pristine state of affairs, and ordering in ever greater detail and precision the sacrificial and priestly cult, through all sorts of ritualistic rules and regulations. Tensions between a type of belief with a more universalistic, and one with a more particularist, tendency were therefore bound to arise. They are indeed a characteristic feature of the whole future course of events, as will subsequently appear (see p. 258f.).

This is in part connected with the fact that after the destruction of Jerusalem the simple people and the poor stayed behind. The Babylonians deported especially the upper strata of the population and left the lower classes in the country, so as not to let it fall into total decay. It has actually been estimated[4] that about 20,000 people must have remained in the country. This remnant, naturally enough, made some sort of recovery in the course of two generations, although trouble with intruders belonging to the surrounding peoples— Ammonites, Moabites, Edomites (see Obadiah and Ezekiel 25 and 35) and Samaritans—did not exactly make life easier for them. The bards or singers responsible for Lamentations probably lived among them; and they had an intense longing to see the temple restored.

One thing may be taken as characteristic of this whole period: namely, that the whole nation was possessed with a continuous yearning for Zion. After the destruction of the temple, the faithful, even from the former Northern kingdom, persisted in coming to the temple ruins, to perform there, in so far as was possible, the business of the cult (Jer. 41:5ff.), even though the number who did so was small (Lam. 1:4). The Lamentations give expression to this great longing for Zion. The prophet Ezekiel not only feels profound sorrow at Jerusalem's downfall but suggests a quite novel scheme for restoring the temple and reconstituting the country and the nation. Deutero-Isaiah also speaks repeatedly of the new Zion, the dwelling-place of Yahweh, and proclaims that city and temple are to be rebuilt. Lyrics such as Psalms 126 and 137 can still give one a lively sense of the exiled Judeans' tremendous nostalgia for their holy city.

It goes to show how much Jerusalem had become for Judah *the*

symbol of God's election and his covenant; and it is very understandable, not only in consequence of the Deuteronomic Reformation
but also because of the importance that Solomon's temple, with the
ark of Yahweh Sebaoth, had acquired in the life of the Judeans. This
was especially so since the collapse of the Northern kingdom and the
wonderful deliverance in 701. Jerusalem was the tangible link in the
chain of historical traditions binding them to the distant past of
David and Moses. All this made of Jerusalem the visible, and for
many the indispensable, pledge and warranty of Yahweh's faithfulness toward his people. That is why, after Jerusalem had gone under,
there remained for so many nothing that they could hold on to.

Those who remained true to the faith clung to the tradition, which
from that time on was assiduously cultivated. The ancient sources
were assembled, and being now combined were re-issued as the
religious and spiritual annals of Israel (the Deuteronomic history).
The utterances of the classical prophets, which events had shown to
be indeed words of God, were also brought together. In priestly and
Levitical circles the old cultic, liturgical (Psalms) and juridical texts
were passed on both orally and in writing; and so the foundation was
laid for the collections of cultic laws such as we find in the oldest
section of the Priestly Code, in the Law of Holiness and in the first
collections of Psalms. In this way the tradition was able in some degree
to assume the place of the temple, the cult and, in part, of prophecy
too.

It was not only thus that men applied themselves to cultivating the
tradition. They also maintained it at a practical level in their daily
lives and in their religion. Great emphasis came to be put on observance of the Sabbath and on circumcision particularly, as signs of
membership of the people of God. The importance of these factors is
underlined by the link which priestly theology establishes between
them and the earliest periods of history. The so-called Priestly Code,
which must have been drawn up partly during the exile, treats the
institution of the Sabbath as the final purpose of Creation (Gen.
1–2:4a), and circumcision as having been already established by
Yahweh at the time of Abraham (Gen. 17). It is possible that even
during the Babylonian exile the tradition was studied and nurtured in
people's homes on the Sabbath day by the recital of classical texts and
that from this there arose later on, when the Torah had come into
being as a book, the custom of meeting together in a separate building:
the synagogue. At what juncture this came about we do not know;

but it is quite likely that it first came into vogue in the Eastern diaspora.[5]

What lies at the back of the restoration idea, then, is a keen desire for Zion to be restored and the interest concentrated around the tradition.

Where the Jews in exile were concerned, the effect of the prophet Ezekiel's activities was in the same general direction. The final part of the sketch of the restoration of the land in the book which bears his name ends with a description of the gates of the holy city. Its closing words are: 'the name of the city from that time on shall be: Yahweh is there' (48:35). Even though the chapters here may be his disciples' rather than his own, this is symptomatic of the place that Jerusalem has in his expectations of salvation. All his preaching turns upon Israel as God's nation and on the holy city at its centre. In all kinds of ways Ezekiel set the scene for the restoration; and he has not without justice been called the father of Judaism. It is remarkable how little this prophet, who after all lived for many decades in foreign parts, has to say about the nations of the world. He alludes almost exclusively to the old enemies of Israel round about Palestine, the small neighbouring states of Moab, Ammon, Edom, Philistia, Tyre, Sidon and Egypt; and he gives sentence upon them all. For Nebuchadnezzar he has a promise in store (29:19f.; 30:10). Like Jeremiah, Ezekiel sees him as the man singled out to execute judgment on Israel and on the other peoples too. The latter only come into the picture in so far as they have some involvement with Israel. Ezekiel lacks all universality of outlook.

As a priest, he was deported to Babylon, along with about 11,000 other eminent citizens of Jerusalem, in 597. He remained a priest at heart, even though after five years in Babylon he was called to be a prophet. In the vision through which he received his call Yahweh appeared to him in all his majesty as a Being of Fire in the likeness of a man, enveloped in a rainbow-coloured mist and seated on a throne of azure, resting upon a carriage borne along by four cherubim. Although the prophet realizes that what he has seen of Yahweh is but a pale reflection of the reality of his Being (he keeps saying. 'it was as though', 'it looked like'), this revelation gave him the complete assurance of the mobility and omnipresence of the celestial Majesty, the comforting beauty and humanity of the God of Fire and his affinity to man. Ezekiel is himself not infrequently addressed as man,[6] which expresses the fact that his nature is bounded by his creatureliness and dependence upon the great God. Thus the absolute character of the divine majesty is one of the leading motifs running through the whole of Ezekiel's preaching. He has been sent to his nation, although, as has been revealed to him, it will hardly listen to him, with the instruction to fulfil his task despite everything, so that the exiles will bow to the will of God. Should he default in his duty to warn his people, the blame for the sin of the godless will devolve upon him (chs. 1-3). Ezekiel, then, is held personally responsible and accountable in his capacity as a prophet. From then on he is at work all the time and in a variety of ways, proclaiming the word to people who seek him out, performing symbolic actions, making songs and writing down the revelations accorded to him, in order to prepare the exiles for the approaching destruction of Jerusalem and to make them realize that the sin of Israel is the sole reason for the Lord Yahweh's (Adonai Yahweh) judgment. This ancient cultic form of address, which has a peculiarly solemn ring about it, is used by Ezekiel as a stereotype name for God and expresses the deep reverence and awe in which the prophet holds him.[7]

When the siege of Jerusalem became a reality, the prophet was smitten with dumbness (probably to be understood as a symbolic gesture; cf. 3:22-27; 24:25-27; 33:21f.).[8] When his wife died, he was not permitted to utter any lamentation, in token of the speechless grief that was to overcome his nation at the destruction of their city. Simultaneously with the grief felt at his beloved wife's death there came upon him all the misery that was to descend upon the city; and it rendered him speechless (24:15f.). Ezekiel suffered deeply, therefore, in his own person under the realization of the message of judgment which for six years he had been obliged to convey.

When after nearly five months the news of the fall of Jerusalem reached the exiles (Ezek. 33:21f.; cf. with Jer. 52:6, 12), Ezekiel was once more called to speak (33:21f.). He then found the exiles beginning to take his words seriously—in the sense that they had now come to credit them—but he could not help observing at the same time that the majority did not contemplate applying them in their own lives (33:30ff.).

We know of only a few prophecies of judgment uttered by Ezekiel after the destruction of Jerusalem, and these are concerned with particular sections of the nation (in 33:23ff. with profiteers in the home country; and in 34 with what had formerly been the governing classes in Jerusalem). Otherwise, the substance of his preaching is of a quite different order. From now on he has leave to speak to the nation of salvation and recovery. The judgment over and done with, Yahweh's constructive work can now begin. He himself takes up the search for his sheep (the people which had been led astray), offering them new possibilities of living (34:11ff.). Cleansed and purified, Israel will be brought home by him (36). God will raise her, so to speak, from the dead (37). Just as God's holiness had first required that judgment be executed upon an unfaithful people, so from now on he will glorify his holy name among the nations by his total redemption of Israel. Ezekiel well knows that all this rests with Yahweh alone and that it will be solely his doing. Along with this strongly theocentric emphasis the accent falls on the note of personal responsibility (18), which Ezekiel propounds in order to prevent his companions in adversity from taking refuge in a pessimistic and amoral fatalism.

His final work was to commit to writing a visionary plan of the future temple, a new ordering of the duties of a prince and of the priests, and of the festivals and sacrificial rites. As he had described (in ch. 10) how Yahweh in all his glory had left the temple, so now (in chs. 43:1ff.; 44:1ff.) he records how Yahweh will return to it, and how with that the desert from Jerusalem up to the Dead Sea will become a fertile garden, a paradise, fed by a stream of living water which will spring out of the temple-mountain. In these pictorial terms he expresses his hope and expectancy that the new temple will be the source of life for a people renewed.

With Ezekiel the visionary elements loom large. Among the accounts of his experiences are some that remind one of ecstatic situations, as on those occasions when he feels himself taken up by God's Spirit and transported from Babylon to Jerusalem (8:3; 2:1; 3:24; 43:5; cf. 3:12f.). Although some of his symbolic actions are presented in such a way as to suggest the idea of psychic disturbances[9] (dumbness, see above, p. 246; lameness, ch. 4), it is hard to lay down the law about this, because the data can be interpreted in so many different ways.

The last of his datable prophecies belongs to the year 571 (29:17). Ezekiel must, therefore, have lived c. 635–570, which would make him a younger contemporary of Jeremiah. When he was carried off in 597 he must already have been a priest of influential standing; and in his early years he must have been one of Jeremiah's opponents. Jeremiah did not affect him to any great extent, therefore, although

here and there the older man's influence is detectable.[10] Their
personalities were too dissimilar, and in many respects their lives
were too far apart in the course they took. Whereas in Ezekiel's case a
priestly cast of thought was always predominant, even when he
became a prophet, with Jeremiah it was just the other way round. At
the personal level Jeremiah gives the impression of a very sensitive
man, even in his choice of words. Ezekiel is a far more angular,
uncompromising figure, sometimes crude, even, in his manner of
expression (16:23) and symbolic gestures (4:5). That is the more
extraordinary in that he is nonetheless a real poet. His thinking is
couched in rigorous contrasts of black and white; and this betrays
him into making one-sided assertions that are in contradiction with
each other. Thus on the one hand he thinks in highly collective terms
(e.g. 15; 16 *et passim*), yet on the other passes such thoroughly
individualistic judgments that no room is left for collective guilt at all
(18). He is also the only prophet who can say of one of God's commandments that Yahweh gave it in order thereby to delude his
people, as punishment for their sinful behaviour (20:25f.). With this
assertion, which makes historical Israel carry the penalty incurred by
their forefathers in the desert, the prophet comes sharply into conflict
with his own individualistically conceived message in chapter 18. He
is, then, a complex personality and so by no means always easy to
understand. One has to take seriously the polarities in what he
utters and hold them, in their paradoxical character, firmly together. Perhaps the psychological explanation of all this lies in
the fact that with all its inflexibility his personality is so highly
emotional too.

The message propounded by Ezekiel is governed principally by the
thought of judgment, by the threatening calamity; although for him
also there is a break-through to the certitude of renewal. In his last
dated prophecy (of 571; 29:17ff.) he believes that he can connect its
fulfilment with a historical event which he definitely expects to happen.
It turned out to be a prophecy unfulfilled; for it was not the Babylonian king Nebuchadnezzar, the conqueror of Egypt, but the
Persian Cyrus, destroyer of Babylon, who proved to be the restorer
of Israel.

The fairly rapid dismembering of the new Babylonian kingdom
after Nebuchadnezzar's death will of course have revived hopes of
liberation among the Jews living in Babylon, who naturally were
familiar with the predictions of the pre-exilic prophets and of Ezekiel

that salvation would come. Entirely new prospects were opened up by the unexpected successes of the Persian king, who disposed of one power after another and within a short time (by 539) had subjugated the Babylonian empire.

It was at this period that there appeared a prophet, probably among the Babylonian Jews, to whom history will never be able to put a name. Apparently because so much in them was felt to have an affinity with the sayings of Isaiah (for instance, in both of them Yahweh is habitually referred to as the holy One of Israel), this man's collected prophecies were tacked on to the Book of Isaiah. Thus nearly all scholars have come to speak of him as Deutero-Isaiah, although others call him the prophet of the exile. He must have been close to the historical events which occurred in and around the year 539; but we should be on our guard against the theory that he played an active political role in them.[11] We must even be chary, as in the case of Amos and Isaiah (see above, pp. 216, 221), of seeing the events of history as the spring-board of Deutero-Isaiah's preaching[12] and the prophet as simply interpreting them. In his case also, what lay right at the root of his preaching ministry was the call through which he received the divine word impelling him forward (Isa. 40:3ff. and 6ff.); and it was only thereafter that he recognized in what was happening the activity of God himself. In the light of his call and of the revelation that came with it, that Yahweh was now actively fulfilling his message of salvation which the earlier prophets had spoken (verses 5 and 8; cf. verse 2), the prophet surveys the events of his time. He proclaims the deliverance which step by step Yahweh has brought nearer in Cyrus's conquests (41:1-7, 25-29; 45:1-8; 46:11; 48:14f.).[13] Yet still in all this it is Yahweh alone who is at work. Cyrus, although he does not know Yahweh, is his servant, his anointed (45:1ff.).

Thus Deutero-Isaiah is the prophet of 'imminent eschatology'. His book starts, therefore, with the message that Israel's time of suffering is over (40:2), that God is returning to dwell in Zion, there to govern his people. The prophet can only set it all in this light because for him, as for Isaiah and Ezekiel, Yahweh is sole and absolute ruler in the world. With him more than with any other prophet of Israel Yahweh is pre-eminently the creator of all things. Yahweh is not only creator and governor of the entire world and the whole of history, but wishes to enter into contact with all mankind. This message has a leaning to universalism which is seen especially clearly in 45:22ff. All the ends of the earth are implicated in salvation (verse 22), all shall one day bow before Yahweh (verse 23) and acknowledge that mighty acts of salvation rest with Yahweh alone.[14] The whole world is envisaged as waiting expectantly for Yahweh's *torah* (42:4; 51:4f.); and Israel (the Servant of Yahweh) is regarded as having a duty to that world to 'bring forth God's justice' to the nations (42:1, 4)[15] and to be a light to the nations (42:6; 44:6; 55:4f.). A positive duty in the world devolves upon Israel: to be an active witness to Yahweh's revelation. In 51:4f. Yahweh himself causes justice and revelation to go forth to the nations.

Since the aim of Yahweh's dealings in world history is the salvation of Israel, this in turn must come to have a significance for the world's peoples. They are to have their part in it and so come to know and worship Yahweh. They will recognize what he has accomplished in Israel as being indeed his own mighty acts. Yahweh will make of Israel, which is so despicable in the world's eyes, a thing of glory.

Over against the prophet's rapture lies the impotence of the nation to which he makes his appeal. They react to his call for faith with something hardly distinguishable from disbelief (42:18ff.; 49:14; 50:2f.; 51:12ff.). This is particularly evident in the second group of the Servant (*Ebed Yahweh*) Songs, as they are called (50:4ff.; 52:13ff. and 53:1ff.): the nation, summoned by the prophet to a new splendour, must itself first be renewed through those who, as 'servant of Yahweh', hear and answer the call and in a representative capacity actually fulfil the task of Israel. In 50:4ff. the prophet, who has thought of himself primarily as Yahweh's servant, gives an account of the violence that he has experienced. In 52:12ff. and 53:1ff. he pictures what he regards as the way of the servant of Yahweh and the outcome of his work. If the liberation and vindication of Israel is to become a spiritual reality, this can only be through the sufferings of the servant of God.

There are, then, various layers and motifs in the prophecies of this extraordinary man of God. Some are of a spirituality so profound that they find scarcely an echo in the centuries that follow; but there are hints of them in Zechariah (2:7—if literally translated: 'thou inhabiter, daughter of Babylon'; 8:13, 20ff.; 9:9f.) and in a Psalm such as 87.

On the other hand his Zionist expectations were certainly not altogether vain. He must have been partly responsible for the return of many an exile to his country, for which he had appealed with so much passion (48:20f.; 52:11f.; cf. 51:9–52:10). We may suppose that 52:11f. was uttered with regard to the departure of the first batch of exiles (under Sheshbazzar in 537), who were allowed to take with them the holy objects belonging to the temple, which Cyrus had already given back (cf. Ezra 1:7ff.). Verse 12 in this passage is surely most indicative in that it provides a good illustration of the fact that Deutero-Isaiah connects up directly with the tradition regarding the exodus from Egypt, which was a hurried business and an occasion when by means of a column of cloud and fire Yahweh proved to be the protector of the fleeing Israelites (cf. Ex. 12:11; Deut. 16:3; Ex. 13:21f.; 14:19f.). It is evident in Deutero-Isaiah again and again to what a large extent his nation's history is a vital force in his experience. It is, however, a past that for him is also present. It is Yahweh's immediate presence in the here and now that he experiences; and this means for him that past and future fuse into a single present reality.

That the once-given word is actualized in the history of his people comes to be the sign of Yahweh's activity as Creator and Lord. It confirms the prophet's message of the immediacy of God's relation with Israel, which he had expressed at the very start of his preaching ministry in the words: 'See, here is your God' (40:9; cf. 52:7).[16]

The number of people who returned at once to Jerusalem in 538 cannot be determined;[17] but it was probably not very considerable. We can assume that as time went on there were further expeditions. Many of the exiles felt an attachment to Babylon and did not move, at least not immediately. Deutero-Isaiah gives the impression that a majority of the exiles were indifferent to his message. Many had found in Babylon a second homeland.

At the command of Cyrus (cf. Ezra 6:3ff.), whose religious policy was very different from the Babylonians' and by whom sanctuaries were therefore being restored in a number of countries, the new arrivals promptly set about rebuilding the temple at Jerusalem. They did not, however, get beyond clearing and restoring the foundations and a part of the walls. Apparently, the funds needed were not forthcoming; and despite the fact that a few had speedily contrived to work themselves into a condition of great prosperity, the economic situation of the Jews, whether of the immigrants or of those who remained behind, was not a very rosy one (Hag. 1).[18]

Not until after 521 did things change, probably because then the main group of immigrants led by Zerubbabel arrived and because the prophets Haggai (who was possibly one of the earliest group of immigrants) and Zechariah (only just returned from Babylon) spurred on the immigrants' leaders, prince Zerubbabel, grandson to Jehoiachin, and Joshua, the high priest, to build the temple (Ezra 5:1ff.; Hag. 1:1).

Haggai, in his prophecies uttered during the year 520, drew attention to the fact that people were indeed working for their own economic advantage, but not on Yahweh's temple. He explained the bad harvest of that year as a divine punishment and so urged the people, in words of some force, to take the rebuilding of the temple in hand again and to press on with it. His words struck home; and in the very same month when the first of them were spoken (September 520) the rebuilding started. A month later another exhortation was addressed to the leaders (Hag. 2:1ff.), as enthusiasm had evidently begun to flag somewhat, when the ruins had been cleared away and it was realized that to rebuild the temple in all its glory would not be possible. Haggai then predicted that at a future time the temple would rise more glorious than it had ever been. Some months later still Haggai warned the people, on the strength of a priestly declaration about cultic uncleanness, which lays it down that whilst 'holiness' cannot be transferred, 'uncleanness' certainly can be, against letting themselves be polluted in this way (2:11ff.), thereby tilting, apparently, at the practice of establishing contact with sections of the population such as Samaritans and Jews who had commingled with them. This means that on the question as to who is allowed to belong to the new temple-community the ritual-cultic viewpoint is declared to be the decisive factor: only those qualify who are cultically clean. Obviously, Isaiah 56:1ff., which places the emphasis on keeping the Sabbath and holding fast to the covenant, and on the fact that the temple ought to be a house of prayer for all nations, gives a different, more broad-minded answer to this question, which probably conflicts, even, with Haggai's.

Moreover, on the same day, the 24th of the 9th month (December 18-19, 520), the day on which the new building was begun[19] (after the rubble had been cleared), Haggai uttered a prophecy which shows that he had aspirations of a political kind; for in it he pointed to Zerubbabel as the future Messianic prince (2:22ff.). Because of these pronouncements this became the day—formally, at any rate—from which the opposition between the Jews who lived by the cult and ritual and the other groups aforementioned took its beginning. From it dated also the open hostility of the latter party to the further construction of the temple (see Ezra 4:1–6). The Messianic saying about Zerubbabel gave them a handle for their complaint to the Persian authorities.

Zechariah, although a priest's son and sincerely attached to the temple and its cult, is not so one-sidedly intent on the building of the temple and on the ritual as Haggai. We get the impression that his attitude is very much that of Jeremiah toward the Deuteronomic Reformation: he accepts them but does not regard them as the key to a final solution.

In Zechariah's preaching there is more of the spirit of Deutero-Isaiah than in Haggai's. To go by the dates assigned to the prophecies and by the summary account in Ezra (who always puts Haggai first; 5:1 and 6:14), the latter prophet appeared first; and only later on did Zechariah come to join him.

The first prophecy incorporated in the Book of Zechariah, and the one bearing the earliest date, was received when the building of the temple was beginning, although it does not actually relate to the matter of the building. It comprises an exhortation, supported by an appeal to the pre-exilic prophets, to true repentance. It looks very much as though, in the face of the all too activistically orientated religious trend of the time, Zechariah wished the old prophetic note sounded by Isaiah and Jeremiah to be heard once more. Such an accent is clearly audible in chapter 7, when some years later, in answer to people who come seeking an oracle regarding the resumption of a fast-day, he declares that Yahweh is not concerned with fasts but with love and righteousness.

His prophecies relating to the temple and to Jerusalem come only second. The first of these pertains to the 24th of the 11th month (is thus dated February 519), two months after the last prophecy delivered by Haggai (1:7). Zechariah's utterances evidently belong to the tense period that started when the Persian authorities, incited by the rural population and the Samaritans, began to take a hand in the matter of the building (Ezra 5:3ff.). At that time Zechariah had three visions, of which only the first bears a date, in which he received, successively, the assurance of Yahweh's loyal attachment to Zion and his anger at the self-assured, arrogant behaviour of the surrounding peoples (1:12ff.), his resolve to break all opposition (1:18ff.) and his promise to restore Jerusalem itself as a spacious, open city which would enjoy the protection of his own presence in it (2:1ff.). Jerusalem is described as a religious metropolis for the nations of the world (2:6ff.).

At the centre of all this lies the truly prophetic notion that Yahweh dwells in the midst of the nation at Jerusalem (2:5, 10f.; 8:7f.). Zechariah obviously carried on working in conformity with Haggai (8:9ff.), but time and again sounding a note that derives entirely from the early prophets. In chapter 3 he may have Joshua, as high priest, clothed in new garments (apparently as a sign that along with the new temple the priesthood also has been clothed anew by Yahweh himself) and furnished with special divine insignia (the stone with seven eyes is worn by him as Yahweh's plenipotentiary; see 4:10c); but then in verse 7 this man is admonished to walk in the ways of Yahweh and so to be faithful in his service. In chapter 4 Zerubbabel and Joshua are presented side by side as the anointed pair. From this it would appear that beside God's 'temporal' anointed one (formerly the king had been the special anointed one) Zechariah recognizes the high priest to be in a like state. The latter came to stand next in dignity to Zerubbabel, whom he avowed to be the Messianic prince (3:8; 6:9ff.). They are both, therefore, 'the anointed' (bearers of oil, olive trees) and as such are hallowed by the Spirit of God. It is in this connexion that Zerubbabel is emphatically told: 'Not by power nor by force, but by my Spirit, says Yahweh Sebaoth' (4:6);[20] and here, of course, the reference is to utterances by earlier prophets (Isa. 11; 42). In this fashion the prophet denies to the designated Messianic prince any claim to a show of political strength.

To what extent the Messianic hope which Haggai and Zechariah pinned on Zerubbabel had a directly political background and so issued in a rebellious movement (as has certainly been postulated) we cannot now be sure. One may perhaps infer from the words of warning spoken by Zechariah that danger did threaten in that direction and that the prophet wanted to avert it. It is at any rate a noteworthy fact that Zerubbabel and Joshua, who had so much to do with building the temple, are neither of them mentioned in the Book of Ezra in connexion with the temple's dedication. Whether, prior to that time, he had perhaps already been recalled by Darius because the Persian court found it safer to have him nearer to hand is, of course, a question, but one that cannot be answered with any degree of confidence.[21] Certainly, there could have been reasons enough: the fact that he was grandson to one of the earlier kings of Judah, the Messianic hope associated with him, the idea that the dedication of the temple might well provide opportunity for political demonstrations.

The dedication took place in the spring of 515, to the accompaniment of large-scale sacrifices (Ezra 6:15ff.). There joined in the Passover feast that followed, besides the former exiles, those Jews who had gone on living in the country but had dissociated themselves from the syncretism all around them. The sacrifices were provided at public expense, just as the state had financed the building (Ezra 6:3ff., 9), in order that prayers might be said in the temple for the Persian king (Ezra 6:10).

The rebuilding of the Jerusalem sanctuary within seventy years of its destruction proved to be of major importance for Judaism. The temple once more became the central point even for the Jews who continued to live in the diaspora. Thus there went out from it a great force pointing back to the centre. The temple had this large significance not only for the national existence as such but more especially for the spiritual development of Judaism. We cannot, of course, say that it came to dominate everything, for during the exile the tradition had acquired great importance in its own right; and this it continued to have in appreciable measure even later on. Nevertheless, the temple became more than ever the centre of religious life (excepting, perhaps, the period between 621 and 609). In particular, the place assumed in the community by the priesthood, with the high priest at its head (this title also was new), was preponderant to a degree unknown before in Israel. From the exile on, one may justifiably speak of a theocracy, or better of a 'hierocracy'. The circumstances primarily contributing to this were, of course, the fact that world power was now exercised by the Persians, whilst Israel was to have no more princely rulers until the Maccabean period, and also that the voice of prophecy had slowly begun to relapse into silence.

There were only two more prophets who were to leave behind them collections of divine sayings: Malachi and Joel. The former was a man who, looking forward to the Day of Yahweh, campaigned vigorously with the priesthood for a pure cult and with the people for a stringent code of marital ethics. Joel was someone whose thinking was more in the vein of the early prophets; and we may regard him as a transitional figure forming a bridge to apocalyptic. We shall come back to these two later on.

With the temple and priesthood the cult assumed a central place. During the Babylonian exile after Ezekiel the ordering of it was thoroughly prepared. It is highly likely that at least the oldest part of the Priestly Code, as it is called, originated in Babylon during the period between Ezekiel and the restoration of the temple. To this priestly source of the Pentateuch belong, for example, a description of the oldest sanctuary that was supposed to have been made in the desert, the tabernacle (Ex. 25ff.), and above all certain parts of the cultic legislation, in particular of the laws of sacrifice in Lev. 1–7. The first five chapters here form a sort of cultic manual for lay people; and chapters 6 and 7 are a collection of more detailed directions for priests about various types of sacrifices. There would, of course, have been many more detailed regulations for priests and Levites, connected with the business of slaughtering and other cultic actions; but these were too technical to be incorporated in the Torah (Law or Pentateuch). The sacrificial laws, as we saw earlier on, followed the ancient ritual practices in vogue during the period when the first temple was standing; but there are definite indications warranting the assumption that when it came to the ordering of sacrificial worship the criticism voiced by the prophets had been taken into account. Thus the fact that sin- and guilt-offerings are regarded as a group on their own is apparently something new. Again, the practice of splashing the blood in the direction of, or actually upon, the mercy-seat, which in the case of sin-offerings preceded the propitiatory act and signified the consecration of the blood, is probably a new rite; likewise the stipulation that sin-offerings can only be made for sins committed unintentionally. When it came to the observance of the great Day of Atonement, new elements were again added to the ancient rites, a probable instance being that atonement was made for the nation as a whole, whereas originally what had taken place on that day was a solemn purification of the sanctuary.[22]

Later on, as we said, these laws were still further elaborated and brought up to date. It meant that a new constituent was added to the gathered corpus of earlier tradition; and this, which was given the overall name of the Priestly Code, was eventually included with the collected tradition to form the Pentateuch. We cannot say for certain that when Ezra came from Persia to Jerusalem in the 5th century he carried with him the whole of the Pentateuch and that the Jerusalem community received it at his hand.[23] Although at one time that was fairly generally assumed to be the case, many today would deny it. Some scholars nowadays believe that what he brought with him is more likely to have been the Priestly Code, in whole or in part, and that the Pentateuch as a corpus of writings must have come into existence in Jerusalem.[24] If so, this could not have happened much later than at the end of the 5th century or, at the outside, the beginning of the 4th; for it was during the latter century that the Pentateuch in its complete form was taken over from the Jews by the Samaritans. This must have been an accomplished fact in the middle of the 4th century at the very latest; for in all likelihood the Samaritan temple was, or was being, built just at that time[25] (the Samaritan 'schism' had already been well under way much earlier, in the period between Zerubbabel and Ezra-Nehemiah).

The Priestly Code (and thus also the Pentateuch as a whole) makes a direct connexion between the cultic legislation and the actual institution of the religion by Moses. It is envisaged as having been given directly at Sinai (Ex. 25ff.; 35ff.; Lev. and Num. 1–10:11). The whole construction and design of the tabernacle, the laws concerning the priests and the high priest, the sacrificial system, rites of purification, festivals and so forth, are included, and everything is represented as having been given directly by Yahweh to Moses. The priesthood is seen as stemming from Aaron, Moses' brother. Even the Zadokite priests are regarded as having sprung from Aaron (via Eleazar), (1 Chron. 24:3).

In the foregoing chapters we have already described, albeit fragmentarily and often enough on a hypothetical basis, how the cult and the priesthood evolved; and it then became apparent that for the most part the cultic regulations must have arisen during the course of events in the land of Canaan. The evolution of Israel's religion came to a head, cultically speaking, when all this ritual was centralized around the Sinai-revelation, on the presuppositions of the Priestly Code. Thus the cult was in fact declared to be the aim of the whole revelation to Moses and the end to which the covenant had been concluded.

The man especially responsible for the fact that things turned out this way, whether we follow tradition in putting him before Nehemiah (458) or give a later date to his activities (either c. 435 or c. 398),[26] was Ezra, the son of a priest in the 5th century. On the instructions of Artaḥshashta (Artaxerxes)[27] he came to Jerusalem to conduct an investigation into the affairs of Judah and Jerusalem on the basis of the Law of God which he had with him (Ezra 7:14; cf. vs. 25f.); and he had sweeping powers to see that this Law was implemented among his people (Ezra 7:23ff.). It is more than likely that he was able to

R

carry out his commission effectively only after the arrival of Nehemiah, who as governor of Judah (Neh. 5:14)[28] was able to wield real political authority.

The acceptance of the Law took place in a solemn act of covenant-renewal, after expression of penitence, public reading and explanation (cf. Ezra 9f. and Neh. 8ff., who between them offer divergent accounts of what took place, which are not easy to harmonize).

To a greater extent, even, than in Haggai's time Ezra purified and renovated the cult, at the same time separating the Jews completely from the rest of the population. To bring this about he took the radical step of requiring all Jews married to foreign women to divorce them or suffer the penalty of being expelled from the national religious community.

Both measures were at the time a dire necessity, if the tiny Jewish community were to remain in being. It is clear from Malachi's prophecies how slipshod the priests were with respect to the standard cultic regulations (they would make sacrifice of valueless animals, 1:6ff.), how lightly they approached their task of guiding the people by dispensing *torah* (2), and what little came of the practice of tithing for the upkeep of the temple worship and the service of Yahweh generally.

Especially with regard to marriage people were very easy-going. Even those who had formerly been exiles made no bones about taking a divorce and marrying with foreign women (Mal. 2:10ff.). Mixed marriages were increasing hand over fist, as is plain from Ezra 9:1ff. and Neh. 13:23—and this, not only among ordinary people, but among priests and Levites too.

No wonder that those responsible for the Jews took drastic measures to prevent the little community from being swallowed up wholesale in the more substantial, and very mixed, population of Palestine. More than anyone else Ezra deserves to be called the father of Judaism.

We may deplore these measures in so far as they encouraged the isolationist bent in the national structure and mental outlook of Judaism. In fact they entailed the claim to purity of blood 'based on the elect status of the holy seed',[29] thus making participation in the Yahwistic religious community depend in principle on the fact of belonging by birth to the Jewish people. At the same time one can see that other means of preserving the group, socially, at least, and perhaps also in its religion, were hardly feasible. In this way isolation became a source of strength, and antithesis the mark of a devoutly religious approach to life. The national community thereby gained internally in unity and cohesion; but because it cut itself off and was tied down to a cultic-ritualistic pattern of religion, it was in danger of losing contact with the world around and becoming a sect.

It was inevitable that this narrow particularism should arouse considerable domestic opposition and provoke strong reaction on the part of non-Jewish sections of the people.

It should be noted that the high priest Eliashib took a stand against the measures adopted by Ezra and Nehemiah (Neh. 13:4ff., 28). He was related to two of Nehemiah's greatest enemies: the Ammonite governor Tobiah and the latter's Samaritan colleague, Sanballat. This high priest, therefore, deliberately opened the way, which was to be followed on many subsequent occasions in leading priestly circles, to fully open intercourse with the ethnic groups and cultures all around.

During a further stay after 432 Nehemiah again implemented Ezra's earlier policies (Neh. 13) and endorsed all the steps that had been taken regarding the cult, tithing, observance of the Sabbath, the dissolution of mixed marriages and the ostracizing of non-Jews and of Jews married to foreign women. Although the evidence is scanty, we ought not to be surprised that these measures, which went so much against the grain with the governing classes and the general population, were not in the long run extremely effective, except among a small group of people assiduously devoted to the Law. People found all kinds of ways to break through the isolationist policies or to counteract them. There were those who wanted to pursue the more universalist line of the prophetic message proclaimed by Deutero-Isaiah and his disciples (see above, p. 241). In such circles were written books such as Jonah, which expresses the idea of co-responsibility toward the non-Jewish world, and Ruth, which by appealing to the celebrated example of David's ancestry registers opposition to the policy regarding marriage and argues for admitting those foreigners who, like Ruth, declare their earnest wish to participate to the full in the life of the national and religious community (1:7-18).

In the study of wisdom also more universalist tendencies were not repudiated. Although on the one hand the religious element was given more prominence than before (cf. Prov. 1-8 with chs. 9ff.), on the other hand foreign sages and writings showing the influence of foreign wisdom were not banned (Prov. 22:17ff.; 23f.; 30f.). Moreover, new ideas found their way into this literature (Job); and later on, under the influence of foreign (and Western) schools of philosophy in the Hellenistic period, one can even notice a leaning toward scepticism (Ecclesiastes).

We shall have to come back to this in the next chapter, and also to apocalyptic, which begins to make its presence felt in this period and is by now coming to be the primary spiritual refuge for those who, while clinging loyally to their beliefs, find no satisfaction in the way things had moved in a cultic and theocratic direction. One of the forerunners of this development was the prophet Joel,[30] who was probably writing round about the year 400. His preaching revives the theme of the proximity of the Day of Yahweh; but he sees it not only as bringing judgment upon Israel but also as threatening the whole cosmos with dissolution (2:10, 30f.; 3:15). He calls upon the nation, which has already been visited with a plague of locusts and has found itself on the verge of economic ruin as a result, to make an act of contrition before it is too late (chs. 1f.). When the people and priesthood have responded to this, he is able once more to proclaim the time of salvation to Israel and envisage the approach of the day when the whole people will share together the Spirit of God, and the gift of prophecy will descend upon them all, from the least to the greatest. Externally too, the particularist policy in religion had powerful repercussions, especially in the Samaritan camp. Samaria had long been the central seat of government for Palestine (see note 28, p. 258). Judah and Jerusalem came under the Samaritan governor Sanballat, until Nehemiah was able to arrange for the Jewish community to have a governor of their own. No wonder, then, that Sanballat proved to be Nehemiah's toughest opponent, and the Samaritan section of the population, knowing that they were officially outcast where the Jewish community were concerned, gradually set about organizing themselves on an independent basis (see p. 257). Thus particularism stirred up an antagonist on its own doorstep, who from then on continued for centuries to wage political war against the Jews in Palestine. In the spiritual realm this group made no distinctive contribution of its own but based itself—at any rate in a later period and to an ever greater degree—entirely on the Jewish *torah*. Of their religious life in the earlier period between 600 and 400 there is little that can be said. Although they will have conserved many of the constituent aspects of their early ways over a pretty long period, under the influence of the renewal of religious life in Jerusalem they probably followed increasingly the example set by the Jews. To what extent they maintained religious as well as political contact with the old North Israelite military colony at Yeb-Syene (Elephantine) in Egypt it is impossible to say (see below). This group certainly appealed to the sons of Sanballat, governor of Samaria, to back up their plea addressed to the Persian governor for the restoration of the temple, which had been destroyed in 410. They had previously made a similar request of the high priest at Jerusalem; but he had sent no reply.[31] The priest at Elephantine thereupon turned to the Persian governors of Jerusalem and Samaria—or at least to the sons of the latter, who perhaps still bore the title of his office but whose place had in effect been taken by his sons (in 410 Sanballat must already have seen more than thirty-five years of service). These men supported his plea with a letter of recommendation to the governor in Southern Egypt. Apparently, this petition of theirs did help; for the temple was later on again in service, if only for a brief period. It is important to understand that the Jewish community in Jerusalem wished to have no contact with the one at Elephantine, but that the Samaritans certainly did so (and likewise the governor at Jerusalem, although he was a Persian). This shows that the Elephantine temple was under boycott in Jerusalem; and it was evidently cold-shouldered not simply on account of the strongly deviationist form of religion practised there. In Samaria, however, some obligation was felt to offer moral support to the Jewish religious community in Southern Egypt. Of course, in the year 410 this did not signify a great deal for the religious relationship between the two parties. One should in any case not put the Samaritan worship at that period in the same category with that at Elephantine.

In origin, however, the form of religion there was quite probably related to that carried on at Bethel after the destruction of Samaria. It was clearly both syncretistic and polytheistic in character. Yahu (who was probably also venerated under the name of Bethel) was the chief god; and next to him were two other deities: Asham-Bethel, a goddess who would seem to have been his consort, and Anath-Bethel or Anath-Yahu, who was almost certainly considered to be the daughter of this pair. Then there was yet another god, Haram-Bethel by name. In addition to these some Egyptian gods were recognized too. Thus a certain Giddel, a Jew, writes to a fellow Jew, Micaiah: 'I bless thee by Yahu and Khnub'.[32] It would appear that animal sacrifices had at one time been made in this temple (it was already in existence by 525, when Cambyses conquered Egypt); but after it was destroyed in 410, things changed. At all events, the priest promises the Persian governor that when the temple has been rebuilt no more bloody sacrifices will be offered. The promise was made, of course, to conciliate the Persian, whose religion did not allow that the sacred fire be polluted by contact with dead creatures. Here we get a good idea of the cultic group's capacity for suiting itself to the wishes of the overlord. The principal Jewish feasts, such as the Sabbath, Pesaḥ and Massoth, were probably kept.[33]

The relationship between this congregation and the Jews in the motherland may not be clear; on the one hand the religion derived wholly from Bethel, on the other the members described themselves, ethnically, as Jews. However, Vincent and Albright's view is the most likely one: namely, that the group came from what had been the Northern kingdom and from the neighbourhood of Bethel, and that they perpetuated the type of syncretism which sprang up in the period following the destruction of the kingdom of Israel.[34] If that is right, this form of religion offers a splendid illustration of syncretism in Samaria after 722, and up to a point gives us a picture of the kind of religion obtaining in Bethel during the final years of the North-Israelite kingship. It thus puts us in the way of a satisfactory explanation for the prophets' hostility to the syncretism of their day in its various forms. Between Jerusalem and Bethel there really was an enormous and unbridgeable gulf. The strong feelings of disapproval that one may well entertain toward the intolerant spirit and separatist consequences flowing from particularism must surely be modified when one stops to consider just what of Yahwism did remain when this syncretizing process had done its work.

The danger of syncretism should be regarded, therefore, as one of the main reasons for the growth of isolationist Yahwism as we find it in Judaism. At any rate, if the preservation of the Jewish community as an ethnically independent social group was the end in view, there was basically no escape from particularism in the state of defensiveness in which Yahwism now found itself placed.[35] This was partly for extraneous reasons (the greater strength of the opposition) and partly because, owing to internal weaknesses, the nation just could not rise to the new spiritual task which the prophetic vision of Deutero-Isaiah had set before it. Thus the period of renewal proved to be a time for much rejoicing and yet also one of profound frustration. What the reactions to this were we shall see in the final chapter.

CHAPTER 11

Centralization and Disintegration

AUTHENTIC SOURCES FOR the political history of the Jewish community between Nehemiah and the time of the Maccabees are few and far between. So far as this period is concerned, we have in the main to rest content with a few pages of Flavius Josephus's *Jewish History*, which are by no means always based on reliable sources. Fortunately, where the history of their religion is concerned, the position is somewhat different; for various books and parts of books in the Old Testament can be ascribed to this latest period. Among those dating from the 4th century are, for instance, the Isaiah-Apocalypse and the Chronicles, along with Ezra. From the 3rd century we have the last chapters of Zechariah, and Ecclesiastes; and from the 2nd come Daniel and a part of the extra-biblical apocryphal literature, besides a few documents known as pseudepigrapha and the Dead Sea scrolls, with perhaps the Book of Esther too. These writings are extremely variegated in character and content. They make us realize immediately what a great diversity of spiritual and intellectual currents existed in Israel between 350 and 150.

That is the fascinating thing about this epoch. In this respect it is indeed an extension of the age that went before it. The turn taken by the development of Israel's religion in the time between Haggai-Zerubbabel and Ezra-Nehemiah evidently determined the course which matters took in the period that followed. The opposing parties and spiritual movements which, however feebly, had given token of their presence at that time now came to full strength. Little enough, no doubt, was happening in the political arena, at all events until about 180; for Israel had a merely passive role in the major fluctuations of world politics, in the course of which the great powers, the Persians, Alexander the Great with his Greeks, and after him the Ptolemies and the Seleucids, displaced one another in rapid succession. Yet in the things of the mind and spirit there was considerable fluidity and indeed friction. Judah may have been politically immature; but

263

spiritually she had regained her self-reliance and inner assurance, and these she was determined stubbornly to defend, meticulously thrusting away whatever might bring about a modification in her religious structure.

It was an attitude calculated to reinforce the tensions among the Jews themselves which in the century of Ezra and Nehemiah had already become noticeable. Many of them wanted to take part in the cultural developments of their age and refused to allow themselves to be saddled with ancient restrictions and usages. The old question of isolation or adaptation came up all over again, especially in the period after Alexander the Great, when Hellenism was advancing through the known world, particularly the Orient. The trouble was that as with Israel, so also for the Hellenistic world culture and religion were so much bound up together that it was not feasible to take on the one without the other. For example, the Greeks' pursuit of sport had an unmistakably religious background and was permeated with all kinds of symbolism which made it impossible for the Jews to participate without abrogating their laws.

The fact that in the gymnasium sport was practised in a state of nudity was probably enough in itself to make any law-abiding Jew recoil in horror. This is only one point, of course (albeit one which gave occasion for acute conflicts); but there were plenty more that had the same effect. Again, the food- and cleanliness-laws tended to create division between the Jews and the non-Jewish world. As these regulations could no longer be fully observed, once the culture of Hellenism had been adopted, it meant in practice that the Law had to be set aside and the religion in that way repudiated. The plain fact of the matter was that by this time 'the faith' and the observance of the Law amounted to one and the same thing. There is no better term for the religious aspirations of Judaism after Ezra's time than the word 'nomocracy'. M. Avi-Yonah, in his recently published book *Geschichte der Jüden im Zeitalter des Talmud*,[1] was well justified in reviving the use of this term to typify the religious life of the Jews at that time. Sellin, for example, had used it already in the thirties, when he covered the latest period of Israel's religious history in a chapter entitled *Jüdische Gesetzesreligion*. As a way of characterizing the religion Sellin's term is very much to the point, even though he started with it rather too far back in the age prior to the Deuteronomic Reformation.[2] The be-all and end-all of religion was indeed the keeping of the Law.

In the Torah as committed to writing in the Pentateuch, which was received as the canon when Ezra appeared, or not long afterwards (see the previous chapter), people had the revelation of Yahweh presented to them in written form. In the latest additions to Deuteronomy (Deut. 4, which was incorporated during the period after the exile) the idea is already clearly expressed of the great advantage that Israel enjoyed over other nations, and the riches that she possessed in the Law of the Covenant. The consciousness of this grew stronger still when the whole Torah as a corpus of divine revelation came into use.

From now on nothing in this Law was to be altered, nothing added or taken away; for the book provided in itself the final and decisive word of God. From the fact that the Samaritans have handed down practically the same book as the Jews (but for a few typical exceptions where, apparently with deliberate intent, the Samaritan version has been modified along the lines of the cult orientated on Shechem), and from the further fact that the Greek translation, the Septuagint,[3] which appeared soon after the schism, follows the Hebrew text very faithfully (where it does show slight discrepancies, these can be traced back, so far as the Torah is concerned, to textual variants that occur in such manuscripts as were currently in use), one may conclude that for the Jewish people of those days the Torah was the unalterable, unshakeable word of God.[4]

It is not to be wondered at, therefore, that once this had become fixed, the activity of the Spirit of God in vision and revelation by prophecy, which had been a persistent experience right down to the 4th century, now ceased. Prophecy disappeared, not through any lack of spirituality but because of the now paramount authority of the written word of revelation, which was preserved in the temple and expounded by priests and scribes, so that little room was left for personal inspiration. Moses, the deliverer, is at once lawgiver and interpreter of the Law (Deut. 1:5). The mediator of the covenant is now also the founder of the cult. Thus the Israelite religion comes to be envisaged as linked *ab initio* with the cult itself. For prophecy as such little or no place remains, and it becomes almost entirely an adjunct of the temple worship. At the time when Chronicles was written it was the Levitical temple-singers who were regarded as the people who prophesied (cf. 1 Chron. 25:1–3, 5; 2 Chron. 20:20; cf. verse 14ff.; 2 Chron. 29:25, 30; 35:15).[5] In support of this view the writer can certainly appeal to the pre-exilic manifestations of cultic

S

prophecy. Then too there is a sharp rejection of free prophetism in Zechariah 13, partly, it would seem, because in this period after 400 it fell more and more under the spell of syncretism (cf. 13:2 and 6). We know that some centuries later the conviction prevailed among the rabbis that prophecy had been brought to an end with Ezra.[6] If reference was still sometimes made to the activity of the Spirit of God, it was always in connexion with eschatological, and especially Messianic, expectations.

None of this implies that in fact the voice of prophecy had been altogether reduced to silence. We can point to a number of chapters in the prophetic writings which date from the time of Joel, and even later (see above, p. 260), such as the so-called Isaiah-Apocalypse (24–27), Zechariah 12–14, Daniel and so on. In more recent times, however, these have been rightly categorized not simply as prophetic but as apocalyptic writings; because, however much we may see them as akin to prophecy and even as an offshoot from it, they already exhibit so many positive traits of later apocalyptic that we can no longer count them as prophecy. Indeed, Jewish tradition itself did not do so—not at least with Daniel and certain other writings which stayed outside of the Old Testament: like the books of Enoch, the Testaments of the Twelve Patriarchs, some Sibylline books and a few writings from Essene circles, including the Damacus-document and the Scroll of the battle of the children of light with the children of darkness.[7] We may take this apocalyptic, or better, perhaps, these apocalyptic trends and currents, as in a way making up for the absence of prophecy and as a reaction against the preponderant nomocracy and hierocracy.

The latter was rooted deep in the events of history. It was intimately connected with the certainty that after the judgment suffered in the exile the age had dawned when a living fellowship with God would be restored. What Ezekiel had spoken of as lying in the future and Deutero-Isaiah had announced to be close at hand and beginning to be realized; what Haggai and Zechariah saw as coming to pass before their eyes (Hag. 2:21ff.; Zech. 1:16f.; 2:1ff.; 8:1ff.)—namely, the time when the promise of salvation would be fulfilled—became and continued to be the basis of that faith by which the renewed people of God lived their lives. The reorganization carried out by Ezra and Nehemiah had revived this idea once more. The covenant made with Yahweh had served to confirm it; and the adopted law set out the conditions and fundamentals of it. *Fellowship with God and his people had to come to be wholly a matter of obedience to the Law; and this was now the decisive factor.* The new Israel saw itself as Yahweh's chosen people still (Zech. 1). In Jerusalem stood the throne of his kingdom, as once it had in David's time.

In essentials this is the faith set out in the Book of Chronicles, the author of which we must probably look for among the inferior priests, the Levites, and more specifically among the temple-singers. For him the primary aspect of the temple worship is the offering of praise to God. This comes before anything else, even sacrifices. Generally speaking, he looks with a kindlier eye upon the Levites than on the priests. Hence his emphasis on the fact that the temple choirs had been David's special care, having been instituted by him in person. Indeed, according to him everything needful so far as the temple was concerned had actually been provided for by David in advance; so that people really had him to thank for the building of it. For this author David is the great central figure; and it is to David's spiritual and temporal authority that he appeals when he glorifies Jerusalem as the city of God. Here David sat upon the throne of God (1 Chron. 17:14; 28:5; 29:23). Jerusalem is the centre of the theocracy. It had been so, as he saw it, in David's day; and after the renewal of the 'partnership' with Yahweh in Jerusalem, it must be so again. The negative thrust of this theology, with its lionizing of Jerusalem, is aimed first and foremost at the Samaritan claims to recognition, but over and above that it has a positive purpose: to affirm and confirm faith in Jerusalem's restitution as the city of God. Jerusalem restored had one thing above all, therefore, to do; and that was to show herself faithful to the Word of Yahweh (see Zech. 1:4).[8]

For all its profound seriousness this outlook entailed great drawbacks. Anything gained in the way of fidelity to the Law was offset by the loss of any forward-looking vision. The prevailing theocracy and nomocracy were not seen merely as the kingdom of God in process of realization, but in fact as that kingdom already realized. The eschatological hope was overlaid by men's confidence that they knew and possessed the truth. The idea of election degenerated and became more the assurance of a privilege conferred than of a call to be answered.[9] What chiefly constrained men to keep the Law was the fear that God would exact retribution for sin, whether collective or individual. To conserve what was laid down in the Torah became the only rule of life. The Law came to be identified with a pre-existent wisdom, and even the Spirit, of God.[10] What followed quite logically from that was the necessity for every religious and social aspect of existence to be insulated from all that was new, different or non-Jewish. Conservatism and separatism became the hallmark of the Jewish community, which thus discharged with utter singleness of means and purpose its duty of obedience to God's Word and of loyalty to him. It is not to be denied that this rigid kind of fidelity to the Law helped to preserve the Jerusalem community (as we saw from its attitude to the Samaritans and other groups in Palestine); but it did so at the price of much tension and of rebuffing many who felt themselves attracted to other types of culture.

Just how true it was that this attitude in matters of religion proved an effective safeguard is evident from the fact that in two centuries of Persian domination the influence of Parseeism on the Jews was quite negligible.[11] Only on the periphery are traces of it detectable, in demonology and angelology (for example, the emergence of personal and national tutelary angels), in its influence on specific sects and in the heightening of a certain element of dualism in them, and in the 'periodizing' or cyclical view of world history which is a feature of some writings. Many of these influences are noticeable only at a late stage (Daniel, and apocalyptic generally) and in documents kept out of the Bible (cf. for angelology, the Book of Tobit); and they are so elusive, anyway, that it is always a question whether, and in what respect, there is any indebtedness to Iranian ideas at all. Some notions which have been imputed to that source, such as the emergence of the figure of Satan, can also be accounted for as a purely internal development in Judaism. It is probably fair to say that the bent toward a dualistic world view, which in certain (apocalyptic) types of belief does threaten to become the basic way of thinking about things, could generally have its origin in Parsee dualism, and that this must in that case have reached the Jews in Palestine via their compatriots resident in Persia and Babylonia.

These last would appear, on the whole, to have felt sufficiently at home in those places, although anti-Jewish movements were not unknown to occur there from time to time, as we find in the Book of Esther. That story may well be founded on what are definite historical reminiscences, although it is no longer possible to pin them down and although they have been poured into a curious, half-mythical, half-legendary mould. It would make this one of the earliest instances of anti-Semitism in the ancient world. Only later on do such things occur in other parts of the world, where the Jews entrench themselves as a self-sufficient group, unwilling to be assimilated (not least in Alexandria and other Hellenistic cities during the 1st century A.D.). Before then, of course, there had been traces of anti-Jewish sentiment that one can pick out in certain writings, as e.g. in those of Manetho, the Egypto-Hellenic author who lived in the 3rd century B.C.[12] This hatred of Jews was connected, no doubt, with the non-Jewish world's antagonism toward the Jewish claim to have a special, God-given task and again toward the fact that in consequence the Jews shut themselves off from the people all around them. The feeling was, however, above all connected, as Holsten[13] so rightly says, with the non-Jews' secret objection to the exclusive character of the God of Israel, which was so utterly different in kind from the nature-gods of the gentiles.

Their deliverance from the imminent danger of a pogrom in Persia induced the Jews there to celebrate the feast of Purim on the 14th and 15th Adar, when the Book of Esther was read as the *Festlegende*. This feast, which for some considerable time must have been observed only by the Eastern Jews, did not make its way into the West until the close of the 2nd century. At any rate, by the beginning of the 1st century the book had come to be known there. From then on Purim was permanently included among the Jewish feasts.

As we remarked in the opening section of this chapter, there were, in this period as in the preceding one, groups who felt unhappy about the way things were going and unhappy with the conservative emphasis on hierocracy and legalism. On the one hand there were those who wanted to move with the times and so tried to combine the contemporary culture with the faith of their fathers; but there were also those who, struck by the imperfections of the divine State, expected a fresh crisis and saw salvation as something still to come (cf. Zech. 12–14; especially 14). Alongside orthodox or 'orthoprax' Judaism, therefore, more liberal or independent currents arose, on the right and on the left, some sympathetic to cultural and humanistic trends, others sectarian in aim and purpose.

In the Old Testament a good example of the former interest is the book 'Ecclesiastes', which is an abstruse writing, the work of an elderly sage of, probably, the 3rd century, who is evidently steeped in the wisdom of many schools but who seems to have been influenced especially by that of Graeco-Hellenism.[14] For a long time he is tossed to and fro between this belief and that, one thought and another. Life, human destiny, has become an enigma for him. Yet in spite of all he clings to a view of God as Maker of the world. Certainly, God is far off, transcendent, so that man cannot see him or know him. Neither in the life of the individual nor in the processes of history is there any demonstrable sign of his governance. Contrary to the Old Testament Book of Proverbs, there can therefore be no question of retribution on his part. So far as the Preacher's belief is concerned, the whole salvation-history of Israel ceases to have any meaning. He reasons from personal experience; and on that basis all that he can retain is his belief in the Creator. Even so, we should not simply call him a sceptic, as some have done.[15] If that were the case, he would surely not have been included in the canon. To give him a place in it was not at all an easy thing to do. Obviously, it came about only in virtue of the fact that somebody contrived to append to his book a brief, fairly positive résumé of his argument, in the words of 12:13 and 14: Of all that we have heard this is the conclusion: 'Fear God and keep his commandments; for this is the duty of every man'. One cannot say that the teachers of wisdom were, in general, 'left-wingers'. The whole point about Jesus Sirach, who wrote his adages at the beginning of the 2nd century, is that he set out to reconcile wisdom and the Law.[16]

Still, the Preacher certainly did not stand alone in his own time. That much is clear from the fact that round about 200 (when control over Palestine passed from the Ptolemies to the Seleucids, and so to King Antiochus III, 198), and thereafter, there was great dissension among the most senior functionaries of the priesthood in Jerusalem as to whether it was possible to accept the Hellenistic culture so strongly championed by the Seleucids. One party wanted to accommodate it, and even asked the king to depose the high priest, Onias, who in their eyes was too conservative. Although the Syrian rulers did not at first agree to this, because complete freedom was permitted to the Jerusalem community in cultic matters, Antiochus IV allowed himself—on receipt of considerable bribes—to be induced to depose Onias and to install as high priest first his brother Jason and then later on yet another, Menelaus.[17]

Both were much disposed to favour Hellenism and made all kinds of innovations, in particular the practice of sport. It was above all the name of Menelaus that so greatly antagonized the Jews, because his very origins were evidently held to disqualify him for the high-priestly office. Guided by his successive high-priestly advisers, Antiochus IV, in the belief that the majority of the Jewish people were longing to be Hellenized, proceeded to impose this on the Jewish community;[18] but by carrying on in this unconsidered fashion he simply unleashed the Maccabean war. When the temple had been despoiled and eventually desecrated, the whole Jewish cult actually abolished and the Jews required to sacrifice to the state gods (between 170 and 168), the loyal Yahwists were driven to rebel.

Antiochus must soon have realized how wrong his policy had been. The radical Hellenist group was only a small one. Beside it there was the religious sect of the Ḥassidim (Asideans, the pious ones), who on the whole contented themselves with a demand for the restoration of the laws, including those of freedom of religion, which had been secured in 198. Alongside and out of this sect there sprang up a religio-nationalist grouping, the Maccabees, whose aim was the total independence of Israel. The issue was virtually decided within a few years; and after only three years it was possible to reconsecrate the temple. This took place on the 25th Chislev 165, the day observed ever since as the feast of the renovation of the temple (Ḥanukkah).

During this time of great anguish and tension the apocalyptic movement, which had long been in process of development, gave birth to a succession of writings, the oldest of which, from the pre-Christian period, have already been mentioned above (p. 266). Of these the earliest is probably the Book of Daniel (c. 166). It has a two-fold purpose. The stories which tell of the steadfastness of the pious and of how they were delivered amid the greatest peril were meant to strengthen the spirit of resistance; and the picture presented of the course of world history pointed to the downfall of the world empires and presaged the speedy arrival of the Kingdom that God was to establish under the rule of the zealous in Israel. With all this the book gives us a good idea of what apocalyptic is really trying to do: to find and offer comfort in a difficult time when Israel is living under foreign domination. It does this by pointing men to the coming fulfilment of their eschatological hopes and by visualizing the time of salvation itself. Worked into the book are all sorts of calculations regarding the time of its dawning (cf. Daniel 9:24ff.) and all kinds of ideas borrowed often enough from non-Israelite mythologies and world views, which give an extraordinarily confused and extremely vague character to the whole thing. Most of them are expressed in the form of visions as-cribed to very early figures of some spiritual magnitude, such as Enoch, Moses, Isaiah and Daniel. In this manner the secrets of history are disclosed to the faithful; and they are offered the consoling prospect of a new world soon to arrive and prepared by God in the heavens. This new world (the 'olam habba') comes to birth only after the present evil cosmos (the 'olam hazzeh) has been consigned to the rubbish-heap and totally destroyed. This conception was obviously not unconnected with the increasingly influential dualistic outlook on the world and history, and with a view of God which was tending to become more and more highly transcendental.[19] Along with all this the expectation of a coming Messiah as the prince destined to usher in the new age takes on a fresh meaning. Sometimes he is presented as a national figure, sometimes also as a celestial one.

The literature of apocalyptic was embraced only in part by all religious groups (e.g. Daniel); and much of it was used solely by sectarian elements.

The party of the pious or zealous ones soon fell to pieces. After the temple had been retrieved and an acceptable high priest (Alcimus) nominated, one group retired from the struggle, as they did not support the nationalist demands of the Maccabees.

It was from this group that there arose in the middle of the 2nd century a movement under priestly direction, probably at the time when the Maccabees started staking a claim to the high-priesthood (in 153 Jonathan was recognized in that capacity by the Seleucids), which later became known as the sect of Essenes. They withdrew into the desert region of Judah close to the Dead Sea; and there they founded a community exhibiting a variety of features: it was strongly inclined to apocalyptic views but was also very much addicted to legalism and anti-Hellenism—all of which resulted in a highly ascetic mode of living. They felt themselves to be the true people of the new covenant; and by strict observance of the Law they hoped to bring nearer the Messianic kingdom. Their founder was probably the Teacher of Righteousness so often referred to in their writings (which have become familiar to us since 1947, when they were discovered in the caves of Qumran).[20] They are the best example known of an apocalyptic group. Most of the old, and some new, apocalyptical writings have been recovered from these caves; and one wonders, therefore, whether a great part of this literature might not have originated with them.

Later on there came a further split in the Maccabean ranks, when in 135 the Pharisees (that is, 'the segregated ones') separated off from the rest because the Maccabean commander, John Hyrcanus, resolved his difference with the Sadducean priests, and aspired to great ideals in the political sphere. Like the Essenes, the Pharisees saw the Jews' duty as consisting in a punctilious observance of the Law; but they sought to achieve this by living in loyalty to the temple and to society. They formed cells in which they studied the Law together and so strengthened its application in their daily lives. They were most faithful in attendance at synagogue; and it was chiefly from their ranks that the scribes were drawn. More and more they came to assume a position of leadership among the people. The Sadducees (Zadokites) were the oldest of these groups. Made up of aristocratic priestly families and rigorously cultic in their outlook, they went a fairly long way, culturally speaking, in embracing Hellenism. In their view of scripture and cult they were highly conservative; so that all sorts of new traditions that came into vogue with the Pharisees were repudiated by them: for example, angelology, the idea of resurrection, certain prescriptions regarding cleanness, and so forth.

Although for a brief period under the Maccabean princes the Jews experienced a political revival (for instance, the Samaritan temple was destroyed in 128, the Edomites were subjugated and forced to submit to being circumcised), its internal divisions made it weak; and when half a century later it was confronted with the might of Rome, it was utterly defenceless.

Through its fidelity to the Law Judaism maintained itself, spiritually; but at the same time, because of this bondage to tradition it created, to being with, no new forms of living. The renewal that came with Christianity was repulsed. After the destruction of the second temple Pharisaism was for centuries the undisputed guide and leader of Judaism. Now that we have reached the end of our journey through fifteen centuries of history, it should be possible to draw together a few impressions which have forced themselves upon us in the process.

The first is of the great strength, the 'life force', that was disclosed in Yahwism. It was this strength that made it possible for Yahwism, despite the smallness and cultural dependence of the group who professed it, and despite the severe struggle it had to hold its own against so many and such powerful religious forces of quite another character, to continue in existence all the time growing and evolving. Yet this is not all; for it stood the test even of the political and social dissolution of that group, the people of Israel, and gave them the possibility of renewed existence.

The second impression is that in all this Yahwism displayed a capacity for adaptation and at the same time a critical bent, both in the highest degree astonishing and both indicative of the fact that this religion possessed a power of discrimination and a strength of self-awareness that belong to its peculiar character and must also result from it. By accommodating certain elements of the surrounding religions and cultures and rejecting others Yahwism grew from being a faith that is no longer clearly intelligible in all respects, whilst being firmly based on one prophetic figure's personal experience of revelation and the deliverance which came to a tiny group in that connexion, into a religion which, on the evidence of various writings, rendered increasing account of its essential nature and attained to a theology and a world view all its own.

The third impression is that the key to Yahwism's vital energy must lie in the nature of its belief in and about God, which drew its strength from the recurrent fact that what was felt to be God's dealing in history tallied with what he revealed by the prophets. This made the relationship with Yahweh not only a direct but also a personal and thus a moral one. From it his Being took its exclusive and divine character and a personal aspect which distinguished him fundamentally from the divine powers of the ancient East, bound up as they were with nature.

The fourth point is that Yahweh's relation to Israel has a historical basis, and not an essentially national one. The patriarchs were not initially involved in this relationship until J made them party to it, as he did for mankind as a whole, even Cain and Enoch, Adam and Eve. Again; in the desert period the Kenites share the knowledge of Yahweh, even if the mode of their relationship with him is not further specified. Yahweh always remains, therefore, essentially the God of Sinai.

In Canaan, of course, as a result of the struggle for Yahweh and against the other gods, the exclusive status of Yahweh as God is more and more centred on Yahweh's relation with Israel, although Amos (9:7) clearly puts the matter otherwise. It was this that engendered the strong tension between what we call particularism and universalism.

The fifth point is that Israel never completely managed to escape from this tension; and it continued to govern the history of her religion. Isaiah resolved it in eschatology, and Deutero-Isaiah (followed at some remove by Zechariah), when speaking of the new life for

Israel, called upon his people to see that the nations had their share in it. Eventually, the exclusiveness of the relationship between Yahweh and Israel came to the fore once again with the restoration of Jerusalem (the privileged condition of the elect, theocracy, nomocracy). Then because on the one hand the state of affairs in the religious sphere was fixed for all time in Scripture, in the *Torah*, and on the other the reins of office were held by a priestly aristocracy which was conservative and dominated by a lust for power, the growth of Yahwism was put under severe restraint and brought almost to a standstill. This meant that any sort of drastic renewal such as Yahwism had undergone more than once already had become impossible. Because of this negative attitude to all further development, and at each rejection of new elements, all sorts of unresolved tensions arose in the spiritual sphere; so that the only possibility of avoiding a total impasse was the formation of various sects. This determined the kind of life led by the Qumran community, which advocated a wholesale purifying of the governing priesthood and of the nation. It also determined the attitude adopted toward the Christian community, which stood for a much more radical renewal. This latter group was felt by Judaism to constitute a plot against its own existence and was therefore rebuffed. That settled the relationship between Judaism and primitive Christianity. They could only continue to exist as two ramifications of the *corpus Jahwisticum*, developing in contrary directions.

Notes

CHAPTER 1

1. C. J. Bleeker, *Op zoek naar het geheim van de godsdienst* (second edition, 1961), 199.
2. Cf. G. W. Anderson, 'Hebrew Religion', in H. H. Rowley, *The Old Testament in Modern Study* (1951), 309.
3. Cf. S. H. Hooke (ed.), *Myth, Ritual and Kingship*, Essays on the Theory and Practice of Kingship in the Near East and Israel (Oxford, 1958), 13ff.
4. Also, e.g., G. W. Anderson, *op. cit.*, 285.
5. Cf. M. Noth, *Die israelitischen Personennamen im Rahmen der gemein-semitischen Namengebung* (1928), 90, 107.
6. English translation (1949) of *Der Glaube der Propheten*.
7. Thus around 970–950. For more detailed evidence regarding the source material, cf. my small book, *Literatuur van Oud Israël* (second edition, 1961), or other Introductions to the Old Testament.
8. In particular through the studies of Von Rad and Noth. We may mention here the latter's *Überlieferungsgeschichte des Pentateuch* (1948). For the rest, see p. 126ff., and the works cited in the notes to that passage.
9. The *traditionsgeschichtliche* method, so called, which takes the tradition as a whole apart into its separate strands and gives these mutually independent *'Einzeltraditionen'*, one by one, their own *Sitz im leben* (usually on an etiological basis), without giving enough attention to the context in which the several traditions occur. Yet we must take into account the possibility that the whole (the framework, at least) was prior to, and had a different (non-etiological) provenance from, the parts.
10. The earliest collection of traditional material (J) gives a good deal of space to the Moses-figure. It is itself a literary elaboration of a number of ancient (not just etiological but also historical) folk-stories.
11. Cf., e.g., K. Kenyon, *Archaeology in the Holy Land* (1960), and *Digging up Jericho* (1957); but she is very cautious in her view of any conclusions that might be drawn from the excavations.
12. *Theologische Rundschau* (1929), 161ff; see further 142ff.
13. We should ponder and take to heart what that great master of Old Testament scholarship in the second half of the last century, A. Kuenen, wrote about this in an article on *Kritische Methode*, originally published in English ('Critical Method', *The Modern Review*, I, 1880, pp. 461–488) and translated by K. Budde, *Gesammelte Abhandlungen* (1894), 96. Kuenen wrote: 'But it is at once apparent from this what an important role the personality of the historian does play; for what I have just been describing as the character of the fact is essentially his understanding of it; and that depends on what part of the reality gets through to him—but at least as much on himself, on the experience which he brings to it and

277

on the "singleness" of his vision. We may deplore it as much as we will; but the historian—even the totally impartial historian—already as regards the representation of the naked facts is something other than a funnel through which the reality comes to us. How much greater, however, does his personal share become when, turning to the task which it is his real business to perform, he proceeds to portray, with or within the body of reality, its soul also, the very life of the past! For there he can offer nothing more and nothing other than his personal interpretation of the image reflected in his mind. Almost everything here depends upon his inward man.'

14. The official religion—and so what is already 'orthodox Judaism'—is very good at giving the cold shoulder to the forms of religion which it finds inimical or displeasing. One recalls the fact that the Essene writings remained buried for eighteen centuries, until they were in part recovered not very long ago. Something of what this literature contained was known from Philo and Flavius Josephus and a few non-Jewish historians; but in the writings of rabbinical orthodoxy they were all but ignored.

CHAPTER 2

1. As J. Hempel again does in his 'Altes Testament und Religionsgeschichte', in *Th. Lt. Zt.* (1956), 259ff.

2. Leipzig (1913), V.

3. Cf. H. Frankfort, *The Problem of Similarity in Ancient Near Eastern Religions.* The Frazer Lecture, 1950 (Oxford, 1951).

4. *The Old Testament against its Environment* (1950), 102.

5. Cf. J. Begrich, 'Vertrauensäusserungen im Israel. Klageliede', in *Z.A.W.* (1928), 230ff., and Gunkel-Begrich, *Einleitung in die Psalmen* (1933), 213ff.; also A. van Selms in *De babylonische termini voor zonde* (1933), 76f.

6. I.a. O. E. Ravn in an article 'Henvendelse till Guddommene', in *Øst og Vest.* Festschrift A. Christensen (1945), 118ff., and W. G. Kunstmann, *Die babylonische Gebetsbeschwörung* (1932).

7. A. Ungnad, *Die Religion der Babylonier und Assyrer* (1921), 177; cf. also Ravn's first examples in the above-mentioned article by him, 118.

8. Ungnad, 180ff., and in a prayer of Nebuchadnezzar's, cf. Ravn, 118f.

9. Cf. his essay, 'Sumero-Akkadian interconnexions: religious ideas', in *Aspects du contact Suméro-Akkadien*, viii (Geneva, 1960), 272ff., in particular 279; cf. also T. Jacobsen, 'Formative tendencies in Sumerian Religion', in *The Bible and the Ancient Near East*, Albright Festschrift (1961), 276, and especially *The Assyrian Dictionary*, vii, sub *ilu* b).

10. 'Morals in Ancient Mesopotamia', in *J.E.O.L.* (1957–58), 184ff., esp. 194.

11. For this cf. especially, A. Alt, 'The God of the Fathers', *Essays on Old Testament History and Religion*, Oxford 1966. Also Starcky, *Palmyre* (1952), 84f., and his contribution, 'Palmyréens etc.', in M. Brillant and R. Aigrain (eds.), *Histoire des religions* IV, (1957), 220; see also some instances, i.e., from 'Mari', given by J. Ph. Hyatt in *V.T.* (1955), 131; and *Assyrian Dictionary, loc. cit.*

12. 'The God of the Fathers', p. 45ff.; see also Chapter 4, p. 119ff.

13. See the story of Wen-Amon, cf. *A.N.E.T.*, pp. 25ff.

14. Cf. C. Westermann, *Grundformen prophetischer Rede* (1960), 70ff.

15. Cf. J. Hempel, 'A.T. und Religions-geschichte', in *Th.Lt.Zt.* (1956), 271ff, and Westermann, *op. cit.*; see also below, Chapter 8, 170f.

16. The territorial god of Moab.

17. The verb at the end of line 8 and beginning of line 9 is more likely Hi (from *šub*=return) than Qal (from *yašab*=dwell).

18. A word inserted, illegible in the text.
19. An undetermined word.
20. E. A. Speiser, 'Ancient Mesopotamia', in R. C. Dentan (ed.), *The Idea of History in the Ancient Near East*, (1955), 56ff.
21. Lambert, *op. cit.*, 5f.
22. Cyrus-Cylinder, see, i.a., trans. *A.N.E.T.*, 315f.; *D.O.T.T.*, 92ff. R. Kittel, *Geschichte des Volkes Israel*, III, (1927), 16ff.
23. Cf. W. von Soden, *Herrscher im Alten Orient* (1954), 70f.
24. A. Goetze, *Kleinasien* (1957), 91.
25. A. Goetze, 'Die Pestgebete des Muršiliš', in *Kleinasiatische Forschungen* i (1930), 161–251; cf. A. Malamat, 'Doctrines of causality in historiography', in *V.T.* (1955), 1ff.
26. Cf. O. Gurney, *The Hittites* (1952), 157f.
27. *Op. cit.*, 159f.
28. *Bab. Wisdom Lit.*, 4; cf. also Speiser, *op. cit.*, 57.
29. D. O. Edzard, *Die zweite Zwischenzeit Babyloniens* (1957), 53ff.; cf. also T. Jacobsen, "Formative tendencies in Sumerian Religion', *op. cit.*, 277. According to the late-Babylonian 'Sargon-Chronicle' (*A.N.E.T.*, 266f.) Marduk also took his revenge on Sargon I after that monarch had captured and desecrated his city.
30. A. Malamat, *op. cit.*, rightly points to the story in 2 Sam. 21 as a clear parallel to the case mentioned by Murshilish.
31. For this term cf. H. Frick, *Vergleichende Religionswissenschaft* (1928), 16. Frick distinguishes between what he calls 'analogous' phenomena—that is, those which fulfil certain similar functions in the religions—and 'homologous' ones, which have a similar origin (occupy the same position in the basic morphological pattern of the religion) but have acquired a totally different functional significance in the various religions.
32. Cf., e.g., for the Sumerian religion, which forms the basis of the Babylonian, the aforementioned article by T. Jacobsen in the Albright Festschrift, 268ff.
33. J. Hempel, 'Gott, Mensch und Tier im A.T.', in *Z.f.syst.Th.* (1931); reprinted in *Apoxysmata* (1961), 198ff.; also Jacobsen, *op. cit.*, 269f.; for Egypt cf. S. Morenz, *Ägyptische Religion* (1960), 19, 148f.
34. Hassuna, Jarmo in Mesopotamia, Jericho in Palestine. Cf. K. Kenyon, *Archaeology in the Holy Land* (1960), 58ff.; S. Lloyd, *Foundations in the Dust* (1955), 237f.; see also the outline in F. R. Kraus, *Wandel und Continuität in der Sumerisch-Babylonischen Kultur.* Inaugural Lecture at Leyden (1954), 9f.
35. Cf., i.a., C. J. Gadd, *Ideas of Divine Rule in the Ancient East* (1948); H. Frankfort, *Kingship and the Gods* (1948); M. Noth, 'God, King and Nation in the Old Testament', in *The Laws in the Pentateuch and other Essays*', London and Edinburgh, 1966. E. A. Speiser, 'Ancient Mesopotamia', in R. C. Dentan (ed.), *The Idea of History in the Ancient Near East*, idem: 'The Biblical Idea of History,' on *I.E.J.* (1957), 204; J. de Fraine, *L'aspect religieux de la royauté israélite* (1954); K. H. Bernhardt, 'Das Problem der altorientalischen Königsideologie im A.T.', in Supplement to *V.T.* VIII (1961). For the various gradations of the divine character of the Egyptian kingship see S. Morenz, *op. cit.*, 35ff.
36. Cf. S. H. Hooke *et al.*, *Myth, Ritual and Kingship* (1958); I. Engnell, *Studies in Divine Kingship* (1943); A. R. Johnson, *Sacral Kingship in Ancient Israel* (1955).
37. In Ps. 45:7 the rendering most to be preferred is: 'your divine throne is for all time and eternity'; and in verse 8: 'therefore has God (originally: Yhwh), your God, anointed you.'
38. See, i.a., J. de Savignac, 'Essai d'interprétation du Ps. CX à l'aide de la littérature égyptienne', in *O.T.S.*, IX (1951), 107ff. As to whether there was a direct

borrowing we cannot be sure, because one must bear in mind the possibility of some borrowing from the Canaanite ceremonial of the former Jerusalemite kingship. To what degree this again was of Egyptian origin is difficult to determine, although (as has become evident from the El-Amarna letters) Egypt was able to make her influence felt effectively in the Syro-Palestinian city-states over several centuries. That Egyptian influence made itself felt within the state of Israel—especially in Solomon's time—is for the rest certain. Up to a point it even became a determining factor in public life.

39. Cf. F. R. Kraus, *op. cit.*, 19f.; W. von Soden, *Herrscher im Alten Orient* (1954), 56f.; C. J. Labuschagne, *Die Onvergelijklikheid van Jahwe in die Ou Testament*, diss. (1962), 86ff.

40. G. van der Leeuw, *Achnaton* (1927), 20ff.

41. J. B. Pritchard, *A.N.E.T.* (1950), 12ff.; H. W. Obbink, *De magische betekenis van de naam, inzonderheid in het Oude Egypte* (1925), 4ff.

42. A. Erman, *Die Religion der Ägypter* (1934), 350f. For the rest, cf. the above-mentioned book by S. Morenz, 144ff., in which an important attempt is made to describe the relation between the unity and multiplicity of the gods in Egyptian religion. The author stresses the fact that in Egypt the unity was attained more by way of syncretism, the merging together of divine personages (on the basis of their common participation in the one divine essence; the Egyptians set greater store by the concept of 'power (energy)' than by the personal character of the gods) than by constructing a hierarchically constituted pantheon.

43. A. S. Kapelrud, *Baäl in the Ras Shamra texts* (1952).

44. O. Eisfeldt, *El im ugaritischen pantheon* (1951); F. Løkkegaard, 'A plea for El, the bull and other Ugaritic miscellanies', in *Studia Orientalia Ioanni Pedersen* (1953), 219ff. A centre position is held by J. Gray, 'The legacy of Canaan', in Supplement to *V.T.*, V (1957), 113ff. See also Eissfeldt in *F.u.F.* (1962), 328ff.

45. Cf. again the above-mentioned lecture by Kraus (p. 279, n. 34).

46. W. G. Lambert, *Wisdom*, 4ff.

47. E. A. Speiser, *op. cit.*, *I.E.J.* (1957), 203.

48. *Idem*, in *The Idea of History*, 43, 68.

49. Anat V, 33f., according to Gordon's numbering.

50. Cf. Marduk as Allgott; text available in translation in *A.N.E.T.*, 69ff.; B. Meissner, *Babylonien und Assyrien*, II, 48f.; J. Hehn, *op. cit.*, 69ff.

51. Meissner, *loc. cit.*; see in general *R.G.G.* (Third edition), IV, sub Monotheïsmus.

52. O. Eisfeldt, *El im Ugaritischen Pantheon* (1951), 65ff.

53. G. van der Leeuw, in his *Achnaton*, speaks of monotheism; cf. E. Otto, 'Monotheistische Tendenzen in der ägyptischen Religion', in *Die Welt des Orients*, II, 99ff.; Morenz, *op. cit.*, 154ff., envisages a sort of trinitarianism.

54. H. Th. Obbink, *De godsdienst in zijn verschijningsvormen* (Second edition) (1947), 130f.

55. Deut. 10:17; Ps. 136:2.

56. Ps. 29:1.

57. Ps. 82:1.

58. The word 'gods' in the Hebrew text has a multiple meaning. It can even be used to signify the spirit of a dead person (1 Sam. 28:13).

59. In practice it only comes into play when some evil has to be taken into account, for which Yahweh cannot be held responsible (1 Kings 22; Job 1f.) or in certain mythological reminiscences (Ps. 82; cf. Gen. 6:1ff.; Gen. 3:22, etc.).

60. See C. J. Labuschagne, *Die Onvergelijklikheid van Jahwe in die O.T.*, diss. (1961).

61. Cf. W. A. Irwin, 'The Hebrews', in H. Frankfort *et al.*, *The Intellectual Adventure of Ancient Man* (1946), 225f.

62. C. J. Bleeker, *De overwinning op de dood* (1942), 13; the ensuing quotation is from p. 40; cf. also H. Frankfurt, *Similarity*, 13ff.

63. Perhaps the first of these was originally a non-Egyptian deity; cf., i.a., C. J. Bleeker, *Die Geburt eines Gottes* (1956), 97; the second was probably drawn into the 'dying and rising life' milieu under the influence of the Osiris-religion; Van der Leeuw, in his *De Godsdienst van het oude Aegypte* (1944), 71ff., speaks of the 'solarization' of the Osiris-religion, and De Buck—in a critical discussion of this work, *Bi.Or.* (1944), 66—of the 'osirianization' of the sun-religion.

64. Cf. Van der Leeuw, *op. cit.*, 63-71.

65. De Buck, *op. cit.*, 66. Cf. Gertrud Thausing, 'Die Religion der Aegypter', in *W.Z.K.M.* (1953), 19: 'Osiris ist das Leben, ist die Materie, das "Stirb und Werde", die Natur in ihrem ewigen Wandel, der Nil im Steigen und Fallen, der Mond mit seinem Zu- und Abnehmen, das Korn mit seinen Wachsen und Geschnitten werden—mit einem Wort die Lebensseiten oder der weibliche Pol im Kosmos.'

66. Van der Leeuw, *op. cit.*, opts for his having been initially a human being, although he takes full account of the vegetative aspect; A. Erman, *Die Religion der Aegypter* (1934), 68, likewise—but on other grounds.

67. The oldest version appears to entertain the idea of the resurrection of Osiris himself; Erman, *op. cit.*, 70.

68. *Op. cit.*, 69.

69. *Op. cit.*, 68 note. The dating here, however, may well be a thousand years too early; A. Scharff, 'Die Frühkulturen Ägyptens und Mesopotamiens', in *Der Alte Orient*, Bd. 41 (1941), 36f. At all events excavation at Helwan has disclosed graves from the beginning of the historical period, with the sacred signs of Isis and Osiris; see K. Lange, *Egypte* (Dutch trans.) (1953), 220.

70. Cf. the Babylonian version of Ishtar's journey into hell, *A.N.E.T.*, 109.

71. Cf., e.g., in the Old Testament Ezek. 8:14. Old Sumerian Tammuz-liturgies: see A. Falkenstein and W. von Soden, *Sumerische und Akkadische Hymnen und Gebete* (1953), 32f., 34f., 73f. (364); 90ff. (367), 185f. (375f.), 344 (405); see also S. H. Hooke, *Babylonian and Assyrian religion* (1953), 31, 36ff.

72. See *A.N.E.T.*, 265f.; in the lists of Babylonian kings he appears (*a*) before the Flood as a herdsman who reigned for 36,000 years in Bad-tibiza, (*b*) after the Flood as a fisherman who reigned for 100 years in Erech.

73. T. Jacobsen, '*Formative Tendencies*, etc.', *op. cit.*, 272, translates the name as: '(he) who engenders the life of the child'.

74. See S. N. Kramer, *Sumerian Mythology* (1944) ,13. A collection of Tammuz-liturgies was published by Witzel in 1935; see further literature in E. Dhorme, *Les religions de Babylonie et d'Assyrie* (1945), 134f.

75. See especially the critical observations of F. R. Kraus in *W.Z.K.M.* (1953), 36ff., and of A. Parrot in *Bi.Or.*, VI (1949), 176ff., on the book by A. Moortgat, *Tammuz, Der Unsterblichkeitsglaube in der altorientalischen Bildkunst* (1949), and the articles 'Auferstehung I' and 'Tammuz', in *R.G.G.*, 3.

76. Jacobsen in *Intellectual Adventure*, 198f., and in 'Formative Tendencies', 272f.

77. *A.N.E.T.*, 52 and 109, and the places specified in Falkenstein-Von Soden.

78. R. Frankena, *Takultu* (1953), 85 n.44.

79. See S. N. Kramer, *Aspects du contact suméro-akkadien* (1960), 277.

80. See J. Bottéro, 'Les divinités sémitiques anciennes en Mésopotamie', in *Le antiche divinità semitiche* (1958), 17ff.; and the afore-mentioned article by S. N. Kramer.

T

THE RELIGION OF ANCIENT ISRAEL

81. Cf. also the comment by Falkenstein-Von Soden, *op. cit.*, 33: 'Das Bild der eigentlichen Dumuzi-Lieder mutet fast wie ein erratischer Block aus einer früheren Epoche der religiösen Entwicklung Babyloniens an.' Also T. Jacobsen, *op. cit.*

82. Additions to the Second edition of J. Pedersen, *Israel III–IV* (1959), 794; cf. also J. Gray, *The Legacy of Canaan* (1957), 57f., and W. W. Baudissin, *Adonis und Esmun* (1911), 111.

83. As is evident enough when one compares the book by Gray, already mentioned, with, e.g., G. R. Driver, *Canaanite Myths and Legends* (1956).

84. J. Pedersen, *Israel*, III–IV (Second edition), 791ff.; J. Gray, *op. cit.*, 29ff., 120ff.; W. Schmidt, *Königtum Gottes in Ugarit und Israel*, in *B.Z.A.W.*, 80 (1961), 9ff. Løkkegaard takes a contrary view, *op. cit.*, 232, although he recognizes, 231, that there is a certain correspondence between Baal and the cycle of the seasons. The biblical data too, which repeatedly link Baal-worship with sexual-cum-agrarian fertility motifs, point in that direction. Cf. Schmidt in *Z.R.G.*, XV (1963), 1ff.

85. See above (p. 40).

86. It is this seven-yearly period which Løkkegaard cites to support his argument that Baal, who dies and rises annually, is not a fertility-god. If we may regard this battle in the seventh year as the final one, then there is no contradiction, either, between the character of Baal in the Baal-cycle and in Aqht-text, where Baal is seen as the undying god (2 Aqht VI, 27ff.). As in the case of Osiris in Egypt, we must see the death of the dying god in Phoenicia not as opposed to the life but as joined in polarity with it. It is precisely as the deity who goes through, and vanquishes, death that Baal can be the symbol of life and immortality.

87. Cf. Lucian, *De Dea Syra*, 6, 7; see trans. by C. Clemen, 'Lukians Schrift über die syrische Göttin', *Der Alte Orient* 37, 3/4 (1938), 8 (cf. 31ff.); also the book by Baudissin, referred to above.

88. O. R. Gurney, *The Hittites* (1952), 184ff.

89. Cf. H. Gressmann, 'Hadad und Baʿal', in *Abhandlungen zur semitischen Religionskunde*, Festschrift W. W. Baudissin; *B.Z.A.W.*, 33 (1918), 191ff., whence it appears that, among others, the inhabitants of Akko, Taanach, Megiddo, Shechem, Lachish and other places in Southern Palestine bore theophorous names compounded with Baal (or Hadad).

90. In the Old Testament: Baalah=Baal-judah; Baal-gad, Baal-hamon, Baal-hazor, Baal-peor, Baal-perazim, Baal-shalisha, Baal-tamar; in addition, some names compounded with Baalah, Baalath and Bealoth.

91. Thus in the patriarchal period this was not yet the case. The absence of allusions to Baalism is nothing strange, therefore. For a long time the old Hebrew tribes retained their desert traditions, as did the Rechabites in a later period. Assimilation followed only upon the change to a sedentary way of life.

92. See further below, 110f., 132ff.; and J. Pedersen, 'Canaanite and Israelite cultus', *Acta Orientalia*, 18 (1939) 1ff.

93. In spite of the objections voiced by J. J. Stamm, in *Z.A.W.*, 57 (1939), 266ff., to Baudissin's exegesis in *Adonis und Esmun*, 407ff., the prophet is evidently alluding here to the still lively and popular belief that just as with the world of nature-deities, so with Israel's God there is a polarity of death and life.

94. F. F. Hvidberg, *Weeping and Laughter in the Old Testament*, Leyden, 1962.

95. We shall come back later on to the notion of the underworld.

96. A. Erman, *Die Religion der Ägypter*, 14ff., 209f., 441.

97. For the Babylonians, cf., i.a., B. Meissner, *op. cit.* and E. Dhorme, *op. cit.*

98. A. de Buck, *Bi.Or.* (1944), 65 (in a review of G. van der Leeuw, *De godsdienst van het oude Aegypte* (1944)).

99. Although Egyptian religion is usually described in terms of the idea of the life-and-death relation (W. B. Kristensen, *Het leven uit de dood*), we must always bear in mind that in fact this is only 'one viewpoint' (as G. van der Leeuw, *op. cit.*, 12ff., recognizes), or 'a bright beam' in a composite whole (as A. de Buck, *loc. cit.*, has it). Even in Egypt death and life were not always seen as going hand in hand together. On the contrary, there is just as much sense of death as an enemy; cf. J. Zandee, *Death as an Enemy* (1960). Here again, it seems, nature proved stronger than theory.

100. Cf. *A.N.E.T.*, 6; see also H. Frankfort, *Similarities*, 11.

101. J. Zandee, *De hymnen aan Amon van Papyrus Leiden*, I, 350 (1948), 84 Bf.; A. de Buck, 'Egyptische Godsdienst', in *De Godsdiensten der Wereld*, I, 77ff.

102. *Op. cit.*, 85A.

103. 'Egypt', in H. Frankfort, *op. cit.*, *The Intellectual Adventure*.

104. *Ibid.*, 363.

105. *Enuma eliš*, VII, 130ff.; see translation by R. Labat, *Le poème babylonien de la création* (1935), 171.

106. See H. L. F. Lutz, *The Concept of Change in the Life and Thought of the Babylonians* (1939), 15.

107. *Intellectual Adventure*, 125ff.

108. See my 'De overwinning van het tragische levensgevoel in Israel', in *Kernmomenten der antieke beschaving* (1947), 33ff. Cf. also F. M. Th. de Liagre Böhl, 'Das Menschbild in babylonischer Schau', in *Suppl. Numen*, II (1955), 28ff., esp. 44f.

109. See Jacobsen, *op. cit.*, 125, Gilg. epic IV, 7–8 (Old-Bab.).

110. Although it was not until fairly late on that many gods in the Sumerian world assumed anthropomorphic forms, of the Babylonian ones this can on the whole be maintained; cf. Jacobsen, 'Formative tendencies', etc., in *The Bible and the Ancient Near East*, 268f.

111. See, e.g., G. W. Lambert, *Babylonian Wisdom*, loc. cit.; S. N. Kramer, *Sumero-Akkadian Interconnections; Religious Ideas* (see above, p. 281, note 79); Th. Jacobsen, 'Formative tendencies', *op. cit.*, 267ff.; Bottéro, 'Les divinités sémitiques anciennes en Mésopotamie', in *Le antiche divinità semitiche* (1958), 17ff; F. R. Kraus, *Wandel und Kontinuität*, 9ff.

112. According to Kramer, *op. cit.*, 277, alongside the Sumerian deities An, Enlil and Ninhursag, the following Semitic gods were taken into the Babylonian pantheon: Ea, Sin, Shamash, Ishtar. Bottéro, *op. cit.*, 50, evidently disagrees with this, because he regards Enki as a Sumerian god and beside the three 'astral' gods names also Apsu and Ilu.

113. W. G. Lambert, *op. cit.*, 5ff., is probably right in seeing Semitic influence here. He speaks of the amoral character of the Sumerian gods, whereas there is a more moral strain present in the Semitic variety. Compare with this what Jacobsen says in the Albright Festschrift about the original character of the Sumerian gods as a pure force of nature, and about the anthropomorphizing process as a late development.

114. See, i.a., C. J. Gadd, *Ideas of Divine Rule*, 39.

115. Cf. above p. 33, and the literature mentioned in note 35 of this chapter.

116. *A.O.T.z.A.T.* (Second edition), 130f.

117. Cf. simply the judgment of Gilgamesh in the Assyrian epic on Ishtar.

118. W. G. Lambert, *op. cit.*, 96ff., especially 105 (see also B. Gemser, 'Spreuken II', in *Tekst en Uitleg* (1931), 53, 1.86ff.):1.135, every day worship your god; 1.139, prayer, supplication and prostration offer him daily; 1.140, and you will get your reward; 1.141, Then you will have full communion with your god.

119. Cf. 'the Discourse of master and slave', e.g., in W. G. Lambert, *Bab. Wisdom Lit.*, 139ff.

120. Cf., i.a., the following books: R. Dussaud, *Les religions des Hittites, des Hourrites, des Phéniciens et des Syriens*, Mana II (1945), 356ff.; S. Moscati, *The Face of the Ancient Orient* (1960), 194ff.

121. Lucian, *The Syrian Goddess:* see C. Clemen, *op. cit.;* Eusebius, *Praeparatio Evangelica* (cf. ed. E. H. Gifford, 5 parts, 1903ff.; text, translation and notes), who elaborates upon the evidence of Philo Biblius and Sanchuniaton; cf., i.a., C. Clemen, 'Die Phönikische Religion nach Philo von Byblos', in *M.V.Äg.Gesch.*, 42, 3 (1939).

122. In the Yehimilk-inscription of Byblos (see *A.N.E.T.*, 499, also the Zakir-inscription of Hamath, *A.N.E.T.*, 501) probably appearing as Baalshamem, whilst he is elsewhere identified with Hadad; see i.a., Albright, *A.R.I.*, 73. Eissfeldt, 'Ba'alshamem und Jahwe', *Z.A.W.* (1939), 1ff.; J. Starcky, *Palmyre* (1952), 98ff.; K. F. Euler, 'Königtum u. Götterwelt i. d. altaram. Inschriften Nordsyriens', in *Z.A.W.* (1938), 272ff. (especially 307B). Cf. above, p. 34.

123. Cf. O. Eissfeldt sub 'Ba'al', *R.G.G.*, I (Third edition), 805f., and 'Hadad', *R.G.G.*, III (Third edition), 7f. He appears frequently in the Amarna-letters. In the North and East Semitic world he is a storm- and rain-god rather than a god of fertility. By being identified in the West Semitic world with Baal he comes to share there Baal's vegetative character (cf. Zech. 12:11; and cf., e.g., F. Horst, his commentary on this text in *Handbuch z. A.T.* (1938), 248). For Baal cf. further J. Pedersen, *Israel* III–IV, 467ff., 506ff. and 793ff.; and M. J. Mulder, 'Baal in het O.T.', *diss. V.U.* (1962). Regarding Adonis and his connexion with Baal we have had something to say already, p. 41. Associated with him is the god Eshmun (cf. W. W. Graf von Baudissin, *Adonis und Esmun*, 203ff.), a Semitic god found only among the Phoenicians. He is the city-god of Sidon (two kings bear the name of Eshmun 'azar). At a later time he turns up as Eshmun-'Adon. Both are gods of life and death. In the Hellenic period Esmun comes to be identified with Asclepius.

124. See above, pp. 40f.; for El see illust. No. 16 and *A.N.E.P.*, 493; for Baal, idem, 490.

125. Cf. O. Eissfeldt, sub 'Aschera', in *R.G.G.* I (Third edition), 637f., and J. Gray, *op. cit.*, 130ff.

126. 1 Kings 16:33; 2 Kings 13:16; 24:4 and 6.

127. O. Eissfeldt, *op. cit.*, 661; J. Gray, *op. cit.*, 129.

128. More often mentioned in the Amarna-letters. She gives the king 'potency' (either 'strength' or 'vital energy', called *bashtu*) and is thus a warrior goddess and goddess of fertility as well. Whether she is a fusion of Astarte and Anat or of Asherah and Astarte is uncertain. In that case she would be an Atargatis-figure and so related to the (later) chief goddess of Ptolemaïs-Akko, who is reckoned to have been the spouse of Hadad (see M. Avi-Yonah, 'Syrian Gods at Ptolemaïs', in *I.E.J.* (1959, 1ff.). The Old Testament speaks of Astarte as the goddess of the Sidonians (cf. 1 Kings 11:5, 33 and 16:31). See also Pritchard, *Figurines*, 70f., who feels certain of the connexion between Ba'alat of Gubla and Asherah. A representation of her is to be found in *A.N.E.P.*, 477, cf. *A.O.B.z.A.T.*, 516. Here she is seen wearing a Hathor-crown, because she is identified with the Egyptian Hathor. Excavations at Byblos have disclosed a temple of Ba'alat at different levels. She must have been one of the principal deities of Byblos from the earliest times (cf. *R.G.G.*, I (Third edition), 1557, sub 'Byblos'). According to Lucian the cult of Adonis was practised here.

129. See the names, p. 252, note 90.

130. Cf. 1 Kings 16:31ff.; and R. de Vaux, *Ancient Israel, Its Life and Institutions*, London, 1962, p. 261; W. F. Albright, '*Archaeology and the Religion of Israel*' (hereafter *A.R.I.*) (1946), 77ff.

131. See below, p. 61.

132. In Egypt becoming 'Antart', in Syria 'Atargatis'; see *A.R.I.*, 74.

133. J. Gray, *op. cit.*, 32ff., 52ff., 77ff., 127ff.; Albright, *A.R.I.*, 75ff.

134. *A.N.E.T.*, 136B.

135. R. de Vaux, *op. cit.*, 350. The same term is used for this as for a part of the (high) priest's clothing in the Bible.

136. J. Gray, *op. cit.*, 128.

137. Cf. Josh. 19: 38; Jer. 1, *et al.* According to J. Gray, *op. cit.*, 151, a stele has been discovered at Beth-Shean, which was erected in honour of Anat, under the name of Antit.

138. Cf. *A.N.E.P.* No. 473 (with lance and shield in her right hand, brandishing a cudgel above her head) and possibly 492, in which a full-clothed goddess is wrapped in a garment consisting of a falcon's wing. Is she also the naked goddess on horseback, *op. cit.*, 479? For Astarte see above, note 128.

139. Cf. M. J. Dahood, *op. cit.*, 77ff.; S. Moscati, in the same work, 130f.; R. Frankena, *op. cit.*, 36; von Soden, sub 'Dagon', in *R.G.G.*, II (Third edition), 18f. On a Phoenician seal an ear of corn is the emblem of this god. In the East he is often identified with Enlil and Hadad. It seems not unlikely that at a later time Baal outstripped the older Dagon, who had been so great over a long period.

140. Bottéro, *op. cit.*, 55.

141. J. Gray, *op. cit.*, 123ff. In the North he occurs relatively seldom; but see G. Rÿckmans, *Religions arabes préislamiques*, 23 (21); very common in South Arabia.

142. Cf. what is said about the gods of life and death in Egypt, p. 38ff.

143. See J. Gray, *op. cit.*, 96 note 2. Cf. for Mekal *A.N.E.P.*, 487.

144. Cf. below, p. 287, note 193.

145. The mention in Ezek. 28:11–19 of the king of Tyre was perhaps originally a reference to this god, Melkart; see J. Dus, 'Melek Sor-Melqart?', in *Archiv Orientální* (1958), 179ff.

146. Cf. J. Gray, *op. cit.*, 132f.

147. J. J. Stamm, 'Der Name des Königs Salomo', in *Th.Z.*, 16 (1960), 290. The word for 'the red light of dawn' in Hebrew is *Shaḥar*. In my view, the identification of the names with the morning- and evening-stars is a less happy one; for these, Ugarit already had the gods Ashtar and Astarte. The name 'Shalem' apparently has to do with the fact that a red sunset is a sign of good weather (cf. Matt. 16:3). *Shaḥar*, the red of dawn, spells bad weather (Matt. 16:3) and could very well be connected, therefore, with the verb *shaḥar*=to grow dark. (Albright, *A.R.I.*, 73, 195 note 10, associates *Shalem* with the Accadian *shalam shamshi* (sunset). He regards as totally separate from this the other names like *Shalim*, *Shalman*, which he connects with 'wellbeing, prosperity', *op. cit.*, 79.

148. See Böhl, *Opera Minora*, 380ff.

149. Cf. Malkiṣedeq (Gen. 14), Adoniṣedeq (Josh. 10).

150. See M. J. Dahood, *op. cit.*, 92f.; J. Gray, *op. cit.*, 133ff.

151. See G. E. Wright, *Biblical Archaeology* (1957), 136ff.; also *B.A.* (1941), 20ff.; Albright, *A.R.I.*, 142ff.; A. Parrot, *The temple of Jerusalem*, 1957, 23ff.

152. See J. Gray, *op. cit.*, 140ff.

153. Peace-offering. Ugarit had the same names for these as the Hebrew.

154. J. Gray, *op. cit.*, 142; cf. C. H. Gordon, *Ugaritic Literature* (1949), 108ff.

155. *A.N.E.T.*, pp. 25ff.

156. *A.N.E.T.*, 499f.

157. *A.N.E.T.*, 502.

158. See St. Yeivin, *A Decade of Archaeology in Israel*, 1948–1958 (1960), 22f.

159. See reports in *I.E.J.* from 1956 on, and Yeivin, *op. cit.*, 24ff.

160. *Op. cit.*, 526f.

161. Cf. also G. Fohrer, 'Die wiederentdeckte Kanaanäische Religion', *Th.LtZt.* (1953), 193ff.

162. See Kupper, *op. cit.*, 109ff., and A. Dupont-Sommer, 'Les débuts de l'histoire Araméenne', in Supplement *V.T.*, I (1953), 40ff.; B. Mazar, 'Aramean Empire', in *B.A.*, XXV (1962), 98ff.

163. See note 123.

164. In the Hellenistic period Adad and Artagatis are the chief gods of Ptolemaïs (Akko); see note 128.

165. See literature above, notes 89, 122 and 123.

166. Text Lidzbarski: *Ephemeris für Semitische Epigraphik*, III (1915), 1ff.; *A.N.E.T.*, 501f.; *D.O.T.T.*, 242ff.

167. Sargon, 'laudatory inscription 33'; Stele 1, 52; Nimrud-inscription 8: 'Jaubi'di and Ilubi'di, *circa* 710' *A.N.E.T.*, 285, 287.

168. M. Noth, *Personennamen*, 110ff.; A. Dupont-Sommer, *op. cit.*, 115.

169. A. Dupont-Sommer, 'Les inscriptions araméennes de Sfiré' (1958), *A.N.E.T.*, 503ff.; first translation by H. Bauer, *A.f.O.* (1932), 1ff.; see the historical discussion of the text by M. Noth in *Z.D.P.V.*, 77 (1961), 118ff. He sees in KTK a South East Aramaean country, and Z. as being on the Euphrates.

170. 'Earth' conjectural here; 'abyss' partly supplied.

171. R. Frankena, *Takultu* 111, note 194; Bottéro, 'Divinità', however, has a West Semitic background in mind.

172. Cf., e.g., W. W. Graf Baudissin, *Kyrios*, III, 81, 115.

173. R. Frankena, *op. cit.*, 117, 236.

174. *A.N.E.T.*, 205; A. Dupont-Sommer, *Sfiré*, 35; also in a treaty between Hannibal and Philip of Macedon. In the case of the new texts discovered at Ras Shamra in 1961, one of the goddesses is called 'daughter of the spring, of the stone, of the heavens and of the ocean' (according to a press report issued in connexion with an announcement made by Virolleaud at the May 4, 1962, session of the Académie des Inscriptions et Belles Lettres in Paris). We may recall an early-Semitic custom, for which cf. that the prophets of the Old Testament call upon heaven and earth (Isa. 1:2, cf. Isa. 2:12; Deut. 32:1), mountains and foundations of the earth (Micah 6:1f.) to pay heed to their message.

175. See M. Noth, *op. cit.*, 163f.

176. A. Dupont-Sommer, *Les Araméens* (1949), 108ff.

177. Cf. A. Parrot, *Malédictions et Violations de Tombes* (1939).

178. Cf. for the text: M. J. Lagrange, *Etudes sur les religions sémitiques* (Second edition) (1905), 492ff.; also A. Dupont-Sommer, *op. cit.*, 116f.

179. This 'with Hadad' is an important addition, which could be very material; but no absolutely satisfactory exegesis is possible.

180. Cf. A. Dupont-Sommer, *Les inscriptions Araméennes de Sfiré* (1958), 19ff.; and see above, p. 58.

181. See in this connexion G. M. Landes, 'The Material Civilisation of the Ammonites', in *B.A.* (1961), 66ff.

182. *Op. cit.*, 74.

183. See, e.g., J. Starcky, 'Palmyréniens, Nabatéens et Arabes du Nord avant l'Islam', in M. Brillant and R. Aigrain, *Histoire des Religions*, 4, 211; O. Eissfeldt, 'Das A.T. im Lichte der safatenischen Inschriften', in *Z.D.M.G.*, 104 (1954), 88ff. (p. 114f.): Allat is invoked as a major goddess also in the North (and Baal too appears).

184. *Op. cit.*, 79; from the 7th century B.C.

185. G. Lankester Harding, *The Antiquities of Jordan* (1959), 45.

186. Cf. the name Mr'il=the man of El (7th century B.C.), *B.A.S.O.R.* (Dec. 1960) 38ff., art. by Hammond.

187. Cf. J. Starcky, *op. cit.*, 204, and J. Ryckmans, 'Het oude Arabie en de Bijbel', *Jaarbericht E.O.L.*, No. 14 (1955–56), 79.

188. E.g. Amminadab; cf. Harding, *op. cit.*, 45.

189. It occurs in Israelite names too; see M. Noth, *Die israelitische Personennamen* (1928), 76ff.

190. M. Noth, *op. cit.*, 78.

191. A. Jamme, *Le Monde divin sud-arabe*, in M. Brillant and R. Aigrain, *op. cit.*, 262ff., 279ff. In early times the name was known also in North Arabia; see G. L. Harding, *op. cit.*, 45 (Ammuladi, king of the Kedar-Arabs). M. Höfner, 'Eine Qatabanische Weihinschrift am Timna'', *Le Muséon* (1961), 453ff., published a text in which 'Athtar and 'Amm occur side by side.

192. Read, with slight modification of the text, *Milkom*, in place of 'their king'.

193. When we remember the gods who acquired the title *melek* (king) in the Ugaritic world, it could be an El-, a Baal- or an Ashtar-figure; cf. W. Schmidt, *Königtum Gottes in Ugarit und Israel* (1961), 17ff. Starcky, with R. Dussaud, thinks El the most likely, *op. cit.*, 224. Could this Molech-El figure have had a solar character, as later on Malachbel did in Palmyra (Starcky, *op. cit.*, 209f.)? Molech would then, on this view, be a parallel of the chief god of Moab.

194. Chemosh Madab and Chemosh Haleth, kings of Moab in Tiglath-Pileser's and Sennacherib's time; cf. G. L. Harding, *op. cit.*, 44f.

195. See Mesha-stone, 1.17 Ashtar-Chemosh, the female (?) counterpart to Chemosh.

196. See Mesha-stone, 1.30, and Josh. 13:17 (Baal Meon); Num. 22:41; cf. 21:19f.; and Josh. 13:17; Bamoth Baal; Baal Peor (Num. 25 and Hos. 9:10).

197. Ashtar-Chemosh may also be a double name—like those which occur, i.a., in Ugarit; and then this figure would be no one other than Chemosh. It speaks in favour of this that in both Southern and Central Arabia the god Ashtar (Athtar) occurs as a male deity, and indeed as morning- or evening-star (whereas in the East Semitic world Ishtar, who is in a similar way associated with Venus, is a female deity. A similar change of sex occurs in the case of the sun-god, who is female in Arabia and male in the East Semitic world). J. Gray, *Legacy of Canaan*, 125—among others—prefers this interpretation. To this, however, it may be objected that both in the Mesha-inscription and in the Bible all further references are to Chemosh only. Cf. also K. Galling, *Textbuch zur Geschichte Israels* (1950), 49, note d–d and fig. 13.

198. See W. von Soden, 'Kamos', *R.G.G.* (Third edition), III (1959), 1105; A. H. van Zÿl, *The Moabites* (1960), 196, with a reference to *R.B.*, 41, 432ff., and Alt, *P.J.B.*, 36, p. 36. Cf. also his *Kleine Schriften*, I (1953), 208ff.

199. Deimel, *Pantheon Babylonicum*, p. 153, No. 1628.

200. Cf. the illustrations in N. Glueck, *The Other Side of the Jordan* (1940), 152ff.; van Zÿl, *op. cit.*, 33f.

201. See J. B. Pritchard, *Palestine Figurines* (1943), especially 100f., and E. Pilz, 'die weiblichen Gottheiten Kanaans', in *Z.D.P.V.*, 47 (1924), 128ff., and table I facing p. 260.

202. Or—if Ashtar is indeed a male deity—perhaps of Astarte?

203. Cf. above, p. 28.

204. The meaning of the word *ryt* is uncertain; for this see C. H. W. Brekelmans, *De Cherem in het Oude Testament*, diss. Nijmegen (1959), 30ff.

205. The word is not clear enough to read.

206. The researches of Brekelmans, *op. cit.*, would indicate that (as far as we know) this was known in the ancient world—apart from Israel—only in Moab.

207. The merciless behaviour in war of Ammonites and Moabites as well as Edomites is stigmatized and condemned by Amos 1:11–23.

208. The evidence of 2 Kings 3 makes such a clear impression, historically, that the fact cannot really be doubted.

209. The only (possible) instance occurs in the story of the sacrifice of Jephthah's daughter (Jud. 11:30ff.), which also takes place in Transjordan.

210. Van Zÿl, *op. cit.*, 197.

211. *Op. cit.*, 199.

212. Num. 25; 31:16 and Hos. 9:10.

213. See M. Noth, 'Israelitische Stämme zwischen Ammon und Moab', *Z.A.W.*, 60 (1944), 11ff., especially 23–30.

214. As Noth has shown in the article referred to; cf. also his *Überlieferungsgeschichte des Pentateuch* (1948), 80ff.

215. Ll.14 and 32.

216. See also A. Bentzen, 'The ritual background of Amos 1:2–2:16', *O.T.S.*, VIII (1950), 85ff.

217. See N. Glueck, *op. cit.*, 154f.; Van Zÿl, *op. cit.*, 34, 201.

218. Gen. 25ff. and 36.

219. As do M. Noth, *Überlieferungsgeschichte des Pentateuch*, 104ff., and V. Maag, 'Jacob-Esau-Edom', in *Th.Z.* (1957), 418ff.

220. Noth also recognizes this when, i.a., he points out that as a clan the Kenizzites are classed with Israel as well as with Edom (Gen. 36:11, 15, 42; Josh. 14:5, 14; 15:17).

221. K. Galling, 'Gemeindegesetz in Deut. 23', in Festschrift für A. Bertholet (1950), 176ff. (in particular 183).

222. Cf. Jer. 49:7; Obad. 8; (Lam. 4:21); the friends of Job and the whole background to the Book of Job; cf. 1 Kings 4:30; Prov. 31:1.

223. Cf. Nelson Glueck, *B.A.* (1947), 83, see below, note 229.

224. Qaus-gaber, see Harding, *op. cit.*, 44; cf. *A.N.E.T.*, 291, 294.

225. Qaus-ʿanal (?), see Nelson Glueck, *Other side*, 110; cf. *B.A.* (1938), 15; (1947), 83. Harding, *op. cit.*, 141, gives besides the name Qaus-geber.

226. Also a North Arabian deity in Palmyra; cf. J. Starcky, *op. cit.*, 218; among the Lihyanites, G. Rÿckmans, *Religions arabes pré-islamiques* (1951), 20; also Harding, *op. cit.*, 44. Is this the same as the West Semitic *Shalim*? De Liagre Böhl argues that Shulman or Shalem was the old city-god of Jerusalem, who had Shulmanitu (an Ishtar-figure) as his female counterpart; cf. *Opera Minora*, 380ff.

227. Melek-Ram; see Harding, 44; for Melek see above, p. 287, note 193.

228. An Aramaean and Mesopotamian god (Adad). In Mesopotamia too Adad is of Semitic origin. Already present in Mesopotomia from before the time of Sargon's dynasty, having made his way in from the West, he attained to great importance in the Accadian period; and the same was still true in the Ammonite period. In particular, Adad is one of the great gods of the Ammonites, having originally come with them from the desert region of Northern Arabia. See J. Bottéro, *op. cit.*, 54, and J. Kupper, *op. cit.*, 149ff. He was venerated especially by the Aramaeans. See also p. 284, note 123.

229. J. Wellhausen, *Reste Arabischen Heidentums*, 67, 209; *Prolegomena* (Fifth edition), 317; also Nöldeke, in a critical assessement of the aforementioned work, in *Z.D.M.G.* (1887), 707ff., especially 714, and *E.R.E.* (1908), 660f.; Albright, 'Islam and the religions of the Ancient Orient', in *J.A.O.S.* (1940), 295, note 39. Whether the name has to do with the Arabic word *qaus* (a bow), and what connexion there is with the old-Arabian deity Quzah, and whether the name Koze,

which Flavius Josephus gives to the Edomite god, rests on a correct identification or not—all this is quite uncertain.

The name is probably the same as occurs in the Minaean texts; see G. Rÿckmans, *Les noms propres sud-sémitiques*, I (1934), 30, 265 and 390, and II, 18.

230. *Z.D.M.G.*, 104 (1957), 88ff.

231. See G. Rÿckmans, 'Het oude Arabië en de Bijbel', in *Jaarbericht E.O.L.* (1955–56), 8ff.

232. It was from this milieu that A. Alt gathered his material for the '*Gods of the Fathers*'.

233. G. Rÿckmans, *Les religions arabespréislamiques* (Second edition) (1951), 14ff.

234. For literature we may refer the reader to J. Starcky, 'Palmyréens, Nabatéens et Arabes du Nord avant l'Islam', in M. Brillant and R. Aigrain, *Histoire des Religions*, 4, 201ff.; *idem*, 'Palmyre' (1952), in *L'Orient ancien illustré*, 7. These are the writings to which we are most indebted for this account of Palmyrene religion.

235. See, i.a., his *The Other Side of Jordan* (1940), 158ff., especially 178ff.

236. Regarding the relation of *du* and *baal* in the names of Arabian gods see, i.a., G. Rÿckmans, 'De maangod in de voorislamietische Zuidarabische godsdienst', in *Mededelingen Kon. Ned. Ak. Wet. Afd. Letterk.* (1948), 7f.

237. Cf. Starcky, *Histoire des Religions*, 230ff.; J. Henninger, 'La religion Bedouine préislamique', in *L'antica Società Beduina* (1959), 126f. This also occurs in Central and Southern Arabia; see Rÿckmans, *Religions Arabes* 8, 28f.

238. See J. A. Montgomery, *Arabia and the Bible* (1934), 155ff.; J. Rÿckmans, *op. cit.*, *J.E.O.L.*, 80ff.; e.g., words for: questions put to an oracle; words like *mslm*, cf. Hebrew *shelem*; *mqtr*, cf. the Hebrew word in Ex. 30:1; et cetera; cf. also G. Rÿckmans, *op. cit.*, 30f., for the terms *liw*' and *liw't* for people consecrated to the service of the deity; cf. R. de. Vaux, *Ancient Israel*, pp. 358ff.

239. G. Rÿckmans, *Religion*, 40; A. Jamme, 'La religion sud-arabe préislamique' in M. Brillant and R. Aigrain, *Histoire des Religions*, 4, 260ff.

240. G. Rÿckmans, *De maangod*, etc., 4.

241. *Loc. cit.*, 15.

242. 'La religion bédouine préislamique', in *L'antica Società Beduina*, Rome (1959), 114ff. For earlier literature the reader is referred to J. Wellhausen, *Reste Arabischen Heidentums* (Second edition, 1929; orig. pub. 1887), which relied on the passages from al-Kalbi cited by the Arabian geogapher, Yakut. Al Kalbi's book (9th century) was recovered at the beginning of this century and published in Cairo in 1913; newly published, translated and annotated by Rosa Klinke-Rosenberger, *Das Götzenbuch, Kitab al-Asnam des Ibn al-Kalbi* (1941). Jamme's and Rÿckmans' studies are an advance, in that these authors have edited and incorporated the newly discovered inscription-material.

243. Cf. E. Mittwoch, *Abergläuberische Vorstellungen und Bräuche bei den alten Arabern* (1913), 2.

244. For this see especially Montgomery, *op. cit.*, 153ff., 187. Henninger, *op. cit.*, 134, explains the phenomenon in terms of a primitive 'high god' concept current among the early Arab nomads—but Wellhausen, *Reste*, 218ff., in terms of a slow, measured process of development of the 'god idea'.

245. See, e.g., G. Beer, *Exodus* (1939), 127ff.

246. See, e.g., Guillaume, *Prophecy and Divination* (138); J. Pedersen, 'The role played by inspired persons among the Israelites and the Arabs', in *Studies in Old Testament prophecy, presented to Th. H. Robinson* (1950), 127ff.

247. Cf. J. Pedersen, *Israel*, I–II.

248. (1934), 185.

249. See also S. Nyström, *Beduinentum und Jahwismus* (1946), 24ff. He instances as typical elements demonstrating the relationship: hospitality; blood-feud;

marriage customs and code of conduct in war. Some earlier books are: M. J. Lagrange, *Etudes sur les religions sémitiques* (Second edition) (1905); W. Robertson Smith, *The Religion of the Semites* (Third edition) (1927); S. I. Curtiss, *Ursemitische Religion im Volksleben des heutigen Orients* (1903). On this last subject— religious life in the present-day Arab world—there exist a number of important works, of which we ought to mention here: Jaussen, *Les coutumes des Arabes*. Finally, we shall mention the names only of T. Canaan and A. Musil. The habits and customs of modern Arab—especially nomad—society afford many illustrations of the spirit and mentality of earlier times; but they cannot be compared— certainly not directly—with life in the ancient Arab and Hebrew world, let alone be equated with it.

250. C. J. Bleeker, *De structuur van de Godsdienst*, 82.

251. *Religion in Essence and Manifestation*, 1938; the will is the divine will, to which man must show himself obedient.

252. *Old Testament Theology*, (1962, 1964), *passim*.

253. *An Outline of Old Testament Theology*, 1958, *passim*.

254. S. Freud, *Moses and Monotheism*, (1939), 95ff. (See also above, p. 36f.).

255. In his article already referred to: 'Ugaritische Probleme und ihre Tragweite für das A.T.', in *Th.Z.*, III (1947), 81ff.—especially 96ff.

256. Although in a somewhat different fashion, V. Maag, 'Malkut Jahwe', Supplement to *V.T.*, VII (1960), 144, also antithesizes the two.

257. Cf. W. Baumgartner, *op. cit.*, 92, who speaks of a third determining factor. V. Maag makes the nomadic-patriarchal age run through, theoretically, into the period of Mosaic history. This would seem to be a less happy option.

258. See my 'De overwinning van het tragische levensgevoel in Israël', in *Kernmomenten der antieke beschaving* (1947), 33ff.

259. See V. Maag, 'Malkut JHWH', *op. cit.*; B. A. van Groningen, *In the Grip of the Past* (1953), 115ff.

CHAPTER 3

1. Cf. 'De compositie van de Samuël-boeken', in *Orientalia Neerlandica* (1948), 167ff., and *De literatuur van Oud-Israël* (1961), 32f., 140ff.

2. As to the connexion between Yahweh and war, see Chapter 6, p. 163ff.

3. Cf. further M. Noth, *Die Ursprünge des alten Israels*, 18ff., especially F. Horst, 'Zwei Begriffe für Eigentum', in *Verbannung und Heimkehr* (1961), Festschrift Rudolph, 135ff.

4. See *B.A.S.O.R.*, 140 (1955), 11ff. Others before him had advanced the suggestion that this was the spot. For further conjectures regarding Gilgal, see H. J. Kraus, 'Gilgal', *V.T.* (1951), 181ff.; and cf. M. Noth, *Josua*. (Second edition) (1953). Cf. also E. Taubler, *Biblische Studien* (1958), 20–29.

5. H. W. Hertzberg, 'Mizpa', in *Z.A.W.* (1929), 161ff., especially 177ff.

6. Cf. for the excavations of J. B. Pritchard, who identified this town with El-Jib in *B.A.* (1956, 1960 and 1961); also his *Gibeon* (1962).

7. H. W. Hertzberg, *op. cit.*; cf. also his *I and II Samuel, A Commentary*, London, 1964, pp. 178f.

8. *Jerusalem und sein Gelände* (1930), 44.

9. Cf. also A. Alt, 'The God of the Fathers'.

10. Near *Ramet el-Khalil*, a few kilometres north of Hebron. This construction is not to be confused with the second splendid sanctuary which Herod caused to be built over the traditional cave of Machpelah. This latter place is to this very day one of the most holy sites for Jews and Muslims.

11. O. Eissfeldt, 'Silo und Jerusalem', in Supplement to *V.T.* IV (1957), 138ff.

12. See Chapter 5.

13. *Personennamen*, 107.

14. That the view of events held by the author of the Saul-David story is so consistent in giving a central place to the figure of Yahweh is yet another consequence of this. Just how this way of envisaging God looked to the rest of Israel, outside Jerusalem, we do not know. It must have been a different story there in many respects. Between Baal and Yahweh there was a much less clear distinction, as is evident from various names compounded with Baal: Ishbaal, Mephibaal. El too is found a good deal in names from the transitional period; so that outside of the Judean-Jerusalemite circle the old syncretistic religious ideas must presumably have lived on.

15. 2 Sam. 6:5; cf., e.g., 1 Sam. 18:6 and Judges 11:34. In this role the ark was even carried into battle; 1 Sam 4. (cf. also Num. 10:35f.)

16. It seems to me untenable—simply because one recognizes that the booth in Ex. 33 which Moses was required to erect was a tabernacle of revelation—to fasten upon the idea that the ark might not be brought into contact with a tent, as Von Rad, *Old Testament Theology*, I, apparently does. On the other hand, I am not sure, either, that R. de Vaux, 'Arche de l'Alliance et tente de réunion' (*A la rencontre de Dieu*, Mémorial A. Gelin), 55ff., is right in thinking that the booth within which the ark stood did service as a tabernacle of revelation (apropos of Ex. 33); cf. also M. Haran, 'The nature of the "*Ohel Mo'edh*"', in *J.SS.*, V (1960), 50ff.

17. A form of expression like the one found in this Judean grotto suggests a narrowly nationalistic religious sense—the kind of thing that one also comes across in contemporaries of Jeremiah, such as the prophet Hananiah (Jer. 28). On this see my *Jahwe en zijn stad* (1962).

18. Cf., i.a., K. Elliger, 'Ephod und Choschen', in *V.T.* VIII (1958), 19ff.; the same author in *R.G.G.* (Third edition), sub 'Ephod'; and R. de Vaux, *Ancient Israel*, pp. 349ff.

19. See also R. de Vaux, *op. cit.*, 355f., who quite rightly understands the priest to be 'the minister of the altar' and not a sacrificer. For the original significance of the show-bread as the gift of a meal to the deity, see W. Herrmann, 'Götterspeise und Götterdrank in Ugarit und Israel', in *Z.A.W.* (1960), 205ff.

20. Cf. Driver, *Canaanite Myths*, 103, Baal-myth 115. A word from the same root is found also in Cappadocian texts, in the sense of 'costly article of clothing'; see *The Assyrian Dictionary*, E, sub '*epattu*'.

21. See A. Bentzen, 'Mitteilung', in *Z.A.W.* (1933), 173ff., and H. H. Rowley, 'Melchizedek and Zadok', in *Bertholet-Festschrift*, 461ff., where on p. 464, note 8, further literature is mentioned.

22. Cf. F. Maass, 'Nathan', in *R.G.G.* (Third edition).

23. For the questions relating to the complex composition of this narrative, see my article, 'De compositie van de Samuël-boeken', *Orientalia Neerlandica* (1948), 167ff., especially 182f., and along with that M. Noth, 'David and Israel in II Sam. 7', *The Laws in the Pentateuch and Other Essays*, pp. 250–259, and H. v. d. Bussche, 'Le texte de la prophétie de Nathan', in *Ephem. Th. Lovanienses* (1948), 354ff.

24. Read verse 4 amended thus: 'Yea, surely, so is my house with God'.

25. Cf. W. Preiser, 'Vergeltung und Sühne im altisraelitischen Strafrecht', in *Festschrift E. Schmidt* (1961), 7ff., who justly observes (38) that what is involved here is not a cleansing of the agent from his sin, but the wiping out of an act endangering the covenant between Yahweh and the nation.

26. *Israel* I–II, 378ff., especially 383ff., 388ff.

27. De Vaux, *op. cit.*, 491.

28. In the pacts between Barga'ayah and Mati'el (published by A. Dupont-Sommer, *Inscriptions Araméennes de Sfiré* (1958), 19 and 99) curses occur at a number (originally seven? the text has been mutilated) of points—maledictions in which the number seven plays a part (example: 'may seven sheep suckle a lamb, and it be not satisfied'). For literature see especially J. Pedersen, *Der Eid bei den Semiten* (1914).

29. In verse 45 the verb *padah*=redeem is used. This word occurs repeatedly in the law in the sense of: to ransom, to give something else in place of the firstborn—(sacrificial) victim. Preiser, *op. cit.*, 23, 27, speaks of the breach of a religious injunction to fast; but what is at issue here is the abrogation of an oath, which entails the imminent danger of capital punishment.

30. See also chapter V, 145; for literature, especially J. Pedersen, *Israel*, I–II; and *Der Eid*.

31. R. Otto, *The Idea of the Holy*; J. Hempel, *Gott und Mensch im A.T.* (Second edition) (1936).

32. As J. Pedersen has it in *Israel*, III–IV, 450ff.

33. See O. R. Gurney, *The Hittites* (1952), 160ff., 164f., where he tells us that in village societies old women were apparently considered to be the ones who had at their command the simplest forms of the secret arts.

CHAPTER 4

1. See, e.g., O. Eissfeldt, 'Religionshistorie und Religionspolemik im Alten Testament', in *Wisdom in Israel and in the Ancient Near East*, Rowley-Festschrift, Supplement to *V.T.*, III (1955), 94ff.

2. The material has been lucidly summarized by Père de Vaux in a number of articles in the *R.B.* (1946, 1948 and 1949). These are now available in a handy German edition which appeared with the title *Die hebräischen Patriarchen und die modernen Entdeckungen* (1961), with a foreword by O. Eissfeldt (De Vaux offers nothing on the religious ideas of the patriarchs). Cf. also H. H. Rowley, 'Recent Discovery and the Patriarchal Age', in *The Servant of the Lord and Other Essays*; M. Noth, *Die Ursprünge des alten Israel im Lichte neuer Quellen* (1961).

3. For detailed information consult Introductions to the Old Testament and that sort of books. We would mention, e.g., O. Eissfeldt, *The Old Testament. An Introduction*, 1965; J. Hempel, *Die althebräische Literatur und ihr hellenistisch-jüdisches Nachleben* (1930–35); Th. C. Vriezen, *De literatuur van Oud-Israël* (1961).

4. 'Das Zeitalter Abrahams', in *A.O.* 29, 1 (1930).

5. *The Prophetic Faith*, 1949, 31ff.

6. *Theologie des Alten Testaments* (1950), 48ff.

7. B. Gemser, *Vragen rondom de patriarchenreligie*, inaugural lecture (1958).

8. *Op. cit.*, 21ff.

9. E.g., E. Sellin, *Israëlitisch- Jüdische Religionsgeschichte*, I (1933).

10. E.g., A. Lods, *La religion d'Israël* (1939); W. O. E. Oesterley and Th. H. Robinson, *Hebrew Religion* (Second edition) (1937) (many reprints).

11. *The God of the Fathers*, pp. 65f.

12. One wonders whether the author was not influenced here by ancient West Semitic traditions—like the Keret and Dan'el legend from Ugarit—having to do with childless princes who also receive certain indications in a dream and either lose their son (Dan'el) or are menaced by him (Keret); cf. J. Gray, *op. cit.*, 73. If one ignores the more or less self-contained story of Sodom and Gomorrah (ch. 17f.), the scheme of the Abraham-narrative between chs. 15 and 22 reminds one very much of the Ugaritic stories, even though it is elaborated in its own

peculiar way. At all events, the theme of the 'want of issue' was a frequently occurring early West Semitic epic motif. There is no call to go along with Alt's explanation, based on sociological considerations (that this is a typical nomad-motif; in Ugarit, at any rate, there was no question of that). It is a more generally human motif, which marks the basic manner in which early West Semitic life was constituted. Viewed thus, the Abraham-and-Isaac story has an obvious back-ground in the life of the ancient East—and both figures have a common origin: that is to say, the Abraham figure from the South and the Isaac figure are related at source.

As against this, however, we may certainly go along with M. Noth (*Über-lieferungsgeschichte des Pentateuch*, 58ff., and Von Rad, *The Problem of the Hexateuch and Other Essays*, 1966, 79–93; on the other side, J. Hoftijzer, *Die Verheissungen an die drei Erzväter*, diss. (1956); see also P. A. H. de Boer, *Gods Beloften over land en volk in het Oude Testament* (1955)) in regarding the theme of the 'promised land' as one of the primal elements in the life of the Semitic nomads, who firmly believed that under divine guidance their meandering existence would eventually end in their taking possession of a homeland that would be their very own.

This latter element of the promise to Abraham may therefore be considered as one of the religious possessions of the early Hebrew tribes in the patriarchal period. Various discoveries during the past few decades make it very likely that we should regard the Hebrews as groups of unsettled, landless people (Habiru) who tried to establish themselves in a number of different countries. They did not originally belong to an ethnic group of clans, although they must have belonged mainly to the Semites who between 2000 and 1300 were for one reason and another out of patience with them; see J. Bottéro, *Le problème des Habiru* (1954).

13. Cf. e.g., J. C. L. Gibson, 'Light from Mari on the Patriarchs', in *J.S.S.* (1962), 44ff., especially 61f.

14. We refer the reader again to the book by S. Nyström; see Chapter 2, note 249.

15. Cf. M. Noth, 'Old Testament Covenant-making in the Light of a Text from Mari', *The Laws in the Pentateuch and Other Essays*, pp. 108ff., cf. also R. de Vaux, *op. cit.*, 74.

16. Cf. R. de Vaux, *op. cit.*, 76–78.

17. See also M. Noth, *Überlieferungsgeschichte des Pentateuch*, 167ff.

18. E has this back in chap. 15; in chap. 20:7 E expressly calls him so.

19. Cf. E. Jenni, *Das Wort 'olam im A.T.* (1955), 53ff.; cf. *Z.A.W.* (1952–53).

20. Cf., i.a., J. Gray, *op. cit.*, 116f., and M. J. Dahood, in S. Moscati, *L'antiche divinità semitiche* (1958), 73. Affirmed by F. M. Cross, 'Yahweh and the God of the Patriarchs', in *H.Th.R.* (1962), 236ff.

21. The end of the Keret-legend is uncertain; possibly it is that the father himself in this case curses his rebellious son and thereby helps to bring about his death.

22. C. van Arendonck linked this up with the *paḥad (fakhid) yishaq*. See also, i.a., J. Pedersen, *Der Eid bei den Semiten*, 151.

23. Cf. the results of M. Noth's researches into Israelitic nomenclature: M. Noth, *Personennamen*, 90ff., and 101ff.

24. Cf. i.a., A. van Selms, 'The Canaanites in Genesis', in *O.T.S.* (1958), 213, although the conclusions drawn by this author from the material are far too sweeping.

25. The name *shaddai*—with two d's—certainly raises problems. Hence all sorts of other conclusions have been tried for; see, e.g., M. Weippert, 'Erwägungen zur Etymologie des Godesnamen 'El Schaddai', in *Z.D.M.G.* (1961), 42ff., who

casting back to the word *shadu* wants to propose 'field-god'. Cf. also Albright, in
B.A.S.O.R. (1961), 163, 48, note 63, and Cross, *op. cit.*, 244ff.

26. See p. 293, note 22, and Chapter 8, p. 305, note 27. With regard to the relation between Isaac and Northern Israel, see W. Zimmerli, *Geschichte und Tradition
von Berseba* (1932), especially 25ff., 31. Isaac seems to have been one of the
early groups, which came up from the South into the North and was there amalga-
mated with the Jacob/Israel group.

27. Se'ir and Edom are not one and the same. Se'ir may be located partly west
and north of Edom. For Esau as a more northerly figure cf. Gen. 33 and V. Maag,
'Jakob, Esau, Edom', in *Th.Z.* (1957), 418ff.

28. The relation between Jacob and Esau is portrayed differently from that of
Abraham, Ishmael and Isaac. With the latter it is a case of direct genealogical
connexion; whereas the former is a brother-relationship which at the same time
contains an oppositive element, standing for the rivalry between brother races or
peoples.

29. Cf. M. Noth, 'Mari und Israel', in *Alt-Festschrift* (1953), 127ff. The name is
not explicable as a Hebrew word. In origin it must be a theophorous name with
the meaning: 'God protects'—a sense of the word preserved only in Southern
Arabic. The Hebrew word for 'slippery customer', 'trickster', cannot be the
original explanation. Obviously, therefore, the name is of ancient, non-Hebrew
origin. It does not occur later on, apparently because people no longer understood
what it meant.

30. Cf. O. Eissfeldt, 'Silo und Jerusalem', in Supplement to *V.T.*, IV (1957),
138ff.

31. This is judged by various people to be the likely translation; see p. 295, note
52; cf. further J. Hempel, *Apoxysmata* (1961), 25f., who is hesitant and opts for the
rendering: 'Herr Jakobs'; E. Jacob, *Ras Shamra*, etc., 69f., who relies in this
connexion on the article by J. Coppens, 'La bénédiction de Jacob', in Supplement
to *V.T.*, IV, 97ff., where additional literature is cited. Verse 24 is quite uncertain
and does not enable us, therefore, to draw a lot of inferences—as V. Maag does,
in fact, in his 'Der Hirte Israels', in *Schw.Th.U(mschau)* (1958), 2ff.

32. For an overall brief survey see H. H. Rowley, 'Recent discovery and the
patriarchal age', also his Schweich Lectures, *From Joseph to Joshua* (1950);
De Vaux's book, already mentioned: *Die hebräischen Patriarchen;* also F. M.
Th. de Liagre Böhl, 'Das Zeitalter Abrahams', in *Opera Minora* (1953), 26ff.;
M. Noth, 'Mari und Israel', in *Alt-Festschrift* (1953), 127ff., '*Die Ursprünge
des Alten Israel im Lichte neuer Quellen*' (1961); 'Der Beitrag der Archäologie
zur Geschichte Israels', in Supplement to *V.T.*, VII, Oxford Congress (1959),
262ff.; L. Rost, 'Die Gottesverehrung der Patriarchen im Lichte der Pentateuch-
quellen', in Supplement to *V.T.*, VII, 346ff.; 'Abraham, père des croyants', ed.
Cahiers Sioniens (1952), wherein J. Starcky, 'Abraham et l'Histoire'; P. Montet,
L'Egypte et la Bible (1959); W. F. Albright's celebrated book, *From the Stone Age
to Christianity* (Second edition) (1946) also deals with the patriarchal age. Cf.
above all his 'The Role of the Canaanites in the History of Civilisation', in
G. E. Wright, ed., *The Bible and the Ancient Near East* (1961), and F. M. Cross,
op. cit.

In passing, perhaps we may just touch upon the most recent effort to set
Abraham within the frame provided by his time. W. F. Albright, in *B.A.S.O.R.*,
163 (Oct. 1961), 36ff., on the basis of the finds made by N. Glueck in the Negeb,
which show that especially in the MB.I-period (2000–1800) a variety of places
were situated here, has tried to establish a connexion between them and Abraham's
journeys. As a caravaneer (that would be the meaning of the word 'Habiru-
Hebrew'), he would have travelled regularly from Mesopotamia into Egypt.

On this trade-route lay Ur, Haran, Shechem, Hebron and Gerar—the towns comprising the chief stopping-places on his journeys.

It seems to me that Albright has himself put a finger on the weak spot in his theory (52), when he declares that in later Hebrew-Israelite tradition nothing of the position which Abraham had taken in the community is any longer to be found—even though that tradition 'faithfully preserved many incidents and phrases which make the original situation clear'. For Albright that is 'not surprising'; but to us it seems not a little 'surprising' that a course of events which has become so unrecognizable in the tradition should have become so 'clear' as Albright supposes it to be. In any case, the whole (semi-) nomads-theory must then come in for a thorough overhaul (cf. Gen. 12f.); and the relation of Abraham to the certainly (semi-) nomadic Jacob- and Isaac-figures becomes a quite remarkable one indeed. Meanwhile, Albright's theory is still worth the effort of keeping in mind, particularly in connexion with the third tradition to which we referred earlier: that of Abraham as a warrior (Gen. 14).

33. For studies of nomenclature, besides the contributions made by Noth and mentioned above, cf. also C. F. Jean, 'Les noms propres de personnes dans les lettres de Mari et dans les plus anciens textes du Pentateuque', in *La Bible et l'Orient* (1955), 129ff. Also his contribution, 'Les noms propres de personnes dans les lettres de Mari', in A. Parrot, *Studia Mariana* (1950), 63ff.

34. See, i.e., M. Noth, 'Mari und Israel', and *Die Ursprünge;* see above, note 32.

35. See, i.a., W. von Soden, 'Verkündung des Gotteswillens', in *Die Welt des Orients* (1950), 356ff.; C. Westermann, *Grundformen prophetische Rede;* A. Parrot, 'Les Tablettes de Mari et l'A.T.', in *R.H.P.R.* (1950), 1ff.; and 'Mari et l'A.T.', in *La Bible et l'Orient* (1955), 117ff.

36. See above, note 15; and his *Die Ursprünge.*

37. J. Ph. Hyatt, 'Yahweh as "the God of my Father" ', in *V.T.* (1955), 13f.

38. M. Noth, *Die Ursprünge*, 19f. Elsewhere the firstborn does sometimes get a double share, i.a., in Nuzu and Alalakh (N. Syria), apparently in communities with a semi-nomadic and agrarian structure (see I. Mendelsohn, in *B.A.S.O.R.*, 156 (1959), 577ff.).

39. *Idem*, 17f., on the basis of a publication by M. du Buit, *R.B.* (1959), 577ff.

40. See in particular, De Vaux, *op. cit.*

41. M. Noth, *op. cit.*, Supplement to *V.T.*; cf. 269ff., especially 271.

42. *Prolegomena to the History of Israel*, 1885, 318f.

43. Address before the Old Testament working conference held in Holland; see J. Pedersen, *Der Eid bei den Semiten* (1924), 151, who had in mind only the first sense of *fakhid:dij*; also in W. F. Albright and, on the same lines, O. Eissfeldt, 'El and Yahweh', in *J.S.S.* (1956), 32, note 2. Cf. also below, Chapter 8, note 27.

44. Cf. Köhler, *Lex.*, sub 'Esau'.

45. Cognate with Lotan, Gen. 36:22; cf. Köhler, *op. cit.*, and O. Procksch, *Genesis*, 2:3, *loc. cit.*

46. See, i.a., Procksch, *op. cit.*

47. Which Israel has in common with Moab. We find it only in the West Semitic world; C. H. W. Brekelmans, *De cherem in het O.T.*, diss. (1959).

48. Cf., e.g., J. Pedersen, *Israel*, I, 378ff.; R. de Vaux, *Ancient Israel*, 10ff., 160ff. Nyström, *op. cit.*

49. R. de Vaux, *op. cit.*, 46ff.; B. Meissner, *Bab. u. Ass.*, I, 394.

50. See, e.g., M. Noth, *The History of Israel*, (Second edition), 1960, 68ff. See also above, p. 108.

51. See M. Noth, *Überlieferungsgeschichte des Pentateuch* (1948), 112ff.

52. See, i.a., F. Dumermuth, 'Zur deuteronomistischen Kulttheologie', in *Z.A.W.* (1958), 59ff., especially 85ff., and M. Weippert, 'Gott und Stier', in

Z.D.P.V. (1961), 93ff., especially 103ff. In point of fact, the bull-image has associations with El as well as with Baal (see pp. 187f.).

53. With O. Eissfeldt, *op. cit., J.S.S.* (1956), 31f., on the ground of Josh. 24:2 and 14f.; cf. C. Steuernagel, 'Jahwe und die Vätergötter', in *Festschrift-Beer* (1935), 62–71.

54. In Hos. 3:4 the *teraphim* is mentioned along with the *ephod* and would appear to have some connexion with the giving of oracles, Ezek. 21:26; Zech. 10:2. See also p. 174. Steuernagel, in the article referred to, posits too direct a connexion between *teraphim* and Father-gods.

55. Thus Buber, *The Prophetic Faith*, 35f.; V. Maag, *Der Hirte Israels, op. cit.,* to similar effect.

56. For Isaac see, i.a., M. Noth, *Pentateuch*, 112ff.

57. Cf. G. W. Anderson, in Peake, *Commentary on the Bible* (1962), the chapter on Patriarchs; V. Maag, *op. cit.*, and F. M. Cross, *op. cit.*

CHAPTER 5

1. Cf. F. Horst, 'Die Notiz vom Anfang des Jahwekultes in Gen. 4:26', in *Libertas Christiana* (1957), 68ff.

2. *Godsdienst van Israël,* I (1930), 36f.; *Religion of Israel* (1947), 15ff.

3. *Jahwe der Gott Kaïns* (1929).

4. H. H. Rowley, *From Joseph to Joshua,* The Schweich Lectures 1948, (1950), 153ff. Especially impressive, in my view, is his stipulation on p. 154f. that the E tradition, which makes Jethro in Ex. 18 return and dissociates the Israel-tribes (=Joseph-tribes) from the Kenites, is the one that assigns Jahweh to Moses and Israel alone, whereas the J tradition of the southern tribes is aware of the Kenite element persisting among them and therefore regards the Yahweh-name as a time-honoured and long-standing inheritance.

5. See Chapter 2, p. 69.

6. B. Rothenberg, *God's Wilderness* (1961); Y. Aharoni, in his article in this book on 'Kadesh Barnea and Mount Sinai', begins by postulating that the most probable location was in the North, in the neighbourhood of Kadesh-Barnea; but at the end of his contribution he reverts—because of a find in the Wadi Feiran (Paran) of a mound of debris which has been found to contain sherds dating from the later iron age—to the Southern Sinai hypothesis. At all events, that is where it must have been located by the time of the Israelite monarchy.

7. Cf. M. Noth, 'Der Wallfahrtsweg zum Sinai (4 Mos. 33)' in *P.J.B.*, 36 (1940), 5ff.; see also A. Musil, *The Northern Hejaz* (1926), e.g., 268.

8. That Ps. 68 is ancient is very likely; according to Mowinckel, *Der 68. Psalm* (1953), even as early as the 11th century.

9. G. von Rad, 'The Form-Critical Problem of the Hexateuch'. *The Problem of the Hexateuch and Other Essays,* Edinburgh, 1966, pp. 1–78.

10. *Überlieferungsgeschichte des Pentateuch* (1948), 63ff. The argument which we give here is that of Noth. With Noth not only Sinai but Moses too practically disappears from the historical version of the deliverance—and as founder of the religion Moses is entirely eliminated; see *op. cit.*, 172. We come back to this question later on.

11. G. von Rad. *op. cit.*, 20ff.; in this connexion he appeals, i.a., to A. Alt, 'The Origin of Israelite Law', (originally 1934) *English Essays on Old Testament History and Religion,* 1966, but bases his case first and foremost on S. Mowinckel, *Le Décalogue* (1927), 114ff. Eerdmans too, although in a different way, refers repeatedly in his writings to the cultic character of the Sinai-narrative.

12. 64f.
13. Cf., his contribution to *Z.A.W.* (1934), 161ff. 'Passahfest und Passahlegende'. As against that see my *De Literatuur van Oud-Israël* (1961), 111f., and also A. Bentzen, *Introduction to the Old Testament* (Second edition), II (1952), 26.
14. See the inaugural lecture by A. S. van der Woude, *Uittocht en Sinai* (1960), and further R. Smend, *Jahwekrieg und Stämmebund* (1963).
15. *Epistulae*, II, 1, 156.
16. W. Baumgartner, 'Ugaritische Probleme und ihre Tragweite für das A.T.', in *Th.Z.* (1947), 81ff.
17. The exposition of 'Yahweh' in the sense of 'He is' includes the following possibilities: (*a*) the somewhat philosophically flavoured explanation generally obtaining in Jewish circles since the 18th century, which is already presupposed in the LXX:Yahweh as the One Who Is, the Eternal (this last expression is that by which Jewry today nearly always renders the name). This is opposed by F. Rosenzweig; see 'Der Ewige', in M. Buber and F. Rosenzweig, *Die Schrift und ihre Verdeutschung* (1936), 184ff. (*b*) the religio-historical interpretation, which understands the 'He is' (and above all the words of Ex. 3:14: I am that I am, or, I will be that I will be) as expressing the notion that Yahweh does not intend to reveal more specifically what his essential being is; (*c*) the theological exposition, which construes the 'He is' to signify 'Here He is!', 'He is present' (i.a., M. Buber). For this interpretation see, i.a., my study *'Ehje asjer 'ehje*, in the *Bertholet-Festschrift* (1950). My personal view is that, theologically speaking, both the last-mentioned elements can be envisaged as being interconnected, at any rate in E's estimate of the name in Ex. 3:14. This writer evidently understands the name 'Yahweh' as the affirmation of God's presence—but at the same time as a refusal by God to disclose what his real name is.
18. Given much prominence, e.g., by W. F. Albright and again by Cross, *op. cit.*, 25ff.
19. As early as the last century, with Ewald; especially with Wellhausen and his school.
20. The natural phenomena described in Ex. 19f.; Ps. 18:8ff., 29 and elsewhere in association with the theophany, and its being connected with the cherubim, do indeed make one think very much in such terms.
21. Cf. Söderblom, *op. cit.* (1916), 310; Volz, *op. cit.* (1924).
22. See G. Gerleman, 'The Song of Deborah in the light of Stylistics', in *V.T.* (1951), 168ff.
23. *The Prophetic Faith.*
24. Cf. R. Smend, *op. cit.*, 20ff.
25. It is only in Gen. 41:38, in the (later) Joseph story, that the divine Spirit appears as the Spirit of wisdom.
26. Just as in the Phoenician world, where the gods are occasionally described as holy (see p. 54), so also in Ugarit already, for El; cf. *Z.A.W.* (1962), 62f., where W. Schmidt deduces far too much from this.
27. As Pedersen, *Israel*, III–IV, 4, also evidently assumes, when he speaks of the disintegration which ensued upon cultural change and the adoption of new gods.
28. Cf. W. Baumgartner, *Ugaritische Probleme, op. cit.*, 99f., and above, p. 73.
29. See, i.a., R. Smend, *Das Mosebild von H. Ewald bis M. Noth* (1959); E. Osswald, 'Moses', in *R.G.G.* (Third edition), IV, 115ff.
30. R. Smend, *Alttest. Religionsgeschichte* (1893), 15ff., 31ff.
31. K. Marti, *Geschichte der Israelitischen Religion* (1897), 54ff.
32. K. Budde, *Die Altisraelitische Religion* (1912), 9ff.
33. *La religion d'Israël* (1939), 50ff.

U

298 THE RELIGION OF ANCIENT ISRAEL

34. *Hebrew Religion*, various editions.
35. *Religion in the Old Testament* (1961).
36. *Religion of Israel* (1947), 26ff.; cf. also his *Alttest. Studien*.
37. *Mose* (Second edition) (1932).
38. See W. F. Albright, *From the Stone Age to Christianity* (1946), 193ff.;
G. E. Wright, *Biblical Archaeology* (1957); J. Bright, *A History of Israel*, 115ff.
39. M. Buber, *Moses* (1947); E. Auerbach, *Moses* (1953); A. Neher, *Moïse et la vocation juïve*; cf. also his *L'essence du prophétisme* (1955); J. Kaufmann, see below, note 42.
40. H. Cazelles, 'Moïse devant l'histoire', in *Moïse, l'homme de l'alliance* (1955), 11ff.
41. *Op. cit.*, 27.
42. Y. Kaufmann, *The Religion of Israel* (1960).
43. *The History of Israel.*
44. Cf. J. Pedersen's critique of Wellhausen, in *Z.A.W.* (1931), 161ff.; *Die Auffassung vom A.T.*, especially 172f. Wellhausen's 'evolutionistic' scheme is not so much grounded in a philosophical view as arising from the general style of thought in the 19th century.
45. *Israelitische und Jüdische Geschichte* (1921), 27.
46. *Überlieferungsgeschichte des Pentateuch* (1948), 190. In the second and subsequent editions of his *Geschichte Israels* Noth allows for the possibility that Moses did play a role in the deliverance from Egypt.
47. It is what is called the 'tomb-tradition', which M. Noth takes as a basis for associating Moses with southern, Transjordanian groups, and so as the basis for acknowledging the existence of an historical Moses-figure.
48. R. Smend, *Das Mosebild*, 62ff. The same idea in Eissfeldt, 'Sinaï-Erzählung und Bileamsprüche', in *H.U.C.A.* (1961), 179ff., specifically 190, who says of Moses and Balaam: 'Mag die Feststellung der Geschehnisse schwer oder gar unmöglich sein, der Nachhall den sie in unseren Erzählungen gefunden haben, legt ein unwiderliegliches Zeugnis dafür ab, dass sie gross und bedeutungsvoll waren'. Moses as a charismatic leader has also been acknowledged in recent years by Alt, in agreement with R. Smend, *Jahwekrieg*, 92.
49. See Köhler, *Lexicon, sub verb.*; P. Montet, *L'Egypte et la Bible* (1959), 34ff.; A. de Buck, 'De Hebreeën in Egypte', in *Varia Historica* (1954), 14, refers us to an article by J. G. Griffiths in *J.N.E.S.* (1953), but refrains from committing himself to a judgment on it; Smend, *op. cit.*, 89.
50. *Überlieferungsgeschichte des Pentateuch*, 184f.
51. *Pentateuch*, 188f.
52. So (correctly) M. Haren, 'The tent of meetings', *Tarbitz*, XXV, 12ff., III–IV, and 'The Nature of the "*Ohel Mo'ed*" ', etc., in *J.S.S.* (1960), 50ff.; cf. also M. Noth, *Exodus, loco*; and Num. 11 and 12. This material is to be regarded as a quite early, more or less independent tradition.
53. Consider too the role discharged by Balaam, and possibly also Moses' part in the battle with Amalek, Ex. 17:8ff.
54. E. Kutsch, 'Lade Jahwes', in *R.G.G.* (Third edition), IV (1960), 198ff. To the point is Smend, *op. cit.*, 56ff., 93ff.
55. *Th.R.* (1929), 161–184.
56. *Th.R.* (1961), 189ff. and (1962), 281ff.; cf. also his *The Ten Commandments in Recent Research*, London, 1967.
57. Cf., i.a., 'Lade und Sterbild', in *Z.A.W.* (1940–41), 197; 'Silo und Jerusalem', in Supplement to *V.T.*, IV (1957), 138ff., especially 144; apparently he does not take this in itself as evidence of a link with Moses. Smend considers that a probability.

58. I.a., J. Morgenstern, in a detailed article: 'The Ark, the Ephod and the tent of meeting', in *H.U.C.A.* (1942–43), 153ff. (1943–44), 1ff.; M. Buber, *Der Glaube der Propheten*.

59. M. Noth too speaks of the 'wahrscheinlich doch vorpalästinische Tradition der Lade' ('Jerusalem und die israelit. Tradition', *Ges. Studien*, 185; see also *Geschichte Isr.*, 79).

60. See my *Jahwe en zijn stad* (1962).

61. Köhler, *op. cit.*, 184; see also F. Horst, 'Dekalog', in *R.G.G.* (Third edition), II (1958).

62. *The Ten Commandments* (1967).

63. *Th.R.* (1961), 226ff.; he ends his examination of the matter by suggesting with some emphasis that there is every possibility of a connexion between the deliverance from Egypt and the events centred on Sinai (*Th.R.* (1962), 305).

64. 'The Origins of Israelite Law', *Essays on Old Testament History and Religion*, 1966, pp. 79–132; see also W. Preiser, 'Vergeltung und Sühne im altisr. Strafrecht', in *Festschrift E. Schmidt* (1961), 7f.

65. The question of capital punishment in this context is crucial for him; and so he is ready to postulate that those transgressions appearing in the decalogue, for which the death penalty is not exacted (e.g. stealing), were initially represented by others. In place of 'Thou shalt not steal', therefore, he postulates an earlier text: Thou shalt not steal a man (i.e. a free Israelite) because the penalty for stealing people is death (Ex. 21:16 and Deut. 24:7); the essential point about the last commandment concerning 'coveting' is the ban on any attempt to appropriate human beings (wife, male or female slave) belonging to the free Israelite. Professor Beek has drawn my attention to the fact that Rashi, in his commentary on the Pentateuch, had already related Ex. 20:5 to the stealing of human beings.

66. Cf., e.g., also Eerdmans, *Religion of Israel*, 26f.

67. Quell, *T.D.N.T.*, II, 119f.

68. E records how a covenant was made (Ex. 24:9–11) which involved a ceremonial, communal meal of the elders with the God of Israel; and likewise D, according to whom the covenant is ratified by a sacrifice and ceremony (Ex. 24:3–8).

69. *Law and Covenant in Israel and the Ancient Near East* (1955).

70. On the question of storing official contracts and the retention of a copy for use see, i.a., R. de Vaux, *op. cit.*, p. 301.

71. It was probably no coincidence, either, that the deuteronomic law was found deposited in the offerings-chest ('*aron*); see Chapter 9, note 2.

72. For what happened in the case of treaties and contracts between states see, besides Mendenhall, especially V. Korošec, *Hethitische Staatsverträge* (1931); for the legislation of Lipit-Ishtar cf. the epilogue, *A.N.E.T.*, 162; see also the epilogue to Codex Hammurabi, end of rev. XXIV and beginning of XXV.

73. For the developing interpretation of the ark cf. M. Haran, 'The Ark and the Cherubim', in *I.E.J.* (1959), 30ff. and 89ff., and the article by Père de Vaux, mentioned in note 85 of this chapter.

74. Cf. also W. Beyerlin, *Origins and History of the Oldest Sinaitic Traditions*, Oxford, 1965.

75. For this see J. J. Stamm's article aforementioned, in *Th.R.* (1961), especially 220ff., and my contribution: 'Litterair-historische vragen aangaande de Dekaloog', in *N.Th.S.* (1939), 19ff.

76. Regarding these see an Introduction to the Old Testament; cf., e.g., O. Eissfeldt, *The Old Testament, An Introduction*, 1965, or my *De literatuur van Oud-Israël* (1961).

77. *From Joseph to Joshua* (1950), 157ff.

78. *The Northern Hejaz* (1926), 262–266.

79. Cf. especially Ex. 18:16b and 20, and, e.g., H. Gressmann, *Mose und seine Zeit* (1913), 422.

80. Since I wrote in 1938 my contribution, 'Literair-Historische Vragen aangaande de Dekaloog', published in *N.Th.S.* (1939), I have changed my view about this. My suggestion then was to regard the two tablets of the decalogue as bearing on the ethical and cultic decalogues and to ascribe both of them to Moses—the one being from Sinai, the other from the Kadesh-period.

81. In this connexion one can also point to the antithetical parallel between Ex. 34:26c (Ex.23: 19c) and an (incompletely preserved) cultic act from Ugarit; cf. G. R. Driver, *Canaanite Myths and Legends* (1956), 121, note 12. Another clue is afforded by the fact that the cultic decalogue (Ex. 20:23; 34:17) is no longer concerned with *pesel* (an image of stone or wood) but with images of metal.

82. See, e.g., G. Beer, *Exodus*, in Handbuch zum A.T., 64f.; R. de Vaux, *Ancient Israel*, 489; E. Kutsch, 'Feste in Israel', in *R.G.G.* (Third edition), s.v.

83. Cf. R. de Vaux, *op. cit.*, 46f.; F. Sierksma, 'Quelques remarques sur la circoncision en Israël' in *O.T.S.*, IX, 136ff.

84. Cf. J. J. Stamm, *Th. R.* (1962), 290ff.; B. D. Eerdmans, *op. cit.*, and 'Der Sabbath', in *Marti-Festschrift* (1925), 79ff.; my 'Kalender en Sabbath', in *N.Th.S.* (1940), 172ff.; R. de Vaux, *op. cit.*, 469, 475ff.

85. I have in mind here the later practice, on the Great Day of Atonement, of sprinkling the blood on the mercy-seat (which was itself a later addition). The question may well be asked whether there may not lie behind this a quite ancient custom whereby a 'blood act' was performed once a year upon the central object of the cult (in order to purify the cultic symbol of Yahweh's presence in the midst of Israel?). On the original connexion between the ark and the tent of revelation ('tent of meeting', *'ohel mo'ed*) see R. de Vaux, 'Arche de l'Alliance et Tente de Réunion', Mémorial A. Gelin, *A la rencontre de Dieu* (1961), 55ff., who maintains this, and M. Haran, *op. cit.*, who denies it.

CHAPTER 6

1. A. Alt, 'Der Rhythmus der Geschichte Syriens und Palästinas', in *Kleine Schriften* III (1959), 19.

2. E. Täubler, *Biblische Studien* (1958), 271ff.

3. C. Snouck-Hurgronje, 'Der Islam', in Chantepie de la Saussaye, *Lehrbuch der Religionsgeschichte* (Fourth edition), I (1925), 648ff., in particular 676f.

4. A. Alt, *Der Rhythmus*, 19.

5. A. Alt, 'Josua', in J. Hempel, *Werden und Wesen des Alten Testaments* (1936), 13ff.; Noth, *The History of Israel*, 93f.

6. Cf. 'Der Beitrag der Archäologie', in Supplement to *V.T.*, VII (1960), 272, note 1.

7. The Leah-tribes, therefore; see Noth, *The History of Israel*, 85f.

8. R. Smend, *op. cit.*, is right in principle when he connects the wars of Yahweh with the earliest, pre-Palestinian Yahwism; but later on they may well have been waged by the amphictyony.

9. These groups cannot, as M. Noth, *The History of Israel*, rightly says, be identified with one of the tribes or with a group of tribes. They have usually been equated with the Rachel- (Joseph-) tribes. At all events, nothing in the tradition justifies our making any such connexion.

10. Like A. Alt.; see, i.a., Noth, *The History of Israel*, 93f.; *Das System der zwölf Stämme Isr.* (1930).

11. See M. Noth, *Überlieferungsgeschichtliche Studien* (1943); *Josua* (Second edition) (1956), *The History of Israel*. Over against that, Y. Kaufmann, *The Biblical Account of the Conquest of Palestine* (1953); cf. also J. Bright, *Early Israel in Recent History Writing* (1956), and Noth's defence, 'Der Beitrag der Archäologie', *op. cit.*

12. M. Noth, 'Der Beitrag', is right in saying that since other groups (the seafaring peoples) were active in South-west Palestine during that period, this coincidence in itself still *proves* nothing, so long as actual vestiges of the Israelites have not been found. K. Kenyon, in her *Archaeology of the Holy Land*, 215 (cf. 231), also gives an indeterminate judgment.

13. Sh. Yeivin, *A Decade*, 25f., who, like M. Noth, 'Der Beitrag', 274, expresses himself with caution on this point.

14. The king of Jerusalem asks for occupying troops to the tune of fifty men (Knudtzon, *El-Amarna-tafeln*, No. 289, 42). One may recall too the story in Judges 18, which tells how six hundred Danites succeed in reducing the city of Laish.

15. M. Buber, *Königtum Gottes* (Third edition) (1956); see also A. Alt, 'The Monarchy in Israel and Judah', in *Essays on Old Testament History and Religion*, pp. 239ff., in particular 353ff.; and J. Hempel, 'Königtum Gottes im A.T.', in *R.G.G.* (Third edition), III, s.v.

16. *Archaeology and the Religion of Israel* (1946), 114.

17. Probably the original meaning was: 'Great be Baal!' (Noth, *Personennamen*, 206f.). For the significance of names compounded with 'Baal', p. 119ff.

18. The relation of the Levites of the later period to the Levi-tribe of early times is one of the most remarkable puzzles in the Old Testament (see, e.g., Noth, *The History of Israel*, 71, note 1; E. Nielsen, *Shechem* (1955), 264ff.; Fohrer, in *R.G.G.* (Third edition), s.v.; R. de Vaux, *op. cit.*, 358ff.

19. Cf. Noth, *History*, 91, who rightly sees as background to this an old tradition of punitive action taken by the amphictyony against one of its disloyal members; for a different view see O. Eissfeldt, 'Der geschichtliche Hintergrund der Erzählung von Gibeas Schandtat', in *Festschrift G. Beer* (1935), 18ff., who thinks that it was simply a matter of a struggle for power between Ephraim and Benjamin.

20. Noth, *Pentateuch*, 16, *Überlief. Studien*, 201ff.

21. Derived from a root signifying either 'to accompany' or 'to borrow (from)'; cf. R. de Vaux, *loc. cit.*; J. Pedersen, *Israel*, III–IV, 170ff., 680; also M. Weber, *Ancient Judaism*, 1952, 182ff. In the law of a later period (Num. 3:2; 8:0) Levites are held to be those Israelites who are taken out of the people in place of the firstborn due to Yahweh.

22. See, i.a., W. H. Gispen, 'Het boek van de oorlogen van Jahwe', in *G.T.T.* (1959), 129ff.; also Caspari, in *Z.W.Th.* (1912), 110ff. For the literary-critical issues raised by this passage see M. Noth on Num. 21, in *Z.A.W.* (1940–41), 175ff.

23. There is no instance of the word 'war' occurring in combination with a divine name other than Yahweh—which makes it perfectly clear that the connexion is with Yahweh specifically.

24. G. von Rad, *Studies in Deuteronomy*, (SBT 9), 1953, 45ff., 30ff.; *Der Heilige Krieg im Alten Israel* (1951); M. Noth, *History*, 107f.; Pedersen, *Israel*, III–IV, 1ff., who makes too much of the primitive, and not enough of the Yahwistic-religious, aspect; Smend, *op. cit.*

25. Cf. Ex. 15:3; Ps. 24:8; Ps. 68. See H. Frederiksson, *Jahwe als Krieger* (1945).

26. Cf. P. Humbert, *La Terou'a* (1946), 27ff.

27. C. H. W. Brekelmans, *De Herem in het O.T.*, diss. (1959).

28. O. Eissfeldt, 'Silo und Jerusalem', Supplement to *V.T.* (1957), 143f.

29. See, e.g., my *Paradijsvoorstellingen der oude Semitische volken*, diss. (1937); J. B. Pritchard, *Archaeology and the Old Testament* (1958).

30. For literature see H. H. Rowley, 'Elijah and Mount Carmel', in *Men of God* (1963), 37ff., who himself finds difficulty with this idea. These rites play a major role in later Judaism; and various rabbis act in the capacity of rain-makers.

31. Strack-Billerbeck, *Kommentar zum N.T.*, II, 491 and 799ff.

32. A. Alt, 'The Monarchy in Israel and Judah', 256.

33. On this topic see B. N. Wambacq, *L'épithète divine Jahwè Sebaoth* (1947); V. Maag, 'Jahwa's Heerscharen', in *Schw.Th.Umschau* (1950), 27ff., and O. Eissfeldt, 'Jahwe Zebaoth', in *Miscellanea Acad. Berolinensia*, II, 2 (1950).

34. Between these laws there are a few unimportant differences, which we have not gone into here. Each of the several wordings has developed along lines of its own. It is debatable whether the items, properly taken together, are exactly ten in number or whether they perhaps amount to twelve (a dodecalogue).

35. Just as Ex. 40:17 implies an altar with steps, the altar in Solomon's temple will have had them too (cf. De Vaux, *Ancient Israel*, 410f.). In that connexion new provisions are laid down regarding the dress of the priests during the cultic action, cf. Ex. 28:42f.

36. For what follows see, i.a., the articles (in which further literature is cited) *Tempel II* and *Tempelgeräte in Israel* (Galling) and 'Heilige Stätten', II (Herzberg), in *R.G.G.* (Third edition), and De Vaux, *op. cit.*, 312ff.

37. G. F. Moore, *Judges* (Second edition), *I.C.C.* (1918), *loco*; E. Täubler, *Biblische Studien* (1958), III, 43ff., 'Micha und Dan'; M. Noth, 'The Background of Judges, 17–18', in *Israel's Prophetic Heritage*, Muilenburg-Festschrift, (1962), 68ff.

38. The evil things (e.g. 17:–4) related of the founder of the sanctuary and about the Danites are probably to be laid at the door of a later redactor, whose intention was to pillory the illegitimacy of the sanctuary at Dan and the treachery and cruelty of the conquerors. We can assume that we are here dealing with a Danite narrative, edited by a critical hand in Jerusalem and later appended to the deuteronomic version of the Book of Judges. M. Noth backs the idea that the story is borrowed from the critical assault on the oldest Danite sanctuary, which must have been launched by the priesthood of the later royal sanctuary at Dan established there by Jeroboam I.

39. The later narrator simply makes it a *pesel*, an image, partly in order to present this sanctuary, from the very earliest times on, in a bad light. Quite probably, therefore, the phrase 'molten image' was added with an eye to the subsequent veneration of the bull-image.

40. See, i.a., H. J. Kraus, 'Die Kulttraditionen des Berges Thabor', in *Basileia*, Festschrift W. Freytag (1959), 177ff.; and cf. E. Kutsch, 'Tabor', in *R.G.G.* (Third edition), with more literature.

41. See, i.a., W. Eichrodt, *Theology of the Old Testament*, I, (1961), pp. 303ff.; J. Pedersen, *Israel*, III–IV, 264ff.; E. Jenni, 'Nasiräer', in *R.G.G.* (Third edition).

CHAPTER 7

1. Cf., i.a., Von Rad, *Old Testament Theology*, I, 56.

2. See, i.a., I. Engnell, *Studies in Divine Kingship* (1943); A. Bentzen, *Det sakrale Kongedømme* (1945); C. J. Gadd, *Ideas of Divine Rule in the Ancient East* (1948); M. Noth, 'God, King and Nation in the Old Testament', pp. 145ff.; J. de Fraine, *L'aspect religieuse de la royauté israélite* (1954); A. R. Johnson, *Sacral*

Kingship in the Ancient Israel (1955); S. H. Hooke, *Myth, Ritual and Kingship* (1958); K. H. Bernhardt, 'Das Problem der altorientalischen Königsideologie', in Supplement to *V.T.*, VIII (1961).

3. Adopting a textual emendation in verse 3. On this Psalm see contributions by M. A. Beek, N. H. Ridderbos and myself in *Vox Theologica* (1944); L. Dürr, *Psalm 110* (1929); G. Widengren, *Psalm* 110 (1941); J. de Savignac, 'Essai d'interpretation du Psaume CX' in *O.T.S.*, IX (1951), 107ff.

4. See, e.g., also B. Gemser, *De Psalmen* III, Text and commentary (1949), 137f.

5. See my *Jahwe en zijn stad* (1962).

6. Cf., i.a., the books on biblical archaeology: e.g., G. E. Wright, *Biblical Archaeology*, and A. Parrot, *The temple of Jerusalem* (1957), and K. Galling, 'Temple in Israel', in *R.G.G.* (Third edition); also Albright, *Archaeology and the Religion of Israel*, 142ff. For a precise, descriptive account we must refer the reader to these.

7. On this issue there is a material difference of opinion. Many scholars have postulated, with H. Th. Obbink, that the bull-figures ought not to have been seen as images of Yahweh ('Jahwebilder', in *Z.A.W.* (1929), 264ff.), but as pedestals for an image (of the god) which was not actually there. Eissfeldt, in the paper to which we have several times referred on 'Lade und Stierbild' in *Z.A.W.* (1940–41), has formulated the theory that the golden calf was a symbol of Yahweh as leader of the people, borne on a standard. This symbol he regards as being already in existence during the desert period. Cf. also M. Weippert, *op. cit.*, *Z.D.P.V.* (1961), 103ff.

8. See W. von Soden, 'Stierdienst', in *R.G.G.* (Third edition).

9. Also von Soden, *op. cit.*, VI, 373.

10. Unless the name 'Samaria' here stands, as perhaps it does in 14.1, for the country. In that case the calf-worship at Bethel could be meant, and could be taken as a symbol for the whole religion of the Northern state.

11. *Der Stadtstaat Samaria* (1954). Also in *Kleine Schriften*.

12. Cf. A. Alt, 'Das Gottesurteil auf dem Karmel', in *Kleine Schriften*, II, 135ff.; O. Eissfeldt, *Der Gott Karmel* (1953); K. Galling, 'Der Gott Karmel und die Ächtung der fremden Götter', in *Alt-Festschrift* (1953).

13. H. H. Rowley, 'Elijah on Mount Carmel'; G. Fohrer, *Elia* (1957).

14. See as well as earlier studies, such as H. Gunkel, *Elias, Jahwe und Baal* (1906); J. J. P. Valeton, *De strijd tussen Achab en Elia* (1900), now also G. Fohrer, *Elia, idem*, art. 'Elia', in *R.G.G.* (Third edition).

15. Cf. also K. Galling, *op. cit.*, 122ff.

16. We might also say: 'between the old militant Yahwism . . .'.

17. See F. R. Kraus, 'Assyrisch Imperialisme', in *Jaarbericht E.O.L.* (1957–58), 232ff.

CHAPTER 8

1. C. Westermann, *Grundformen prophetischer Rede* (1960), 99ff., on the basis of form-critical examination reaches the same conclusion.

2. A. Causse, *Du groupe ethnique à la communauté religieuse* (1937), 95ff.

3. In an address, cf. 'Rondschrijven', No. 11, May 15, 1935, from *Ex Oriente Lux*.

4. *Op. cit.*, 72.

5. E.g., *A.N.E.T.*, 444.

6. Of course, the possibility is not excluded that in formulating their utterances the prophets followed certain literary ideas and schemata well known in their day. Isaiah certainly reflects the influence of the 'wisdom' thought and literature.

7. For these see, i.a., W. von Soden, 'Verkündung des Gotteswillens', in *Die Welt des alten Orients* (1950), 397ff. They have often been brought under discussion—in the Netherlands by, i.a., N. H. Ridderbos, *Israëls profetie en profetie buiten Israël* (1955), and F. M. Th. de Liagre Böhl, 'Profetisme en plaatsvervangend lijden in Assyrië en Israël, in *N.T.T.* (1950), 81ff.

8. See, e.g., A. Neher, *L'essence du prophétisme* (1955), 24f.

9. See, e.g., C. Westermann, *Grundformen*, 70ff.

10. There too the *nabi'* is typically presented as *mešugga'*, as 'raving'. The verb which means 'behave like a prophet' is also the word for the raving of a lunatic.

11. For both texts see *A.N.E.T.*, pp. 320f., 50ff.

12. (1938), 118ff. On the Arabian seers see also J. Pedersen, 'The Role played by inspired Persons among the Israelites and the Arabs', in H. H. Rowley (ed.), *Studies in Old Testament Prophecy*, Th. H. Robinson-Festschrift (1950), 127ff.

13. p. 119.

14. A term for 'soothsaying' which occurs also in Hebrew although from the root of a different verb: *'arif* (Arab.), *yid'oni* (Hebr.).

15. J. Pedersen, *op. cit.*, 133.

16. J. Pedersen, *op. cit.*, 134f.

17. *Idem*, 137.

18. See *Th.W.z.N.T.*, VI, Krämer, sub *Prophetes*, especially 789ff., and E. Fashcer, *Prophetes* (1927).

19. Cf., e.g., H. H. Rowley, 'Old Testament Prophecy and Recent Study', in *The Servant of the Lord* (1952), 91ff., especially 96ff.

20. For the most recent literature on this subject see, i.a., M. Noth, *Überlieferungsgeschichte des Pentateuch*, 80ff.; O. Eissfeldt, 'Sinai-Erzählung und Bileamsprüche', in *H.U.C.A.*, XXXII (1961), 191ff.; S. Mowinckel, 'Der Ursprung der Bileamsprüche', in *Z.A.W.* (1930), 233ff. Mowinckel denies the historical background entirely and sees in these stories only a saga, which must be held to account for the origin of the early lyrics in Num. 24. Was Balaam perhaps originally a prophetic figure active in the cause of Baalism, as one might well conclude from the tradition in Num. 31:8ff., 16? And was his influence felt during a certain period among the eastern tribes of Israel? At all events, Num. 31 associates Balaam with Baal Pe'or (cf. Num. 25), and not with Pethor (Num. 22:5).

21. See R. Press, 'Der Prophet Samuel', in *Z.A.W.* (1938), 177ff.; A. Weiser, '1 Samuel XV', in *Z.A.W.* (1936), 1ff., and especially his *Samuel, seine geschichtliche Aufgabe und religiöse Bedeutung* (Forschungen zur Religion und Literatur des A.u.N.T., 1962), in particular 86–94; H. Wildberger, 'Samuel', in *R.G.G.* (Third edition) (where see further literature) and M. Newman, 'The Prophetic Call of Samuel', in *Israel's Prophetic Heritage*, Muilenburg-Festschrift (1962), 86ff.

22. On this matter cf. besides Hölscher's book, i.a., J. Ridderbos, *Profetie en Ekstase* (1941); J. Lindbolm, 'Einige Grundfragen der alttestamentlichen Wissenschaft', in *Bertholet-Festschrift* (1950), 325ff.

23. At a later time (Jeroboam II) we have Jonah, whose prophecies of salvation were nationalistic in outlook (2 Kings 14:5) and who not inappropriately, therefore, in the legend of the Book of Jonah, appears as the prophet who resists the command to carry the message about repentance to the inhabitants of Nineveh. Thus the authors of that little book were still thoroughly familiar with his reputation as a 'nationalist'.

24. Cf., i.a., H. J. Kraus, *Prophet und Politiek* (1952), 41ff., 53ff.; G. Quell, *Wahre und falsche Propheten* (1952), has justifiably stressed how difficult it is to find a firm basis in any external indications for qualifying prophecy as 'false'.

25. F. R. Kraus, 'Assyrisch Imperialisme', in *Jaarbericht E.O.L.* (1957–58), 232ff.

26. *Ibid.*

27. The usual thing is to alter one letter and read *dodeka*=your beloved (your guardian, patron?). Perhaps, on the strength of the Ugaritic *derek*, we can render this as Mightiness, Monarch, Prince—as E. Jacob does, *Ras Shamra et l'A.T.* (1960), 65f. If it be allowable to read *Dod*, we can regard this divine name as having an affinity with the *paḥad Yiṣḥaq* of the patriarchal age (see Chapter 4, i.a., note 26), which can be rendered as 'kin' of Isaac. We should bear in mind here that Isaac belongs to the neighbourhood of Beersheba; see W. Zimmerli, *Geschichte und Tradition von Berseba* (1932), i.a., 21ff.

28. Besides the books on the History of Israel, see further H. H. Rowley, 'Hezekiah's Reform and Rebellion', in *Men of God*, 1963, 98ff., in which he specifies a great deal of literature.

29. See my *Jahwe en zijn stad* (1962), where I take issue with G. von Rad, who contends in his *Theology* that because we assume a zeal on Isaiah's part for the cult (which would inculcate the tradition of Zion as the unassailable sanctuary), he did not believe that Zion would be destroyed; cf. also my 'Essentials of the Theology of Isaiah', in the *Muilenburg-Festschrift* (1962).

30. *A Decade of Archaeology*, 32f.; R. Amiran, 'The tumuli west of Jerusalem', in *I.E.J.* (1958), 205ff.

CHAPTER 9

1. On this question the reader should consult an Introduction to the Old Testament or a Literary History of Israel (see Chapter 4, note 3).

2. The 'book of the law' was evidently discovered when the offerings-chest, which probably stood next the altar (cf. 2 Kings 12:9), was turned over ('emptied out', 2 Kings 22:9). 2 Chron. 34:14 puts it even more clearly: 'while they were bringing out the money that had been brought into the house of Yahweh'. This would lead us to suppose that the scroll (papyrus) of the book had been deposited in the large offerings-chest. At a pinch it is still possible to think of the scroll's being discovered between the chest and the altar; but the verbs used in the above-mentioned texts make this unlikely.

3. Cf. W. F. Albright, *A.R.I.*, 165ff., and G. Fohrer's and W. Zimmerli's commentaries on Ezekiel. Zimmerli believes that there can be no question of any real movement of reaction against Deuteronomy.

4. See M. Noth, *Überlieferungsgeschichtliche Studien* I, and also the Introductions to the Old Testament.

5. Fourteen MSS of Deuteronomy, as well as twelve of Isaiah and ten of the Psalms; cf. F. M. Cross, *The Ancient Library of Qumran* (revised edition, 1961), 43; still more now, of Deut. and Psalms.

6. Provided the foregoing explanation is the correct one. Many scholars regard the verses 2:ff. as announcing the judgment to fall upon Assur. This seems improbable, because the appearance on the scene of the Babylonians has already been depicted in chapter 1.

CHAPTER 10

1. *The History of Israel* (1960), 259.

2. On this see, i.a., K. Galling, 'Serubbabel und der Wiederaufbau des Tempels in Jerusalem', in *Verbannung und Heimkehr*, Festschrift W. Rudolph, (1961), 67ff.

3. See my *An Outline of Old Testament Theology* (1958), p. 299.

4. R. Kittel, *Geschichte des Volkes Israel*, III (1927), 55ff., who considers that the smaller half of Judah's population went into exile in 597 and 587, as many again were killed, and about one in eight would have been kept behind in the country.

5. See Galling, 'Synagoge', in *R.G.G.* (Third edition), and E. L. Ehrlich, *A Concise History of Israel*, 72.

6. Literally, 'son of man'; but this only means 'a man, someone who is part and parcel of the human race'. It is a form of address used more than ninety times in the book. Cf. also the sketch of Ezekiel by M. A. Beek, in *Inleiding in de Joodse Apocalyptiek* (1950), 19ff.

7. Cf., i.a., F. Baumgärtel, 'Zu den Gottesnamen in den Büchern Jeremia und Ezechiel', in *Verbannung und Heimkehr*, Festschrift W. Rudolph, (1961), 1ff.

8. See G. Fohrer, 'Ezechiel', in *Handbuch zum A.T.* (1955), at these texts.

9. Only very recently K. Jaspers wrote in this vein: 'Der Prophet Ezechiel: Eine pathographische Studie', in *Arbeiten zur Psychiatrie*, usw., Festschrift K. Schneider (1947), 77ff.

10. See J. W. Miller, *Das Verhältnis Jeremias und Ezechiels* (1955).

11. Cf., i.a., Max Haller, 'Die Kyroslieder Dt. Jes. 's', in Festschrift-Gunkel, *Eucharisterion*, I (1923), 261ff., who assigns him a role at the court of Cyrus; or S. Smith, *Isaiah Ch.* 40–55 (Schweich Lectures) (1940, 1944), who sees him as the leader of a secret movement active on Cyrus's behalf. P. A. H. de Boer, *Second Isaiah's Message*, in *O.T.S.*, XI (1956), 118ff., is rightly opposed to this view.

12. As P. A. H. de Boer does, to my mind, in the above-mentioned book, 86ff.

13. The first mention of Cyrus, at 41:2, indicates that he has already embarked on his triumphant course; and it must have been made with an eye to Cyrus's victory over Croesus (546).

14. About the close of this passage many differing opinions have been expressed. Some exegetes want to delete verses 24b and 25 as a later addition. Others argue on the basis of verse 25 that 22ff. do not have a universalist implication, but that the appeal is to the Israelites from all the ends of the earth to come to Yahweh (P. A. H. de Boer, *op. cit.*, 90). The most satisfactory solution is to follow, i.a., J. Muilenburg, *The Interpreter's Bible*, loco, in putting not only verse 24a but the whole of 24 and 25 into the mouth of all the dwellers upon earth and to regard that as being what they swear to. Ehrlich too, *op. cit.*, 76, is very definite in recognizing the prophet's universalism.

15. In regard to these utterances, there is some dispute as to whether Deutero-Isaiah really had in mind a missionary enterprise for Israel. Of course, if one takes the word 'missionary' in its strictly modern connotation (the sending out of 'missionaries'), there can be no question here of mission in that sense. But Israel *is* being made aware here of her duty to acquaint the nations with the salvation that lies in Yahweh and his revelation, Israel *is* being called upon to bear witness to Yahweh and his salvation among the peoples of the world, in order that they may have a share in them (42:6; 45:2; 49:6). See in this connexion my *An Outline of Old Testament Theology*, 362, *et. al.*, and R. Martin-Achard, *A Light to the Nations* (1962), who is not prepared to speak in terms of 'mission'.

16. See B. J. van der Merwe, *Pentateuchtradisies in die prediking van Dt.-Jes.* (1955).

17. See M. Noth, *The History of Israel*, 308; R. Kittel, *Geschichte III*, 2, 319ff.; according to K. Galling, 'Die Exilswende in der Sicht des Propheten Sacharja', in *V.T.*, II (1952), 17ff, and 'Von Naboned zu Darius', in *Z.D.P.V.*, 170, (1954), 26ff., it was not until about 521 that under Zerubbabel's direction the main group, among whom was the prophet Zechariah, arrived in Jerusalem. The tally of 42,000 people (Ezra 2; Neh. 7) was in that case made up between 520 and 515, and

includes the names of those comprising the Jewish community in the country at the time.

18. For the history of the rebuilding see especially the aforementioned article by K. Galling in the Rudolph Festschrift.

19. K. Galling, *op. cit.*, 80.

20. A different translation and interpretation by K. Galling, *op. cit.*

21. K. Galling, *op. cit.*, thinks that the criticism that was engendered in the Jewish community itself allayed the danger of a political Messianism.

22. With regard to the matters above-mentioned, see, i.a., my article 'Hizza' in *O.T.S.*, VII (1950), 201ff.

23. O. Eissfeldt, *The Old Testament, An Introduction*, regards this as probable.

24. Thus M. Noth, *The History of Israel*, 336.

25. H. H. Rowley, 'Sanballat and the Samaritan Temple', *Men of God* (1963), 246ff.; A. Alt, 'Zur Geschichte der Grenze zwischen Judaä und Samaria', in *Kleine Schriften*, II, 346ff., especially 357f.

26. On this point see the books on the History of Israel or an Introduction to the Old Testament.

27. The historical point at issue here, or one of them, is whether the first or the second king of that name is envisaged.

28. On the political relationship between Judea and Samaria cf. especially A. Alt, 'Die Rolle Samarias bei der Entstehung des Judentums', in *Kleine Schriften*, II, 316ff., and 'Judas Nachbarn zur Zeit Nehemias', *idem*, 338ff.

29. Cf. Ezra 9: and M. A. Beek, *Geschiedenis van Israël* (Second edition), 118; A. van Selms, *Ezra en Nehemia*, Tekst en Uitleg (1935), 21f., rightly characterizes the situation thus: 'The one party laboured under a narrow-minded fanaticism, the other under a lack of religious seriousness'. Ehrlich, *op. cit.*, 79ff., would appear to have a very considerably mitigated conception of Ezra's and Nehemiah's measures regarding mixed marriages: cf. Ezra 10:10–16 and Neh. 13. 25ff.

30. Some go back much further into history. Thus M. A. Beek, in his *Inleiding in de Joodse Apocalyptiek*, 25, calls even Ezekiel a progenitor of this movement of the spirit.

31. Cf. *A.N.E.T.*, 492, *D.O.T.T.*, 260ff.

32. The latter name (of an Egyptian god in Elephantine) has not come down to us in its complete form; see *A.N.E.T.*, 491.

33. See E. G. Kraeling, *The Brooklyn Museum Aramaic Papyri* (1953), 83ff.; *idem*, 'Elephantine Urkunden', in *R.G.G.* (Third edition); Albright, *Archaeology and Religion of Israel* (Second edition) (1946), 168ff., who despite everything thinks that the group was monotheistic. A. Vincent, *La religion des Judéo-Araméens d'Eléphantine* (1937); C. G. Wagenaar, *De Joodse kolonie van Jeb-Syene in de 5de eeuw v. Chr.* (1928); E. Meyer, *Der Papyrusfund von Elephantine* (1912).

34. What Albright has in mind, partly because of the results yielded by excavation at Bethel in 1934, is that this place enjoyed a second period of prosperity after the destruction of Jerusalem. See *op. cit.*, 172ff. A. Vincent sees as a background the religious practices obtaining in Bethel prior to 622, when the town was taken by Josiah. So far as pronouncing on the origin of the religious forms is concerned, there is little to choose between these ideas.

35. See A. Bertholet, *Die Stellung der Israeliten und der Juden zu den Fremden* (1896).

CHAPTER 11

1. (1962), 1.

2. *Israelitisch-Jüdische Religionsgeschichte* (1933), 100ff.

3. Translation of the Torah into Greek must have been started in Alexandria at

about the middle of the 3rd century, first orally, as an elucidation of the reading of the Law in the synagogue, but in all probability soon also in a settled, written form. See, i.a., I. L. Seeligmann, 'Problemen en perspectieven moderne Septuagintaonderzoek', in *J.E.O.L.*, II, 6–8, 359ff., with much literature.

4. This strictness with respect to the text of the Torah was very meticulous, although differences of interpretation were still possible. As regards the books not canonized until a later period—the Prophets and the Writings—people in the ancient Jewish world were more free, in the matter of textual transmission as well as of interpretation. Cf. on this, e.g., Strack-Billerbeck, *Kommentar z. N.T.*, IV (1928); 433ff.; I. L. Seeligmann, 'Voraussetzungen der Midraschexegese', in Supplement to *V.T.*, I (1953), 181; G. Gerleman, *Synoptic Studies in the Old Testament* (1948), and above all, a commentary like the *Pesher Habakuk* among the Qumran scrolls. It is noteworthy how in many cases a literal insistence on the text goes hand in hand with a free exegesis—whence it appears that legalism was obliged yet again to concede a degree of liberty.

5. For the exegesis of these texts, interpolated at a later stage, see W. Rudolph, *Chronikbücher* (1955), in Handbuch z. A.T.

6. See Meyer in *Th.W.z.N.T.*, VI, 817ff., also W. Foerster, 'Der Heilige Geist im Spätjudentum', in *N.T.S.*, 8 (1961), 117ff.

7. On these writings see further one of the Introductions to the Old Testament, already mentioned, or one of the books on the 'Dead Sea Scrolls': e.g., J. v. d. Ploeg, *De vondsten in de woestijn van Juda*; for the rest, we mention only F. Cross, *The Ancient Library of Qumran* (Second edition) (1961), and C. T. Frisch, *The Qumran Community* (1956). All these works contain abundant references to further literature.

8. Unfaithfulness indeed, as the Chronicler demonstrates for page after page, had earlier been the cause of all the misery of the exile; for Yahweh requites disobedience with judgment, and fidelity with blessings.

9. See my *Die Erwählung des Volkes Israel* (1953).

10. As happens with Jesus Sirach; see, i.a., R. H. Charles, *Apocrypha and Pseudepigrapha of the Old Testament.*, I, 304ff.

11. Cf. J. H. Moulton, *Early Zoroastrianism* (1913), 286ff., and B. Reicke in *R.G.G.* (Third edition), sub 'Iran IV, Iranische Religion, Judentum und Christentum'.

12. See F. M. Th. de Liagre Böhl, 'Die Juden im Urteil der griechischen und römischen Schriftsteller', in *Opera Minora*, 101ff.; A. G. Roos, 'Joden en Jodenvervolgingen in het Oude Egypte', in *De Gids* (1947), 1ff., A. M. A. Hospers-Jansen, *Tacitus over de Joden* (1949), 35ff. The destruction of the Jewish temple at Yeb-Syene in 410 is not, of course, to be ascribed to religious hatred.

13. W. Holsten, 'Antisemitismus', in *R.G.G.* (Third edition).

14. See my article in *N.Th.T.* (1946), 'Prediker en de achtergrond van zijn wijsheid'.

15. See J. Pedersen, *Scepticisme Israélite* (1931).

16. Cf., e.g., chapters 39 and 44ff. of his book.

17. The first two books of the Maccabees give us a very good notion of this period.

18. Avi-Yonah, *op. cit.*, 3f. See further the books on the History of Israel.

19. See, i.a., H. H. Rowley, *The Relevance of Apocalyptic* (Second edition), (1963); M. A. Beek, *Inleiding tot de Joodse Apocalyptiek* (1950); R. H. Charles, *Religious Development between the Old and New Testaments*, many reprints; D. S. Russell, *Between the Testaments* (1960).

20. Cf. above, note 7 of this chapter, and, i.a., in *R.G.G.* (Third edition), the articles, 'Essener' and 'Qumran'.

Abbreviations

A.N.E.P.	*The Ancient Near East in Pictures relating to the Old Testament.*
A.N.E.T.	*Ancient Near Eastern Texts relating to the Old Testament,* edited by J. B. Pritchard (1950).
A.O.B.z.A.T.	*Altorientalische Bilder* (Second edition), edited by H. Gressmann (1927).
A.O.T.z.A.T.	*Altorientalische Texte* (Second edition), edited by H. Gressmann (1926).
A.R.I.	*Archaeology and Religion of Israel,* by W. F. Albright.
A.T.	*Altes Testament (Old Testament).*
A.T.D.	*Altes Testament Deutsch.*
B.A.	*Biblical Archaeologist.*
B.A.S.O.R.	*Bulletin of the American Schools of Oriental Research.*
Bi.Or.	*Bibliotheca Orientalis.*
B.J.R.L.	*Bulletin of the John Rylands Library.*
B.Z.A.W.	*Beihefte der Zeitschrift für die Alttestamentliche Wissenschaft.*
D.	*Deuteronomist,* Deuteronomy.
D.O.T.T.	*Documents from Old Testament Times,* edited by D. Winton Thomas, 1958.
E.	*Elohist.*
E.R.E.	*Encyclopaedia of Religion and Ethics.*
F.u.F.	*Forschungen und Fortschritte.*
G.T.T.	*Gereformeerd Theologisch Tijdschrift.*
H.Th.R.	*Harvard Theological Review.*
H.U.C.A.	*Hebrew Union College Annual.*
I.C.C.	*International Critical Commentary.*
I.E.J.	*Israel Exploration Journal.*
J.	*Jahwist (Yahwist).*
J.A.O.S.	*Journal of the American Oriental Society.*
J.E.O.L.	*Jaarbericht Ex Oriente Lux.*
J.N.E.S.	*Journal of Near Eastern Studies.*
J.S.S.	*Journal of Semitic Studies.*
M.V.Aeg.Gesch.	*Mitteilungen der Vorderasiatisch-Aegyptischen Gesellschaft.*
N.T.	*New Testament.*
N.T.S.	*New Testament Studies.*
N.T.S. (N.Th.S.)	*Nieuwe Theologische Studiën.*
N.T.T.	*Nederlands Theologisch Tijdschrift* (from 1946).
O.T.S.	*Oudtestamentische Studiën.*
P.	*Priestly Code.*

P.J.B.	*Palestinajahrbuch.*
R.B.	*Revue Biblique.*
R.G.G.	*Die Religion in Geschichte und Gegenwart.*
R.H.P.R.	*Revue d'Histoire et de Philosophie Religieuses.*
Schw.Th.U(mschau)	*Schweizerische Theologische Umschau.*
Th.Lt.Zt.	*Theologische Literaturzeitung.*
Th.R.	*Theologische Rundschau.*
Th.W.z.N.T.	*Theologisches Wörterbuch zum Neuen Testament.*
Th.W.b.z.N.T.	*Theologisches Wörterbuch zum Neuen Testament,* edited by G. Kittel, 1933.
Th.Z.	*Theologische Zeitschrift* (Theol. Fac. Univ. of Basel).
T.D.N.T.	*Theological Dictionary of the New Testament,* Michigan, 1964.
V.T.	*Vetus Testamentum.*
W.Z.K.M.	*Wiener Zeitschrift für die Kunde des Morgenlandes.*
Z.A.W.	*Zeitschrift für die alttestamentliche Wissenschaft.*
Z.D.M.G.	*Zeitschrift der deutschen Morgenländischen Gesellschaft.*
Z.D.P.V.	*Zeitschrift des Deutschen Palästinavereins.*
Z.f.syst.Th.	*Zeitschrift für Religions- und Geistesgeschichte.*
Z.Th.K.	*Zeitschrift für Theologie und Kirche.*
Z.W.Th.	*Zeitschrift für wissenschaftliche Theologie.*

INDEXES

Authors

ALBRIGHT, W. F. 106, 135, 161, 184, 262
Alt, A. 27, 69, 106, 107, 109, 119, 120, 122, 143, 156, 189
Arendonck, C. van 118
Avi-Yonah, M. 264

BAUDISSIN, W. W. 55
Baumgartner, W. 73
Bleeker, C. J. 71
Böhl, F. M. Th. de Liagre 105
Brekelmans, C. H. W. 164
Buber, M. 13, 105, 132
Budde, K. 135
Buck, A. de 200

CAUSSE, A. 199

DALMAN, J. M. 85
Dillmann, A. 135

EERDMANS, B. D. 125, 135, 150
Eissfeldt, O. 35, 65, 66, 106, 121, 142, 166
Erman, A. 39

FRANKFORT, H. 46

GALLING, K. 184, 189
Gemser, B. 105, 120
Gerleman, G. 132
Glueck, N. 68
Guillaume, A. 204

HEHN, J. 23
Hempel, J. 166
Henninger, J. 70
Hertzberg, H. W. 84
Holsten, W. 269
Hooke, S. H. 9, 10

JACOBSEN, Th. 48
Jamme, A. 70
Jaspers, K. 138

KAUFMANN, Y. 135
Kittel, R. 135

Köhler, L. 17, 142
Kramer, S. N. 26
Kraus, F. R. 215
Kristensen, W. B. 38
Kuenen, A. 135
Kutsch, E. 142

LAMBERT, W. G. 26, 29
Lods, A. 135

MARTI, K. 135
Mendenhall, G. E. 145
Montgomery, J. A. 71
Morenz, S. 201
Muilenburg, J. 84
Musil, A. 148

NEWMAN, M. L. 210
Noth, M. 58, 86, 106, 112, 116, 118, 126, 135, 136, 140, 141, 156, 157, 210, 240

OESTERLEY, W. O. E. 135
Otto, R. 99

PARROT, A. 116
Pedersen, J. 40, 71, 95, 127, 131, 132, 134, 194
Pfeiffer, R. H. 135, 166
Pierson, A. 7
Procksch, O. 105

RAD, G. von 71, 126, 164
Ravn, O. 26
Robinson, T. H. 135
Rowley, H. H. 116, 125, 148
Ryckmans, G. 70

SELLIN, E. 135, 264
Smend, R. 135
Soden, W. von 144
Söderblom, N. 131
Stamm, J. J. 142, 143

TÄUBLER, E. 154

VAN DER LEEUW, G. 39, 71, 77
Van Zÿl, A. H. 63

Vincent, A.   262
Vischer, W.   125
Volz, P.   131, 135

WEISER, A.   210
Wellhausen, J.   65, 108, 118, 135, 136
Wilderberger, H.   210

Wilson, J. A.   46
Wright, G. E.   24

YADIN, Y.   55

ZANDEE, J.   46

Gods

ABYSS   57, 58
Adad   57, 202, 203
Adon   61
Adonis   39, 41, 43
Aglibol   67
Allat   60, 61, 66, 68
'Amm   60, 61
Amon   34, 204
Anat   35, 41, 51, 110
Anath-Bethel   261
Anath-Yahu   261
Antu   35
Anu   34, 35, 48, 167
Anunnaki   57
Aphrodite   41
Ares   132
Asham-Bethel   218, 261
Asherah   51, 55, 231
Ashtar   51, 52, 53, 61, 62, 66, 70
Astar   51
Astarte   51, 52, 54, 55, 63, 68, 161, 176
'Atar   57, 58
Atargatis   68
Athene   51
'Athtar   See Ashtar
Aton   34, 35, 36
Attis   39

BAAL   12, 20, 34, 38, 40, 41, 42, 43, 51,
    52, 53, 55, 57, 61, 62, 63, 67, 110,
    121, 122, 123, 127, 133, 134, 155,
    160, 161, 165, 168, 169, 170, 176,
    187, 188, 189, 190 191, 192, 193,
    199, 213, 218, 219, 225, 228, 230,
    231, 232
Ba'alat   51, 54
Baal-Berith   155
Baal Hamman   58
Baal Harran   See Sin
Baal Semed   58
Baal Shamayin (Be'elshamin, Be'el-
    shemayin)   57, 66, 67, 204
Be'er Lahai Roi   121
Bel   67

Bel-Marduk   67
Bol   67
Bolastar   67

CHEMOSH   28, 29, 61, 62, 63, 64, 82,
    204

DAGON   52, 82
Dan'el   15, 16, 110
Day   57, 58
Dionysius   69
Dusares   See Dushara
Dushara   66, 68, 69

EA   167
Earth   57, 58
El   12, 34, 35, 37, 41, 42, 51, 53, 55, 57,
    58, 60, 61, 65, 67, 69, 73, 86, 110,
    111, 113, 115, 121, 122, 123, 129,
    130, 131, 133, 134, 156, 159, 161,
    165, 166, 170, 176, 187
El Abraham   122
Elat   51
El Bethel   114, 121, 122
El Elyon   24, 109, 121, 122, 180
Eloah   12
Elohim   12, 97, 165
El 'Olam   121, 122
El Ro'i   121
El Shaddai   111, 115, 121, 122
Elyon   57, 58, 165, 209
Enlil   35, 74

GAD-'AWIDH   66

HADAD   See Hadad-Rimmon
Hadad-Rimmon   43, 51, 56, 57, 58,
    59, 65, 67, 74
Haram-Bethel   261
Heaven   57, 58
Hobal   69
Horon   53
Horus   39

IGIGI 57
Ilah 66, 69
Ilat See Allat
Ilu-Wer 57
Inanna-Ishtar 40
Ishtar 26, 39, 41
Isis 34, 39, 41
'Itha' 66

JUPITER 34

KERET 15
Khnub 261
Koshar 53

LILITH 58
Lilitu 58

MALAKBEL 67
Manat 68
Manoto 69
Marduk 34, 36, 47, 48, 49, 67
Mars 132
Mekal 52
Melek 61
Melkart 53, 57
Milk 52
Milkom 61, 228
Min 38
Molech 61
Mot 40, 41, 51
Motabah 69

NABU 26
Nergal 62, 227
Night 57, 58
Ninlil 35

Ninurta 35, 36

OSIRIS 38, 39, 40, 41, 45, 48, 234
Ozza 68

QAUS 65

RAKAB-EL 58
Re 34, 38, 47, 48
Resheph 52, 58
Rowda 68

SAHR 57
Sakkuth 227
Salman 65
Sedeq 53
Shahar 53
Shalem 53
Shamash 57, 58
Shapash 52
Shay'-ha-qaum 66, 69
Sibitti 57, 58
Sin 35, 58

TAMMUZ 39, 40, 41, 43, 234
Telepinu 41

VENUS 52, 62, 66, 67, 68, 70
Verah 52

WELL-SPRINGS 57, 58

YAHU 57, 261
Yam 53
Yarhibol 67
Yerah 60, 61

ZEUS 34

Persons

AARON 257
Abiathar 84, 85, 89, 91, 185
Abijah 187
Abimelech 159
Abner 99
Abra(ha)m 24, 85, 107, 108, 109, 110, 111, 112, 113, 115, 116, 118, 119, 120, 136, 244
Absalom 85, 95, 100
Adam 274
Adapa, King 167
Adoni-nur 61
Adoni-Pellet 61
Ahab 8, 12, 20, 189, 192, 193, 197, 212, 214, 225,

Ahaz 220, 221, 222, 223, 226, 228
Ahijah 89, 186, 212
Ahimaaz 91
Ahimelech 84, 89, 91
Alcimus 272
Alexander the Great 263, 264
Amenophis IV (Ikhnaton) 34, 35
Amnon 100
Amon 228
Amos 20, 30, 59, 84, 165, 185, 191, 199, 216, 217, 218, 219, 221, 222, 224, 229, 236, 238, 249, 274
Antiochus III 270
Antiochus IV 270, 271
Apsu 47

x

Arpad 57, 60, 217
Artahshashta See Artaxerxes
Artaxerxes 257
Ashurbanipal 26, 215, 217, 228, 232
Athaliah 192, 193

BALAAM 101, 164, 208
Barak 156, 177
Barga'ayah 58
Bathsheba 92, 100, 143
Benjamin 114, 162

CAIN 108, 119, 125, 166, 274
Caleb 157
Cambyses 261
Cyrus 240, 248, 249, 251

DANIEL 263, 266, 268, 271
Darius 254
David 13, 27, 57, 77, 79, 80, 81, 82, 83, 84, 85, 86, 87, 89, 91, 92, 93, 94, 95, 96, 97, 98, 99, 100, 142, 143, 163, 166, 174, 175, 179, 180, 181, 182, 183, 184, 185, 186, 193, 196, 206, 212, 217, 224, 225, 232, 237, 244, 259, 267
Deborah 156, 157, 160, 169, 176, 191, 205, 208, 209, 210
Deutero-Isaiah 196, 197, 224, 237, 240, 241, 242, 243, 249, 251, 253, 259, 262, 266, 274
Doeg 93

ELEAZAR 257
Eli 84, 177
Eliashib 259
Elijah 8, 12, 20, 162, 189, 190, 191, 192, 197, 199, 208, 209, 211, 219
Elisha 64, 190, 192, 209, 211, 213, 214
Enoch 124, 271, 274
Esarhaddon 29, 65, 217
Esau 108, 112, 113, 118
Eve 274
Ezekiel 16, 43, 53, 111, 145, 197, 199, 211, 229, 234, 238, 241, 243, 245, 246, 247, 248, 249, 255, 256, 266
Ezra 253, 256, 257, 258, 259, 263, 264, 265, 266

GAD 91, 212
Gedaliah 237
Giddel 261
Gideon 175, 191

HABAKKUK 238, 239
Hagar 108, 109, 111, 118
Haggai 252, 253, 254, 258, 263, 266
Hammurabi 49, 144, 145, 146, 181
Hananiah 8

Hezekiah 220, 221, 223, 226, 228, 229, 230
Hiram 53
Hosea 20, 43, 84, 135, 145, 146, 190, 218, 219, 224, 230, 235, 236
Huldah 169
Hyrcanus, John 272

IKHNATON See Amenophis IV
Isaac 107, 108, 110, 111, 112, 113, 116, 118, 119, 120, 121
Isaiah 20, 37, 101, 183, 191, 196, 197, 199, 217, 218, 219, 221, 222, 223, 224, 225, 229, 230, 234, 237, 238, 241, 249, 253, 271, 274
Ishbaal 161
Ishmael 111, 121

JACOB 66, 112ff., 116, 119, 123, 187
Jason 270
Jedidiah 92
Jehoash 193
Jehoiachin 252
Jehoiada 193
Jehoiakim 232, 235
Jehoshaphat 192, 212, 213
Jehosheba 193
Jehu 73, 190, 191, 192, 213
Jephthah 228
Jeremiah 8, 16, 145, 196, 210, 219, 224, 228, 230, 232, 233, 235, 236, 237, 238, 241, 242, 245, 247, 248, 253
Jeroboam I 175, 186, 187, 188
Jeroboam II 193, 215, 216, 219
Jerubbaal 42, 159, 161
Jesse 224, 225
Jezebel 20, 73, 189, 190, 192
Joab 98, 100
Joel 208, 255, 260, 266
Jonah 259
Jonathan 81, 91, 96, 97, 98
Jonathan (High Priest) 272
Jonathan ben Rechab 192
Joram 192, 193
Joseph 113, 114, 115, 116, 156, 157
Josephus 263
Joshua 136, 156, 157, 158
Joshua (High Priest) 252, 254
Josiah 101, 226, 228, 231, 232, 234, 235

LABAN 66, 112, 113, 117
Lamech 119
Leah 113
Levi 114, 156, 162
Lipit Ishtar 144, 145
Lot 108, 109, 118
Lucian 41

MALACHI 208, 255, 258
Manasseh 101, 114, 115, 228, 230
Manetho 269
Melchizedek 24, 109, 181
Menelaus 270
Mephibaal 42, 161
Merneptah 113
Merodach Baladan 220
Micah 88, 183, 218, 222, 224, 225, 228, 229, 236
Micah (the Ephraimite) 174, 175, 176
Micaiah 261
Micaiah ben Imlah 193, 213
Mohammed 103, 119, 155, 206
Moses 10, 15, 16, 17, 37, 73, 74, 103, 104, 105, 125, 131, 135, 136, 137, 138, 139, 140, 141, 142, 143, 144, 147, 148, 149, 151, 152, 155, 157, 163, 175, 178, 190, 191, 208, 210, 234, 244, 257, 265, 271
Murshilish 29

NAAMAN 82
Nabonidus 29
Nahum 238
Nathan 79, 80, 87, 91, 92, 98, 143, 185, 186, 203, 211, 212
Nebuchadnezzar 236, 239, 245, 248
Necho 232
Nehemiah 257, 258, 259, 260, 263, 264, 266

OBADIAH 243
'Omri 28, 189, 192, 225
Onias 270

PANAMMU 58, 59
Pekah 220
Phinehas 162

RACHEL 113
Rahab 165
Reuben 156
Reuel 140

Rezin 220
Ruth 259

SAMSON 164, 178
Samuel 92, 101, 178, 200, 208, 209, 210, 211, 212
Sanballat 259, 260, 261
Sarai 108, 109, 111
Sargon 217, 220, 226
Saul 13, 79, 80, 81, 82, 83, 84, 89, 90, 93, 94, 95, 96, 99, 142, 161, 179, 180
Sennacherib 180, 217, 220
Shalmaneser IV 217
Shemaiah 212
Sheshbazzar 251
Shishak 192
Simeon 114, 156
Sisera 157
Solomon 14, 53, 79, 85, 91, 92, 100, 173, 174, 179, 180, 181, 182, 184, 185, 186, 192, 196, 231, 244

TAMAR 100
Tiglath-Pileser III 30, 215, 217, 220
Tobiah 259
Tukulti-Ninurta I 29

URIAH 92, 100
Urukagina of Lagash 144
Uzzah 86
Uzziah 193, 215, 221

WEN-AMON 54, 203, 206, 211

ZABUD 80, 92
Zadok 91, 92, 185, 257, 273
Zakir 57, 204
Zechariah 252, 253, 254, 263, 266, 274
Zedekiah 212, 232, 235
Zipporah 139, 140
Zephaniah 228, 229, 238
Zerubbabel 240, 251, 252, 253, 254, 257, 263

Places

ACCADIA 167
Ai 108, 158
'Ain Qedeirat 148
'Akaba, Gulf of 125
Aleppo 53
Alexandria 269
Anathoth 51, 235
Antioch 53

Arabah 125
Aram 65, 217
Ashdod 52
Asia Minor 22, 23
Ataroth 62

BAALBEK 60
Baal-Peor 63, 174

Bashan 165
Beersheba 19, 109, 110, 112, 121, 122, 161, 176, 219, 226
Beth Anat 51
Bethel 19, 20, 37, 43, 52, 69, 84, 108, 110, 112, 114, 121, 122, 123, 161, 176, 183, 186, 187, 188, 192, 214, 216, 218, 232, 261, 262
Beth-Horon 53
Bethlehem 93, 99
Bethlehem Ephrathah 225
Beth-Shan 52, 173
Byblos 41, 51, 54, 174, 203, 211

CARMEL 189, 214
Cyprus 51

DAMASCUS 30, 56, 82, 216, 220, 266
Dan 19, 43, 123, 161, 174, 175, 186, 188, 192
Dibon 29, 61, 62

ELEPHANTINE 20, 37, 43, 52, 73, 169, 188, 218, 261
Elim 139
Euphrates 22, 45
Europe 7

FERTILE CRESCENT 22

GAZA 52
Gerasa 59, 60
Gezer 179
Gibeah 94, 161, 162
Gibeon 84, 94, 95, 99
Gilgal 80, 83, 84, 127, 157, 177, 188, 214, 216, 218
Gilgamesh 48, 167
Gomorrah 109

HAMAT 57
Hamath 204, 217
Haran 113
Hauran 65, 67
Hazor 55, 158, 173, 179
Hebron 83, 85, 95, 107, 108, 112, 157, 161, 176, 226
Horeb 190

ISSACHAR 156

JABBOK 113
Jabesh 80
Jebel Tannur 68
Jericho 16, 84, 158
Jerusalem 11, 19, 24, 25, 30, 53, 54, 79, 83, 84, 85, 86, 88, 89, 91, 93, 122, 142, 176, 179, 182, 183, 185, 186, 187, 188, 189, 193, 218, 219, 220, 222, 223, 224, 225, 226, 229, 230, 231, 234, 235, 236, 237, 238, 240, 243, 244, 245, 246, 247, 251, 253, 254, 255, 256, 257, 260, 261, 262, 267, 270, 275
Jethro 140
Jezreel 176, 189, 190
Jordan 136, 152, 186

KADESH 139, 142, 148, 149 151, 152
Kedar 66
Keilah 89
Khirbet el-Mefjir 84
Kiriath-jearim 84
Kiriath Sepher 157

LACHISH 158, 173

MACHPELAH 111, 112
Mahanaim 176
Mamre 85, 108, 121, 122
Marah 139
Mari 15, 28, 52, 60, 116, 117, 200, 201, 203, 204, 206
Mecca 45, 60, 68, 69
Megiddo 43, 167, 173, 179, 232
Mesha 28, 29, 204, 228
Mizpah 161, 218
Moreh 108
Moriah 110
Mount of Olives 83, 85

NABATAEA 60, 66, 67, 68, 69, 119
Nahariya 54, 55
Nebo 62, 204
Nahor 120
Nile 22, 48
Nineveh 117, 232, 238
Nob 83, 84, 85, 89, 91, 93, 176, 177
Nuzi 15
Nuzu 116, 117

OPHRAH 175

PALESTINE 32, 42, 52, 62, 108, 112, 113, 119, 126, 154, 157, 159, 172, 186, 193, 220, 232, 240, 242, 245, 258, 260, 268, 270
Palmyra 59, 60, 66, 67, 68
Peniel 19, 112
Petra 59, 60, 68, 148

QUMRAN 163, 234, 239, 241, 272, 275

RAS SHAMRA 50
Red Sea 139, 151
Rephidim 139

SEʿIR 125, 132
Shara 68
Shechem 19, 107, 108, 110, 113, 114, 121, 122, 146, 155, 156, 157, 159, 161, 162, 173, 176, 183, 184, 186, 265
Shiloh 19, 83, 84, 93, 114, 142, 161, 176, 177, 187, 210
Shur 139
Sidon 51, 245
Sinai 16, 82, 88, 125, 126, 127, 128, 129, 136, 138, 139, 141, 142, 144, 147, 148, 151, 152, 157, 184, 257, 274
Sodom 109
Succoth 113

TABOR 161, 176, 218
Tekoa 97, 100, 181, 216, 225
Tell Beit Mirsim 161
Tell Tainat 53, 55, 184
Tigris 22, 117, 215
Tirzah 173
Transjordan(ia) 59ff., 141, 142, 154, 189, 212, 228
Tyre 53, 189, 245

UGARIT 15, 16, 34, 35, 40, 41, 51, 52, 53, 54, 110, 118, 154, 187

YEB-SYENE See Elephantine

ZEBULUN 156

Subjects

AHLAMU 56
Amalekites 96, 139, 152, 163–4, 210
Amarna Letters 50, 52, 140, 167
Amarna period 154, 159
Ammonites 59, 60–2, 64, 80, 154, 228, 243, 245, 259
Amorites 53
Ancient Near East 8, 11–13, 16, 22–4, 28, 30, 32–3, 36–8, 44, 76, 79, 87, 100, 102, 116, 125, 143–4, 147, 155, 165–7, 175, 179, 181, 184–5, 193–4, 200, 206, 274
Angelology 268, 273
Animal worship 45
Apocrypha 263
Arabia, Arabians 22–4, 27, 32, 40, 45, 50, 52, 56, 58–61, 64–71, 73, 109, 118–19, 124–6, 155, 162, 200, 204–5, 207, 209
Aramaeans 50, 56ff., 64–5, 67, 118–19, 212
Archaeology 20, 50, 106, 158, 161
Ark, the 131, 136, 142, 146–7, 151, 165, 183–4, 187, 196, 244
Art 7, 76
Assyria, Assyrians 10, 14, 23, 26–7, 29, 40, 49, 61, 65, 116–17, 125, 191, 193, 215–18, 220–3, 226, 228–9, 231–2, 239

BABYLONIA, BABYLONIANS 10, 12, 14, 23–7, 29, 32–5, 38–41, 44, 47ff., 56, 65, 68, 72–3, 75, 125, 167, 181, 220, 227, 239, 243–5, 247–52, 255–6, 268
Benjaminites 202
Blood Feud 95, 99–100

Brahminism 103
Buddhism 11, 103
Byzantine Empire 155

CALVINISM 11
Canaan, Canaanites 9, 20, 22, 24, 38, 41–2, 50ff., 56, 60, 72–3, 82–4, 87–8, 90–2, 95, 107–10, 114–15, 117–19, 121–2, 124, 126, 129–33, 136, 138, 140–2, 146–50, 152–5, 159–61, 165, 167, 170–4, 176–8, 180–1, 183, 186, 209, 211, 228, 257, 274
Chaldeans 239
Christianity 10, 12, 77, 103, 191, 224, 241, 273, 275
Chronicles, Book of 88, 185, 263, 265, 267
Church 7
Circumcision 66, 71, 109, 111, 119, 140, 150, 244, 273
Coptic 11
Covenant 97, 111, 122, 126, 135, 139, 145–6, 149, 154, 207, 210, 212, 230–1, 233, 244, 252, 257–8, 265–6
Covenant, Book of 169, 231, 265
Creation 31

DANIEL, BOOK OF 271–2
Day of Atonement 256
Dead Sea 68, 125, 247, 272
Dead Sea Scrolls 263
Decalogue 17, 135, 142–9, 151, 171, 173, 218
Demonology 268
Deuteronomic Reform 11, 144, 176, 198, 226, 232–3, 235–6, 242, 244, 253, 264

Deuteronomic School 17, 19, 126–7, 145–6, 150, 158, 182, 184, 188, 229–31, 233–4
Divine Kingship 33, 39, 45–7
Druses 11

EAST See Ancient Near East
Ecclesiastes, Book of 206, 263, 269
Edom, Edomites 22, 59, 64ff., 108, 112, 118–19, 125, 132, 157, 166, 243, 245, 273
Egypt 10, 12, 14, 16, 20, 23–4, 29, 32–5, 38–9, 41, 44, 45ff., 53–4, 56, 60, 62, 65, 68, 71–3, 75, 82, 108, 116, 119, 126–30, 132, 135, 138–42, 144, 147–8, 150–3, 157, 159, 167, 169, 181–2, 185, 187–8, 200–1, 204, 207, 218, 220, 232, 234, 237, 245, 248, 251, 261
Enoch, Book of 266
Ephraim, Ephraimites 114–15, 157, 162, 174
Eschatology 197–8, 201, 219, 223–4, 237, 249, 266–7, 271, 274
Essenes 266, 272–3
Esther, Book of 263, 268–9
Exile 13, 166, 198, 218, 234, 237, 240–6, 249, 251, 255, 258, 265–6
Exodus, the 9, 126–8, 137, 140, 147, 149–50, 251
Exodus, Book of 104

FAMILY GODS 27, 67
Fertility Gods 40–2, 52, 62, 69, 120, 187

GENESIS 10
Greeks 23, 50, 67–8, 73, 205, 263

ḤABIRU 108, 116, 154, 159
Hamites 23
Hanukkah 271
Hassidim 271
Hebrew tribes 9–10, 13, 22, 27, 41, 71, 79, 105, 108, 120–1, 128–9, 131, 134–5, 140–1, 144, 151–2, 154–5, 157–8, 161, 171, 187, 211
Hereafter, the 31, 45
Hezekiah's Reform 198, 220, 225–6
Historiography 14–16, 18, 79, 108, 118, 126
Hittites 23, 29, 41, 53, 58, 101, 145
Hivites 155
Hyksos 116

IPRI See Ḥabiru
Isaiah-Apocalypse 263, 266
Islam 10–12, 70, 77, 103, 155
Ishmaelites 108–9, 118

JEBUSITES 85, 89, 91, 180–1, 185
Jews 7, 11, 19, 135, 142, 198, 224, 234, 240, 242–5, 248–9, 251–2, 255, 257–60, 262–6, 268–71, 273
Job, Book of 111, 260
Joshua, Book of 16, 84, 156, 158
Josiah's Reform 144, 232, 235
Judah 60, 88, 115, 156–7, 175, 180, 183, 186, 192–3, 212–13, 216, 218–22, 224, 228–30, 233, 237–40, 254, 257–8, 260, 273
Judges, the 9, 18, 79, 110, 133, 142, 160, 165–6, 169, 172, 176, 178, 209–10
Judges, Book of 10, 83, 133

KENITES 108, 118–19, 125, 128, 138, 140, 148, 150–2, 157, 163, 274
Kenizzites 157
Kings, Book of 83, 184, 188, 226, 228

LAMENTATIONS, BOOK OF 238, 243
Law of Holiness 244
Leviathan 165

MACCABEES 255, 263, 271–3
Mesha Stone 61–2, 64
Mesopotamia 22, 28, 32, 34, 40, 48–50, 52, 56, 60, 71, 107–8, 111, 117, 162, 207, 234
Messiah 77, 92, 197, 212, 225, 237, 252–4, 266, 272
Methodists 11
Midianites 119, 139–40
Moab, Moabites 28, 51, 58, 60–1, 64–5, 154, 163–4, 228, 243, 245
Monarchy 13, 18–20, 26–7, 33, 43, 60, 65, 77, 79, 82–3, 86, 88–9, 110, 143, 149, 154, 165–6, 169, 173–4, 177–82, 186, 188, 191–2, 204, 209, 212, 214–15, 217, 235, 262
Monotheism 12, 35–7, 80, 82, 122, 135, 191
Mystics 11, 36, 199

NATIONALISM 132
Nazirites 164, 178, 210
New Year Festival 33

OATHS 95–7

PANTHEISM 36–7, 72
Parseeism 11, 268
Passover 139, 149, 231, 255
Patriarchs 9, 15–16, 66, 85, 87, 103ff., 124, 127, 129, 131, 133, 136, 138, 153, 156, 159, 168, 171, 175–6, 187, 274
Pentateuch 124, 126, 256–7, 265
Persia, Persians 23, 29, 68, 73, 248–9, 253–6, 261–3, 268–9

Pharaoh 46–7, 113, 139, 151
Pharisees 272–3
Philistines 23, 52, 65, 71, 80 ,84, 107, 177, 186, 220, 225, 228, 245
Phoenicia, Phoenicians 16, 20, 24, 28, 32–5, 38, 40–2, 44, 50ff., 56–7, 67, 71–3, 90, 124–5, 154, 181, 184, 189, 203, 207, 217
Politics 7, 12, 24, 79, 89, 99, 134, 183, 185–6, 192–3, 195, 198, 203, 208, 212, 216–17, 221, 223, 225, 228, 232, 240–1, 255, 273
Polytheism 12, 35, 63, 160, 229
Priesthood 19–20, 88, 131, 174–5, 177, 182–5, 191, 193, 201–6, 210, 227, 230–2, 236, 243–4, 247, 254–5, 257–8, 260, 262, 265, 267, 270, 275
Priestly Code 17, 244, 256–7
Prophets 10, 19, 25, 28, 30, 43, 64, 75, 78, 83, 88, 91, 101, 116, 124, 127, 136, 141, 143–5, 161, 176–8, 182, 188–93, 194ff., 229–30, 234–6, 238, 240, 242, 244, 248, 253, 266, 274
Proverbs, Book of 270
Psalms 25–6, 185, 199, 244
Psalms, Coronation 33
Ptolemies 263, 270
Purim, Feast of 269

QUAKERS 11

RECHABITES 87, 156, 182, 192, 199, 217
Reformers 11
Resurrection 273
Ritual observances 31–2, 42, 230, 242–3, 252
Romans 23, 59, 67

SABBATH 150, 244, 252, 259, 262
Sacrifice 25, 58, 61, 63–4, 66, 68, 84, 88, 90, 93–4, 131, 149, 169, 171, 173, 175, 177, 182, 184–5, 188, 195, 199, 202, 216, 218, 220, 225, 228, 231–2, 234, 243, 247, 256–8, 261–2, 267, 271
Sadducees 272–3
Safatenes 69
Sam'al Inscriptions 58
Samaria, Samaritans 20, 188, 192, 214, 217–18, 227, 232, 243, 252–3, 251, 259–62, 265, 267–8, 273
Samuel, Books of 133

Sassanid Empire 155
Satan 268
Scholastics (medieval) 11
Seleucids 263, 270, 272
Semites, Semitic 23, 25, 27, 30, 31ff., 40–1, 45, 49, 52, 56–62, 64–9, 71, 106–8, 117–18, 124, 138, 145, 187, 193, 200–1, 204, 217, 220–1, 239, 268
Septuagint 265
Servant of Yahweh 250
Servant Songs 250
Sheol 44
Sibylline Books 266
Song of Deborah 13, 132–4, 141, 157, 159, 163–4
Sumeria 26, 29–30, 34–5, 39–40, 49
Suteans 56
Synagogue 7, 11, 244, 273
Syria, Syrians 22, 24, 27–8, 51, 53, 56–7, 60, 71, 82, 120, 154, 184, 191, 193, 217, 220, 227, 232, 240, 270

TEACHER OF RIGHTEOUSNESS 272
Temple (in Jerusalem) 19–20, 25, 43, 85, 87–9, 91, 150, 173, 177–9, 182–5, 193, 196, 212, 216, 221, 223–4, 231–2, 234, 236–7, 239–40, 242–4, 247, 251–6, 258, 261–2, 265, 267, 271–3
Testament of the Twelve Patriarchs, the 266
Tiamat 47–8
Tobit, Book of 268
Tutelary Gods 27

VOWS 95

WISDOM LITERATURE 25, 47, 77, 180–1, 201, 259, 269

XENOPHON 215

YAHWISM 9, 11–13, 20, 28, 30, 38, 41–2, 73, 80ff., 88, 90, 92, 104, 111, 123, 124ff., 154ff., 179, 181, 183, 186, 188–92, 195–6, 206, 211, 213, 217, 219–20, 229–31, 235–6, 241, 243, 258, 262, 273–5

ZENDJIRI INSCRIPTIONS See Sam'al Inscriptions

Biblical References

GENESIS

1:	44, 166, 244
1:2	44, 75
1:4ff.	44
1:11ff.	43
1:31	75
2ff.	166ff.
2:	244
4:3f.	166
4:11ff.	166
4:17	166
4:26	124
6:1ff.	168
10:25	107
11:1ff.	107, 166
12ff.	107
12:1ff.	107, 109f.
12:3	197
12:10ff.	108
13:	108
13:18	85
14:	108, 116, 121f.
14:7	148
14:18ff.	53
15:	109, 111, 116f.
16:	109, 117
16:13f.	27, 121
17:	109, 111, 121, 244
17:5	111
18:1	85
18:22ff.	109
19:30ff.	111
20:	111
20:11	111
21:	109
21:9f.	117
21:13	111
21:34	121
22:	110, 111
24:	110
24:62	121
25ff.	113
25:11	121
25:29ff.	117
28:	121
28:3	115
28:10ff.	113, 133
28:17ff.	114
28:20	95
28:29f.	113
29ff.	66
29:1	66
31:	117, 175
31:5	113
31:42	112f., 120
31:53	113, 120
32f.	113
32:9	113
32:14ff.	113
32:33	113
33:10	113
33:20	114
34:	105, 114, 162
35:1ff.	122
35:11	115
36:	108
36:35f.	65
36:38f.	65
38:	105
46:3	114
49:	105, 114
49:5ff.	114
49:24f.	115

EXODUS

1:8ff.	139
2:	139
2:10	140
3:	127
3:4ff.	104
3:14	130
3:19	141
4:19f.	139
4:24ff.	139f., 150
6:1ff.	104, 111
7ff.	139

11:4ff.	139	5:4	96
12:11	251	6:	256
12:21ff.	139	7:	256
12:29ff.	139	18:20	169
13:20	139	19:31	101
13:21ff.	251	20:6	101
14:5ff.	139	20:27	101
14:19f.	251	23:	43
15:	127, 139, 142		
15:21	126	**NUMBERS**	
16:	139	1ff.	257
17:	139	5:21	95
17:8ff.	163	6:	178
17:16	164	10:29	139
18:	140, 148	10:35	151
19ff.	127	11ff.	160
19:	127, 142	11:24ff.	141
19:5ff.	233	12:6f.	141
19:16ff.	190	13:26	139, 148
20:	142f., 145ff., 172	14:	139
20:3f.	148	16:21ff.	139
20:18	190	20:	139, 148
20:23	146, 148, 171	20:13	148
20:24	171f.	21:14	163
21ff.	135, 231	21:29	61
22:16f.	100f., 160	22ff.	64, 164
22:20	160, 189	23:23	101
22:29	229	24:	209
23:	149	24:18ff.	164
23:12ff.	147, 160, 169, 171	25:1ff.	42, 174
23:18ff.	160, 173	25:4	160
24:	139, 142	25:6ff.	162
24:3ff.	145	33:	125f.
24:12ff.	145		
25ff.	149, 265f.	**DEUTERONOMY**	
32ff.	43, 127, 139	1:5	233, 265
32:	162	1:19	148
32:8	187	4:	265
32:27ff.	162	5ff.	234
33:7ff.	141	5:	143, 146
34:	147, 149, 171f.	7:	232
34:10	145	10:2f.	146
34:13	172	11:	232
34:14ff.	147f., 171	11:10ff.	151
34:24	151	12:	230
34:26	173	13:	189, 230
34:27	145	14:	160, 230
35ff.	257	15:12ff.	230, 232, 234
35:3	150	16:	42, 231
		16:3	251
LEVITICUS		16:18ff.	230
1ff.	256		

17:	230
17:8ff.	230
17:14ff.	233
18:	230
18:10f.	101
18:15	141
19:14ff.	230
22:28	100
23:8	64
26:1ff.	170, 231f.
26:5ff.	126f.
31:10ff.	126
33:2	125
33:8ff.	162f.
33:19	177
34:10f.	141
34:18f.	232

JOSHUA

4:19ff.	84
7:	94
9:15ff.	96
24:	156, 158

JUDGES

1:	158
4:	141
4:6	177
4:14	164
5:	82, 126, 128
	133, 164
5:1	178
5:4	125
5:5	125
5:8	133, 160
5:12	164
5:14f.	157
6:	160, 173
6:8	66
6:25ff.	175
7:18	164
7:22	164
8:22ff.	160
8:27	174
8:29ff.	155
9:	155
9:8ff.	160
10:1ff.	210
11:	228
12ff.	177
12:8ff.	210
13:	173
13:25	178
14:6	178

14:19	178
15:14	178
16:23	52
17ff.	162, 174
19ff.	162

RUTH

1:7ff.	259
1:20f.	111
2:16	27

1 SAMUEL

1ff.	83f.
3:20	209
3:33ff.	102
4ff.	164
5:	52
5:5	228
7:	91
8:	160
9:9	207, 209
9:12f.	177
9:22	177
10:	211
10:1	89
10:5ff.	92, 211
11:	80, 187
11:13	177
11:15	83f., 93
12:	143
12:15ff.	101
12:21f.	102
13:	88
13:16	80
14:	187
14:3	89
14:6ff.	80, 164
14:12	80
14:15	80
14:18f.	89
14:20	80
14:23	80
14:24f.	96
14:31f.	90, 99
14:35	88
14:36ff.	89, 96, 101
14:45	80
15:	89, 197
15:2f.	164
16:14ff.	80f.
18:1ff.	80, 97
18:12	80
18:14	80
18:17	163

18:28	80	2:32	102
19:	175, 211	3:3	85
19:9ff.	80f.	3:9ff.	80
19:18ff.	92, 211	3:28ff.	99
19:24	209	3:35	96
20:5f.	93	5:2ff.	80
20:8	81	5:3	85
20:12ff.	81, 96f.	5:19ff.	81, 89
20:23	81	5:22ff.	89
20:42	81, 97	6:	86, 90ff.
21f.	84	6:6ff.	81
21:1ff.	83, 90	6:11ff.	81
21:5	90, 164	6:17f.	85f., 93
21:7	93	6:21f.	80, 92
22ff.	80	7:	87, 182, 186,
22:	91		203
22:3	81, 98	7:4	91, 211
22:5	91, 101, 212	7:6	213
22:10	89	7:6f.	85
22:13	89	7:8ff.	80, 92
22:15	89	7:12	91
22:17f.	89	8:18	91, 185
23ff.	81	9:3	97
23:6ff.	89	9:5ff.	97
23:9ff.	89	11:27	81
23:11f.	89	12:1ff.	91f., 211f.
23:13	81	12:9f.	81, 92
23:16	98	12:11f.	81, 92, 98f.
23:17	97	12:20	83, 85
23:26	81	12:25	212
24:5ff.	89	12:30	61
24:16	81	13:	100
24:20ff.	81	14:	100, 181
25:28	163	14:2	101
25:39	81	14:14	97, 101
26:9ff.	89	14:16	81, 97
26:10	81	15:7ff.	83, 85, 95
26:19	81f., 90, 93,	15:12	93
	97f.	15:24ff.	91
26:24f.	81	15:27	91
28:	100f.	15:32	83, 85
28:6	101	16:8ff.	81, 98
28:13f.	101	16:12	96
30:6	27, 98	16:22	81
30:7ff.	81, 89	17:14	81
30:15	96	17:23	102
30:17f.	97	18:17	66, 102
30:23	81	19:15ff.	84
31:11ff.	102	19:21	89
		19:24ff.	97
2 SAMUEL		19:37	102
1:	185	20:16	101
1:15f.	89	20:19	81, 97
1:26	97	21:	80, 94f., 99f.
2:1f.	89	21:3	81, 94, 97
2:4	85		

21:7	97
21:8ff.	102
23:5	92
23:16f.	90, 93, 99
24:1ff.	81, 91, 212
24:15	93
24:18ff.	90
24:22ff.	93f.
25:	91

1 KINGS

1f.	80
1:	91f.
1:25	93
1:39	89
2:	86, 91
2:5f.	100f.
2:9	101
2:10	102
2:28f.	85, 100
2:34	102
3:	84, 181
4:5	92, 185
4:29	181
6:	183
7:13ff.	53
8:	183
8:5	182
8:14	182
8:22	182
8:54ff.	182
9:15	179
10:	181
11:	65
11:6ff.	186
11:7	61
11:29ff.	212
12:22ff.	212
12:26ff.	43
12:28	187
12:31	162
13f.	188
14:1ff.	212
15:13	73
18:	189, 213
18:34ff.	170
18:39	190
18:46	211
19:	190ff.
19:8	126
19:12	190
19:15ff.	190, 192
19:19ff.	214
21:	189

| 22: | 212 |
| 22:19 | 36 |

2 KINGS

2ff.	214
2:1	84
2:4	214
2:23ff.	214
3:	62, 214, 228
3:6ff.	214
3:13ff.	64, 214
3:15	211, 213
3:27	61f., 82
4ff.	214
4:1ff.	214
4:8ff.	214
4:33ff.	214
4:38ff.	84, 214
5:17	82
6:1ff.	214
6:12	214
6:15	214
6:32	214
7:1ff.	214
8:7ff.	214
8:10	214
8:18	193
9:1ff.	192, 213f.
9:11	211
9:22	73
10:	189
10:29	192
11:	193
12:	193
13:14ff.	64, 214
13:20ff.	214
14:29	216
16:10ff.	220
17:24ff.	227
18:3ff.	225f.
21:	228
21:6	101
22ff.	231
22:14	169
23:	228, 231
23:7	231
23:13	186
23:15ff.	188
23:24	101

1 CHRONICLES

13:	87
15:	87
17:14	267

22:8	87
24:3	257
25:1ff.	265
28:5	267
29:23	267

2 CHRONICLES
8:14	206
20:14ff.	265
20:20	265
28:22ff.	220
29:	220
29:25	265
29:30	265
35:15	265

EZRA
1:7ff.	251
4:1ff.	253
5:1ff.	252f.
6:3ff.	240, 251, 255
6:9	255
6:10	255
6:14	253
6:15ff.	255
7:14	257
7:23ff.	257
7:25f.	257
9:	258
9:1ff.	258
10:	258

NEHEMIAH
5:14	258
8ff.	258
12:24	206
12:36	206
13:	259
13:4ff.	259
13:23	258
13:28	259

JOB
1f.	36
1:3	66
1:6ff.	36
2:1ff.	36

PSALMS
2:	33, 164, 181
20:	164, 185
24:	86
25:2	27
29:	170
35:23f.	27
45:7f.	33
48:	183, 236
65:10ff.	170
67:	43
67:7	43
68:	82, 128, 164
68:8f	126
68:9	125
68:15	111
69:4	27
71:12	27
72:	181
78:60	84
82:1	36
84:4	27
84:11	27
86:2	27
86:12	27
87:	250
89:6ff.	36, 170
89:10ff.	44, 165
91:1	111
104:	170
110:	33, 181f.
126:	243
132:	86
137:	243
143:10	27

PROVERBS
1ff.	259
9ff.	259
12:13f.	270
22:17ff.	259
23:	259
24:	259
30:	259
31:	259

ISAIAH
1:	223
1:10f.	199, 217
2:1ff.	223ff.
2:3	229
2:6	219
3ff.	217
3:4f.	201
3:12f.	229
6:	221

6:8ff.	222	53:1ff.	250
7:8ff.	222	56:1ff.	242, 252
7:18ff.	222	66:1f.	242
8:13ff.	222		
8:19	219	JEREMIAH	
9:1ff.	223	1:	204, 207, 236
10:5ff.	223	2:1ff.	124, 208, 219, 228, 235
11:1ff.	223f.		
11:14	66	3:12ff.	236
11:42	254	3:21ff.	232
13:6	111	4:1ff.	236
14:32	199, 222	4:4	232
17:10f.	43	7:	236
24ff.	266	7:3ff.	143
26ff.	217	7:5ff.	199
27:	16, 166	7:9	143
27:1	44, 165	7:12	84
28ff.	223	7:22f.	149, 236
28:16	223	8:18ff.	235
30:15	191, 222	9:1ff.	149, 235
31:7	219	11:1ff.	233
36ff.	223	11:18ff.	235
40:2	249	13:	236
40:3ff.	249	14:13ff.	236
40:6ff.	249	14:28ff.	236
40:9	251	15:1	210
41:1ff.	249	15:10ff.	235
41:25ff.	249	15:18	235
42:1ff.	242, 250	15:19f.	236
42:4	250	16:	235
42:6	250	18:19ff.	235
42:18ff.	250	19:	236
43:22ff.	242	20:7ff.	235
44:1ff.	242	23:	235
44:6	250	23:5	237
44:28	242	23:9ff.	236
45:1ff.	249	26:	215, 224, 229, 235
45:22ff.	249		
46:11	249	26:6	84
48:14f.	249	26:7	236
48:20ff.	251	27ff.	235f.
49:14	250	27:9	64
50:2ff.	250	28:	199
50:4ff.	250	31:	236
51:	166	31:15ff.	236
51:1	242	31:33ff.	233, 237
51:4f.	250	31:35ff.	237
51:7	242	32:	236f.
51:9f.	44, 165, 251	33:19ff.	237
51:12ff.	250	33:23ff.	237
52:7	251	34:	232
52:11ff.	251	35:	192
52:12ff.	250	36ff.	237

36:22	235	44:1ff.	247
37f.	215, 236	48:35	245
41:5ff.	243		
46ff.	238	**HOSEA**	
48:46	61	1ff.	218
49:1	61	1:4	190, 192
49:3	61	2:	43, 124, 127,
49:28ff.	66		208, 219
52:6	246	2:7ff.	170
52:12	246	2:13f.	170, 219
		2:16	42
		2:17ff.	170
LAMENTATIONS		2:20ff.	43
1:4	243	4:1ff.	199, 218
4:20	181	4:2	127, 143
		4:4ff.	218
EZEKIEL		4:11ff.	218
1ff.	246	4:15f.	84, 188, 218
1:24	111	5:1ff.	177, 218
2:1	247	6:1ff.	43, 218
3:12f.	247	8:1	127
3:22ff.	246	8:4rf.	187, 218
3:24	247	8:11	218
4:	247	8:13	127
8:	234	9:7ff.	211, 218
8:3	247	9:10	42
8:14ff.	43	9:15	84, 177, 188
10:	247	10:4ff.	218
10:5	111	11:1	33
14:	16	11:14	219
15:	248	12:12	84, 188, 218
16:	208, 248	12:14	135, 141
18:	247f.	13:2	184
20:	124	13:4ff.	124, 127
20:25	229, 248	14:6ff.	170
24:15f.	246		
24:25ff.	246	**JOEL**	
25:	243	1f.	260
25:4ff.	66	2:10	260
25:10	66	2:30f.	260
29:17ff.	248	3:15	260
29:19f.	245		
30:10	245	**AMOS**	
33:21f.	246	1:2	217
33:30ff.	246	1:6	65
34:	246	2:1f.	59
34:11ff.	247	2:6ff.	216
35:	243	2:10ff.	124, 178
36:	247	3ff.	216
37:	247	3:2f.	199
40ff.	183	4:1ff.	216
43:1ff.	247	4:4f.	84, 177, 216
43:5	247	5:4	188
		5:5	84, 219

5:18ff.	197	2:21ff.	266
5:21ff.	216	2:22ff.	252
5:25	124, 149		
6:5	185	ZECHARIAH	
7:	204	1:	267
7:1ff.	216	1:4	267
7:9	217	1:12ff.	253
7:10ff.	217	1:16ff.	266
7:11	216	1:18ff.	253
8:	204	2:1ff.	253, 266
8:1ff.	216	2:5	254
8:14	218f.	2:6ff.	254
9:	204, 216	2:7	250
9:3	44, 165	2:10f.	254
9:7f.	199, 274	3:	254
9:11f.	217	3:8	254
		4:6	254
		4:7	254
MICAH		4:10	254
3:12	224	6:9ff.	254
4:1ff.	225	7:	253
6:6ff.	225, 228	8:1ff.	266
6:8	88, 199, 225	8:7f.	254
6:16	225	8:9ff.	254
7:2ff.	201	8:13	250
		8:20ff.	250
HABAKKUK		9:9ff.	250
1:2ff.	239	12:	266, 269
1:12ff.	239	12:11	43
2:1ff.	239	13:	266, 269
2:3f.	239	13:1ff.	211, 266
		13:2	266
		13:6	266
ZEPHANIAH		14:	266, 269
1:1	229		
1:4ff.	228	MALACHI	
1:8	229	2:10ff.	258
		4:4f.	191
HAGGAI			
1ff.	253	MARK	
1:	251f.	9:6	191
2:1ff.	252		
2:11ff.	252	JOHN	
2:12f.	90	7:37	170